shôjo

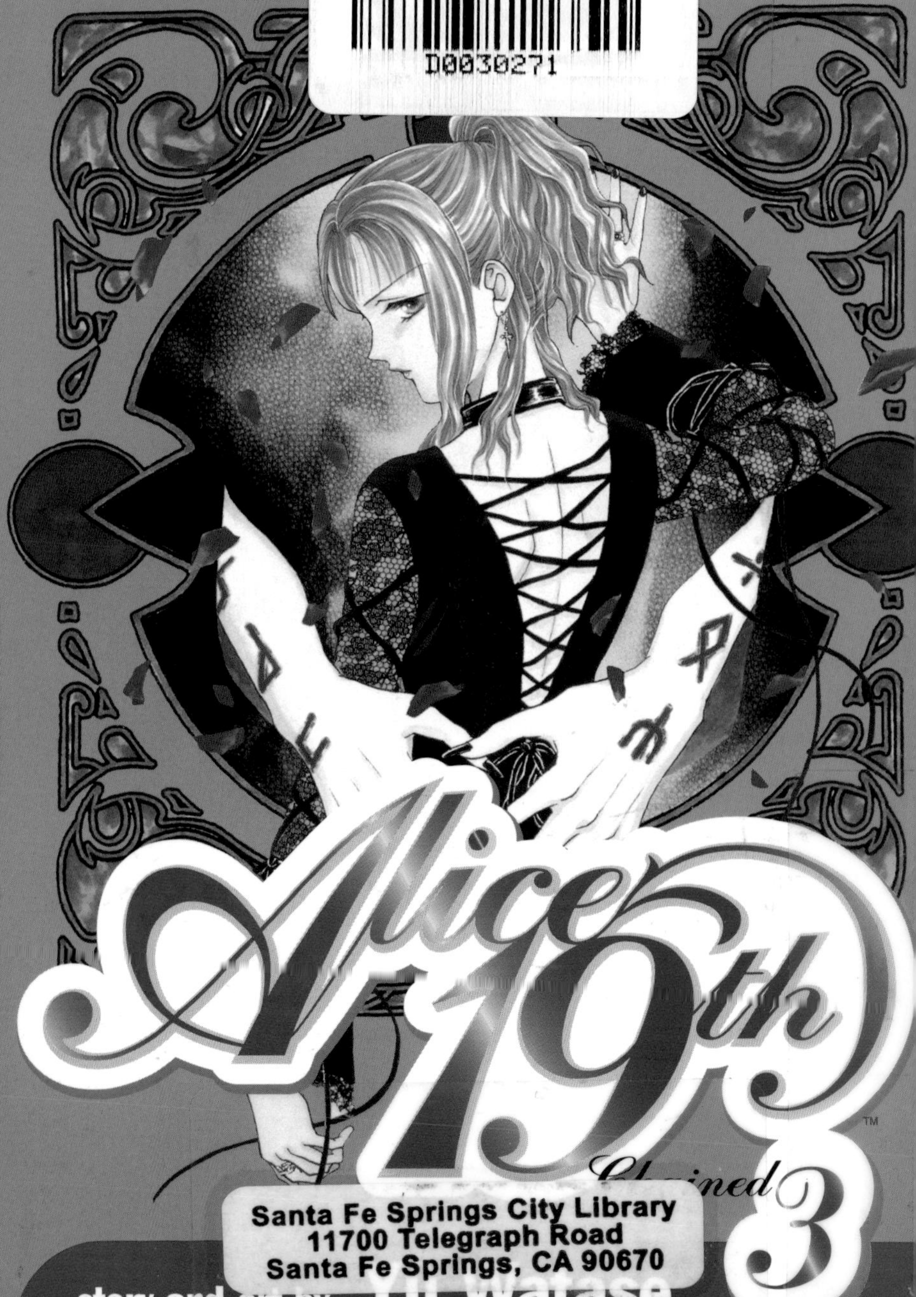

Alice 19th™

Chained 3

story and art by Yu Watase

Alice 19th
volume 3 Chained
shôjo edition

STORY & ART BY
Yû Watase

English Adaptation/Lance Caselman
Translation/JN Productions
Touch-Up Art & Lettering/Walden Wong
Cover Design & Layout/Judi Roubideaux
Editor/Kelli Blackwell

Managing Editor/Annette Roman
Editor in Chief/William Flanagan
Production Manager/Noboru Watanabe
Sr. Director of Licensing/Rika Inouye
Vice President of Marketing/Liza Coppola
Sr. Vice President of Editorial/Hyoe Narita
Publisher/Seiji Horibuchi

Printed in Canada

Published by VIZ, LLC
P.O. Box 77010 · San Francisco, CA 94107

Shôjo Edition
10 9 8 7 6 5 4 3 2 1
First printing, February 2004

www.viz.com   storeviz.com   ANIMERICA
                                ANIME & MANGA MONTHLY

The story thus far:
Alice Seno slowly realizes her ability to use the power of the Lotis and tries desperately to
save her older sister, Mayura, from the darkness. Kyô Wakamiya, Mayura's boyfriend
whom Alice has been in love with, lends an honorable hand in saving Mayura. Out of thin
air, a beautiful Lotis-master named Frey from Scandinavia joins them in their rescue, all the
while, courting young Alice for her hand in marriage. His romantic intentions throw both
Alice and Kyô for a loop but why is Kyô having trouble with Frey's advances?

Alice 19th

volume 3 Chained

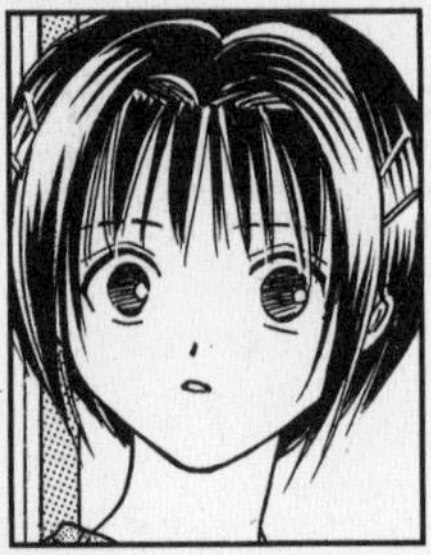
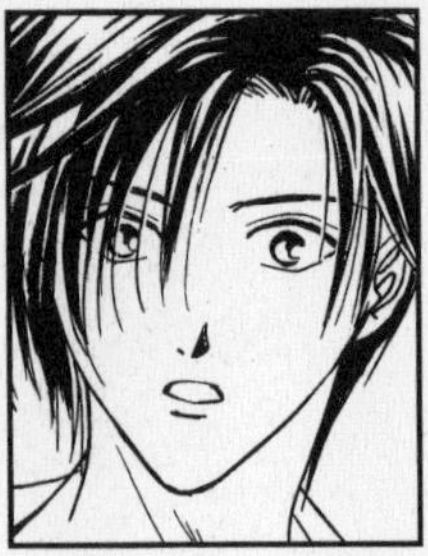
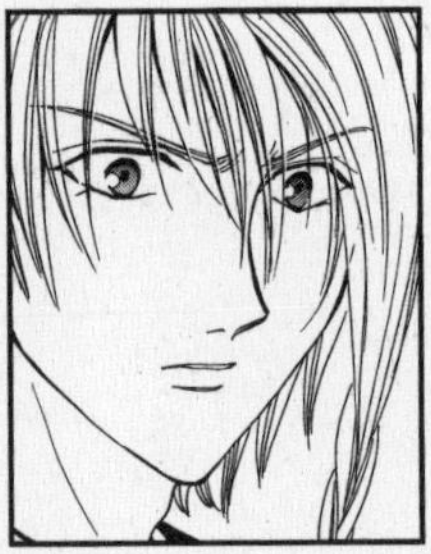
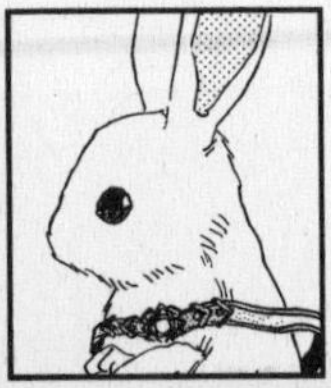
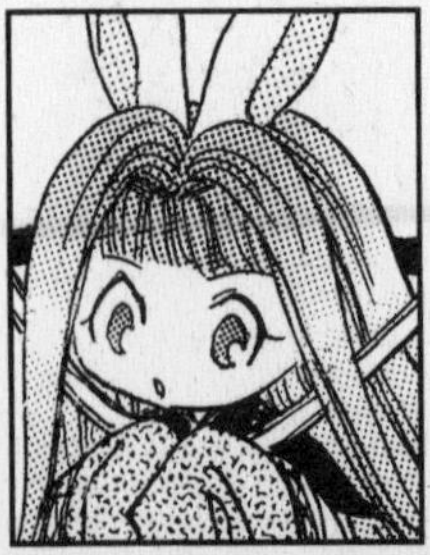

CHAPTER 3

CHAINED: SHACKLED AND BOUND

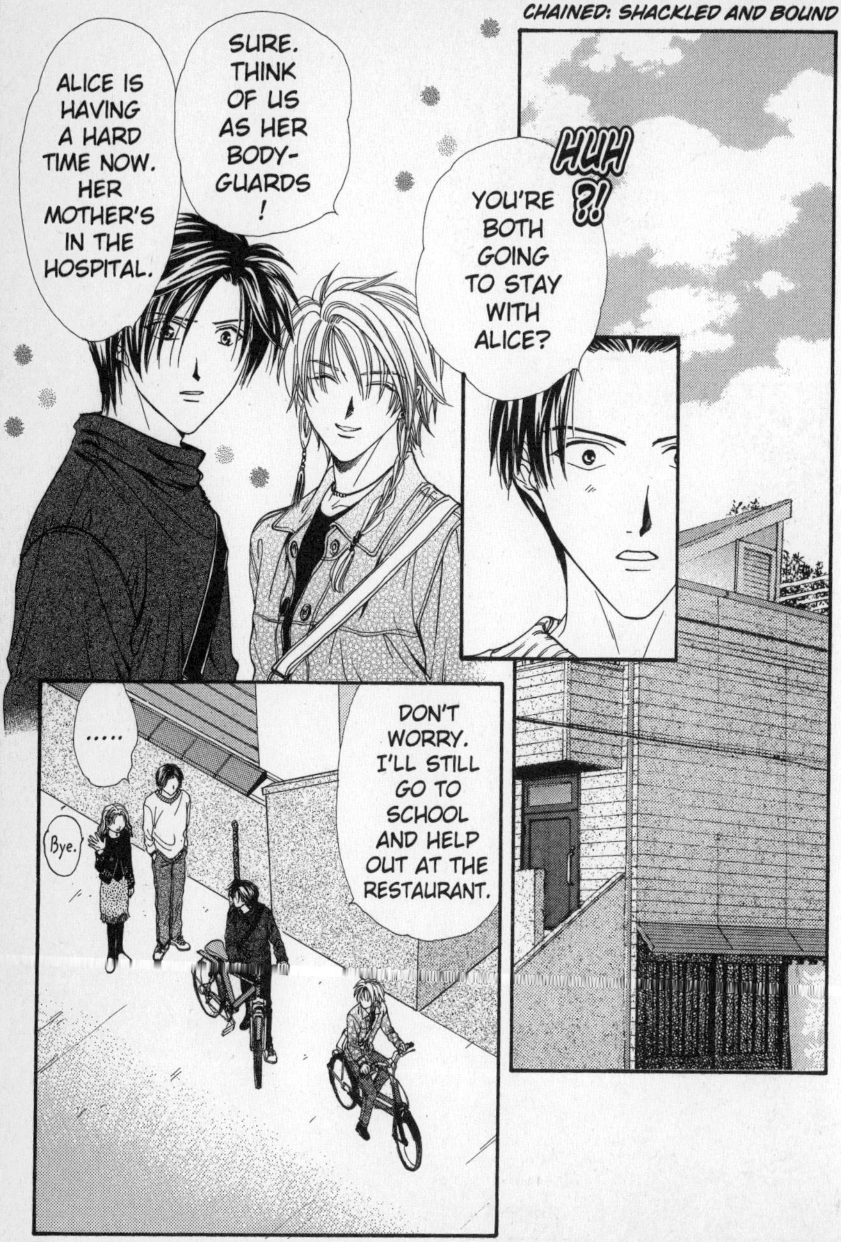
HUH ?!
YOU'RE BOTH GOING TO STAY WITH ALICE?
SURE. THINK OF US AS HER BODY-GUARDS !
ALICE IS HAVING A HARD TIME NOW. HER MOTHER'S IN THE HOSPITAL.
DON'T WORRY. I'LL STILL GO TO SCHOOL AND HELP OUT AT THE RESTAURANT.
.....
Bye.

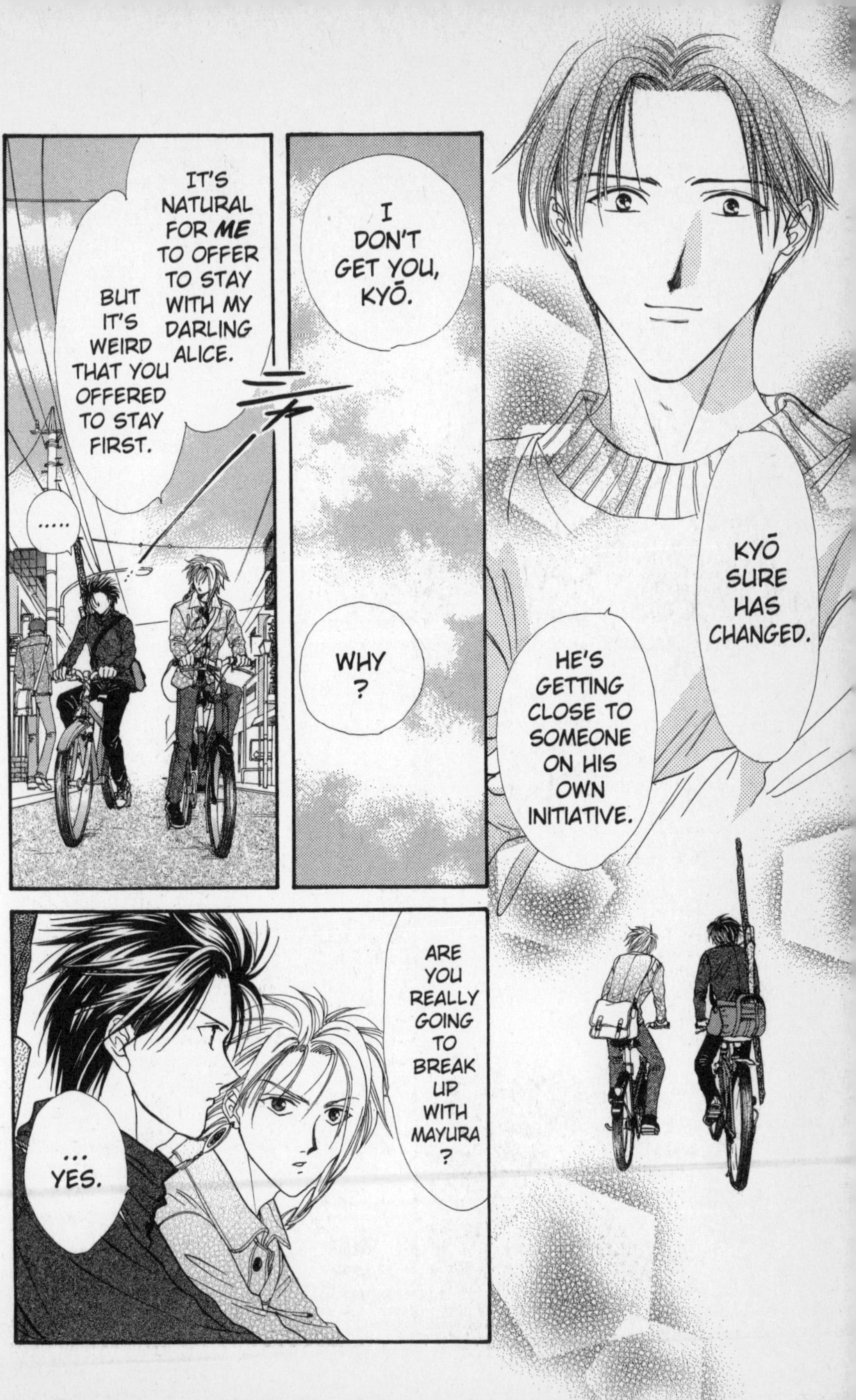
KYŌ SURE HAS CHANGED.
HE'S GETTING CLOSE TO SOMEONE ON HIS OWN INITIATIVE.
I DON'T GET YOU, KYŌ.
WHY?
IT'S NATURAL FOR *ME* TO OFFER TO STAY WITH MY DARLING ALICE.
BUT IT'S WEIRD THAT YOU OFFERED TO STAY FIRST.
......
ARE YOU REALLY GOING TO BREAK UP WITH MAYURA?
... YES.

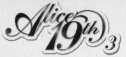

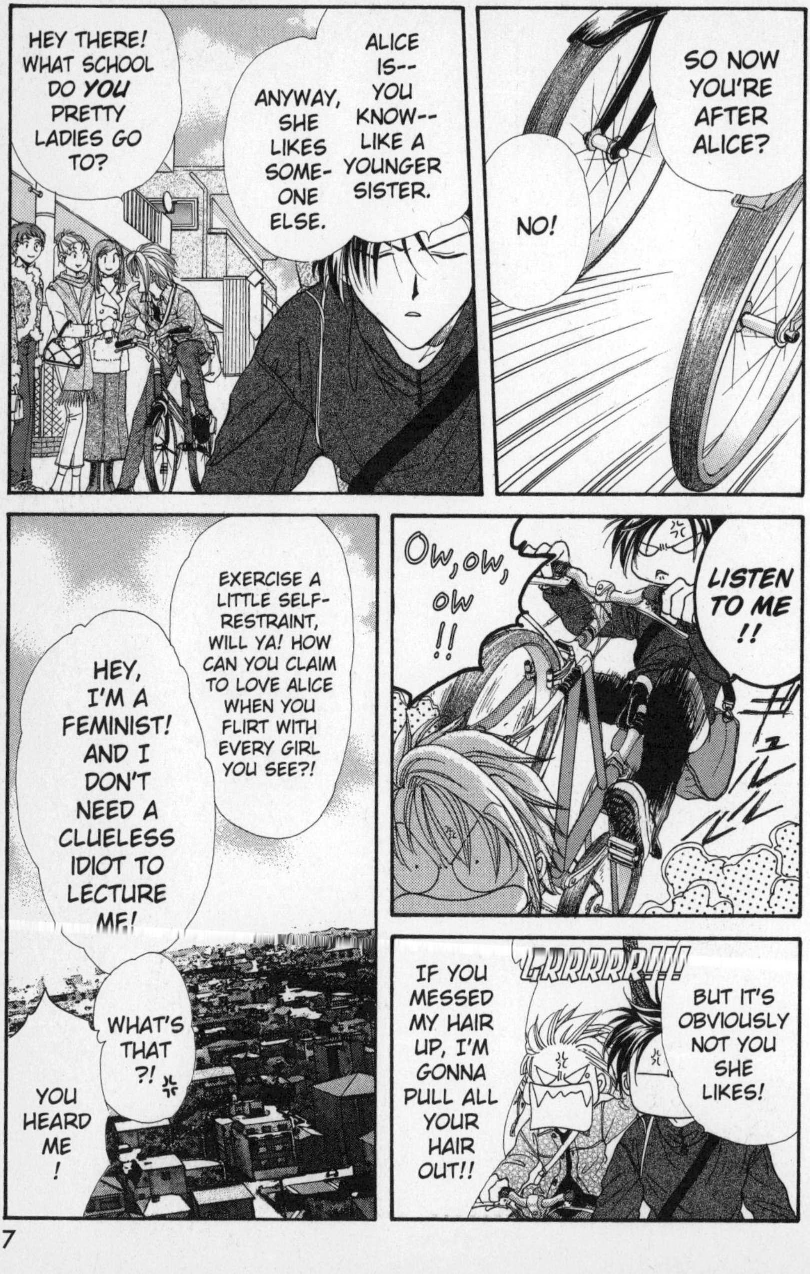
SO NOW YOU'RE AFTER ALICE?
NO!
ALICE IS-- YOU KNOW-- LIKE A YOUNGER SISTER.
ANYWAY, SHE LIKES SOMEONE ELSE.
HEY THERE! WHAT SCHOOL DO *YOU* PRETTY LADIES GO TO?
LISTEN TO ME!!
Ow, ow, ow!!
BUT IT'S OBVIOUSLY NOT YOU SHE LIKES!
GRRRRR!!!
IF YOU MESSED MY HAIR UP, I'M GONNA PULL ALL YOUR HAIR OUT!!
EXERCISE A LITTLE SELF-RESTRAINT, WILL YA! HOW CAN YOU CLAIM TO LOVE ALICE WHEN YOU FLIRT WITH EVERY GIRL YOU SEE?!
HEY, I'M A FEMINIST! AND I DON'T NEED A CLUELESS IDIOT TO LECTURE ME!
WHAT'S THAT?!
YOU HEARD ME!

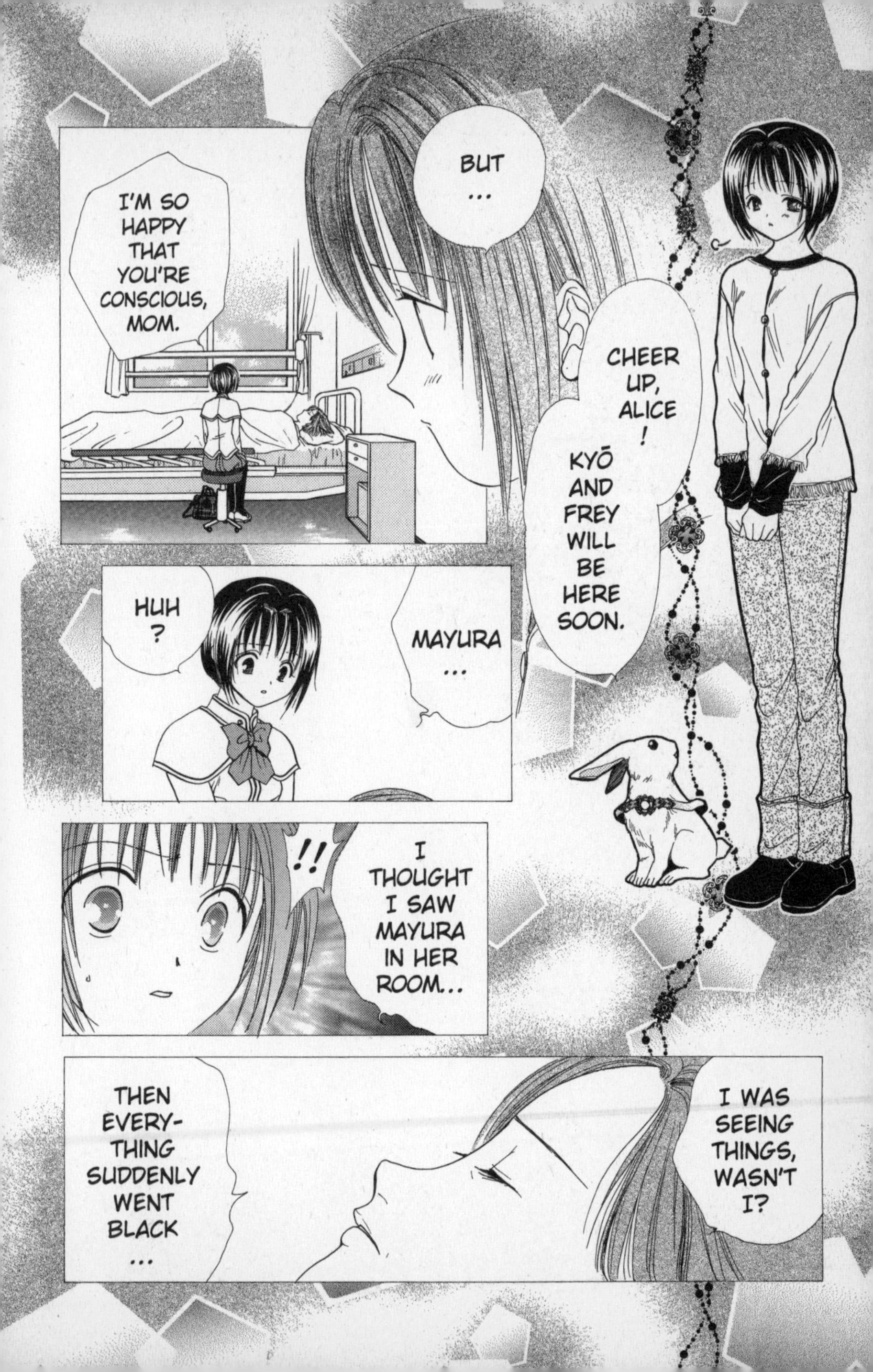
CHEER UP, ALICE!
KYŌ AND FREY WILL BE HERE SOON.
BUT ...
I'M SO HAPPY THAT YOU'RE CONSCIOUS, MOM.
MAYURA ...
HUH ?
I THOUGHT I SAW MAYURA IN HER ROOM...
!!
I WAS SEEING THINGS, WASN'T I?
THEN EVERY-THING SUDDENLY WENT BLACK ...

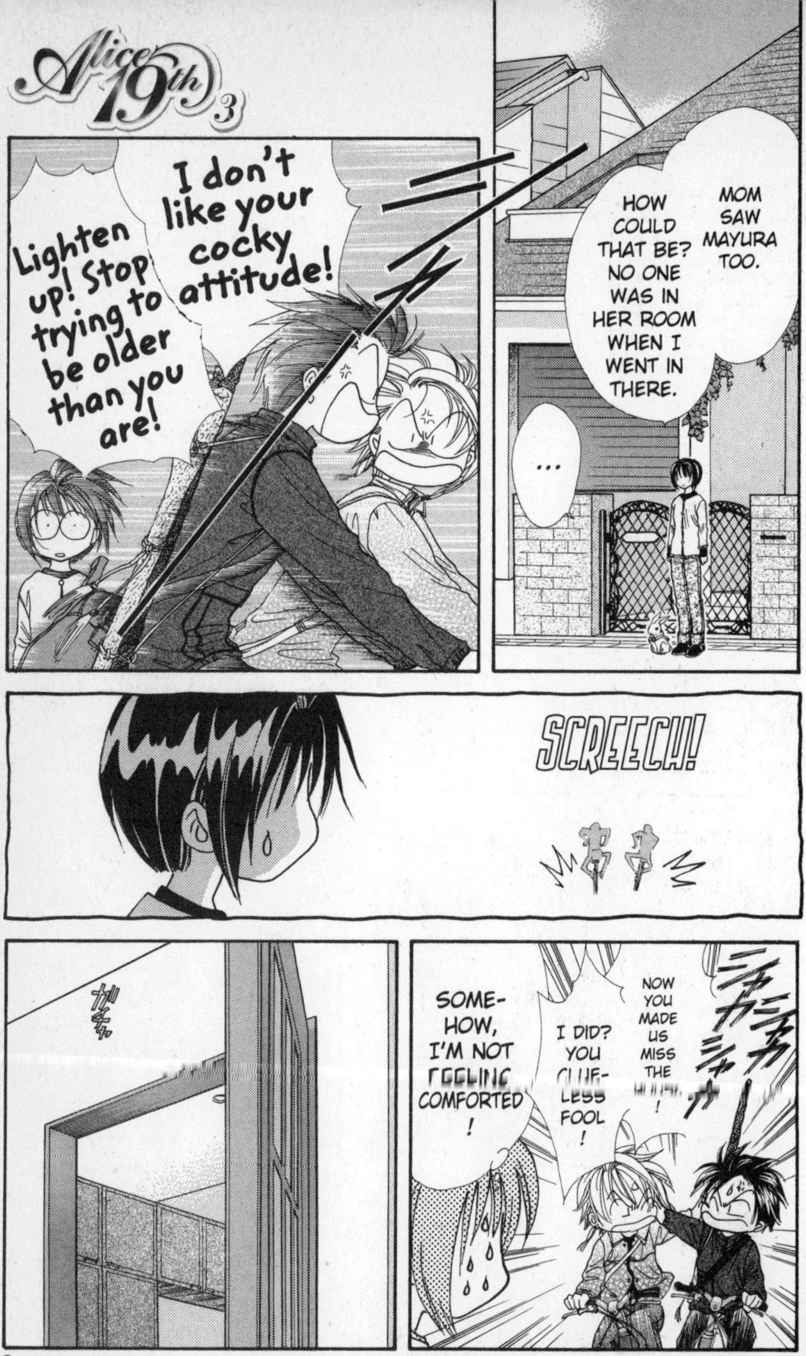
MOM SAW MAYURA TOO.
HOW COULD THAT BE? NO ONE WAS IN HER ROOM WHEN I WENT IN THERE.
...
I don't like your cocky attitude!
Lighten up! Stop trying to be older than you are!
SCREECH!
NOW YOU MADE US MISS THE
I DID? YOU CLUELESS FOOL!
SOMEHOW, I'M NOT FEELING COMFORTED!

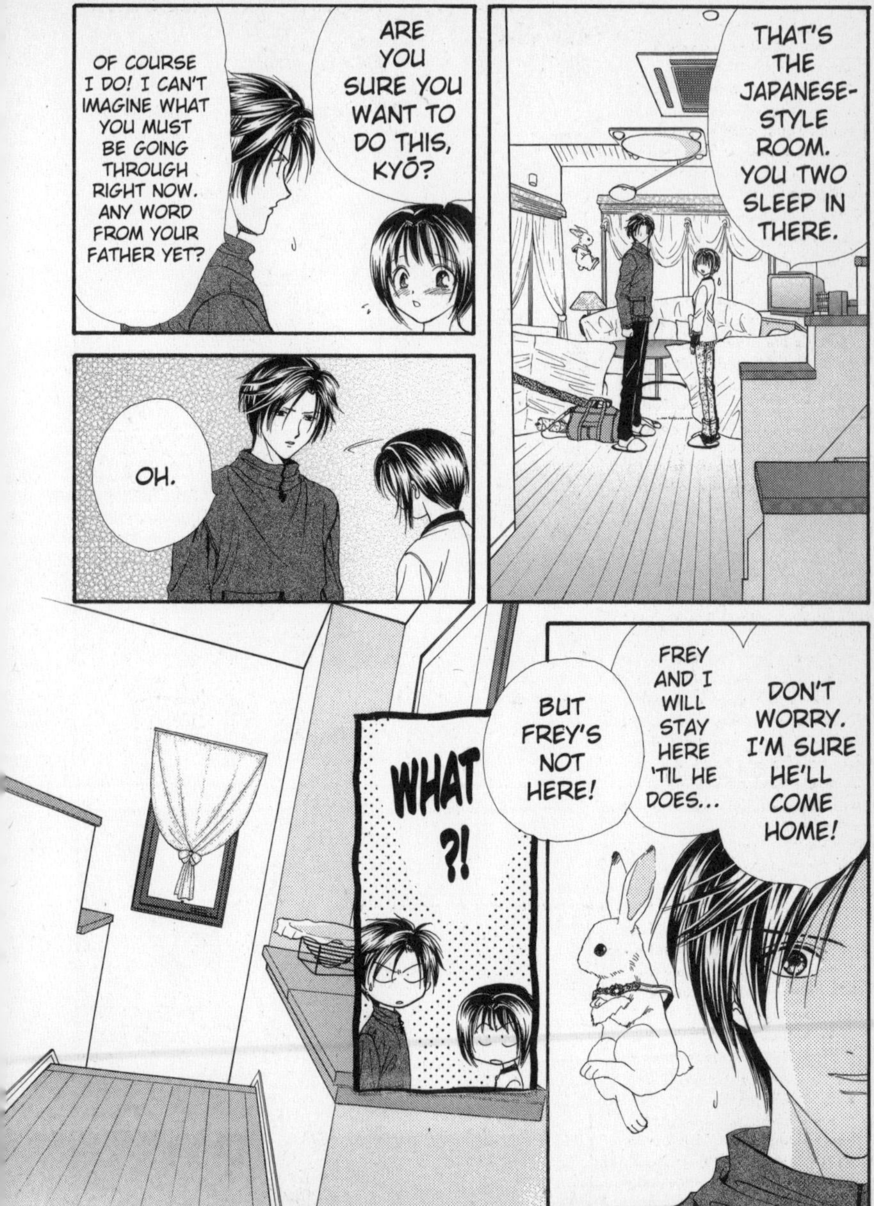
THAT'S THE JAPANESE-STYLE ROOM. YOU TWO SLEEP IN THERE.
ARE YOU SURE YOU WANT TO DO THIS, KYŌ?
OF COURSE I DO! I CAN'T IMAGINE WHAT YOU MUST BE GOING THROUGH RIGHT NOW. ANY WORD FROM YOUR FATHER YET?
OH.
DON'T WORRY. I'M SURE HE'LL COME HOME!
FREY AND I WILL STAY HERE 'TIL HE DOES...
BUT FREY'S NOT HERE!
WHAT ?!

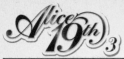

Thanks for reading Alice 19th. Somehow I finished Volume 3. I hope you enjoy it. (Yawn)
Now, when I asked for recommendations for good music before, I received all sorts of replies. I already have music from Escaflowne The Movie and Noir. Noir is dubbed. It is best suited to Ceres. It's edgier.
When you speak of Escaflowne, it's got to be Ms. Yoko Kanno.
All three of us here at my studio are big fans of her (although my assistant is the one who wants her complete collection). From Nobunaga's Ambition to Macross Plus, and from China (the NHK Special) to Cowboy Bebop, I've listened to nearly all of her work. There are so many, I can't name them all!
I'd like to collect them a few at a time, but I already have a lot of CDs and mini-disks, so.... But as her fan, I'd like to get everthing!
I have the two Earth Girl, Arjuna disks, but I've seen only the second half of the main edit...
I think the hero was on the archery team.
I listened to the title song, "Mameshiba," many times as I worked on Alice 19th. The lyrics fit so well.
I really create scenes from music, so I'm pretty finicky about it. (I'm a fanatic, after all.) Ms. Kanno can write all different kinds of music, so she's awesome. (Ah, I wish she would write something for me...)
Personally, my very favorite is probably the soundtrack from Escaflowne (TV and movie releases), probably because it has lots of sad [illegible] Besides, I just like the anime itself. I got hooked on it about three years ago. (That's late!!) I saw the movie twice, too! At an anime event abroad, I was happy that I got to talk to the director, Akane! I even spoke with Yuki, the character designer!! Looking forward to their new work. Starting in spring?
Anyway, changing the subject, I could get hooked on Hikaru Utada's promotion videos...!! Final Distance and Traveling!! They're awesome!

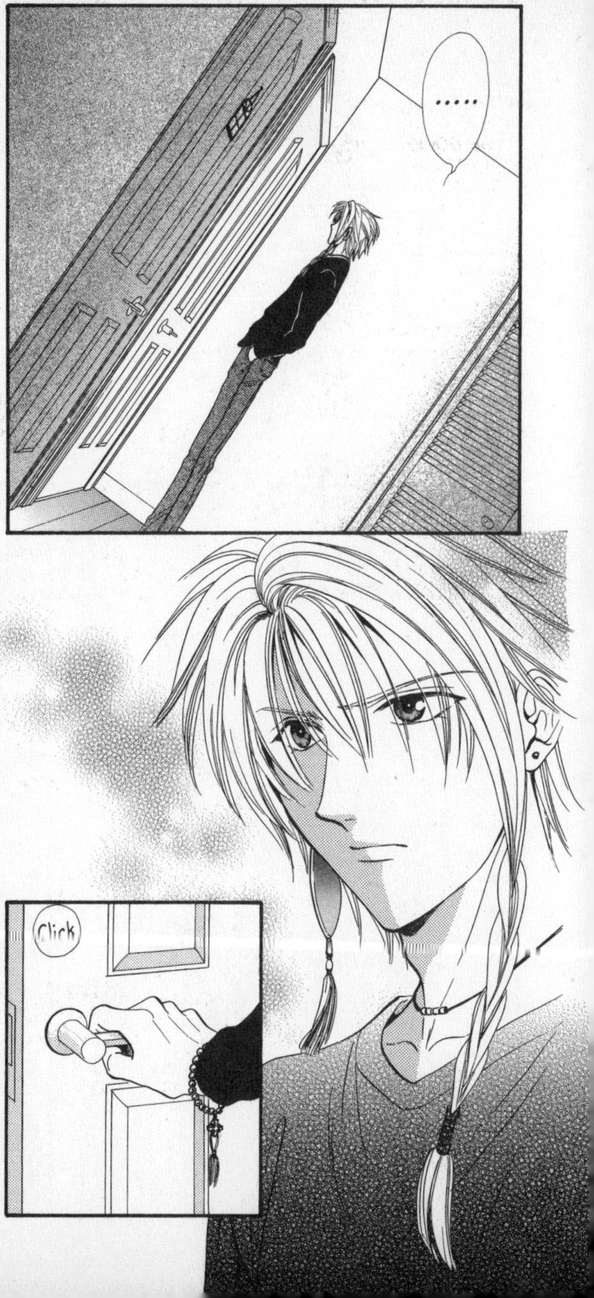

......
Click

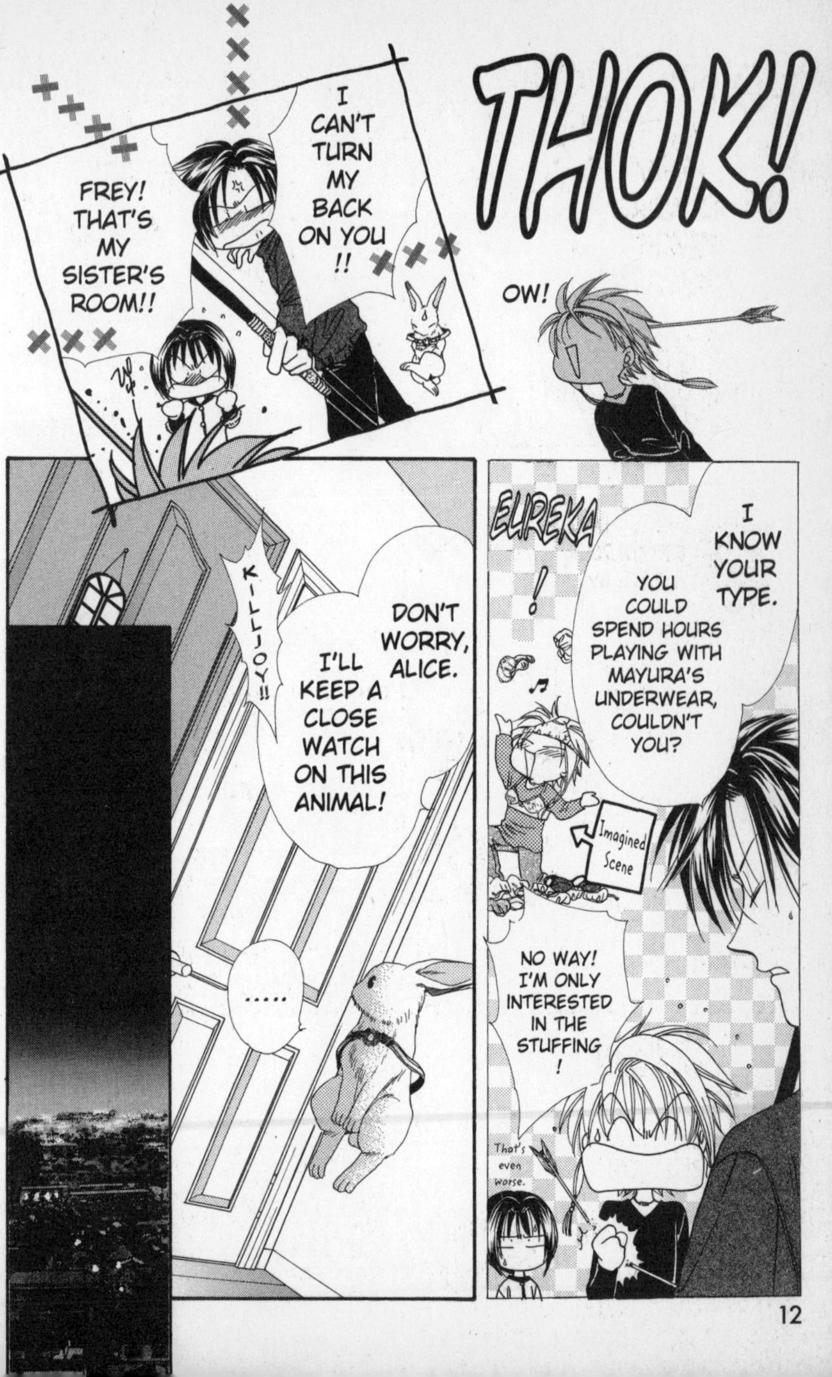
THOK!
OW!
I CAN'T TURN MY BACK ON YOU!!
FREY! THAT'S MY SISTER'S ROOM!!
EUREKA!
I KNOW YOUR TYPE.
YOU COULD SPEND HOURS PLAYING WITH MAYURA'S UNDERWEAR, COULDN'T YOU?
Imagined Scene
NO WAY! I'M ONLY INTERESTED IN THE STUFFING!
That's even worse.
DON'T WORRY, ALICE.
I'LL KEEP A CLOSE WATCH ON THIS ANIMAL!
KILLJOY!!
......

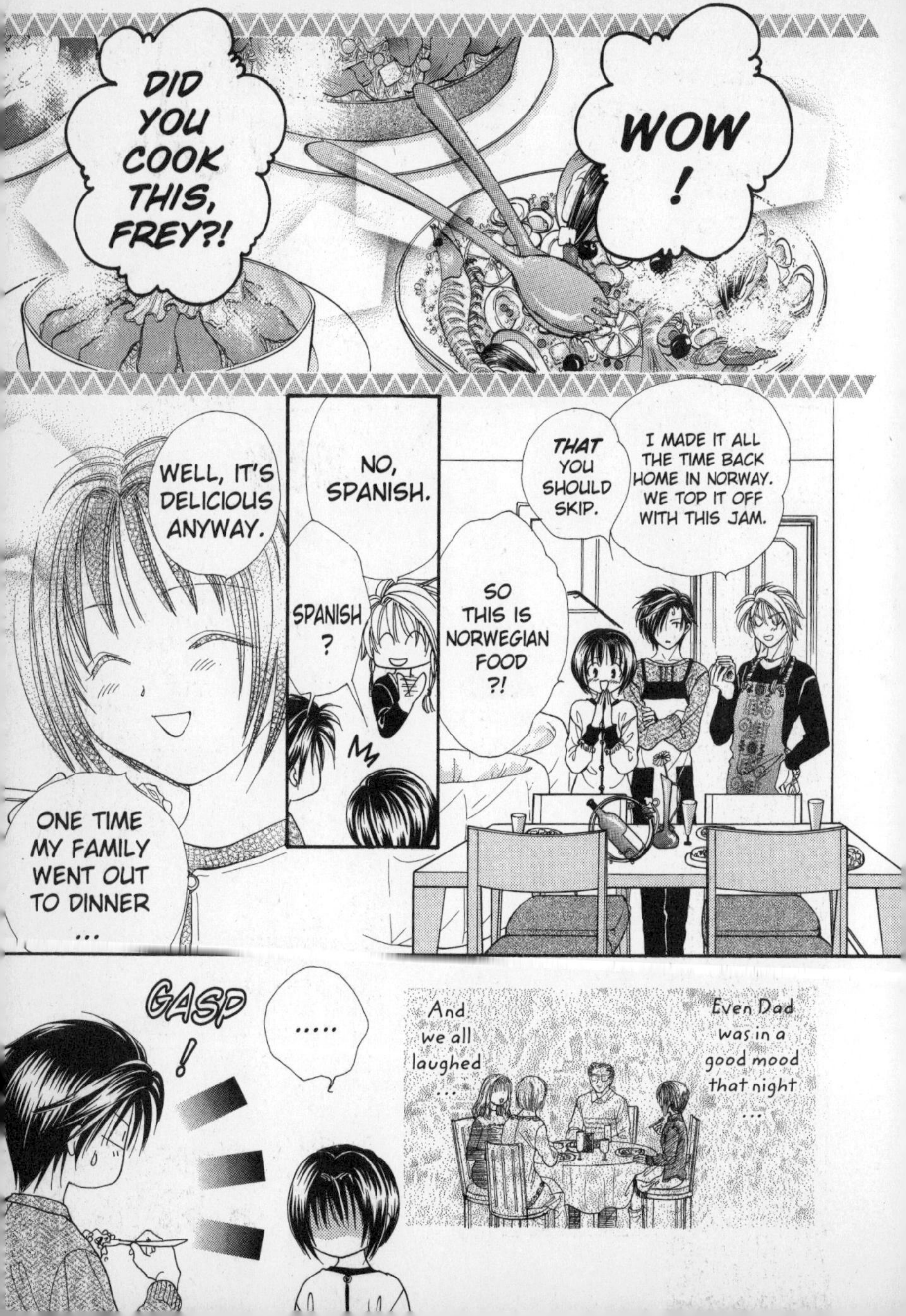
WOW!
DID YOU COOK THIS, FREY?!
I MADE IT ALL THE TIME BACK HOME IN NORWAY. WE TOP IT OFF WITH THIS JAM.
THAT YOU SHOULD SKIP.
SO THIS IS NORWEGIAN FOOD?!
NO, SPANISH.
SPANISH?
MM
WELL, IT'S DELICIOUS ANYWAY.
ONE TIME MY FAMILY WENT OUT TO DINNER ...
Even Dad was in a good mood that night ...
And we all laughed ...
.....
GASP!

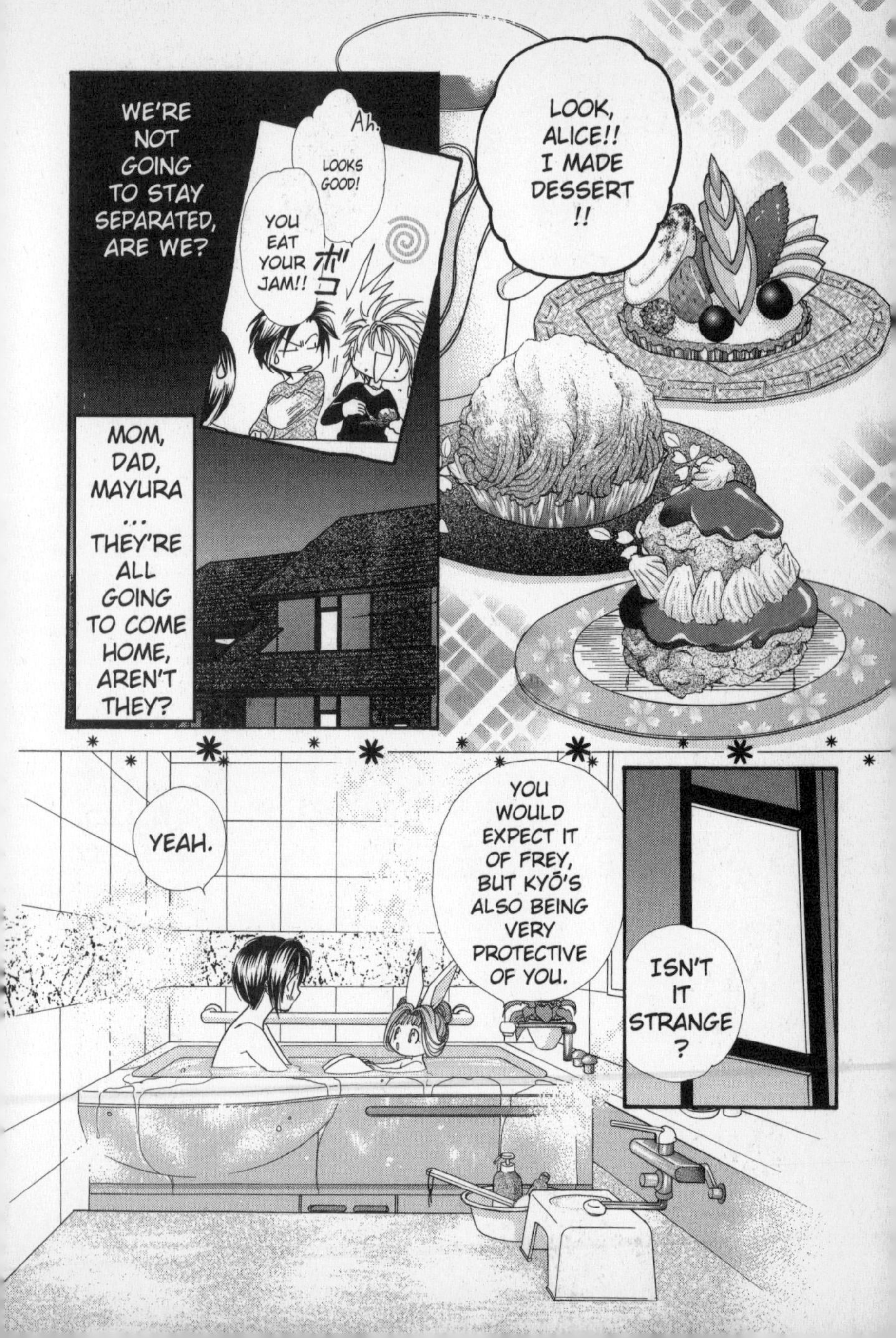
LOOK, ALICE!! I MADE DESSERT !!
WE'RE NOT GOING TO STAY SEPARATED, ARE WE?
Ah.
LOOKS GOOD!
YOU EAT YOUR JAM!!
ボコ
MOM, DAD, MAYURA ... THEY'RE ALL GOING TO COME HOME, AREN'T THEY?
ISN'T IT STRANGE ?
YOU WOULD EXPECT IT OF FREY, BUT KYŌ'S ALSO BEING VERY PROTECTIVE OF YOU.
YEAH.

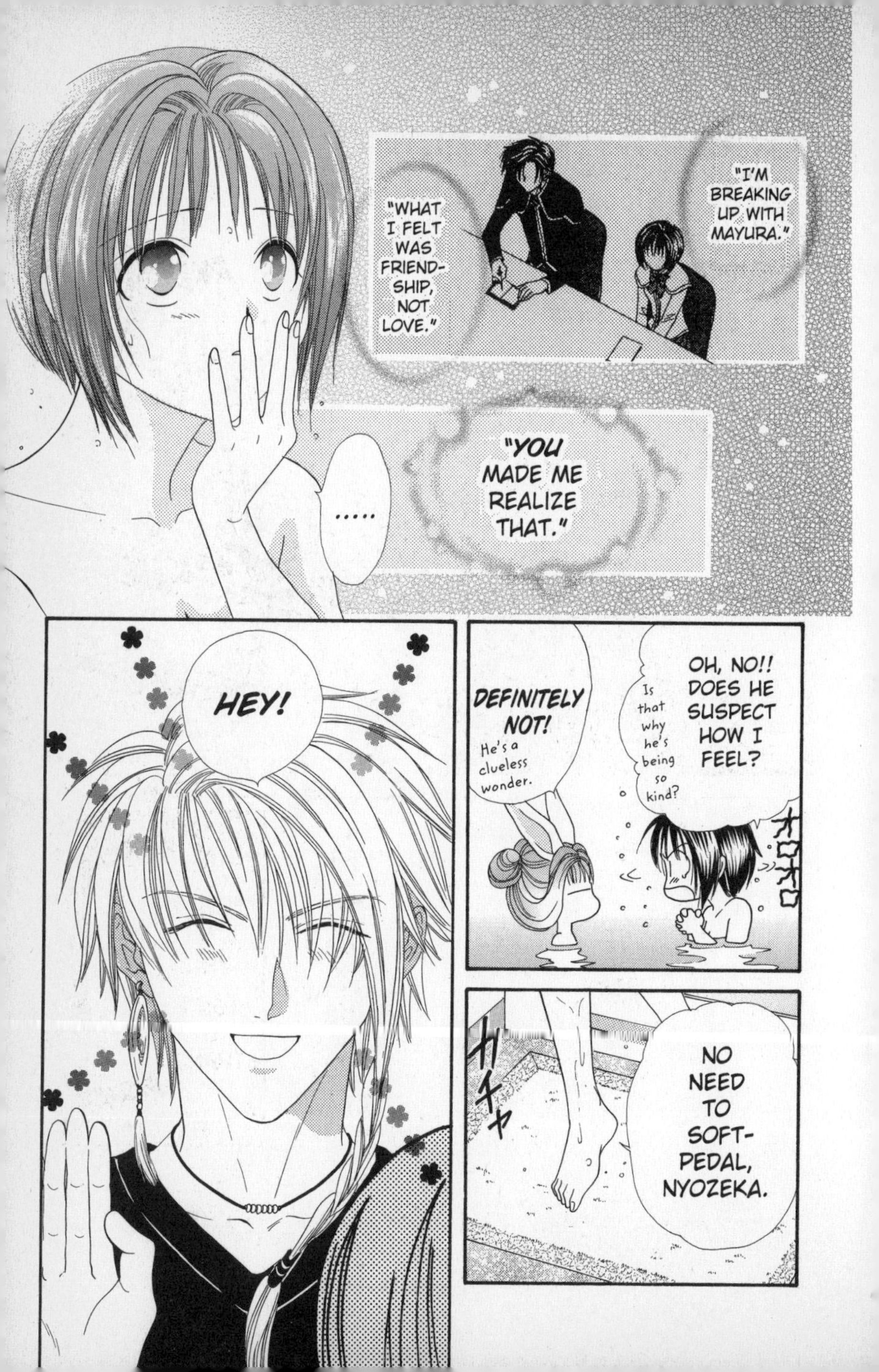
"I'M BREAKING UP WITH MAYURA."
"WHAT I FELT WAS FRIENDSHIP, NOT LOVE."
"YOU MADE ME REALIZE THAT."
.....
OH, NO!! DOES HE SUSPECT HOW I FEEL?
Is that why he's being so kind?
オロオロ
DEFINITELY NOT!
He's a clueless wonder.
NO NEED TO SOFT-PEDAL, NYOZEKA.
カチャ
HEY!

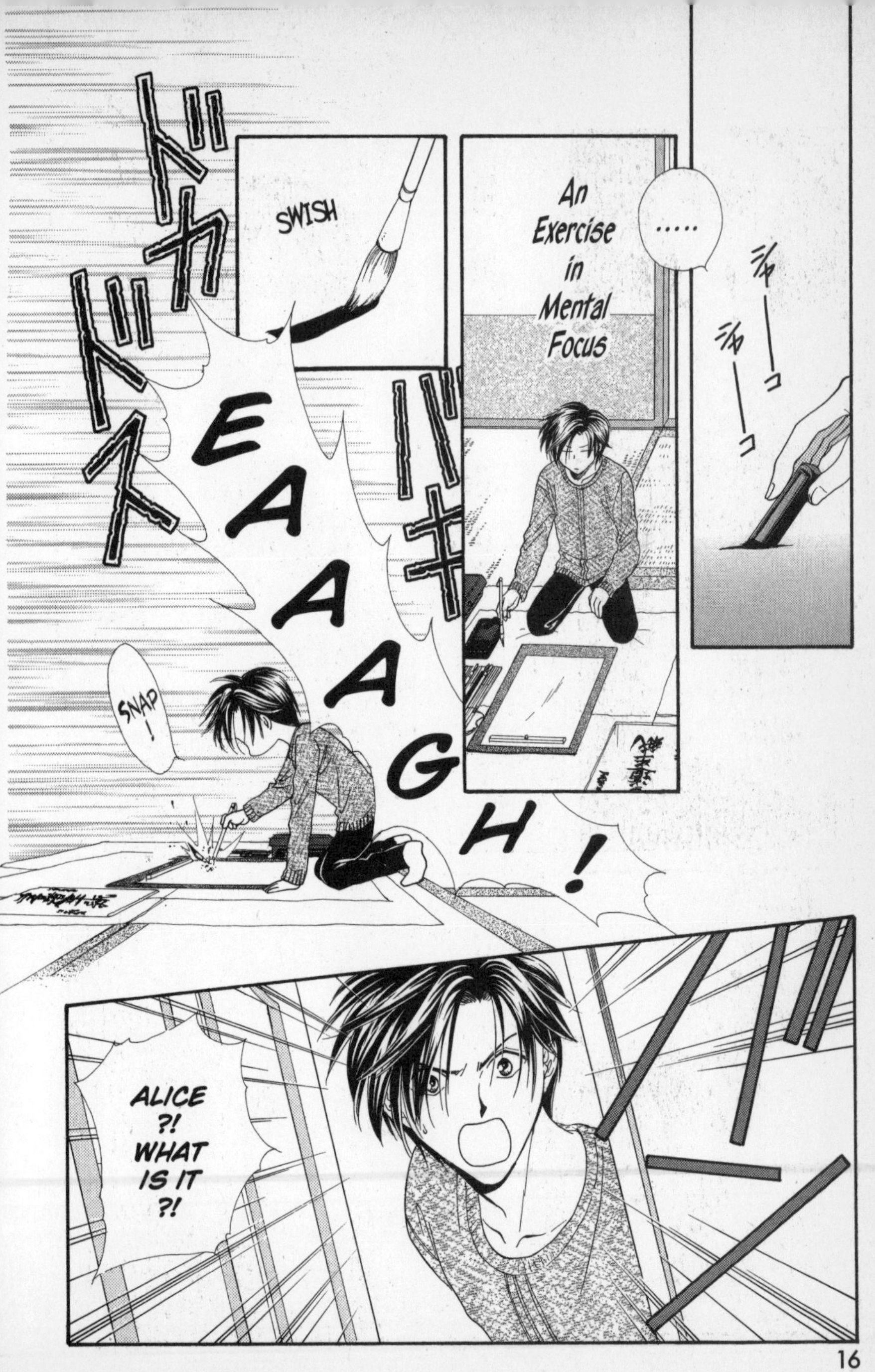
An Exercise in Mental Focus
.....
SWISH
EAAAGH!
SNAP!
ALICE?! WHAT IS IT?!

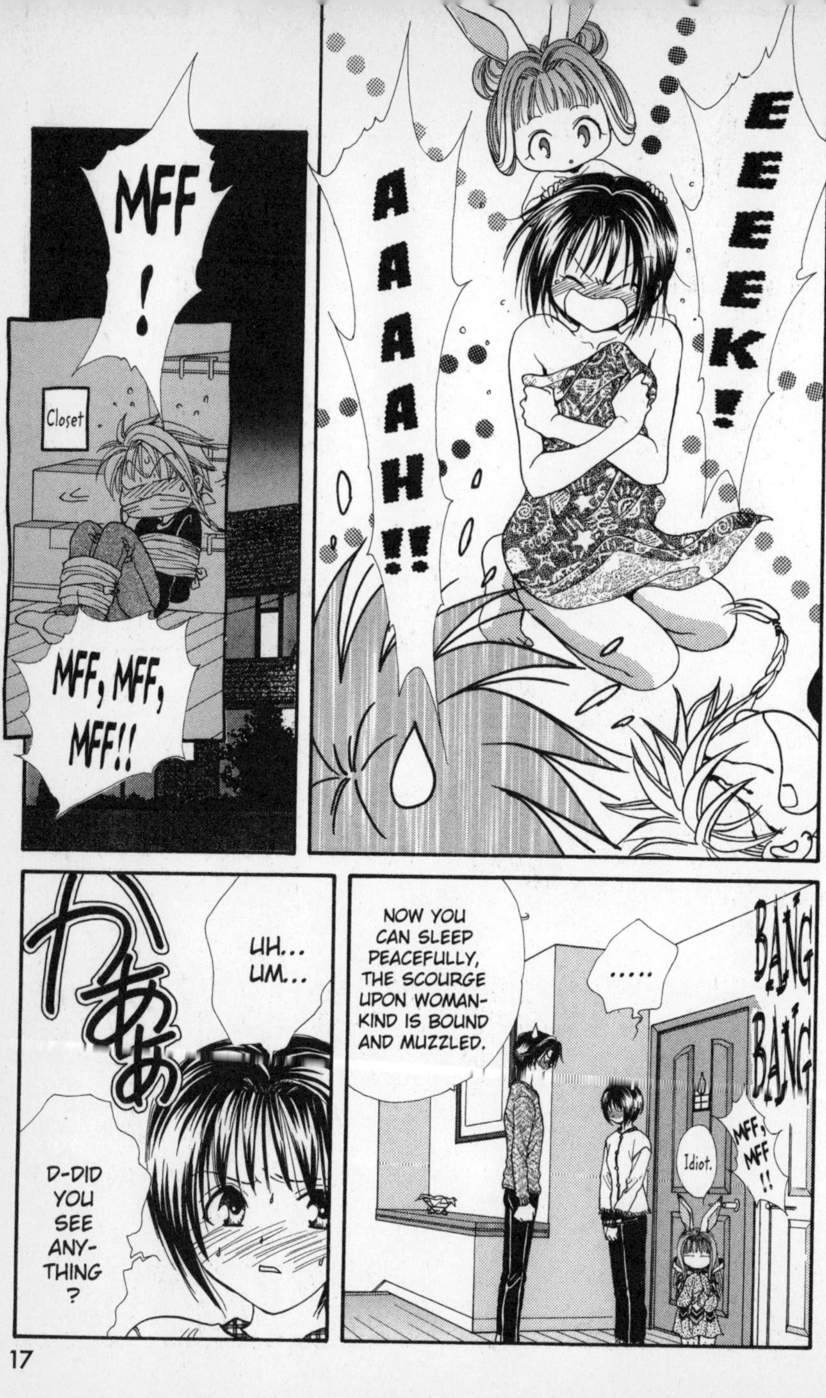
EEEEEK!
AAAAAH!!
MFF!
Closet
MFF, MFF, MFF!!
BANG BANG
.....
NOW YOU CAN SLEEP PEACEFULLY, THE SCOURGE UPON WOMAN-KIND IS BOUND AND MUZZLED.
MFF, MFF !!
Idiot.
わぁあ
UH... UM...
D-DID YOU SEE ANY-THING?

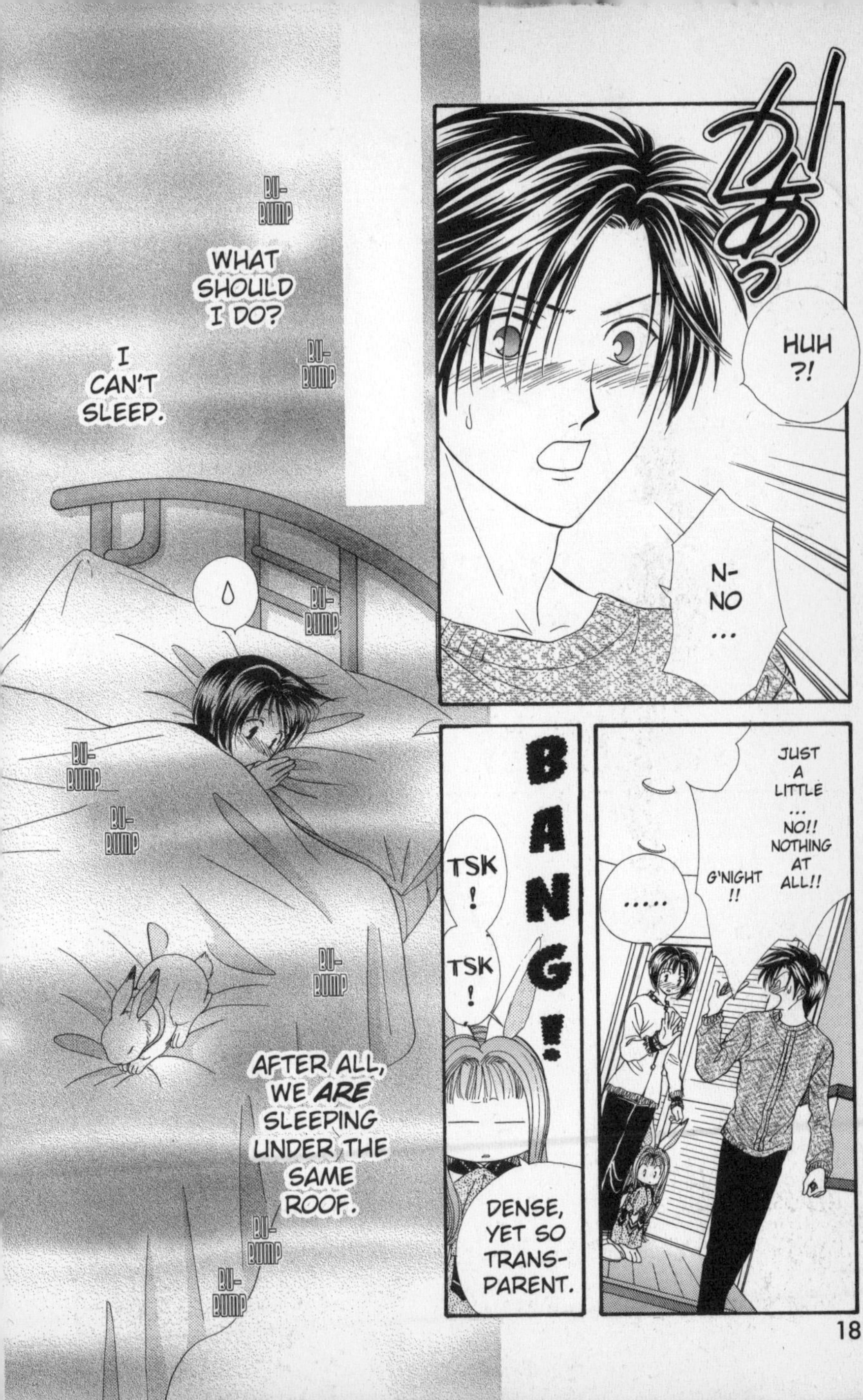
かぁっ
HUH?!
N-NO...
JUST A LITTLE... NO!! NOTHING AT ALL!!
G'NIGHT!!
.....
BANG!
TSK!
TSK!
DENSE, YET SO TRANSPARENT.
BU-BUMP
WHAT SHOULD I DO?
BU-BUMP
I CAN'T SLEEP.
BU-BUMP
BU-BUMP
BU-BUMP
BU-BUMP
AFTER ALL, WE *ARE* SLEEPING UNDER THE SAME ROOF.
BU-BUMP
BU-BUMP

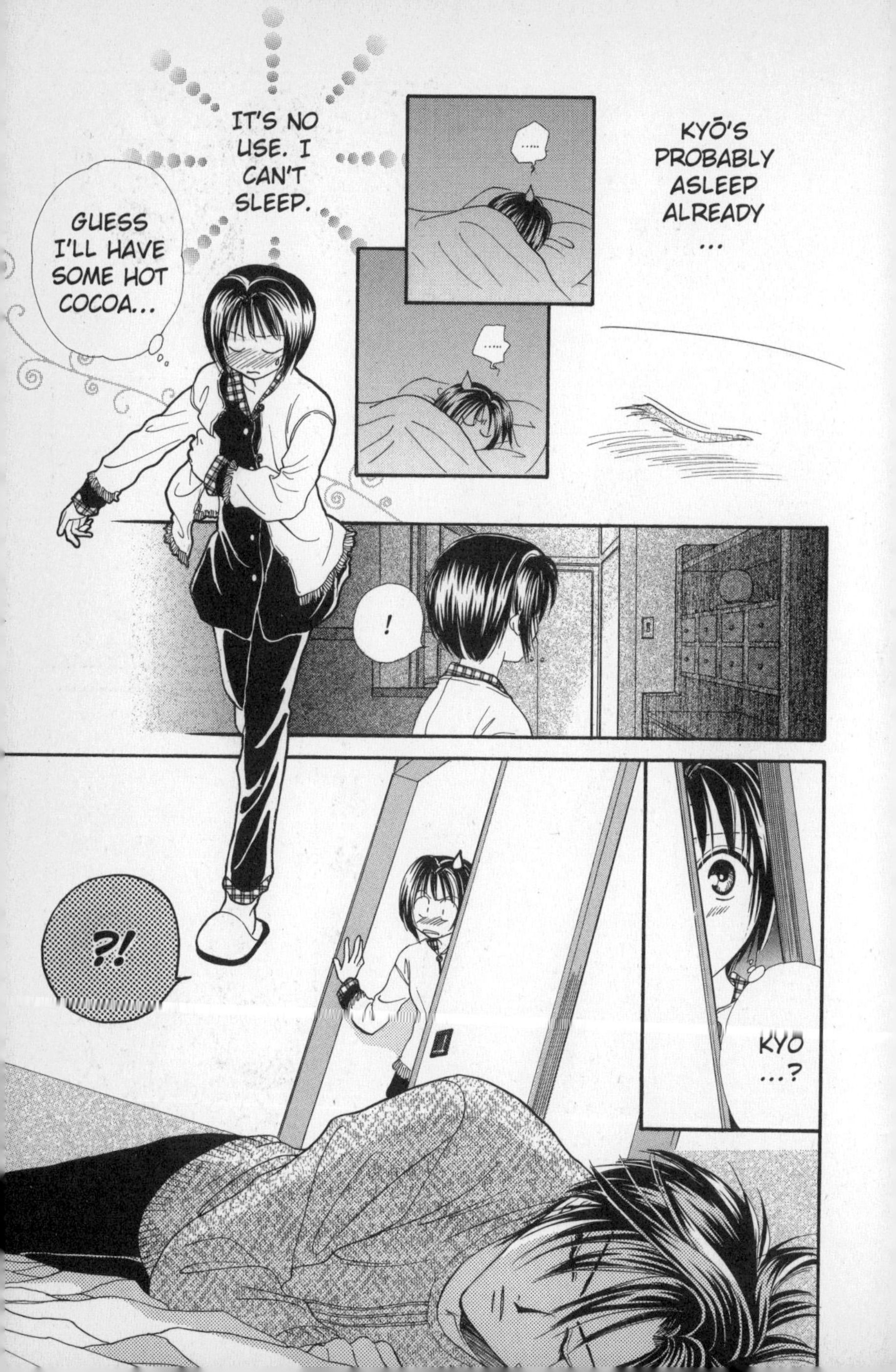
KYŌ'S PROBABLY ASLEEP ALREADY ...
.....
.....
IT'S NO USE. I CAN'T SLEEP.
GUESS I'LL HAVE SOME HOT COCOA...
!
KYO ...?
?!

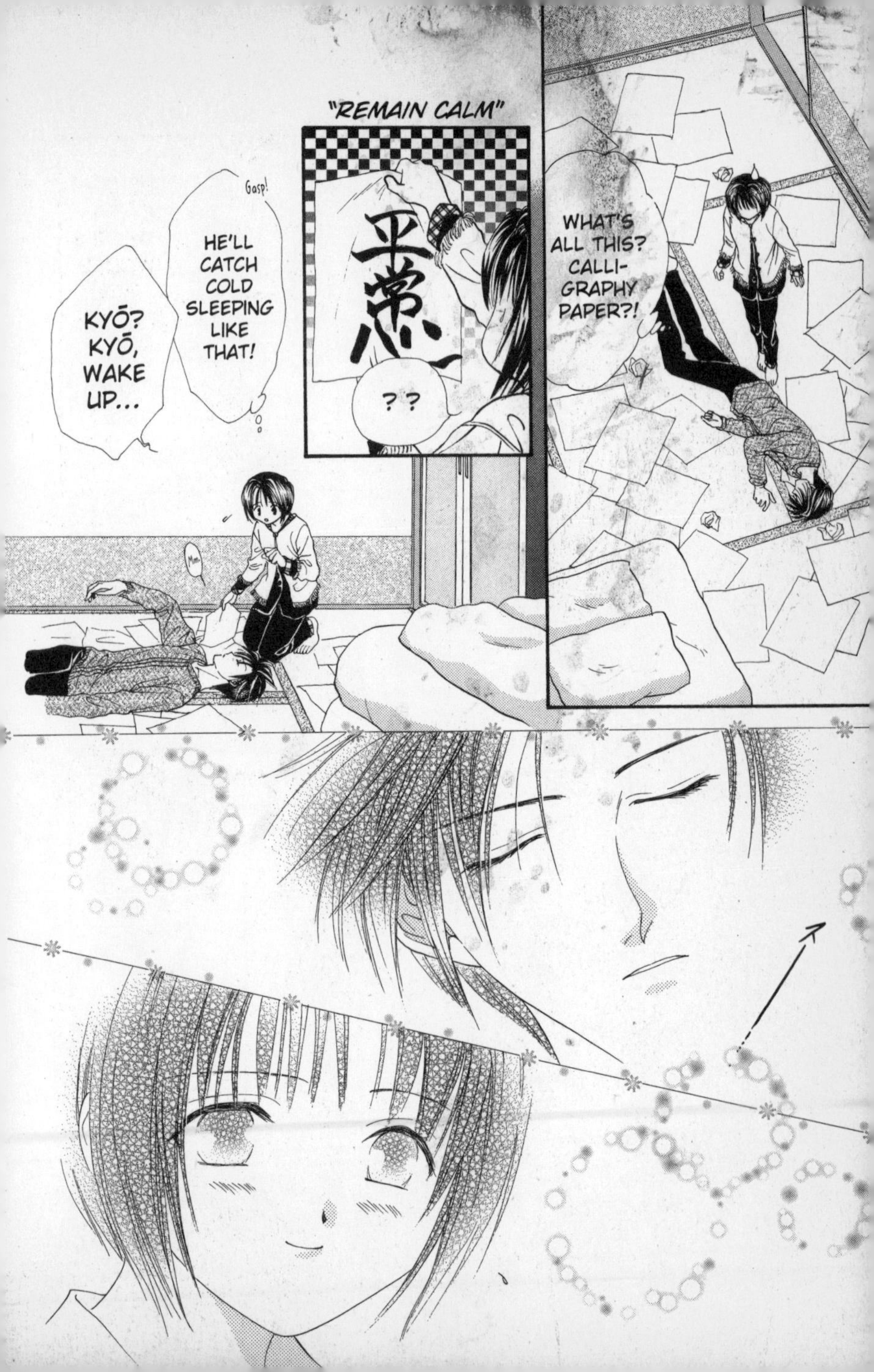
WHAT'S ALL THIS? CALLI-GRAPHY PAPER?!
"REMAIN CALM"
平常心
??
Gasp!
HE'LL CATCH COLD SLEEPING LIKE THAT!
KYŌ? KYŌ, WAKE UP...
Mm.

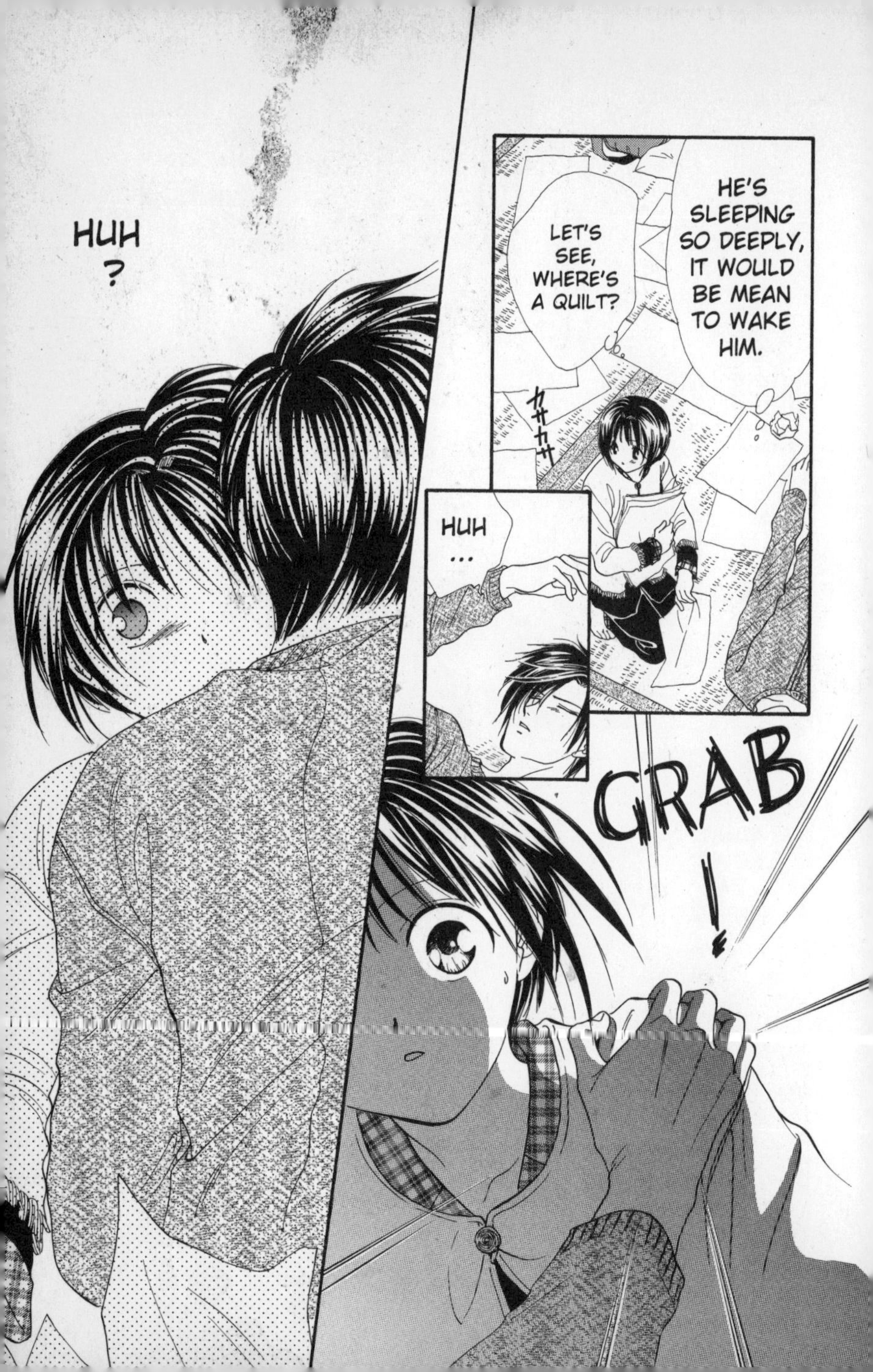
HE'S SLEEPING SO DEEPLY, IT WOULD BE MEAN TO WAKE HIM.
LET'S SEE, WHERE'S A QUILT?
カサカサ
HUH ...
GRAB !
HUH ?

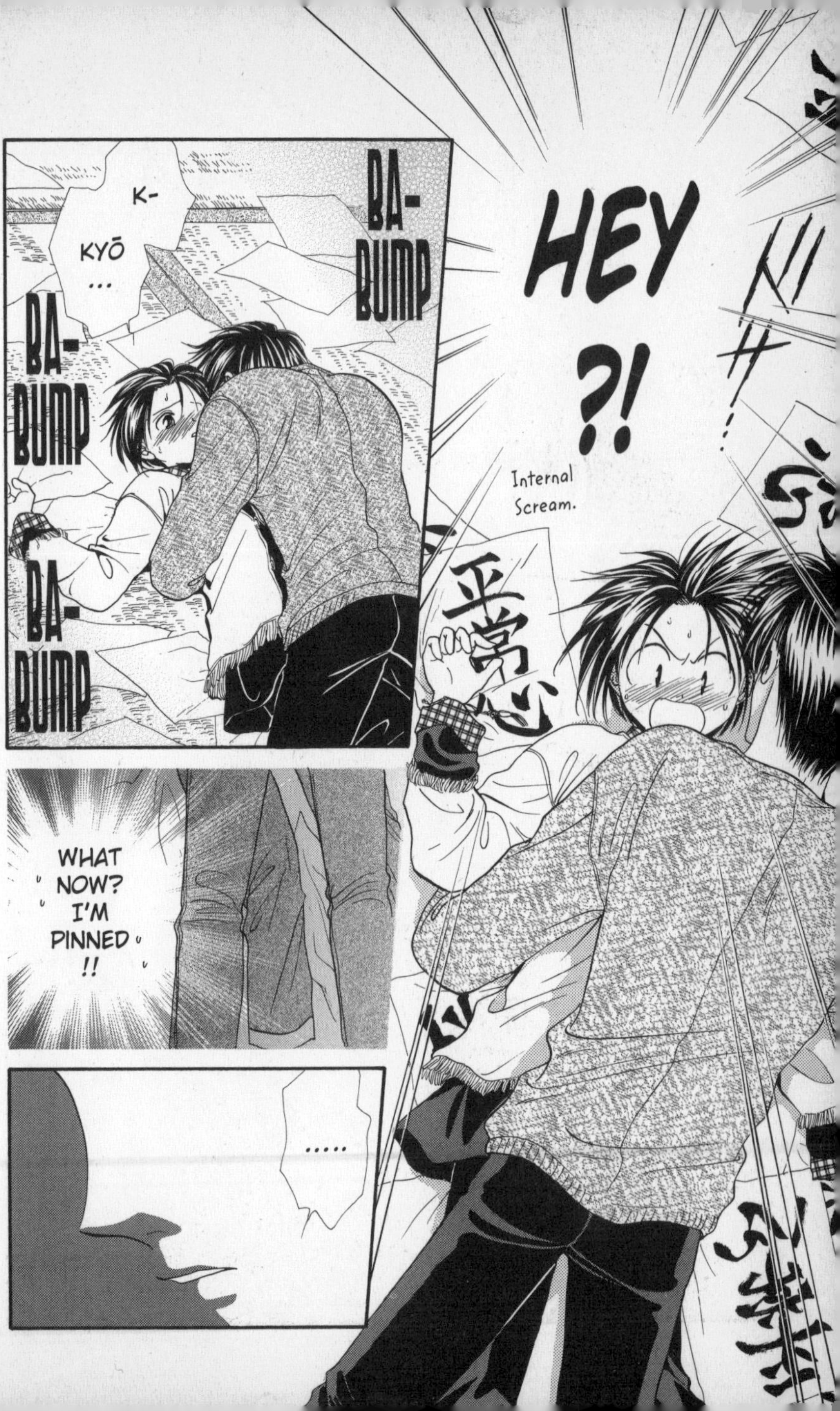
HEY ?!
Internal Scream.
平常心
BA-BUMP
K-
KYŌ ...
BA-BUMP
BA-BUMP
WHAT NOW? I'M PINNED !!
.....

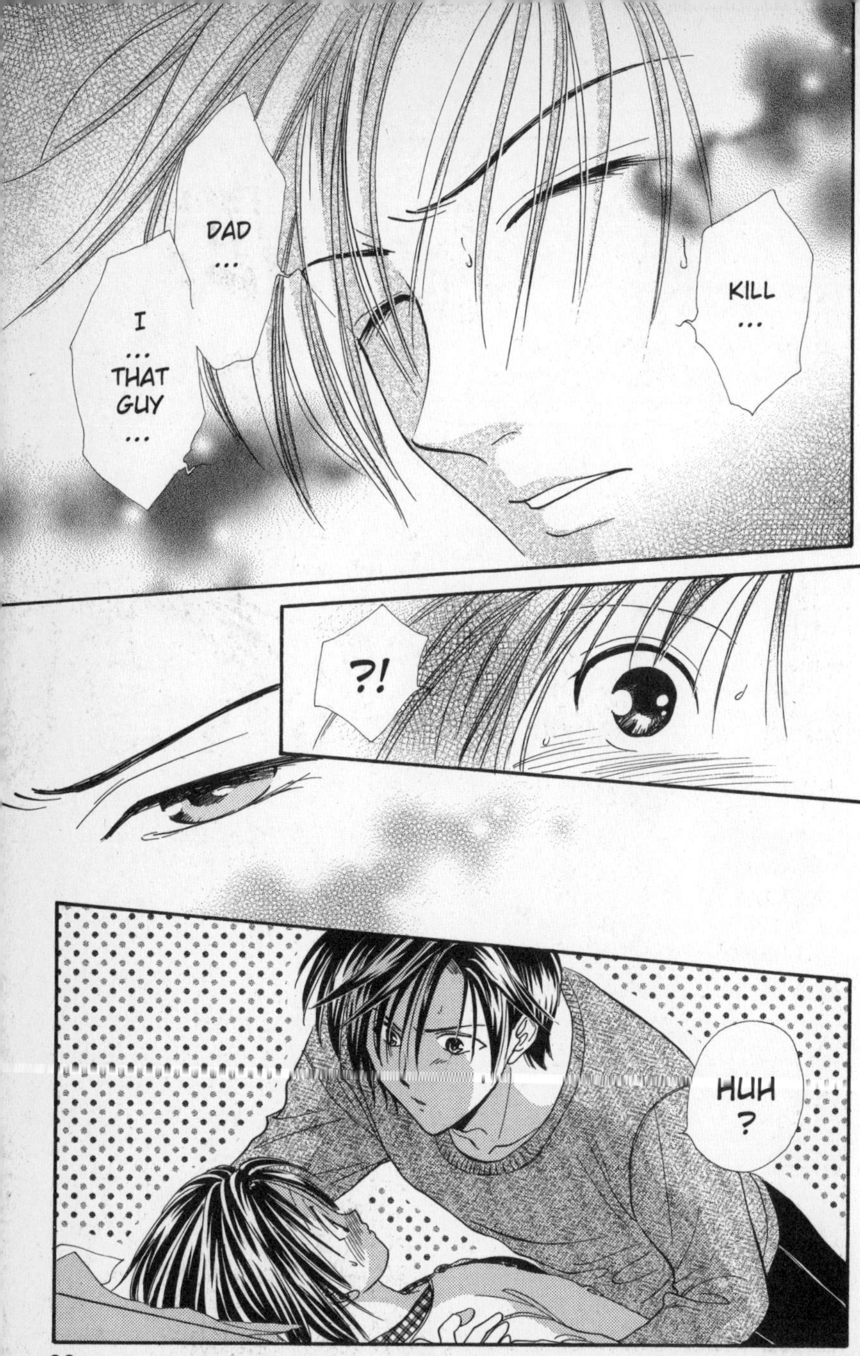
KILL ...
DAD ...
I ... THAT GUY ...
?!
HUH ?

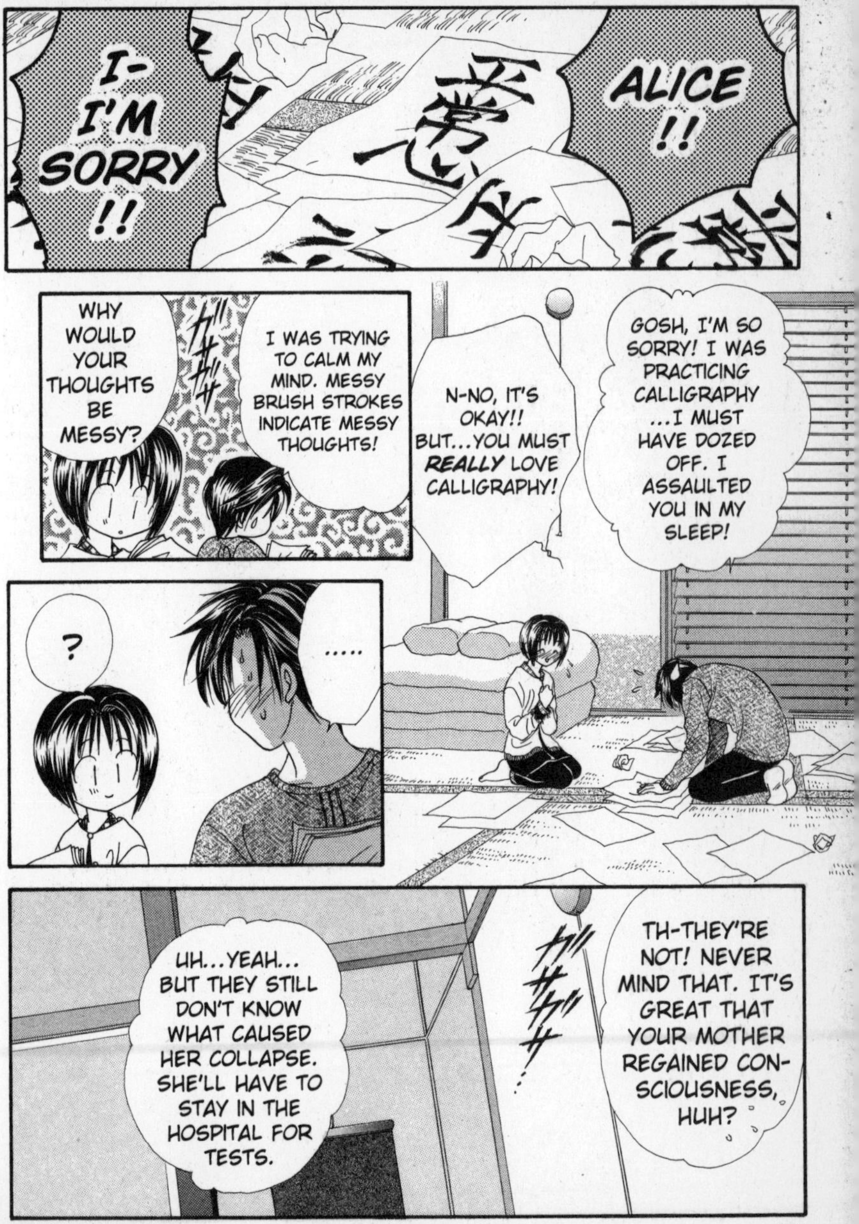
ALICE !!
I- I'M SORRY !!
GOSH, I'M SO SORRY! I WAS PRACTICING CALLIGRAPHY ...I MUST HAVE DOZED OFF. I ASSAULTED YOU IN MY SLEEP!
N-NO, IT'S OKAY!! BUT...YOU MUST *REALLY* LOVE CALLIGRAPHY!
I WAS TRYING TO CALM MY MIND. MESSY BRUSH STROKES INDICATE MESSY THOUGHTS!
WHY WOULD YOUR THOUGHTS BE MESSY?
.....
?
TH-THEY'RE NOT! NEVER MIND THAT. IT'S GREAT THAT YOUR MOTHER REGAINED CON- SCIOUSNESS, HUH?
UH...YEAH... BUT THEY STILL DON'T KNOW WHAT CAUSED HER COLLAPSE. SHE'LL HAVE TO STAY IN THE HOSPITAL FOR TESTS.

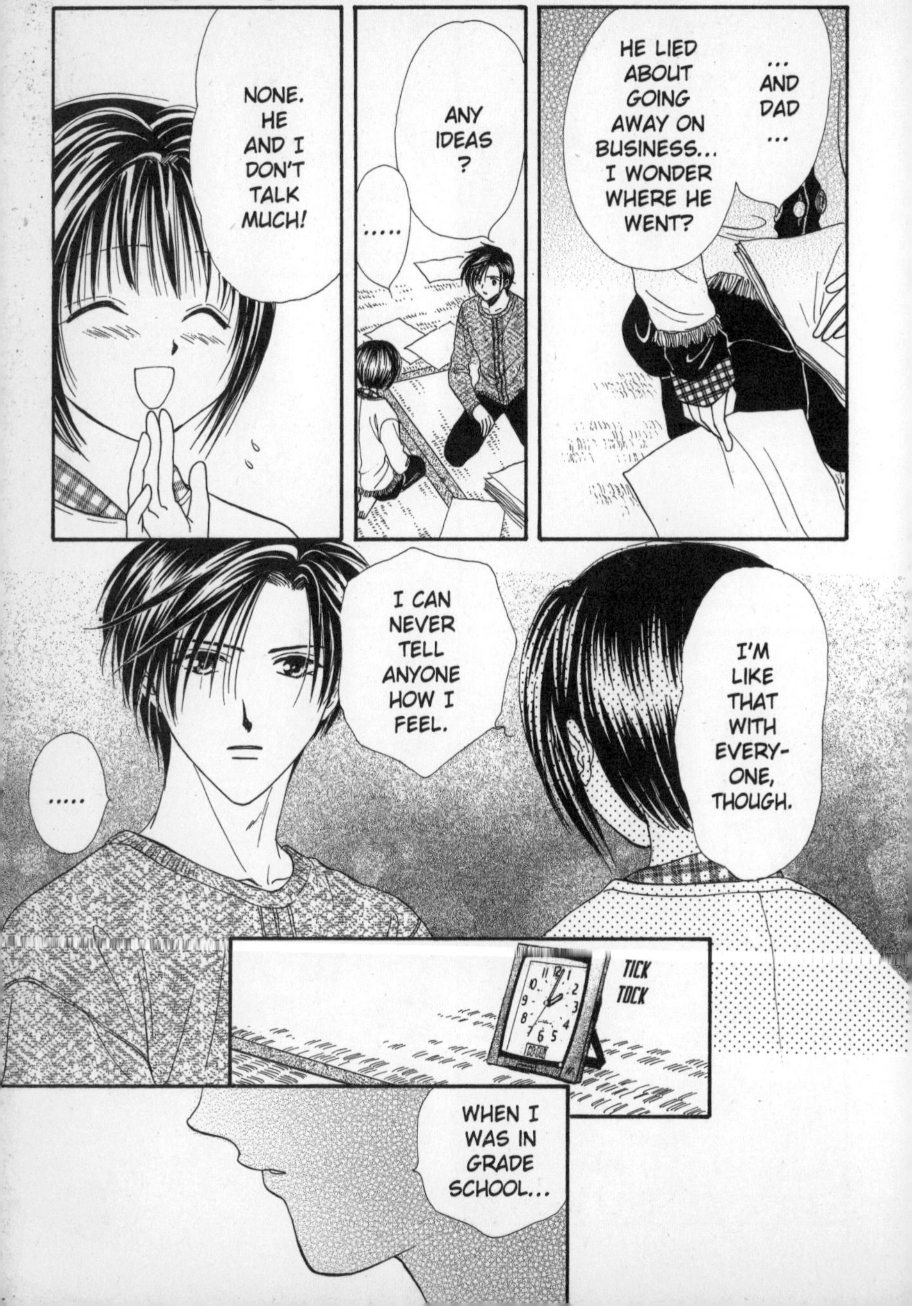
...AND DAD...
HE LIED ABOUT GOING AWAY ON BUSINESS... I WONDER WHERE HE WENT?
ANY IDEAS?
.....
NONE. HE AND I DON'T TALK MUCH!
I'M LIKE THAT WITH EVERY-ONE, THOUGH.
I CAN NEVER TELL ANYONE HOW I FEEL.
.....
TICK TOCK
WHEN I WAS IN GRADE SCHOOL...

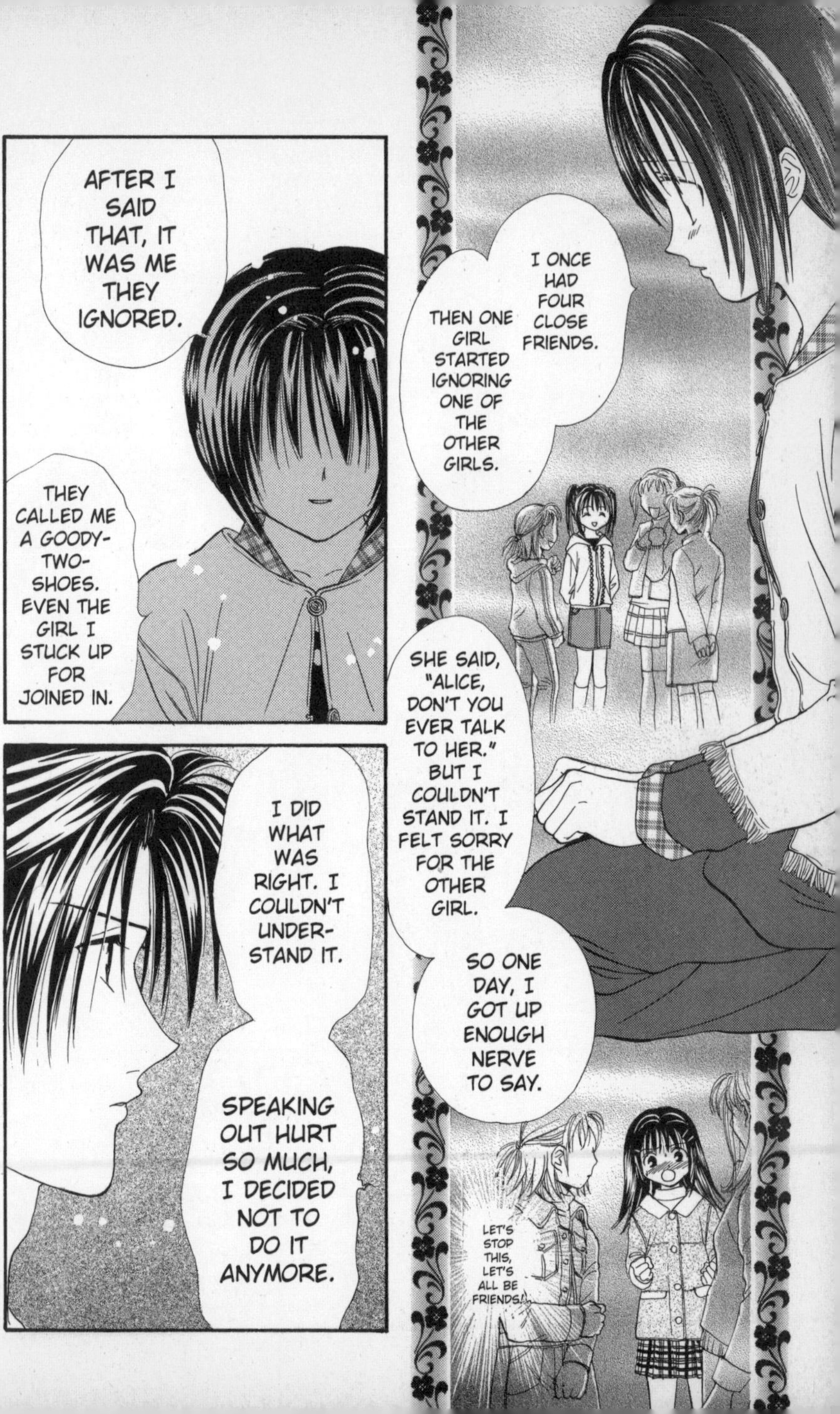
I ONCE HAD FOUR CLOSE FRIENDS.
THEN ONE GIRL STARTED IGNORING ONE OF THE OTHER GIRLS.
SHE SAID, "ALICE, DON'T YOU EVER TALK TO HER." BUT I COULDN'T STAND IT. I FELT SORRY FOR THE OTHER GIRL.
SO ONE DAY, I GOT UP ENOUGH NERVE TO SAY.
LET'S STOP THIS, LET'S ALL BE FRIENDS!
AFTER I SAID THAT, IT WAS ME THEY IGNORED.
THEY CALLED ME A GOODY-TWO-SHOES. EVEN THE GIRL I STUCK UP FOR JOINED IN.
I DID WHAT WAS RIGHT. I COULDN'T UNDER-STAND IT.
SPEAKING OUT HURT SO MUCH, I DECIDED NOT TO DO IT ANYMORE.

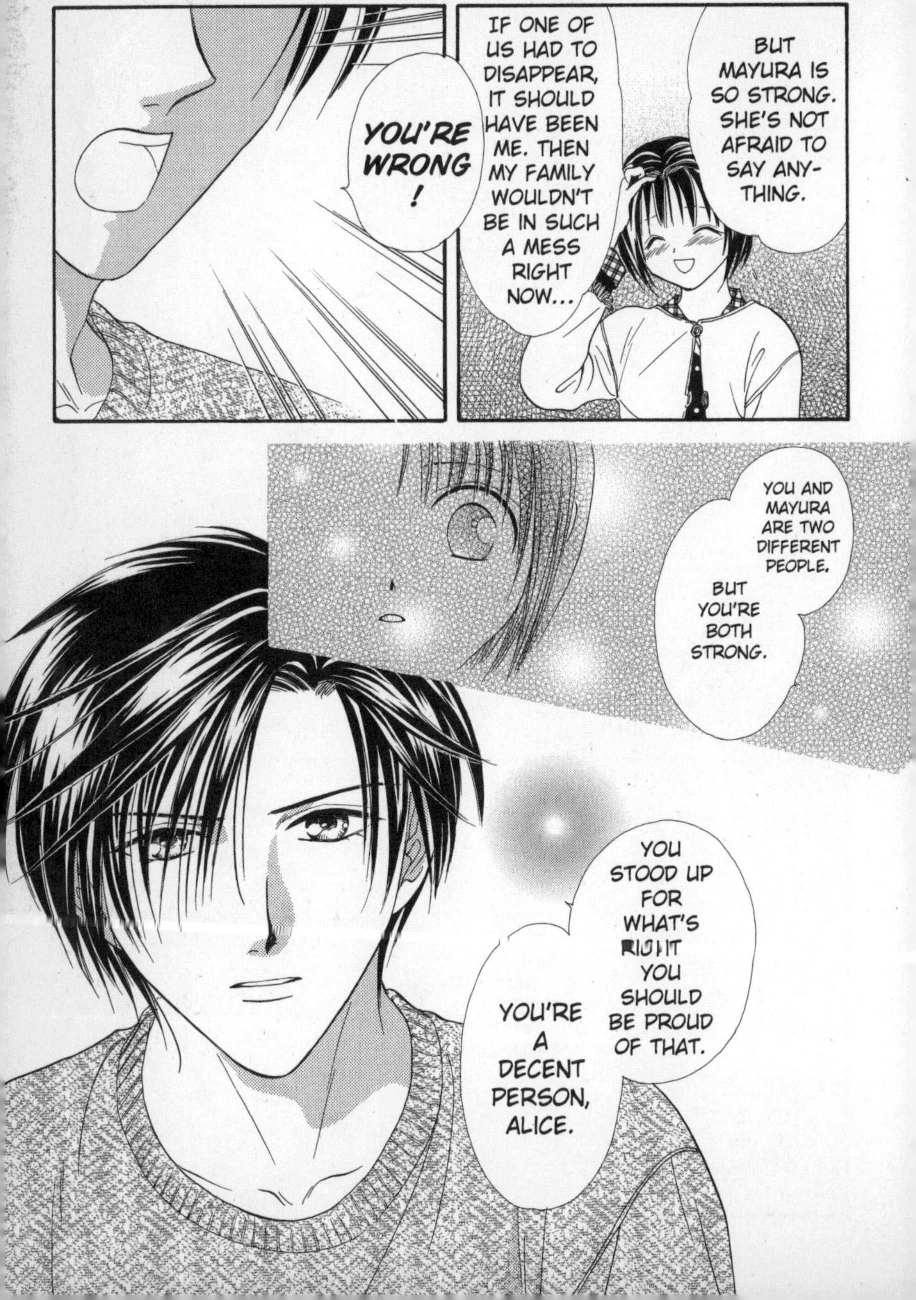
BUT MAYURA IS SO STRONG. SHE'S NOT AFRAID TO SAY ANYTHING.
IF ONE OF US HAD TO DISAPPEAR, IT SHOULD HAVE BEEN ME. THEN MY FAMILY WOULDN'T BE IN SUCH A MESS RIGHT NOW...
YOU'RE WRONG!
YOU AND MAYURA ARE TWO DIFFERENT PEOPLE.
BUT YOU'RE BOTH STRONG.
YOU STOOD UP FOR WHAT'S RIGHT YOU SHOULD BE PROUD OF THAT.
YOU'RE A DECENT PERSON, ALICE.

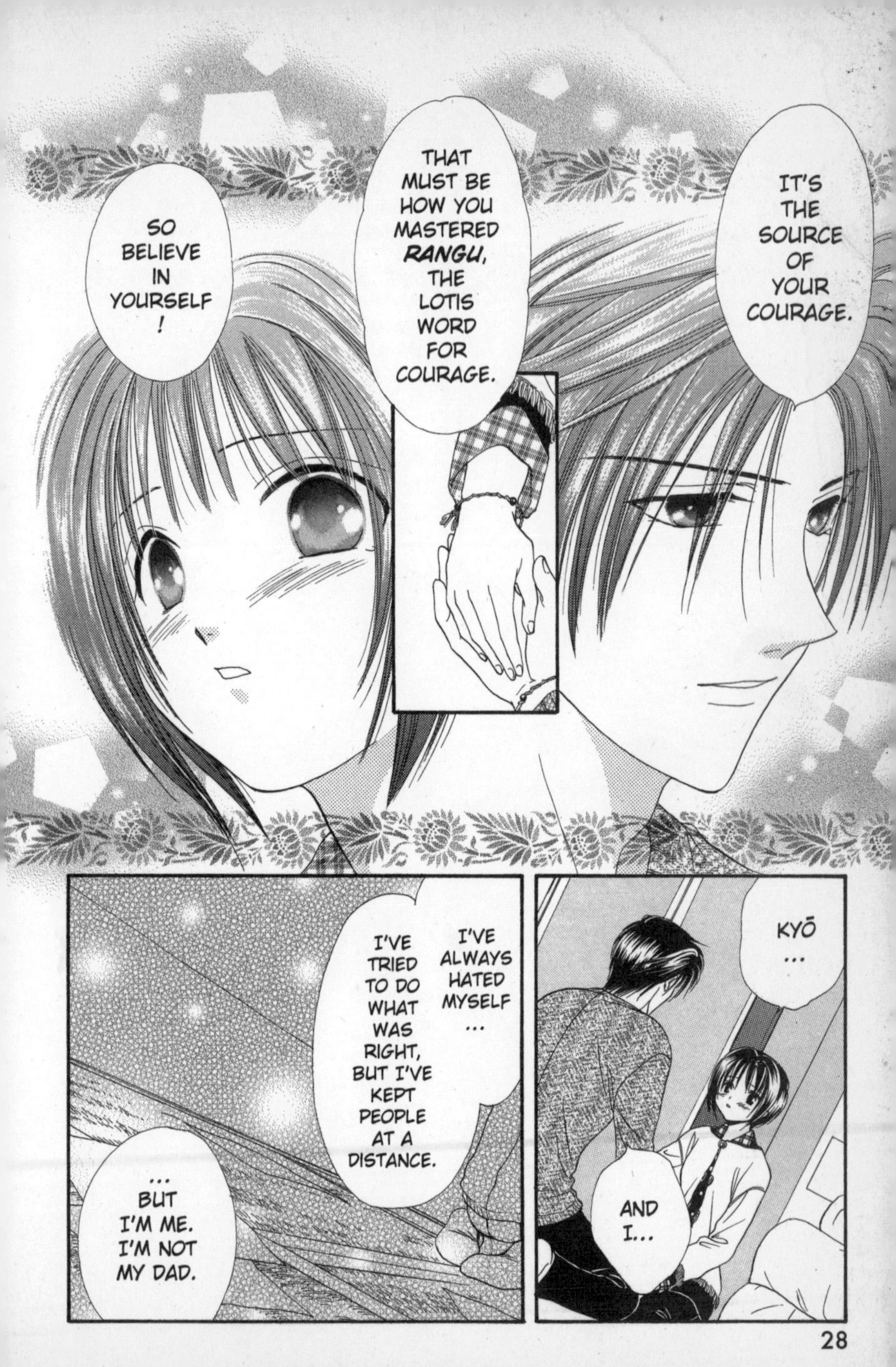
IT'S THE SOURCE OF YOUR COURAGE.
THAT MUST BE HOW YOU MASTERED *RANGU*, THE LOTIS WORD FOR COURAGE.
SO BELIEVE IN YOURSELF!
KYŌ...
AND I...
I'VE ALWAYS HATED MYSELF...
I'VE TRIED TO DO WHAT WAS RIGHT, BUT I'VE KEPT PEOPLE AT A DISTANCE.
...BUT I'M ME. I'M NOT MY DAD.

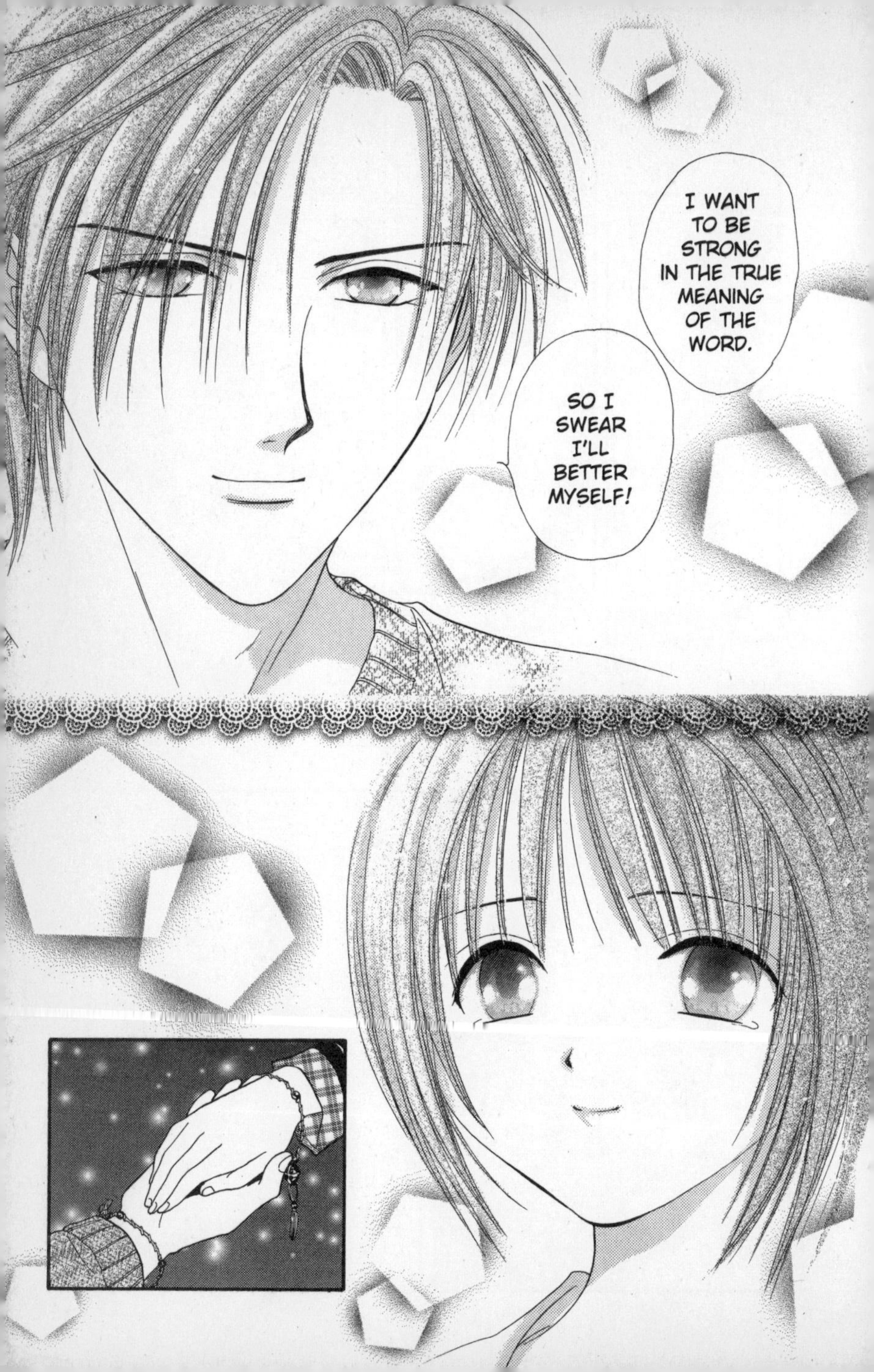
I WANT TO BE STRONG IN THE TRUE MEANING OF THE WORD.
SO I SWEAR I'LL BETTER MYSELF!

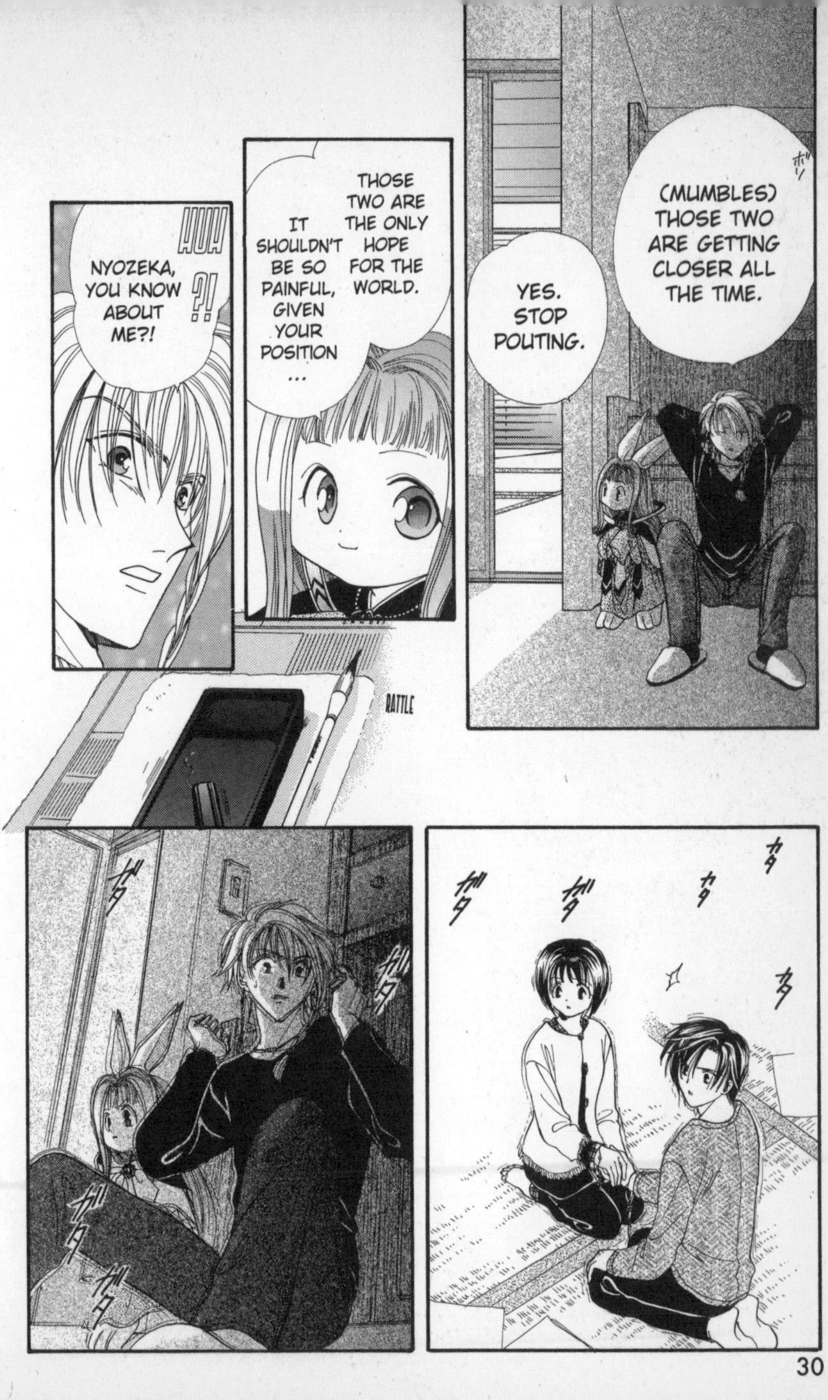
(MUMBLES) THOSE TWO ARE GETTING CLOSER ALL THE TIME.
YES. STOP POUTING.
THOSE TWO ARE THE ONLY HOPE FOR THE WORLD.
IT SHOULDN'T BE SO PAINFUL, GIVEN YOUR POSITION ...
HUH
?!
NYOZEKA, YOU KNOW ABOUT ME?!
RATTLE

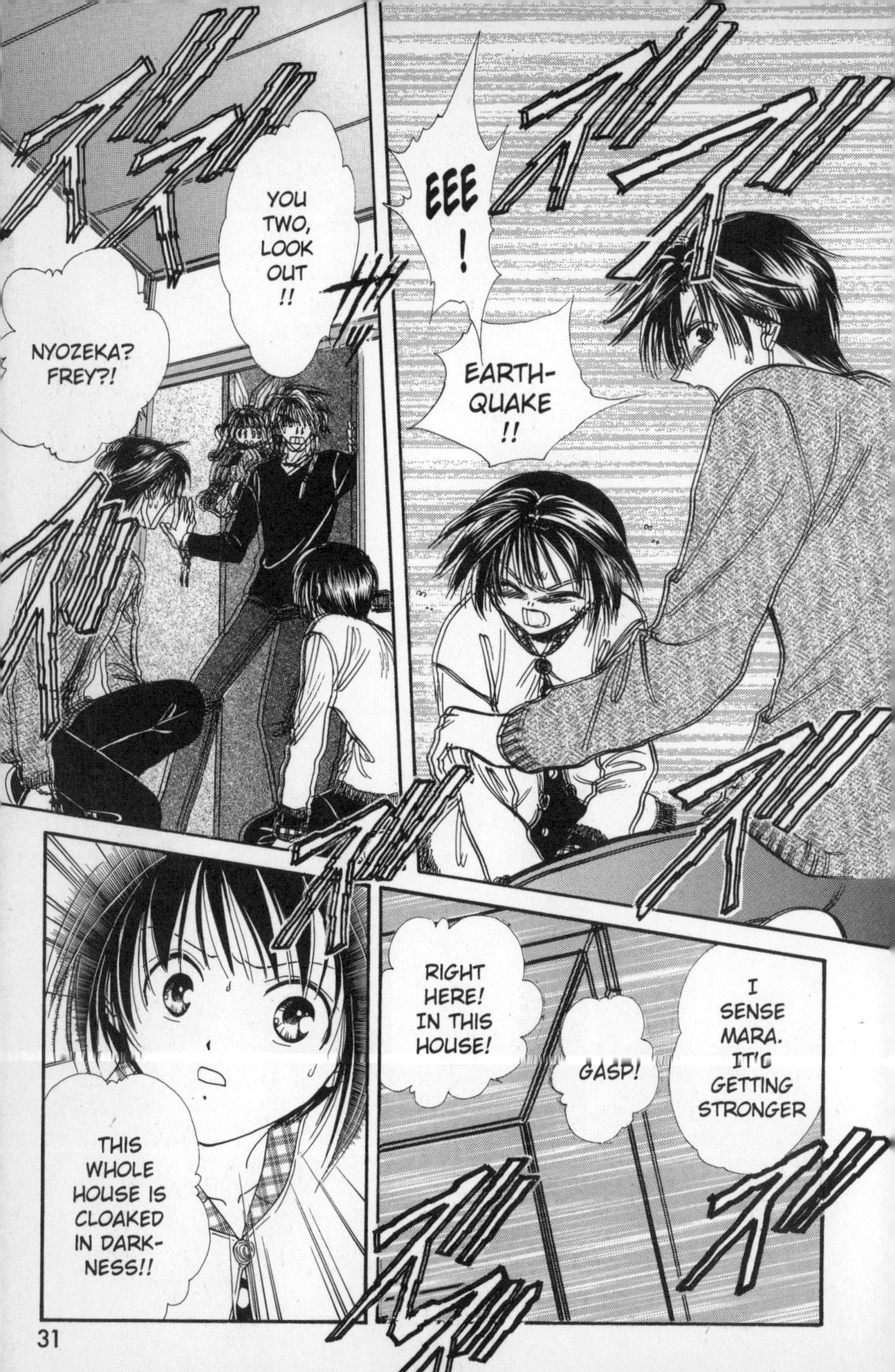
EEE!
EARTHQUAKE!!
YOU TWO, LOOK OUT!!
NYOZEKA? FREY?!
I SENSE MARA. IT'S GETTING STRONGER
GASP!
RIGHT HERE! IN THIS HOUSE!
THIS WHOLE HOUSE IS CLOAKED IN DARKNESS!!

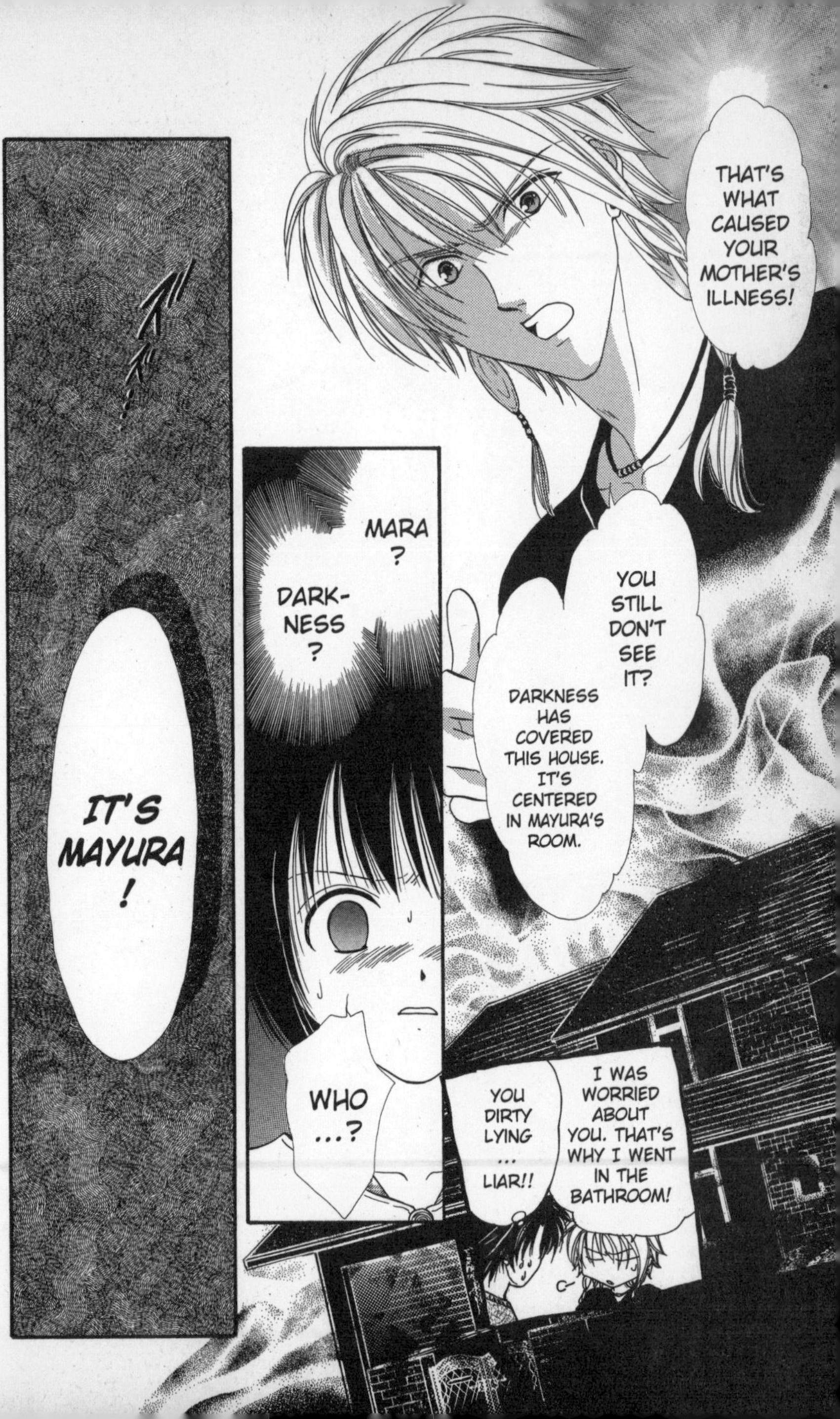
THAT'S WHAT CAUSED YOUR MOTHER'S ILLNESS!
YOU STILL DON'T SEE IT?
DARKNESS HAS COVERED THIS HOUSE. IT'S CENTERED IN MAYURA'S ROOM.
I WAS WORRIED ABOUT YOU. THAT'S WHY I WENT IN THE BATHROOM!
YOU DIRTY LYING ... LIAR!!
MARA?
DARKNESS?
WHO ...?
IT'S MAYURA!

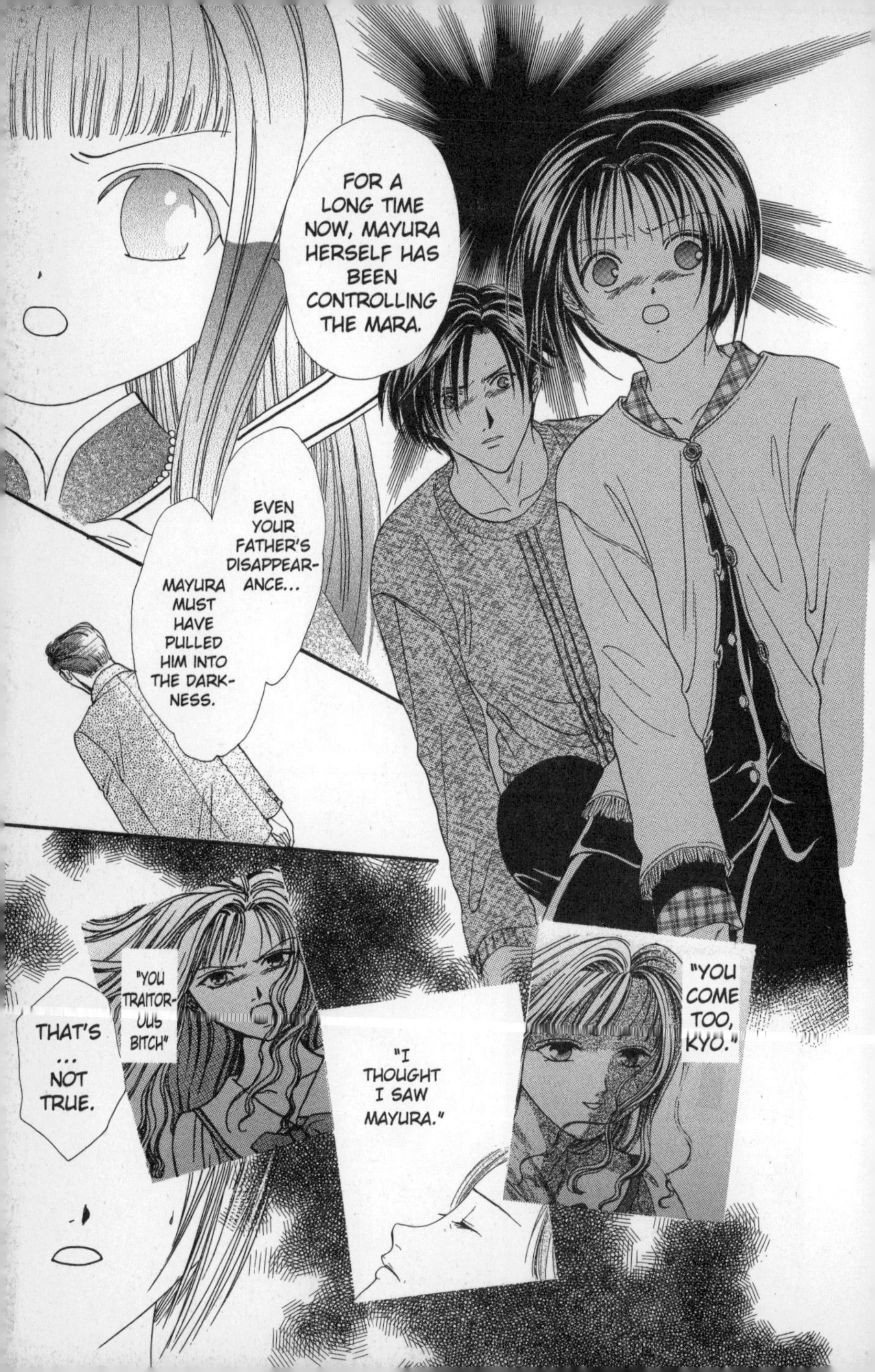
FOR A LONG TIME NOW, MAYURA HERSELF HAS BEEN CONTROLLING THE MARA.
EVEN YOUR FATHER'S DISAPPEAR-ANCE...
MAYURA MUST HAVE PULLED HIM INTO THE DARK-NESS.
"YOU COME TOO, KYO."
"I THOUGHT I SAW MAYURA."
"YOU TRAITOR-OUS BITCH"
THAT'S ... NOT TRUE.

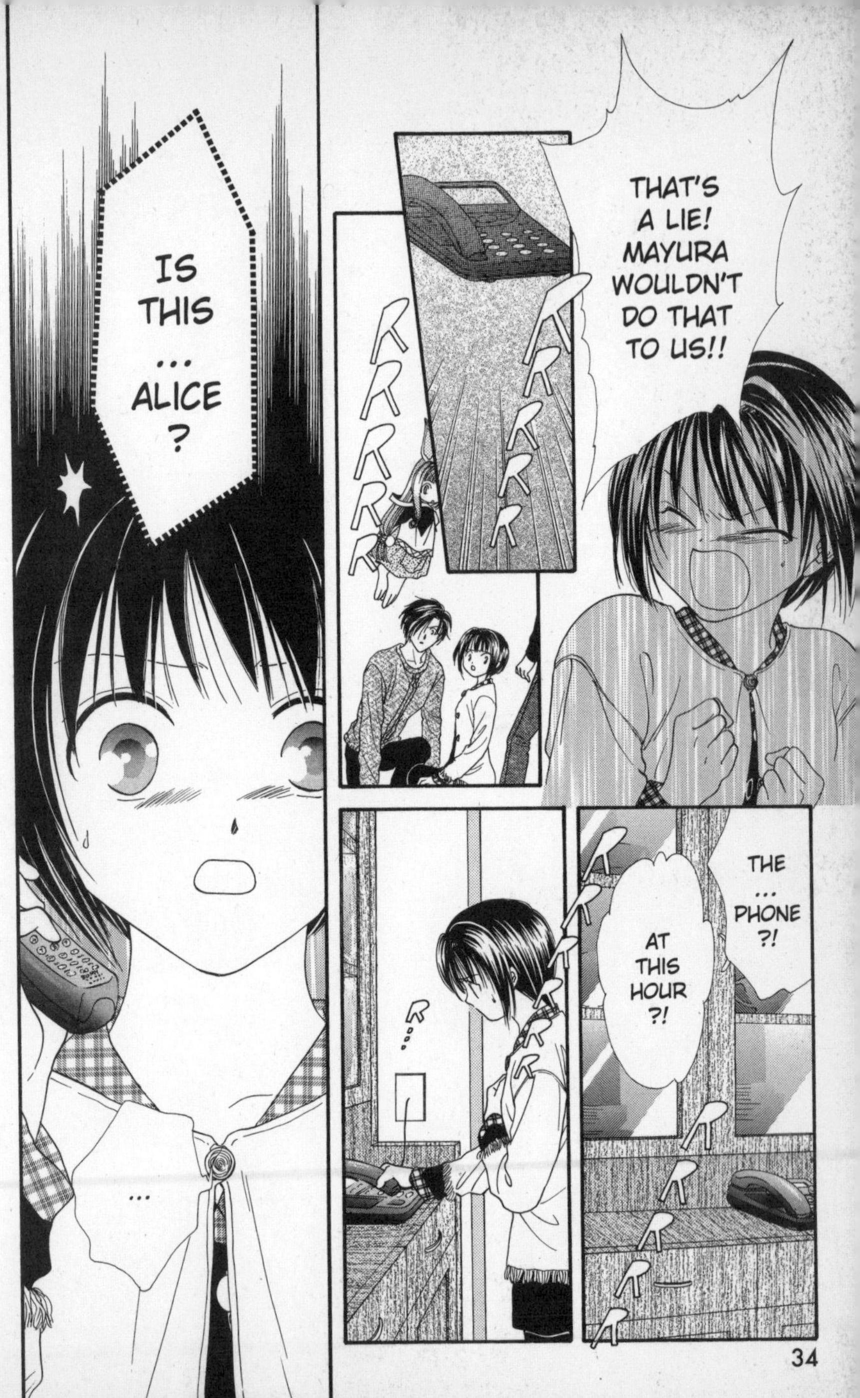

THAT'S A LIE! MAYURA WOULDN'T DO THAT TO US!!
THE ... PHONE ?!
AT THIS HOUR ?!
IS THIS ... ALICE ?
...

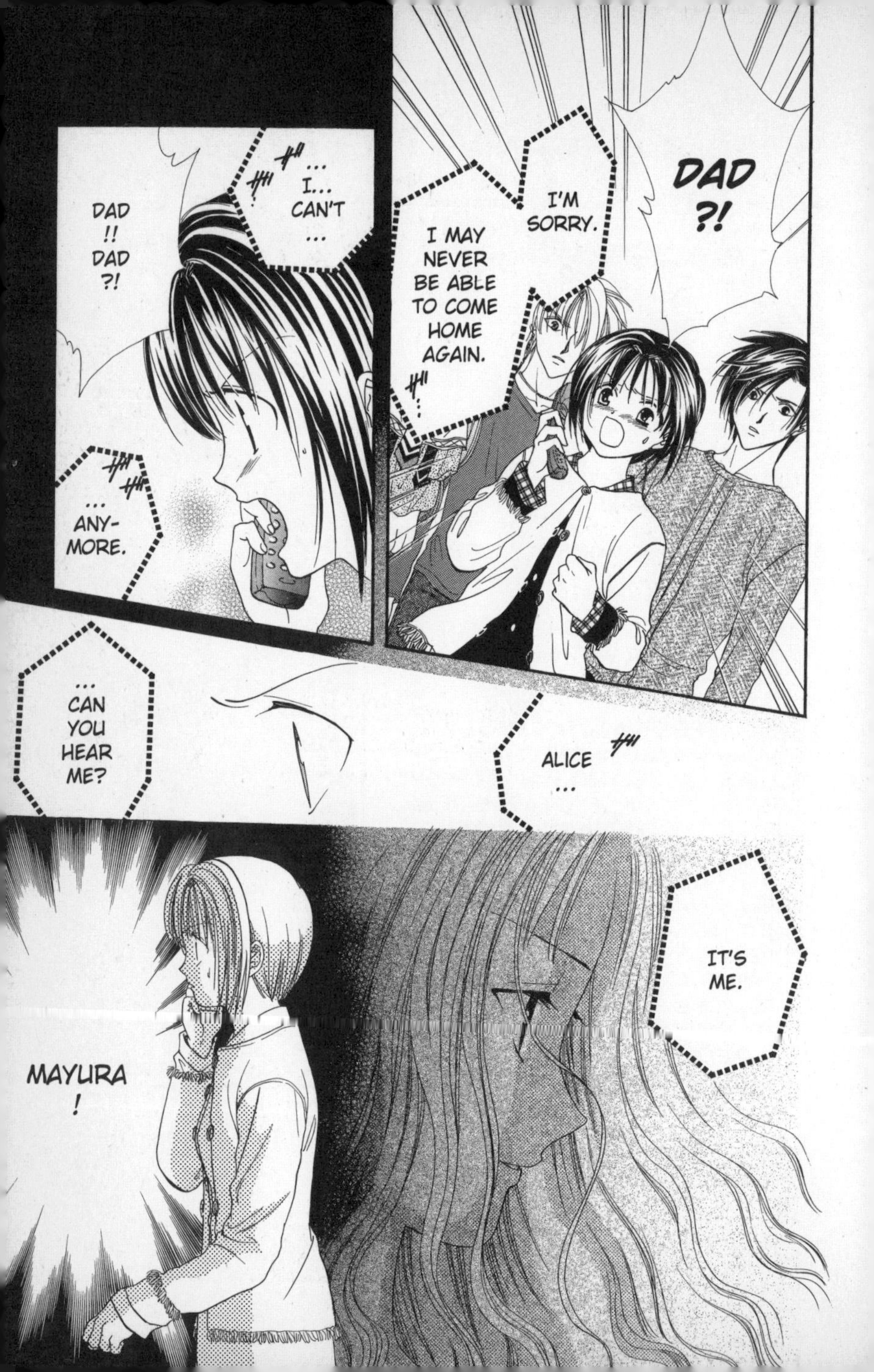
DAD ?!
I'M SORRY.
I MAY NEVER BE ABLE TO COME HOME AGAIN.
... I... CAN'T ...
DAD !! DAD ?!
... ANY-MORE.
ALICE ...
... CAN YOU HEAR ME?
IT'S ME.
MAYURA !

ALICE SENO

🌸 HEIGHT: 158 CM

🌸 BUST: 80 CM. WAIST: 59 CM. HIPS: 88 CM.

🌸 PISCES (3/19)

🌸 BLOOD TYPE A

🌸 INTERESTS: LOVES ANIMALS.

🌸 HOBBY: COLLECTING SMALL, ANIMAL-RELATED THINGS.

🌸 GRADES, PERFORMANCE IN SPORTS: AVERAGE

🌸 QUIRKS: HAS A COMPLEX ABOUT HER OLDER SISTER WHO EXCELS IN EVERYTHING.

🌸 HABITS: SPENDS A LOT OF TIME SENDING E-MAILS AND TEXT MESSAGING, BUT HAS NO FRIEND IN WHOM SHE CAN REALLY CONFIDE. (FEAR OF BEING HURT HAS CAUSED HER TO AVOID CLOSE RELATIONSHIPS.)

🌸 PERSONALITY: SHY, BUT HAS INNER STRENGTH. PURE OF HEART, KIND-HEARTED, CRIES EASILY. USUALLY THINKS TOO MUCH ABOUT OTHER PEOPLE'S FEELINGS AND MISINTERPRETS THEM. SHE'S ALWAYS WANTED TO CHANGE THIS PART OF HERSELF.

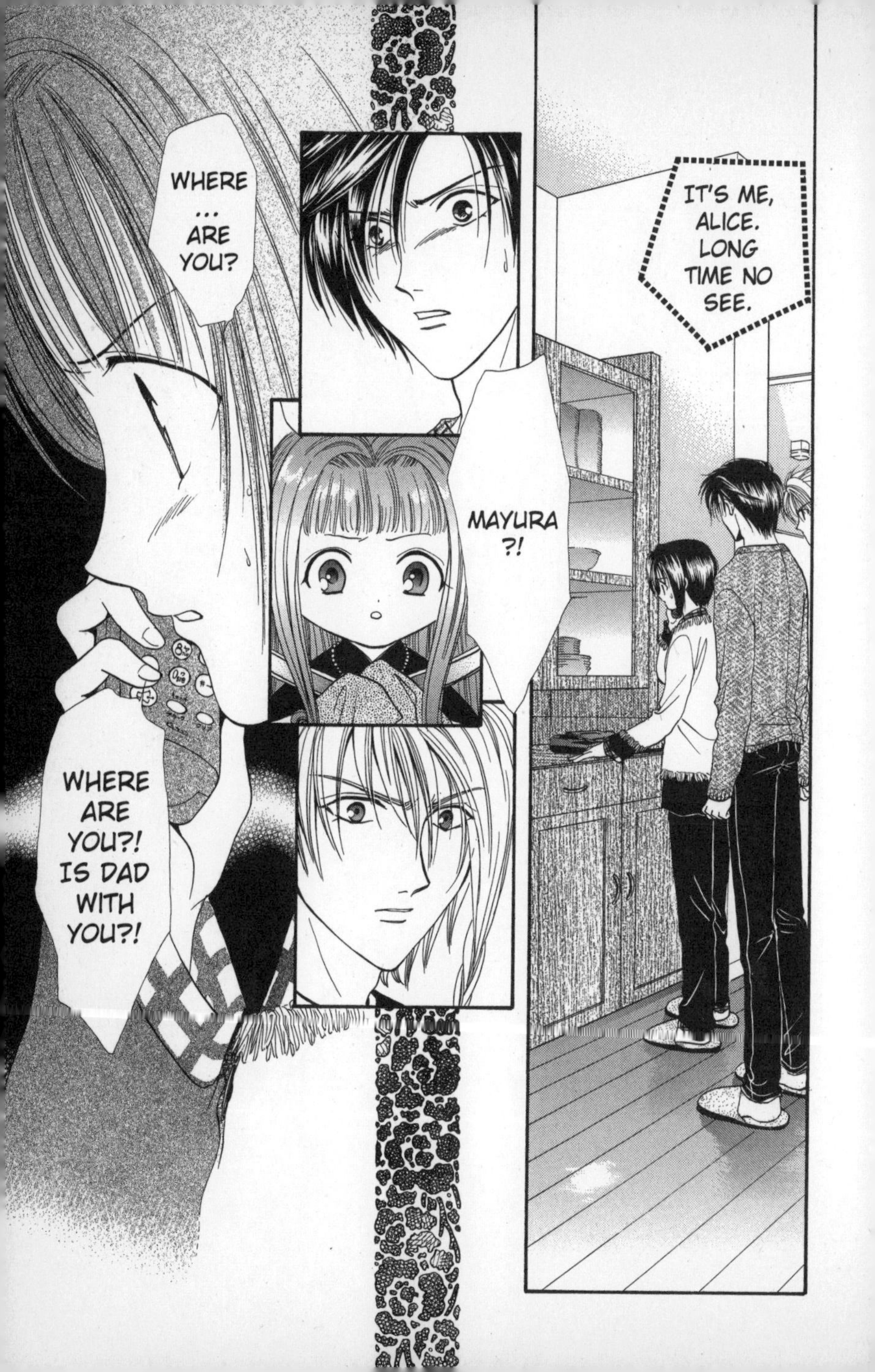
IT'S ME, ALICE. LONG TIME NO SEE.
MAYURA ?!
WHERE ... ARE YOU?
WHERE ARE YOU?! IS DAD WITH YOU?!

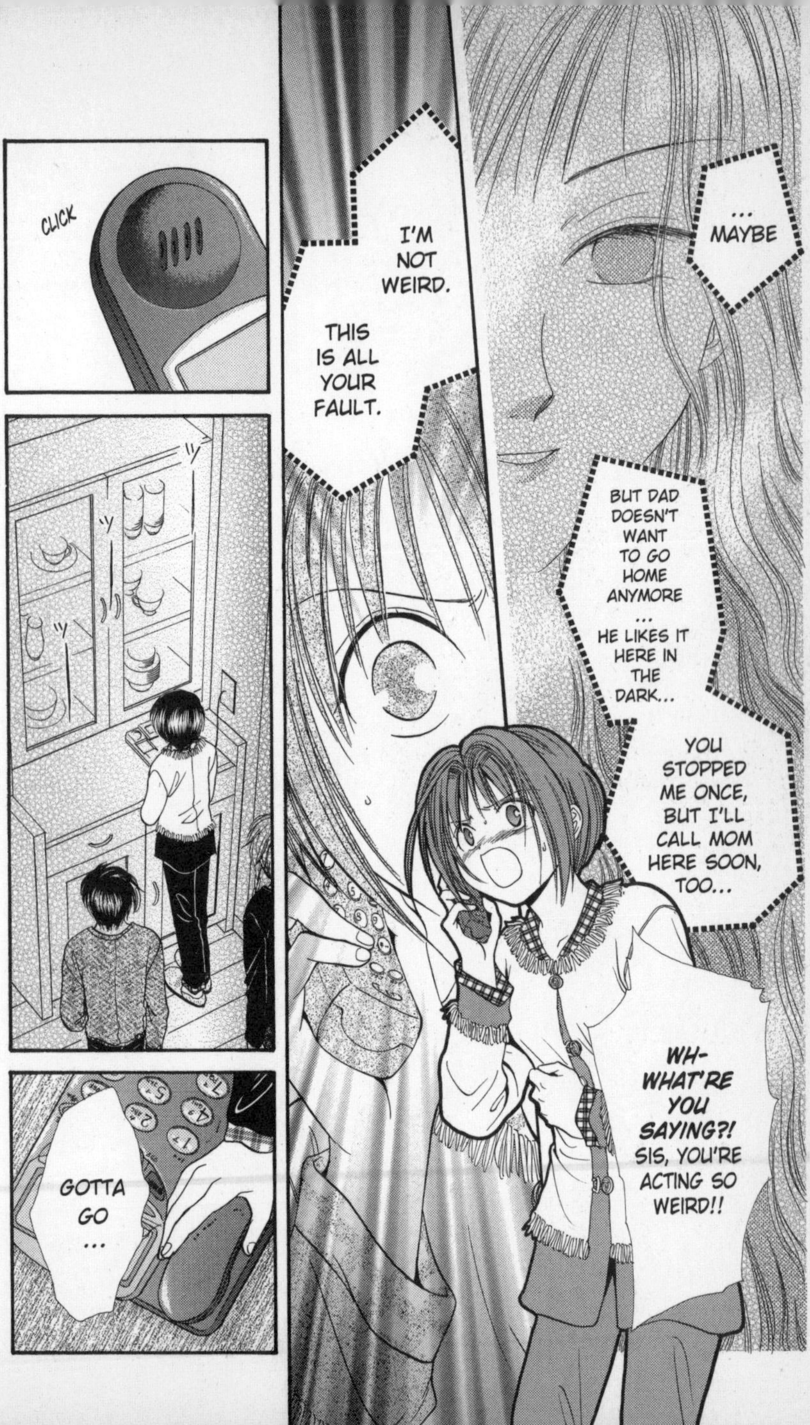
...MAYBE
I'M NOT WEIRD.
THIS IS ALL YOUR FAULT.
BUT DAD DOESN'T WANT TO GO HOME ANYMORE ... HE LIKES IT HERE IN THE DARK...
YOU STOPPED ME ONCE, BUT I'LL CALL MOM HERE SOON, TOO...
WH-WHAT'RE YOU SAYING?! SIS, YOU'RE ACTING SO WEIRD!!
CLICK
GOTTA GO ...

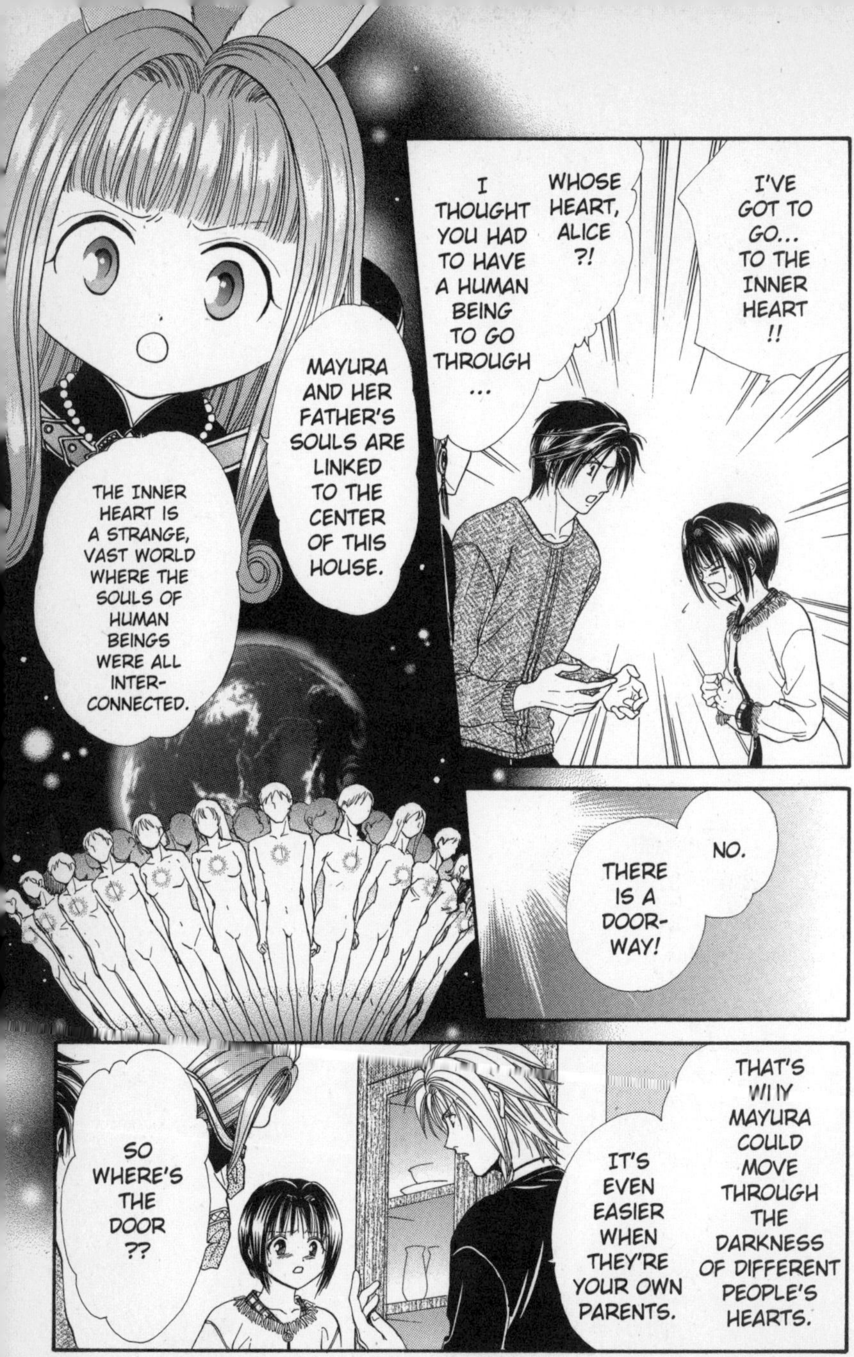
I'VE GOT TO GO... TO THE INNER HEART !!
WHOSE HEART, ALICE ?!
I THOUGHT YOU HAD TO HAVE A HUMAN BEING TO GO THROUGH ...
NO.
THERE IS A DOOR-WAY!
MAYURA AND HER FATHER'S SOULS ARE LINKED TO THE CENTER OF THIS HOUSE.
THE INNER HEART IS A STRANGE, VAST WORLD WHERE THE SOULS OF HUMAN BEINGS WERE ALL INTER-CONNECTED.
THAT'S WHY MAYURA COULD MOVE THROUGH THE DARKNESS OF DIFFERENT PEOPLE'S HEARTS.
IT'S EVEN EASIER WHEN THEY'RE YOUR OWN PARENTS.
SO WHERE'S THE DOOR ??

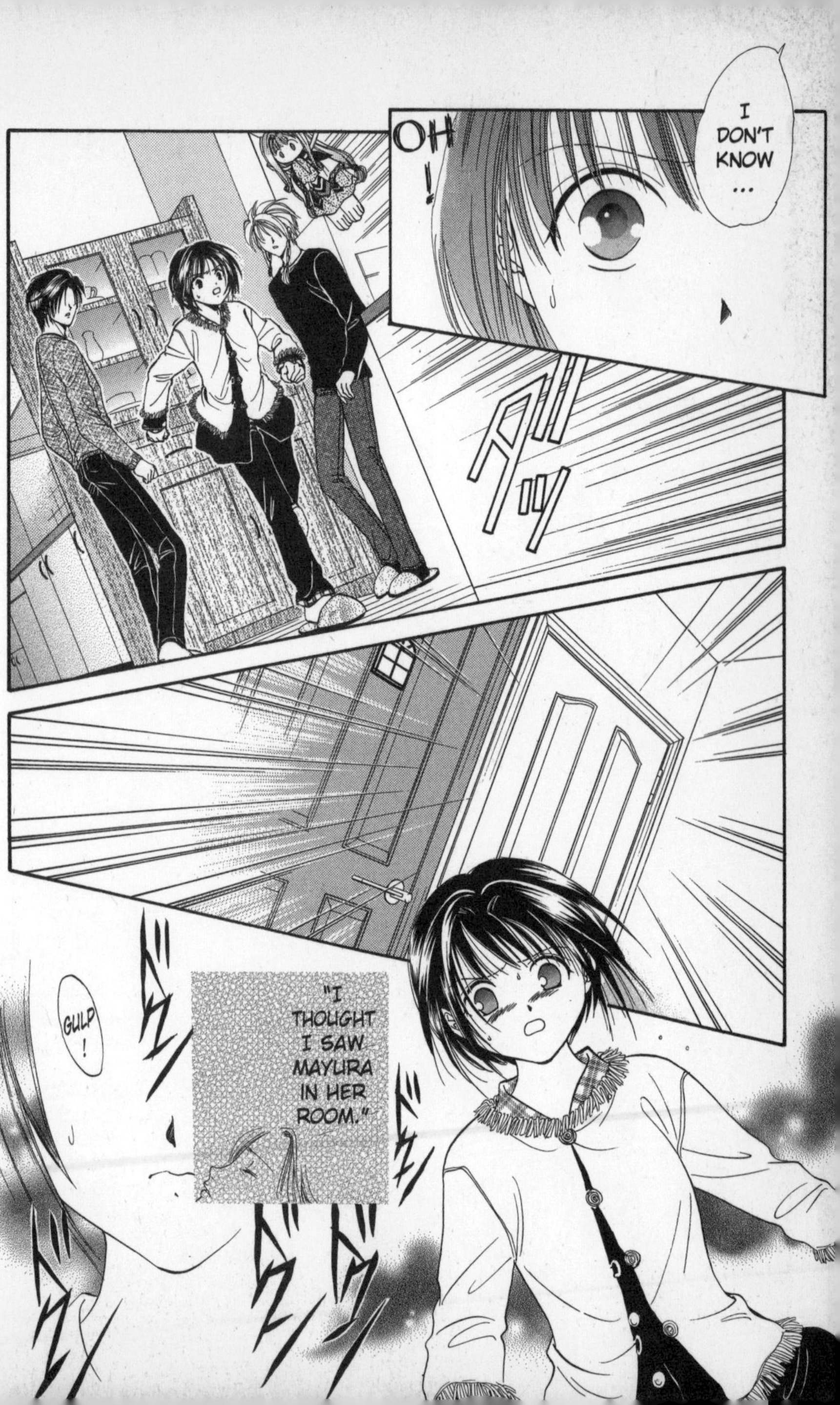
I DON'T KNOW ...
OH !
GULP !
"I THOUGHT I SAW MAYURA IN HER ROOM."

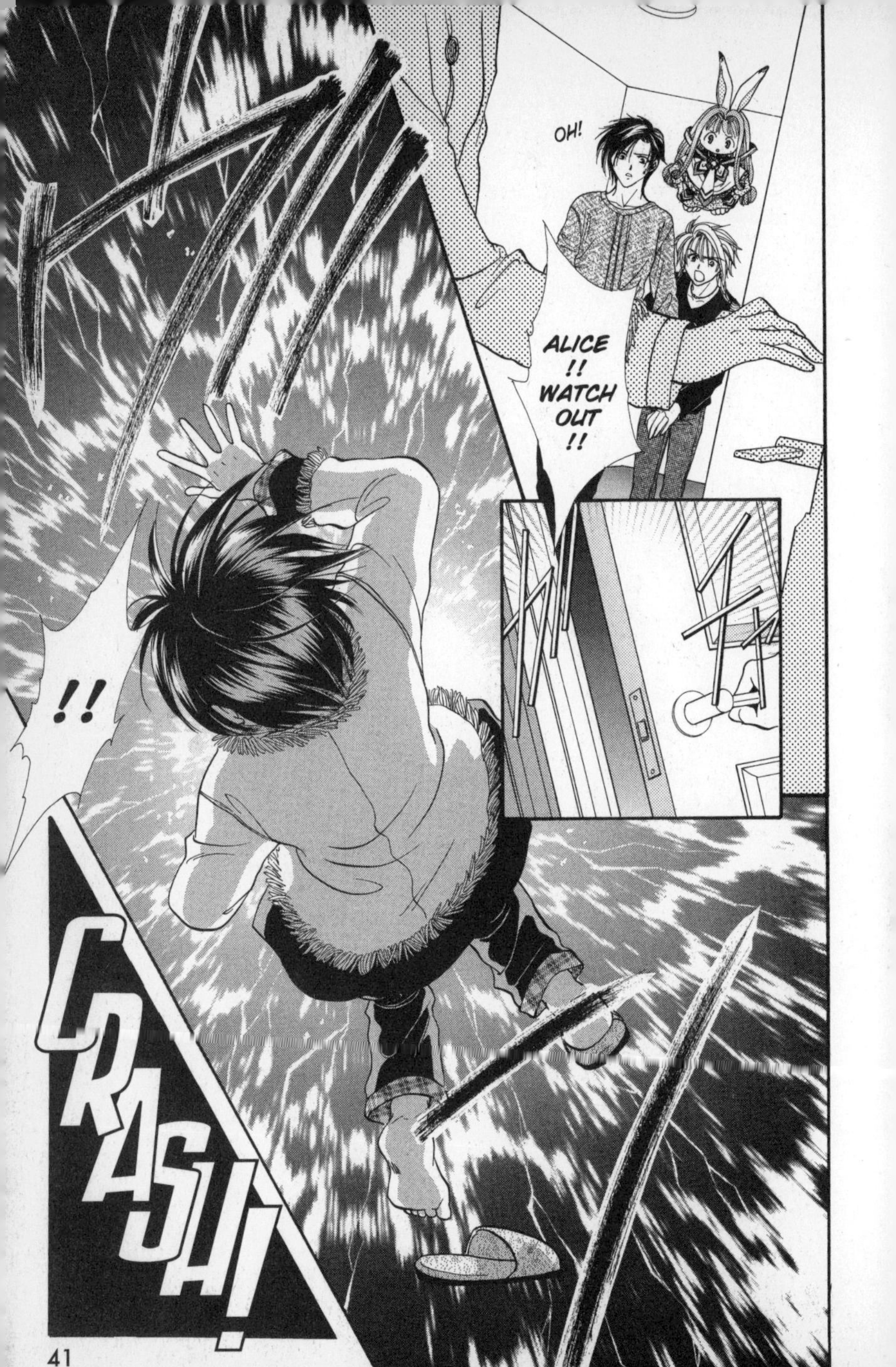
OH!
ALICE !! WATCH OUT !!
!!
CRASH!

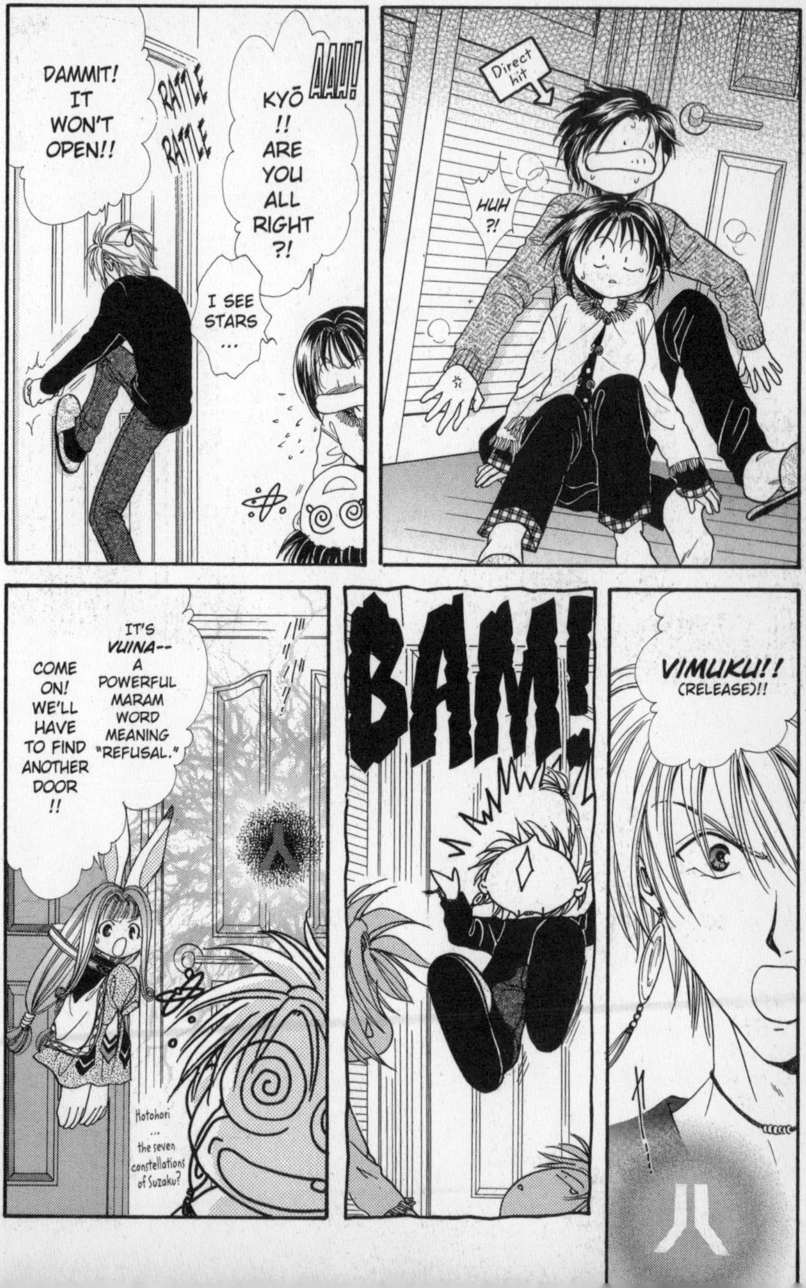
Direct hit
HUH ?!
AAH!
KYŌ !! ARE YOU ALL RIGHT ?!
RATTLE RATTLE
DAMMIT! IT WON'T OPEN!!
I SEE STARS ...
VIMUKU!! (RELEASE)!!
BAM!
IT'S VUINA-- A POWERFUL MARAM WORD MEANING "REFUSAL."
COME ON! WE'LL HAVE TO FIND ANOTHER DOOR !!
Hotohori ... the seven constellations of Suzaku?

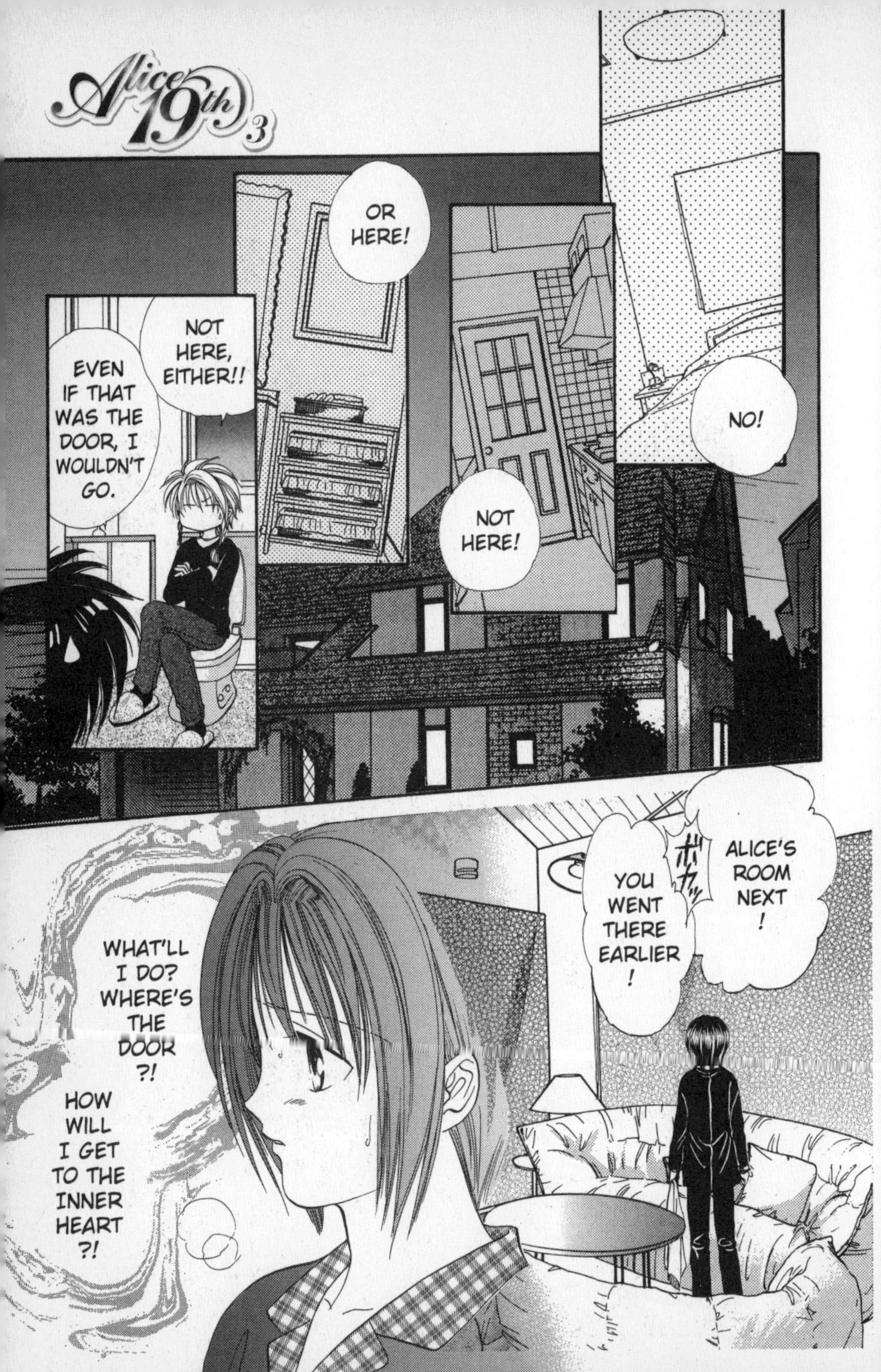
NO!
NOT HERE!
OR HERE!
NOT HERE, EITHER!!
EVEN IF THAT WAS THE DOOR, I WOULDN'T GO.
ALICE'S ROOM NEXT!
ボカッ
YOU WENT THERE EARLIER!
WHAT'LL I DO? WHERE'S THE DOOR?!
HOW WILL I GET TO THE INNER HEART?!

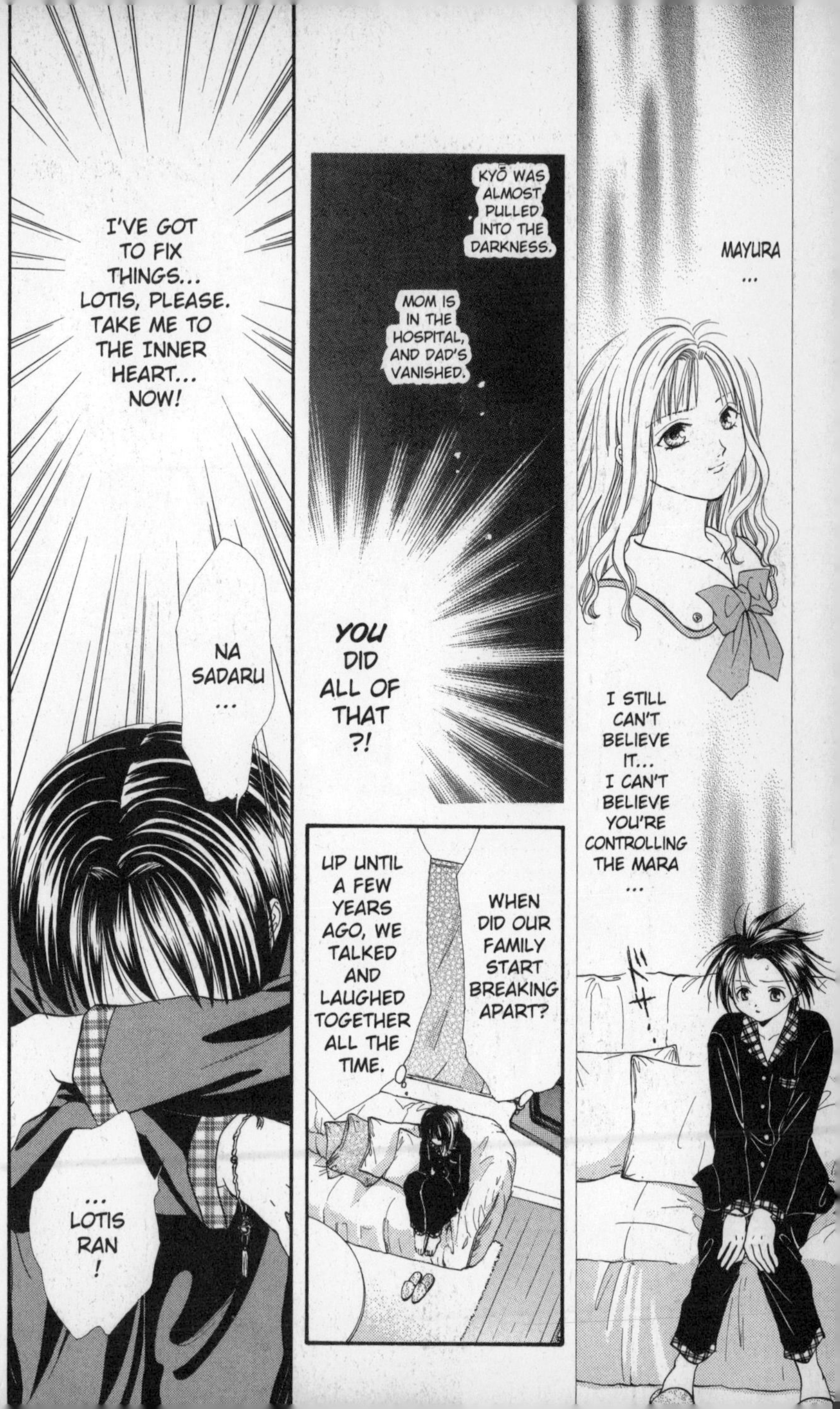
MAYURA ...
I STILL CAN'T BELIEVE IT... I CAN'T BELIEVE YOU'RE CONTROLLING THE MARA ...
KYŌ WAS ALMOST PULLED INTO THE DARKNESS.
MOM IS IN THE HOSPITAL, AND DAD'S VANISHED.
YOU DID ALL OF THAT ?!
WHEN DID OUR FAMILY START BREAKING APART?
UP UNTIL A FEW YEARS AGO, WE TALKED AND LAUGHED TOGETHER ALL THE TIME.
I'VE GOT TO FIX THINGS... LOTIS, PLEASE. TAKE ME TO THE INNER HEART... NOW!
NA SADARU ...
... LOTIS RAN !

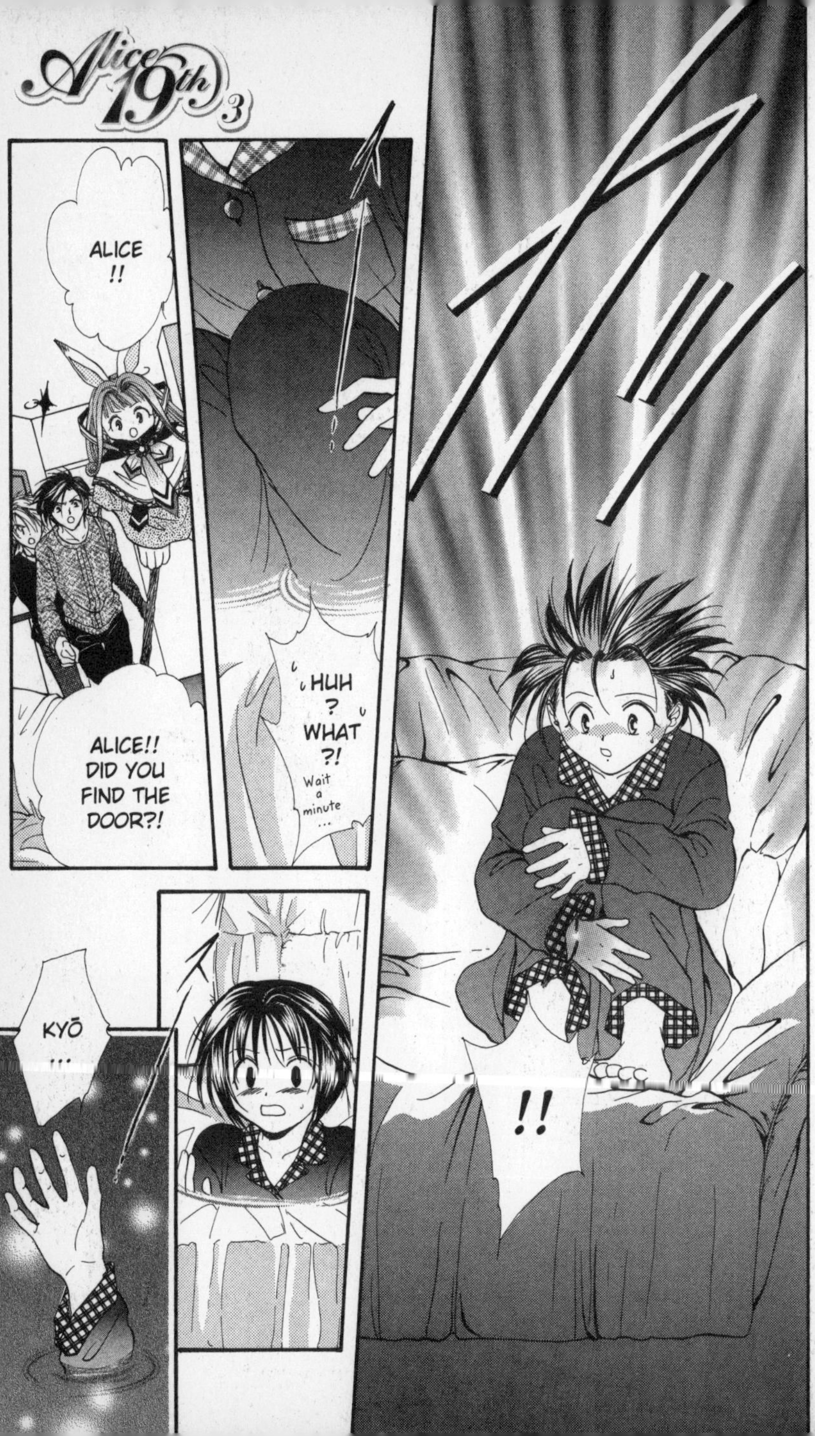
!!
HUH ? WHAT ?!
Wait a minute ...
ALICE !!
ALICE!! DID YOU FIND THE DOOR?!
KYŌ ...

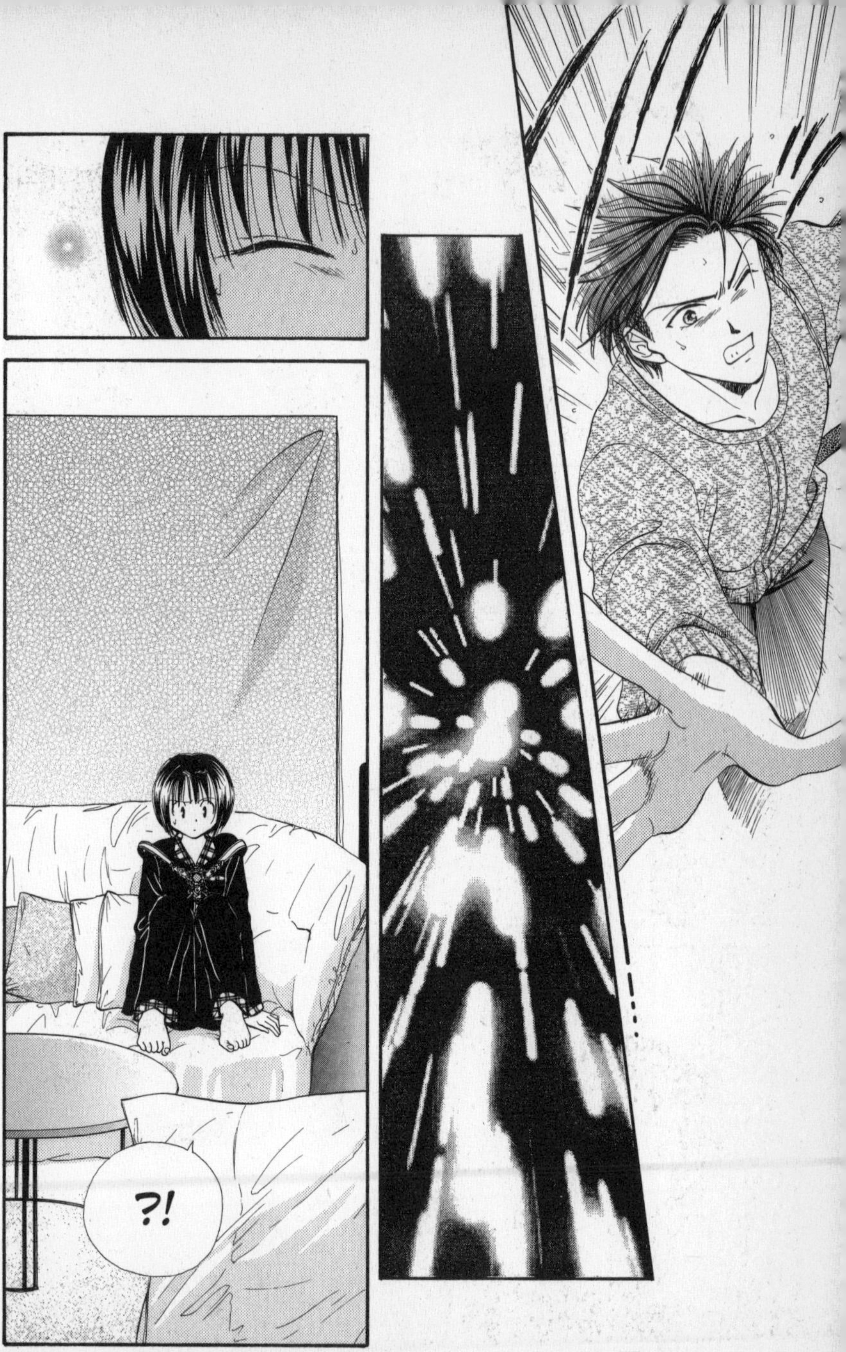
?!

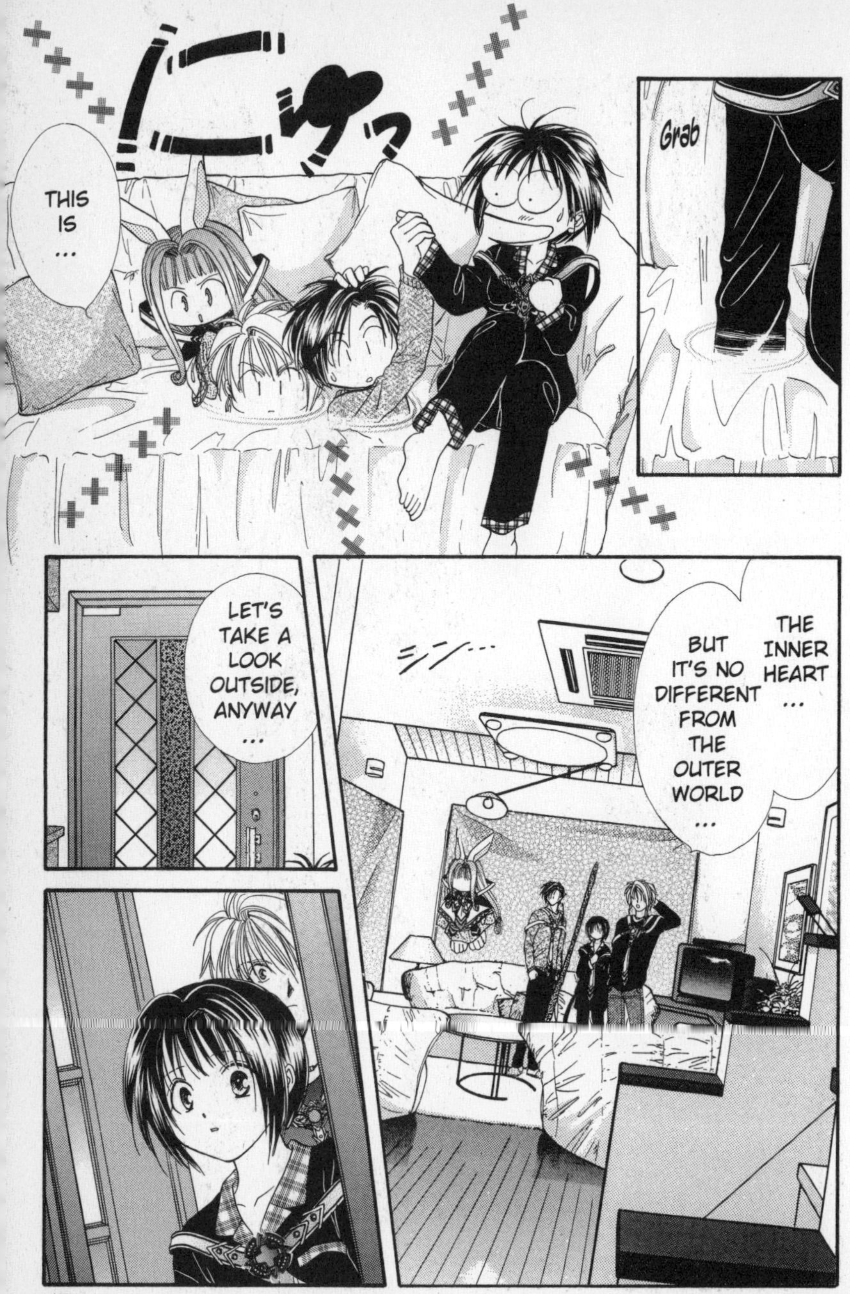
Grab
にゅっ
THIS IS ...
THE INNER HEART ...
BUT IT'S NO DIFFERENT FROM THE OUTER WORLD ...
シーン...
LET'S TAKE A LOOK OUTSIDE, ANYWAY ...

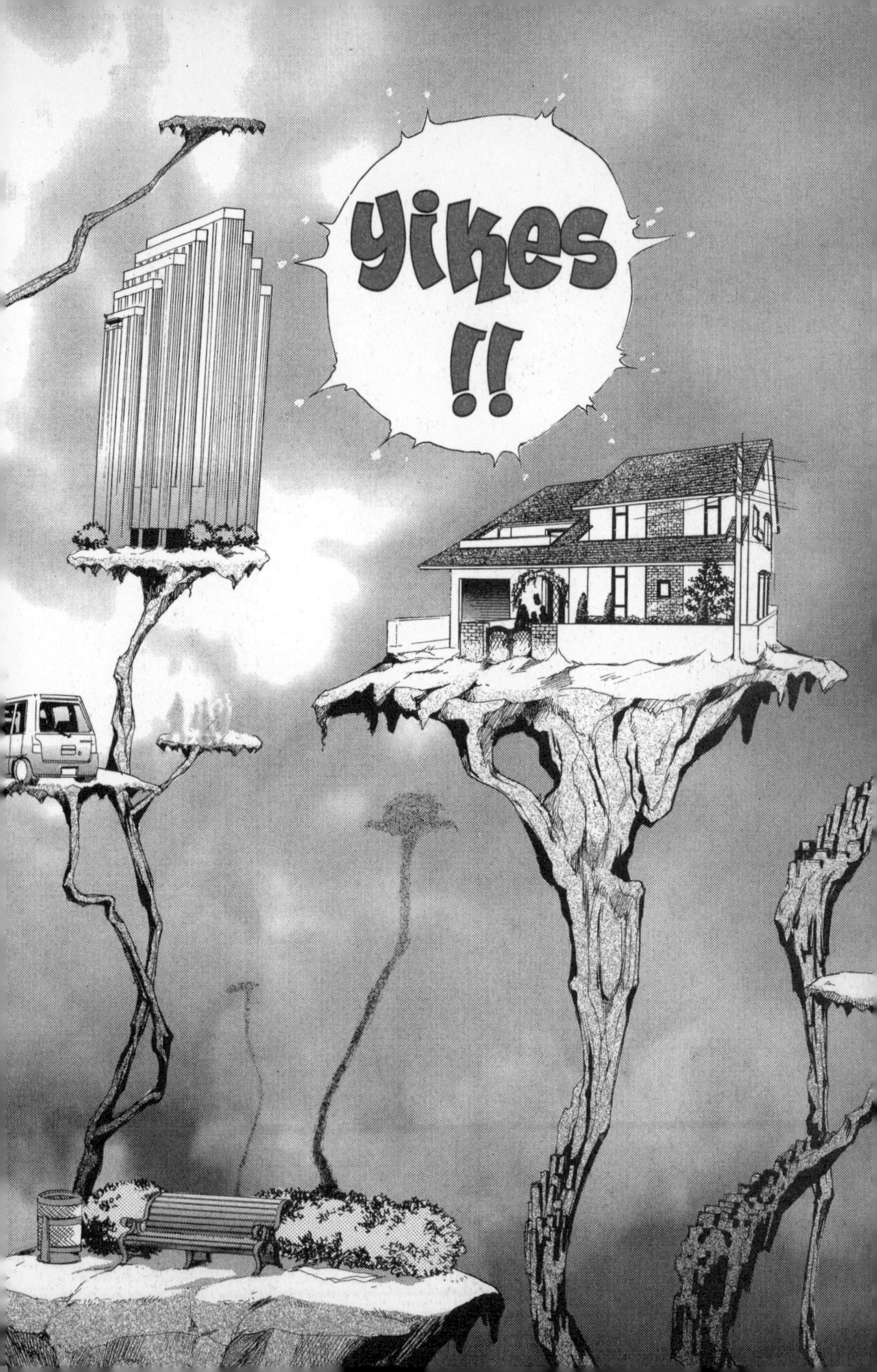
yikes !!

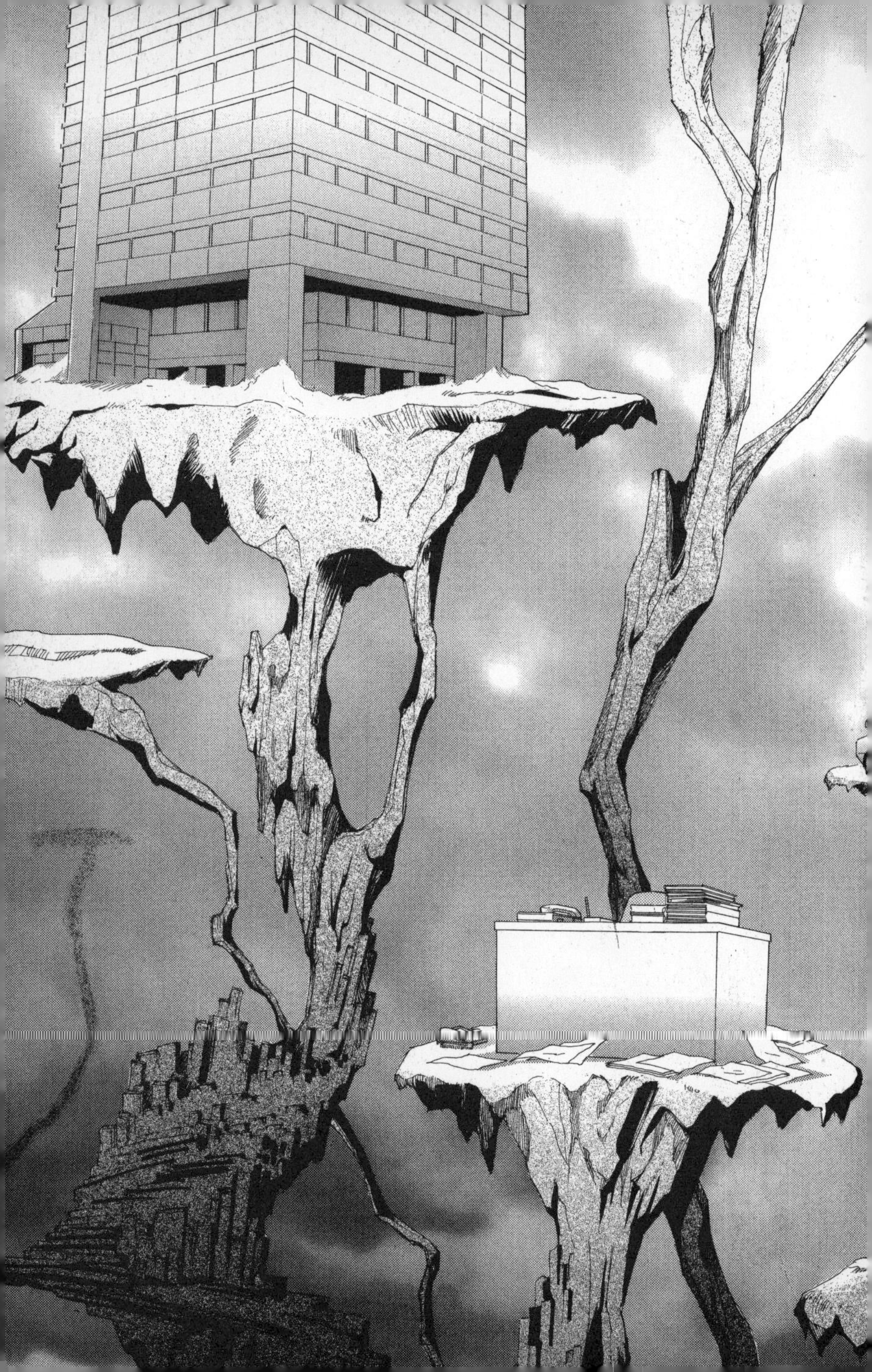

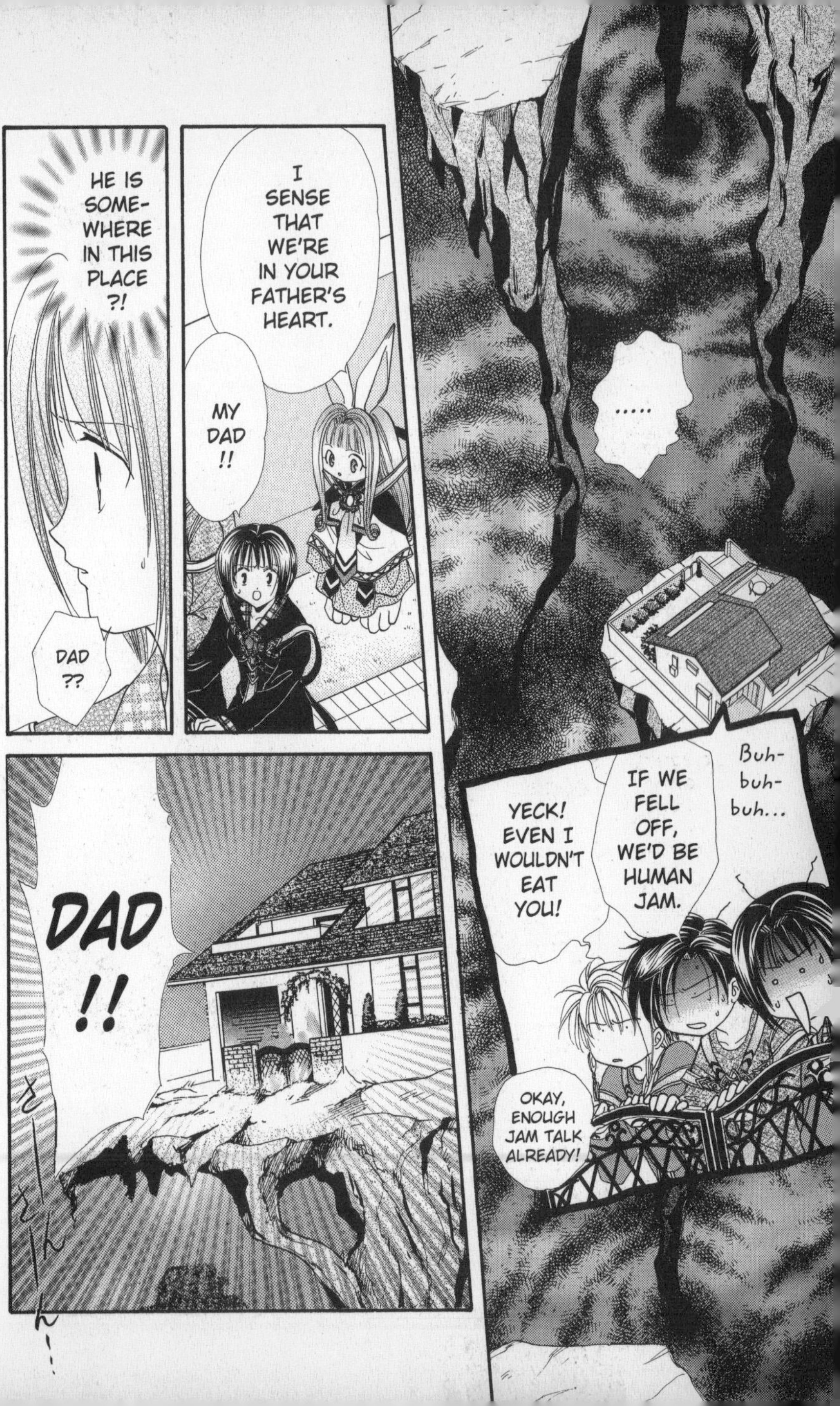
.....
Buh-buh-buh...
IF WE FELL OFF, WE'D BE HUMAN JAM.
YECK! EVEN I WOULDN'T EAT YOU!
OKAY, ENOUGH JAM TALK ALREADY!
I SENSE THAT WE'RE IN YOUR FATHER'S HEART.
MY DAD !!
HE IS SOME-WHERE IN THIS PLACE ?!
DAD ??
DAD !!
とーーん…

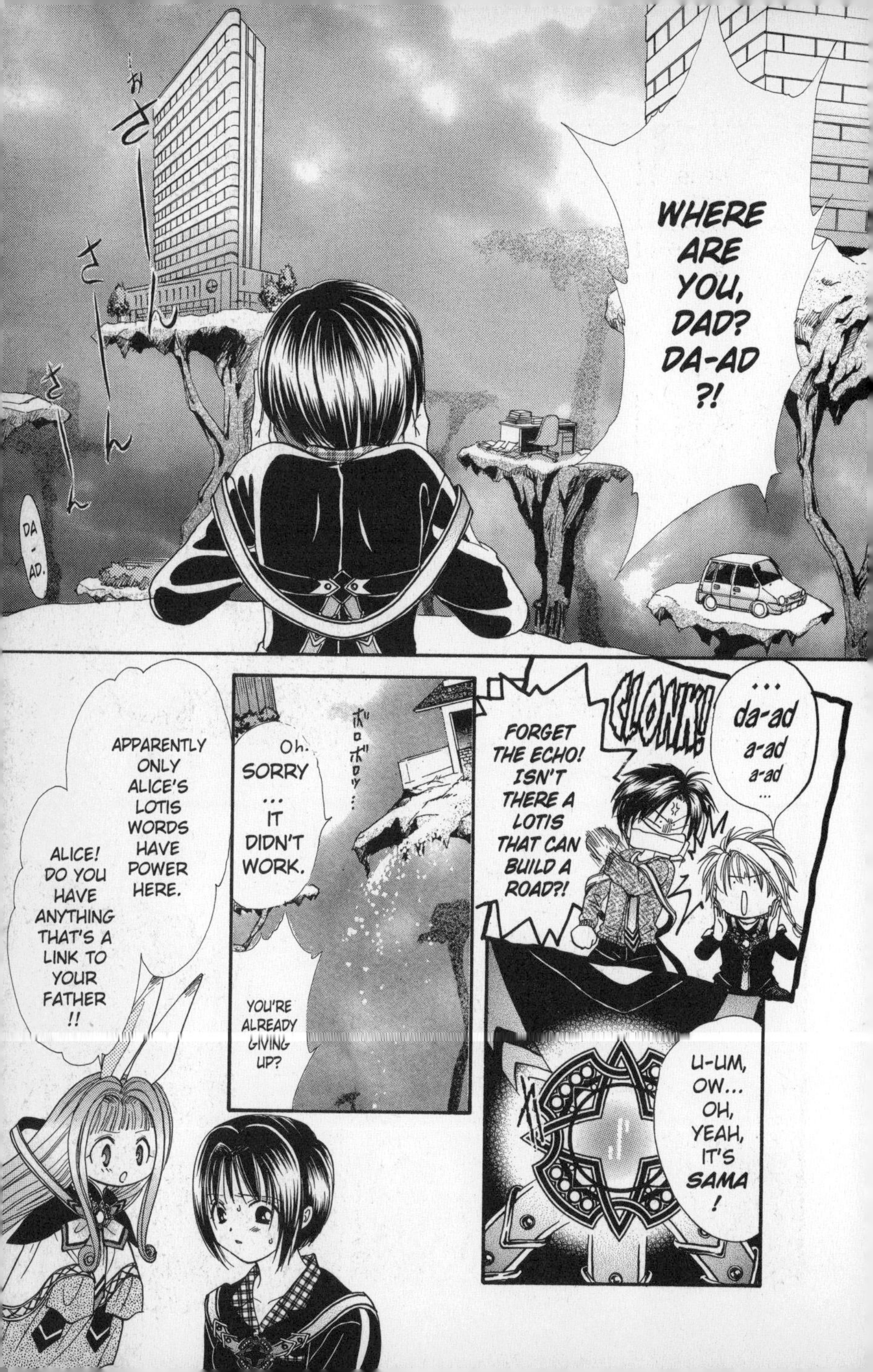
WHERE ARE YOU, DAD? DA-AD?!
…おさーーん
さーーん
さーん
DA-AD.
… da-ad a-ad a-ad …
CLONK!
FORGET THE ECHO! ISN'T THERE A LOTIS THAT CAN BUILD A ROAD?!
U-UM, OW… OH, YEAH, IT'S SAMA!
Oh. SORRY… IT DIDN'T WORK.
ボロボロッ…
YOU'RE ALREADY GIVING UP?
APPARENTLY ONLY ALICE'S LOTIS WORDS HAVE POWER HERE.
ALICE! DO YOU HAVE ANYTHING THAT'S A LINK TO YOUR FATHER!!

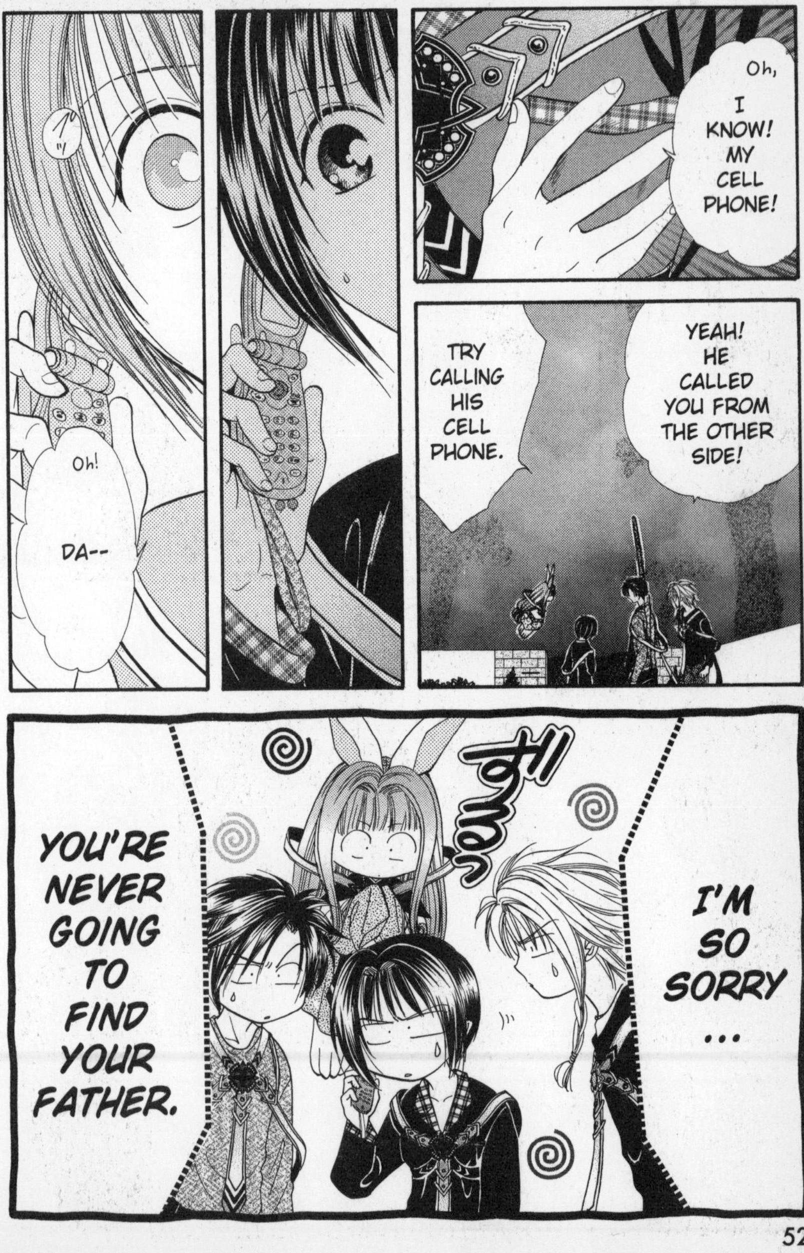
Oh, I KNOW! MY CELL PHONE!
YEAH! HE CALLED YOU FROM THE OTHER SIDE!
TRY CALLING HIS CELL PHONE.
Oh!
DA--
I'M SO SORRY...
YOU'RE NEVER GOING TO FIND YOUR FATHER.

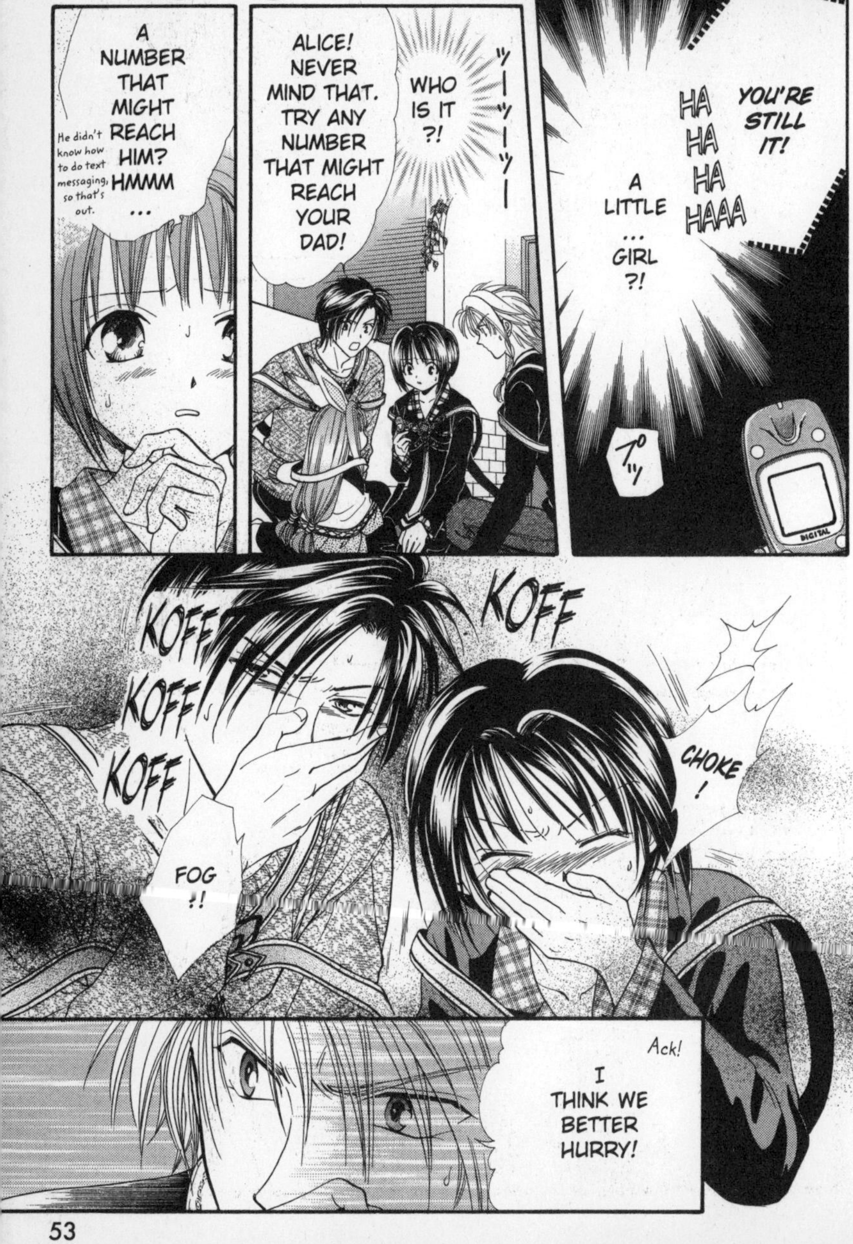
YOU'RE STILL IT!
HA HA HA HAAA
A LITTLE ... GIRL ?!
プッ
ツーツーツー
WHO IS IT ?!
ALICE! NEVER MIND THAT. TRY ANY NUMBER THAT MIGHT REACH YOUR DAD!
A NUMBER THAT MIGHT REACH HIM? HMMM ...
He didn't know how to do text messaging, so that's out.
KOFF
KOFF KOFF KOFF
CHOKE!
FOG ?!
Ack!
I THINK WE BETTER HURRY!

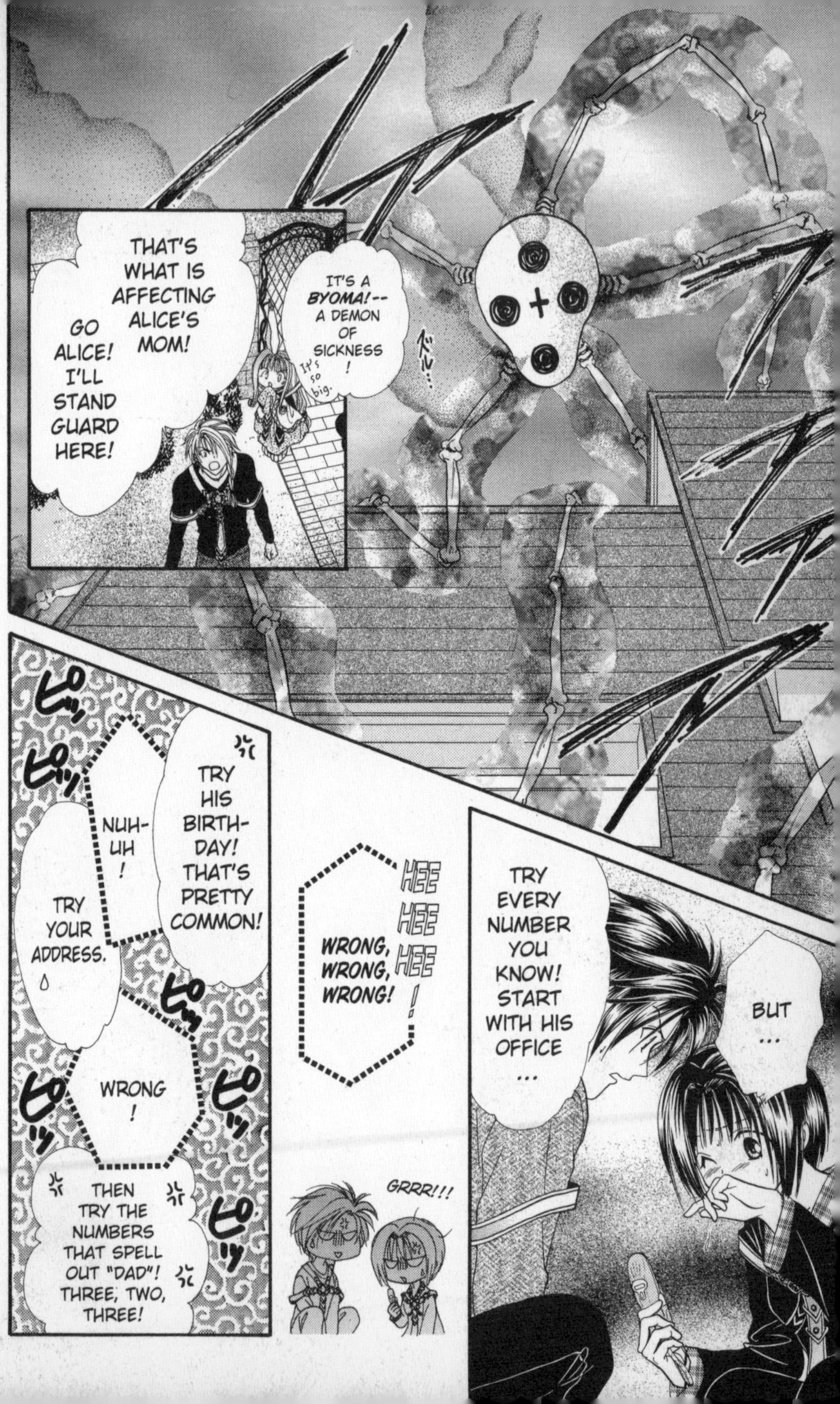
IT'S A BYOMA!-- A DEMON OF SICKNESS!
It's so big.
THAT'S WHAT IS AFFECTING ALICE'S MOM!
GO ALICE! I'LL STAND GUARD HERE!
TRY EVERY NUMBER YOU KNOW! START WITH HIS OFFICE...
BUT...
HEE HEE HEE!
WRONG, WRONG, WRONG!
GRRR!!!
ピッ
ピッ
TRY HIS BIRTH-DAY! THAT'S PRETTY COMMON!
NUH-UH!
TRY YOUR ADDRESS.
ピッ
WRONG!
ピッ
ピッ
THEN TRY THE NUMBERS THAT SPELL OUT "DAD"! THREE, TWO, THREE!
ピッ

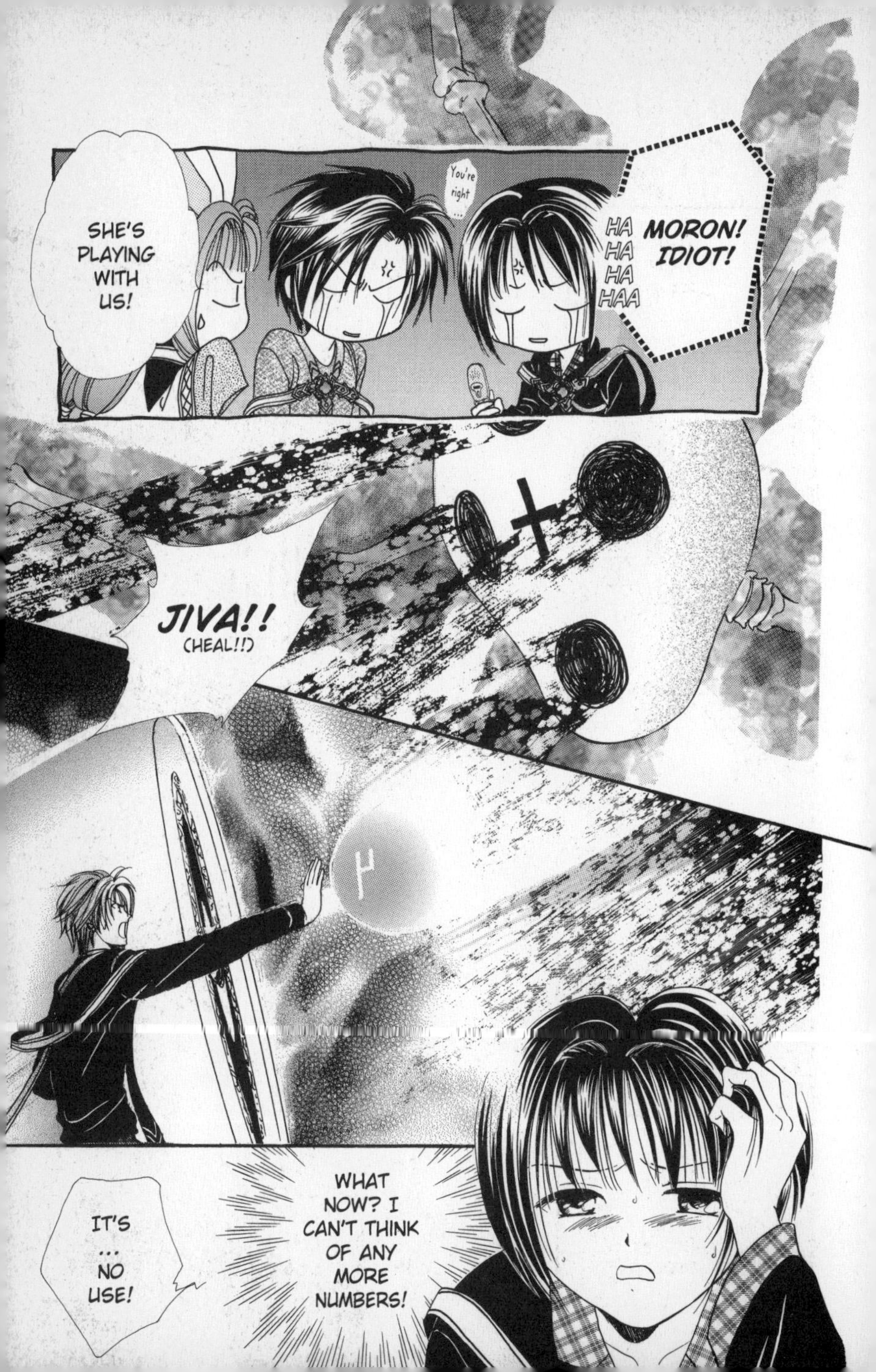

MORON! IDIOT!
HA HA HA HAA
You're right...
SHE'S PLAYING WITH US!
JIVA!!
(HEAL!!)
WHAT NOW? I CAN'T THINK OF ANY MORE NUMBERS!
IT'S ... NO USE!

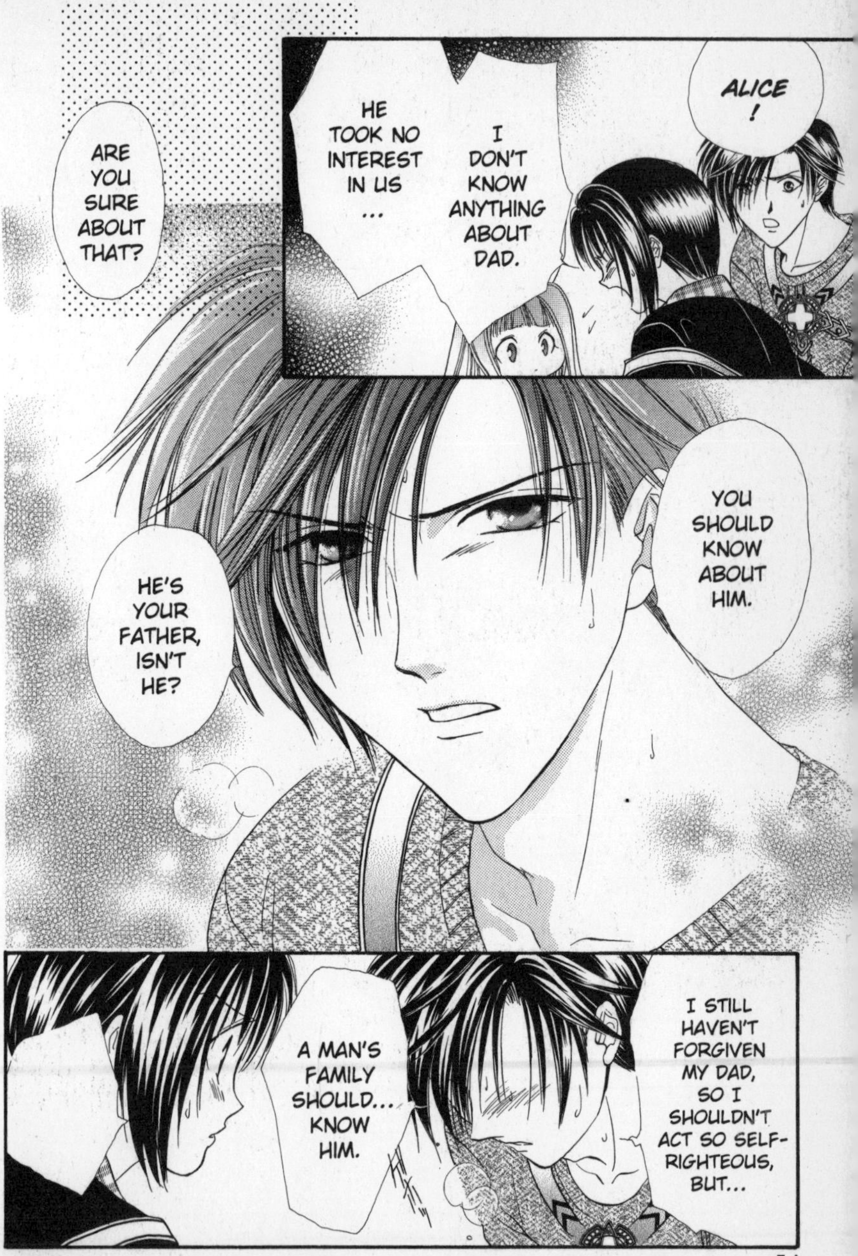
ALICE !
I DON'T KNOW ANYTHING ABOUT DAD.
HE TOOK NO INTEREST IN US ...
ARE YOU SURE ABOUT THAT?
YOU SHOULD KNOW ABOUT HIM.
HE'S YOUR FATHER, ISN'T HE?
I STILL HAVEN'T FORGIVEN MY DAD, SO I SHOULDN'T ACT SO SELF-RIGHTEOUS, BUT...
A MAN'S FAMILY SHOULD... KNOW HIM.

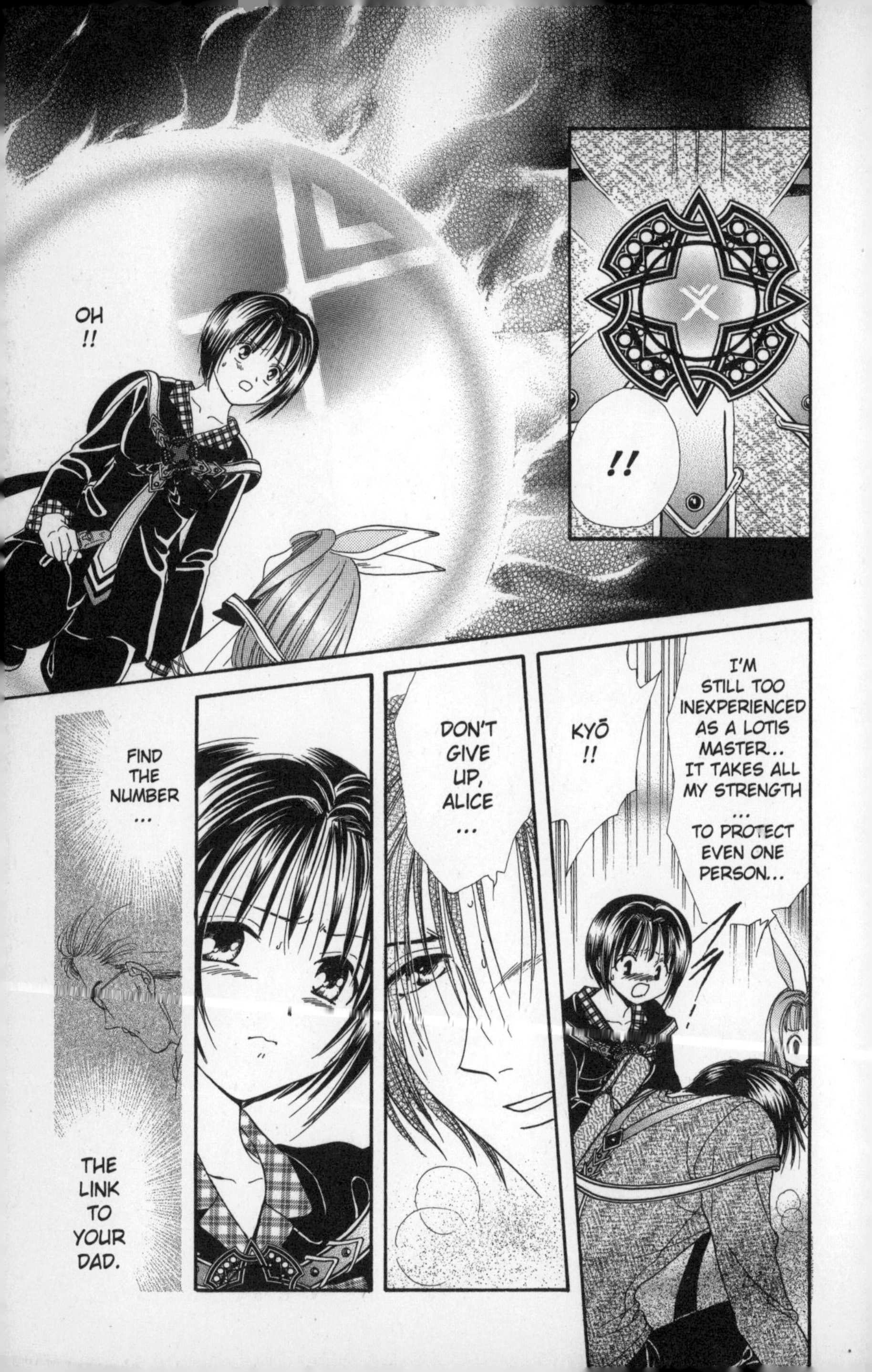
!!
OH !!
I'M STILL TOO INEXPERIENCED AS A LOTIS MASTER.. IT TAKES ALL MY STRENGTH ... TO PROTECT EVEN ONE PERSON...
KYŌ !!
DON'T GIVE UP, ALICE ...
FIND THE NUMBER ...
THE LINK TO YOUR DAD.

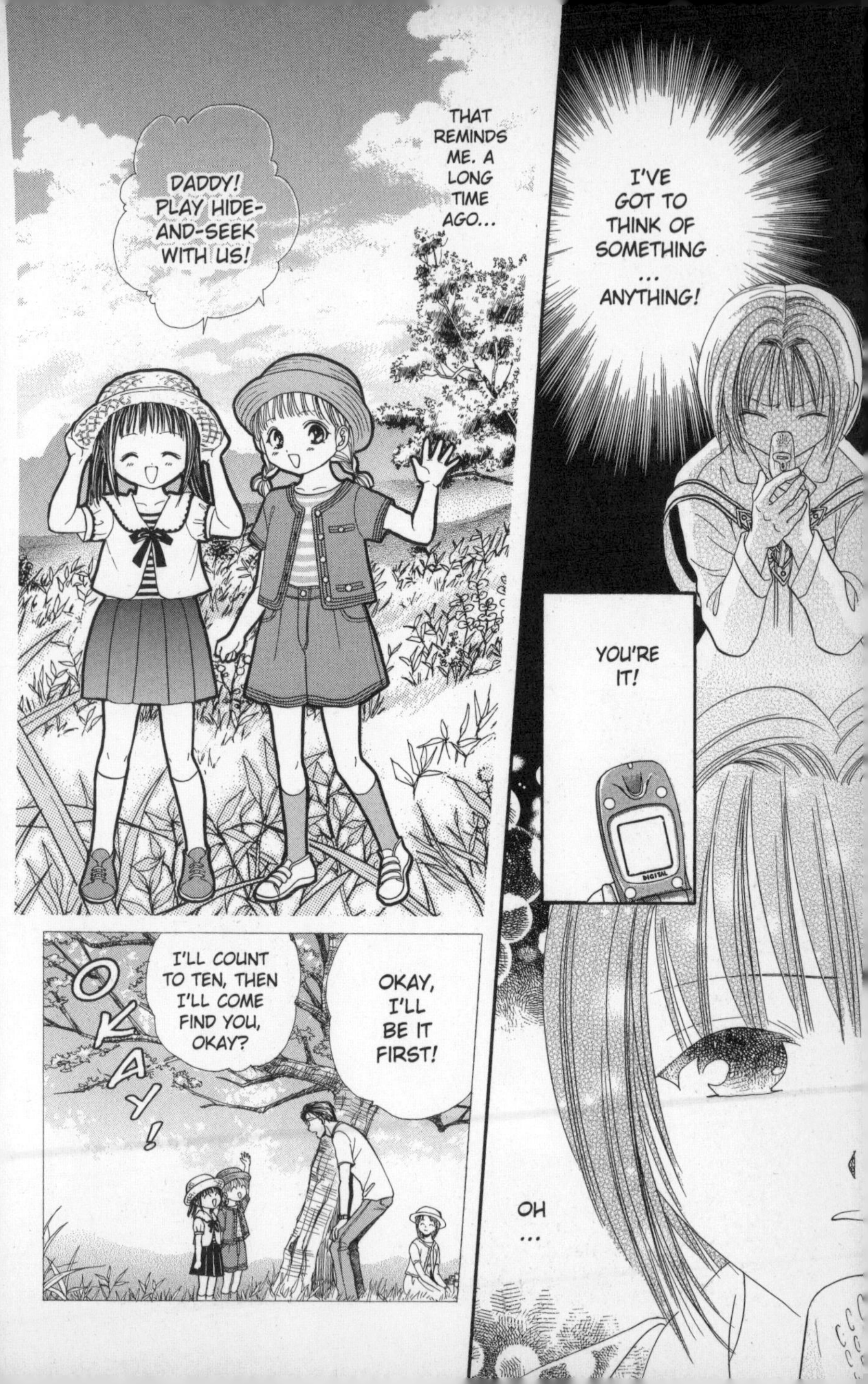
I'VE GOT TO THINK OF SOMETHING ... ANYTHING!
YOU'RE IT!
OH ...
THAT REMINDS ME. A LONG TIME AGO...
DADDY! PLAY HIDE-AND-SEEK WITH US!
OKAY, I'LL BE IT FIRST!
I'LL COUNT TO TEN, THEN I'LL COME FIND YOU, OKAY?
OKAY!

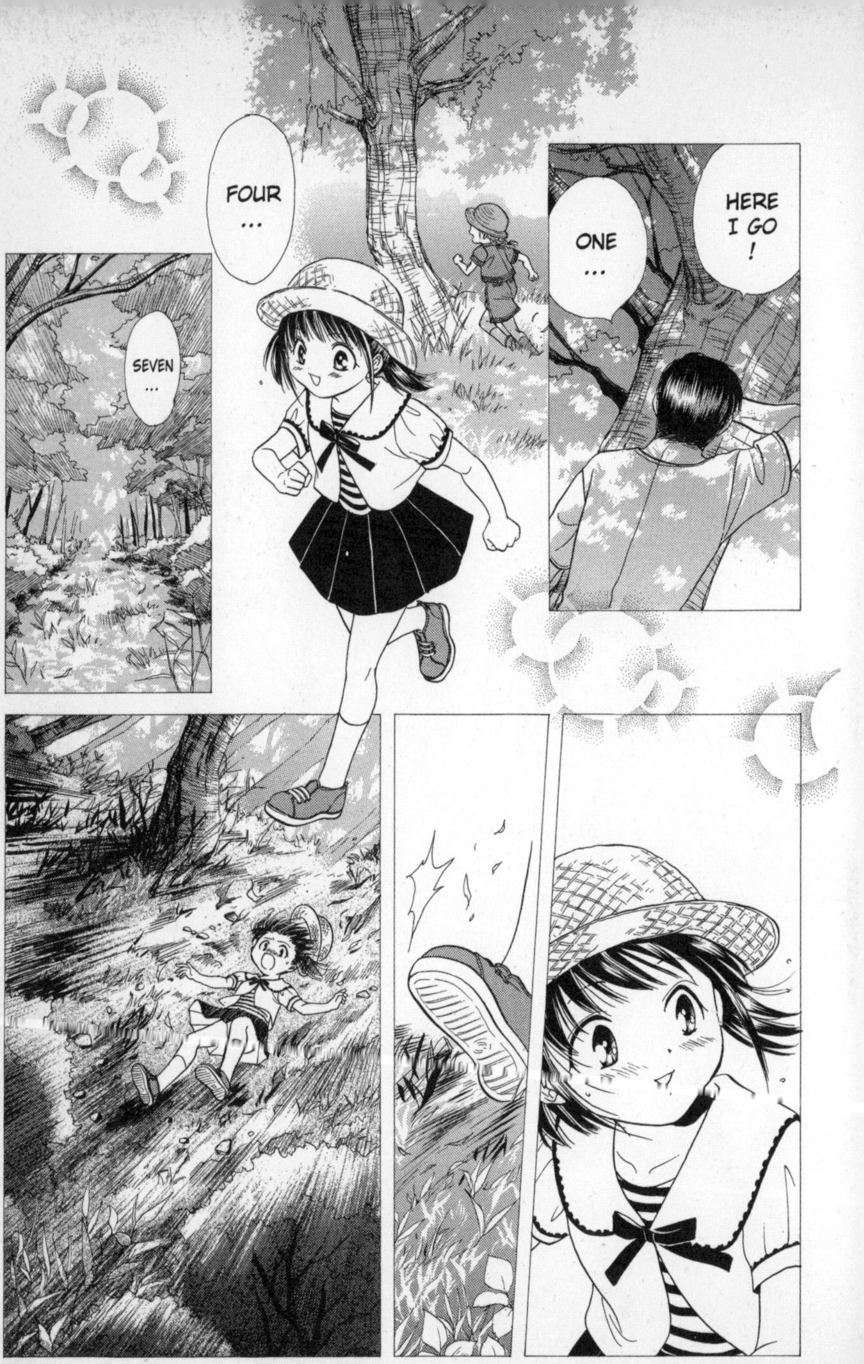
HERE I GO!
ONE...
FOUR...
SEVEN...

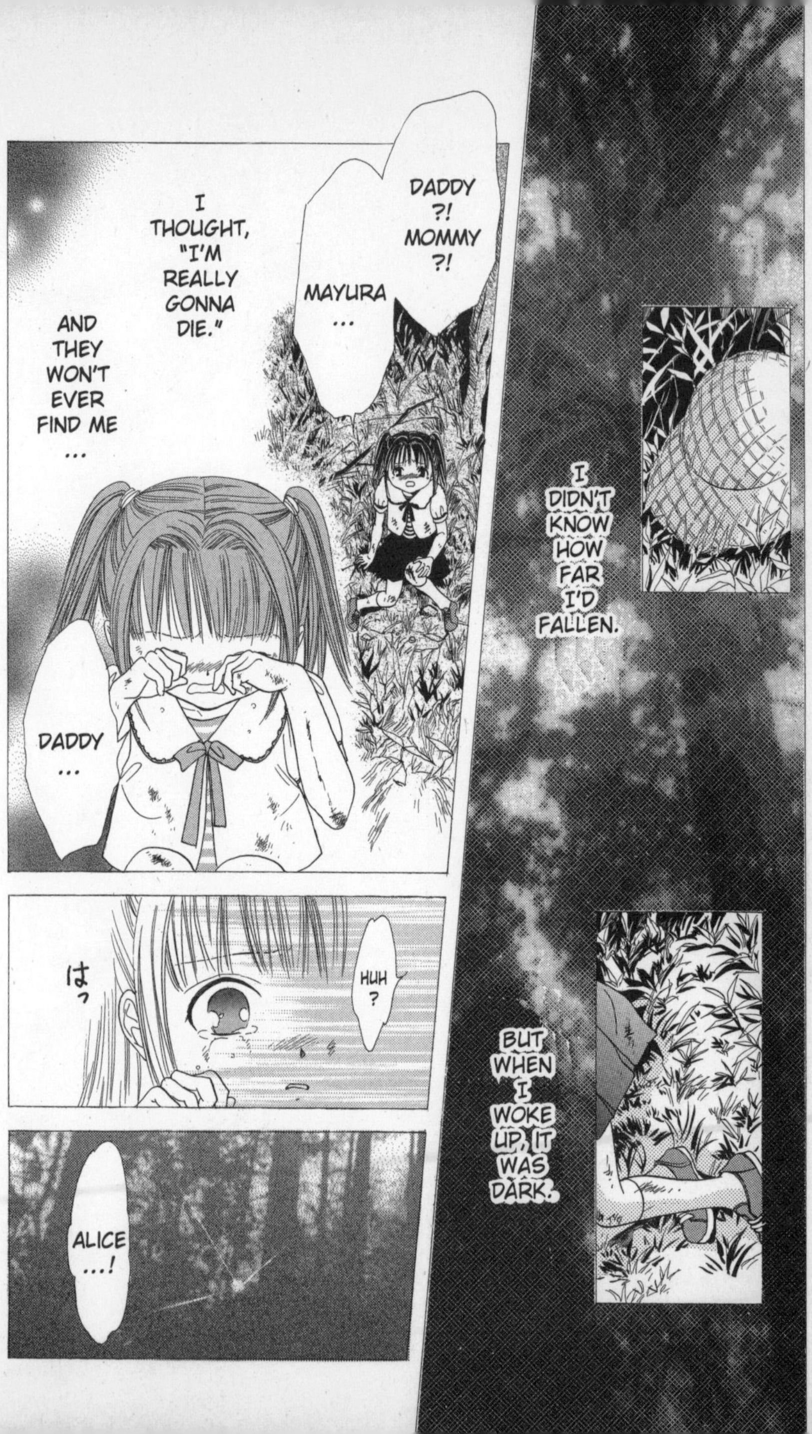
I DIDN'T KNOW HOW FAR I'D FALLEN.
BUT WHEN I WOKE UP, IT WAS DARK.
DADDY ?! MOMMY ?!
MAYURA ...
I THOUGHT, "I'M REALLY GONNA DIE."
AND THEY WON'T EVER FIND ME ...
DADDY ...
HUH ?
はっ
ALICE ...!

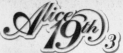

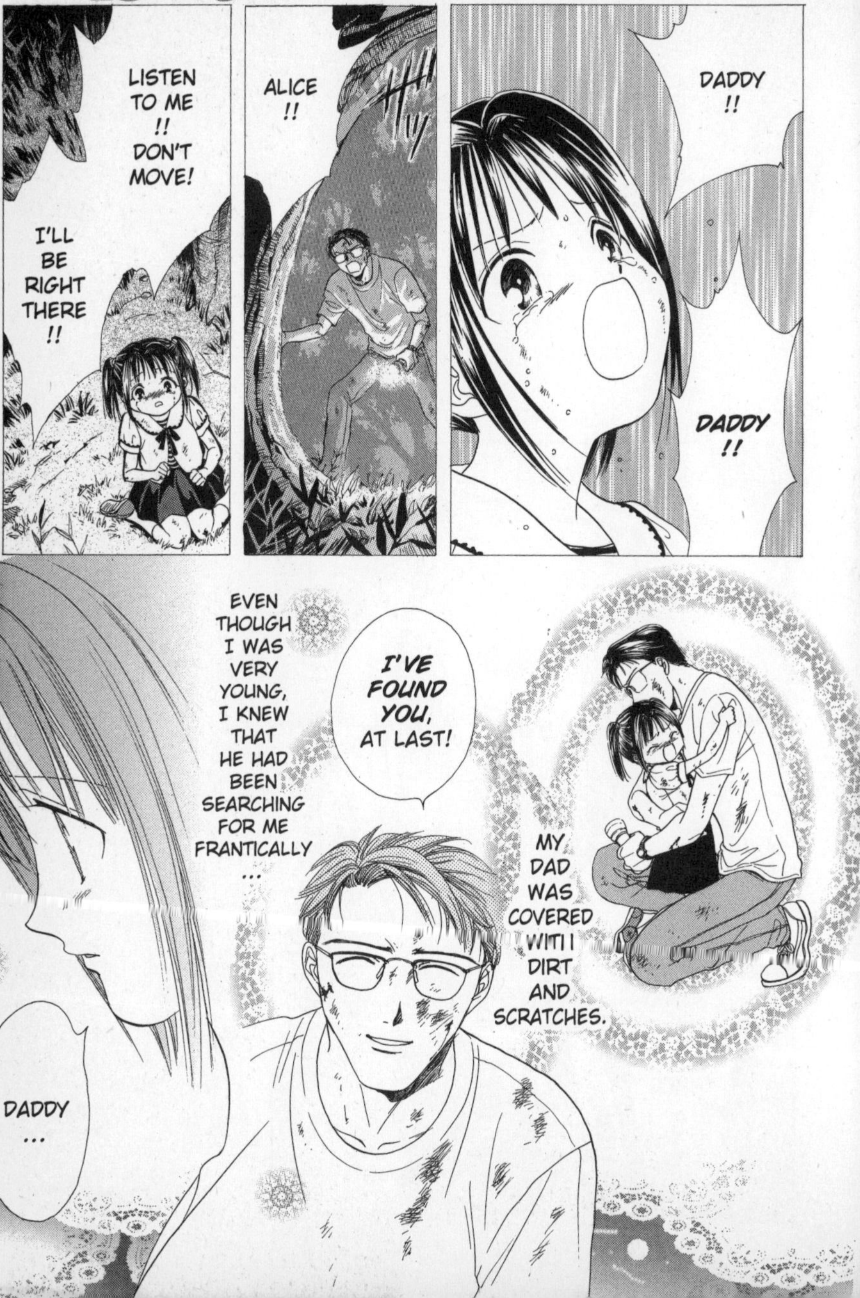
DADDY !!
DADDY !!
ALICE !!
LISTEN TO ME !! DON'T MOVE!
I'LL BE RIGHT THERE !!
EVEN THOUGH I WAS VERY YOUNG, I KNEW THAT HE HAD BEEN SEARCHING FOR ME FRANTICALLY ...
I'VE FOUND YOU, AT LAST!
MY DAD WAS COVERED WITH DIRT AND SCRATCHES.
DADDY ...

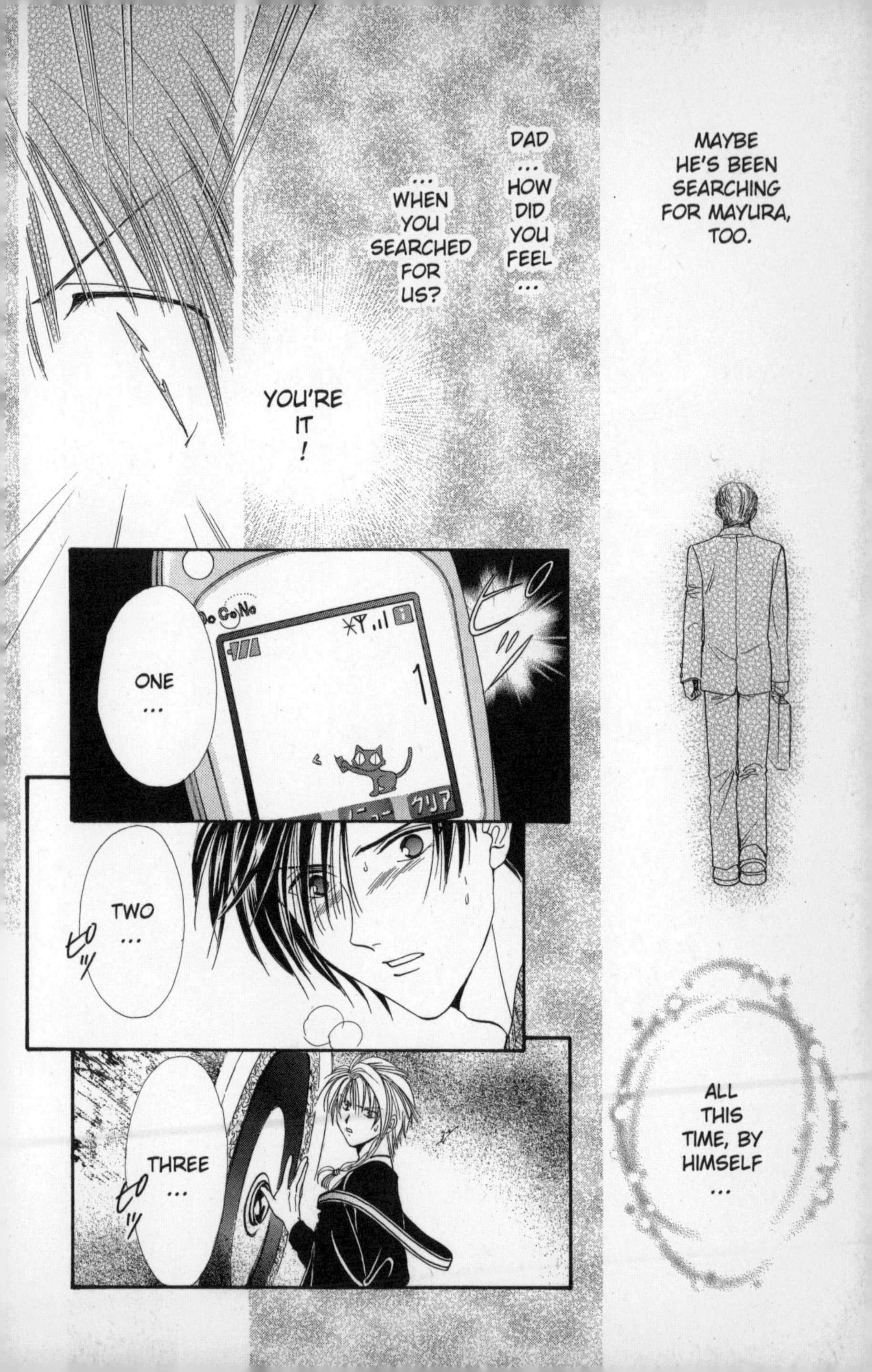
MAYBE HE'S BEEN SEARCHING FOR MAYURA, TOO.
ALL THIS TIME, BY HIMSELF ...
DAD ... HOW DID YOU FEEL ...
... WHEN YOU SEARCHED FOR US?
YOU'RE IT !
ONE ...
TWO ...
THREE ...

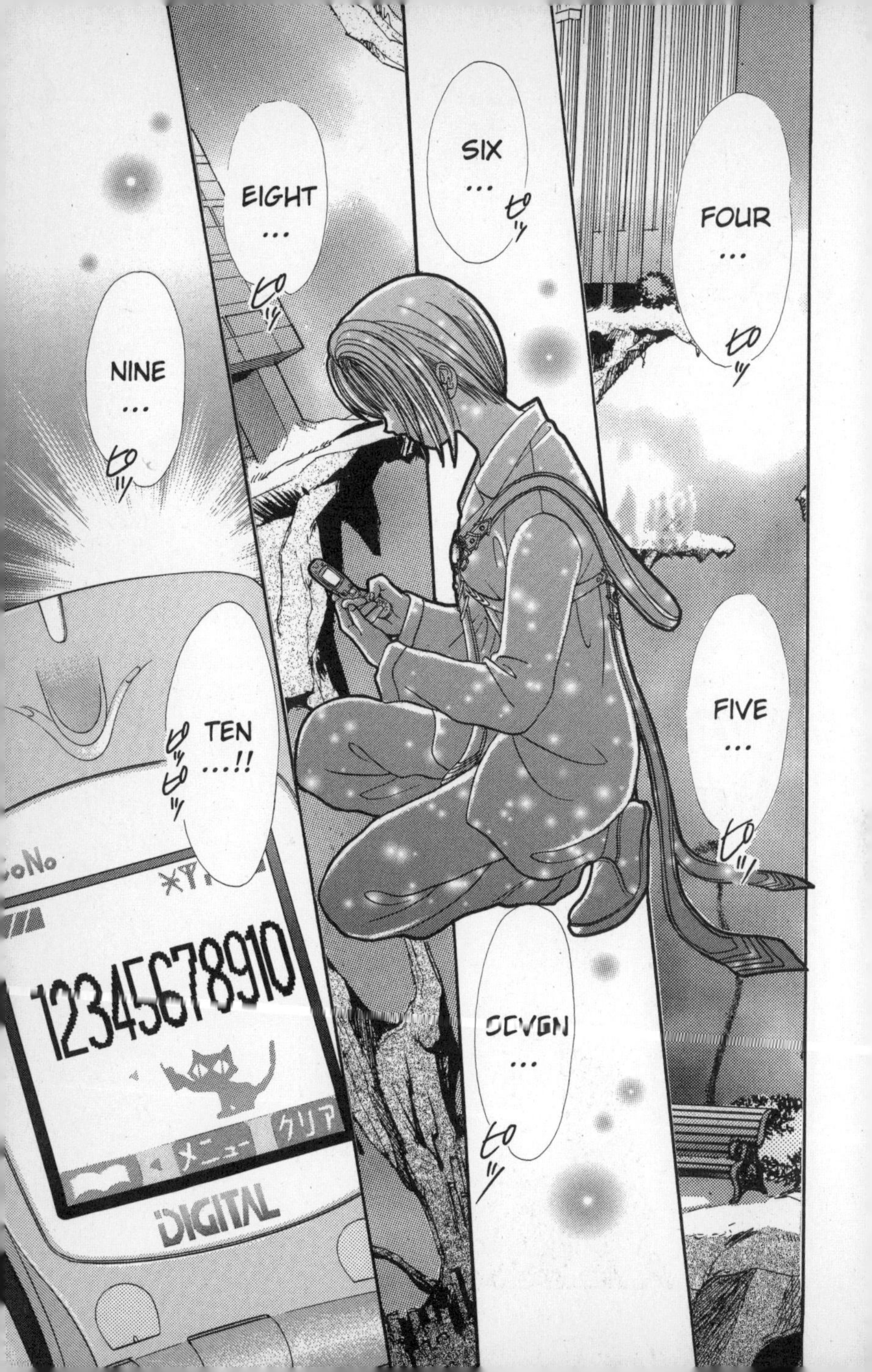
FOUR
...
ピッ
FIVE
...
ピッ
SIX
...
ピッ
SEVEN
...
ピッ
EIGHT
...
ピッ
NINE
...
ピッ
TEN
...!!
ピッ
ピッ
12345678910
クリア
メニュー
DIGITAL

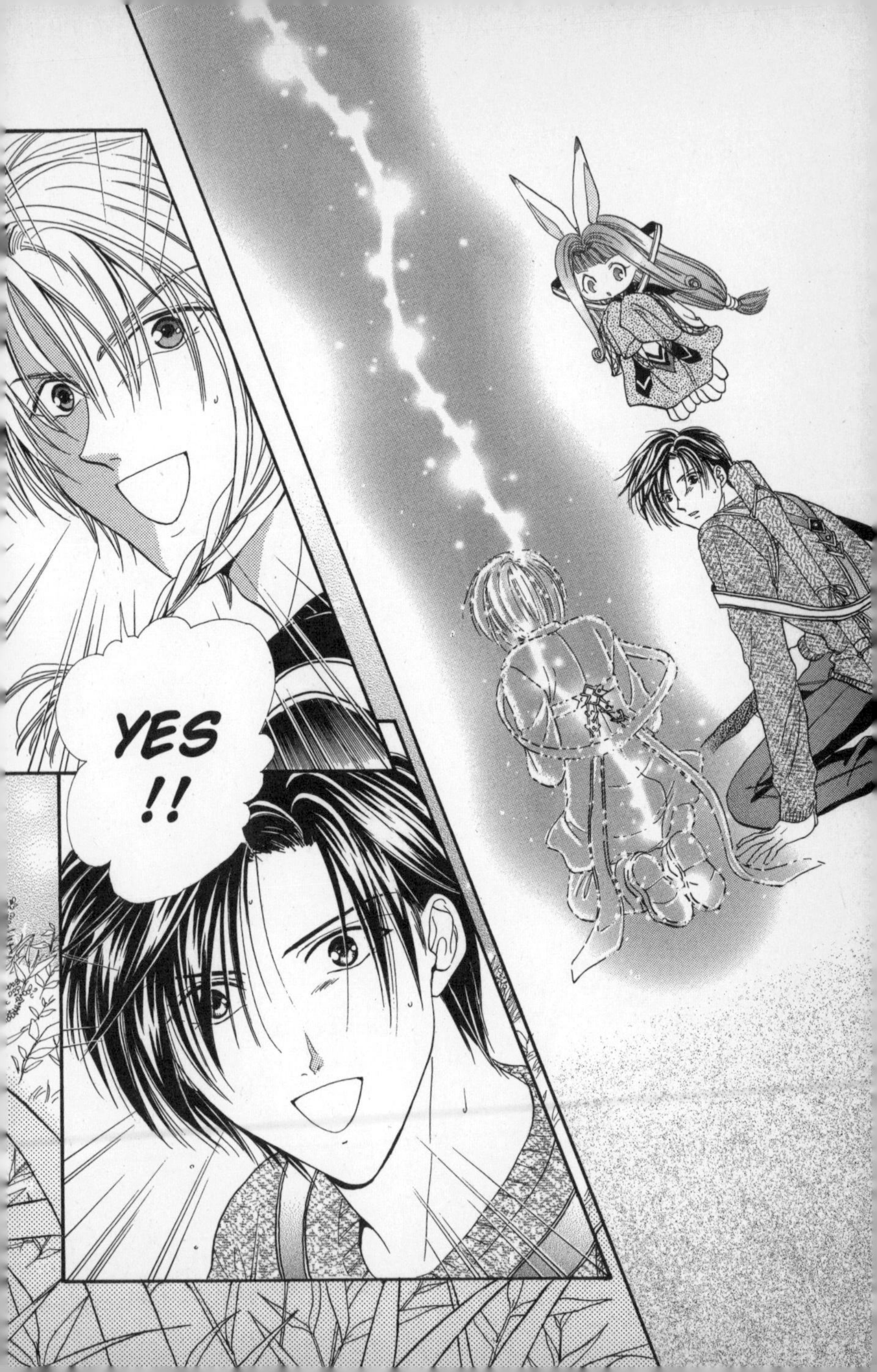
YES !!

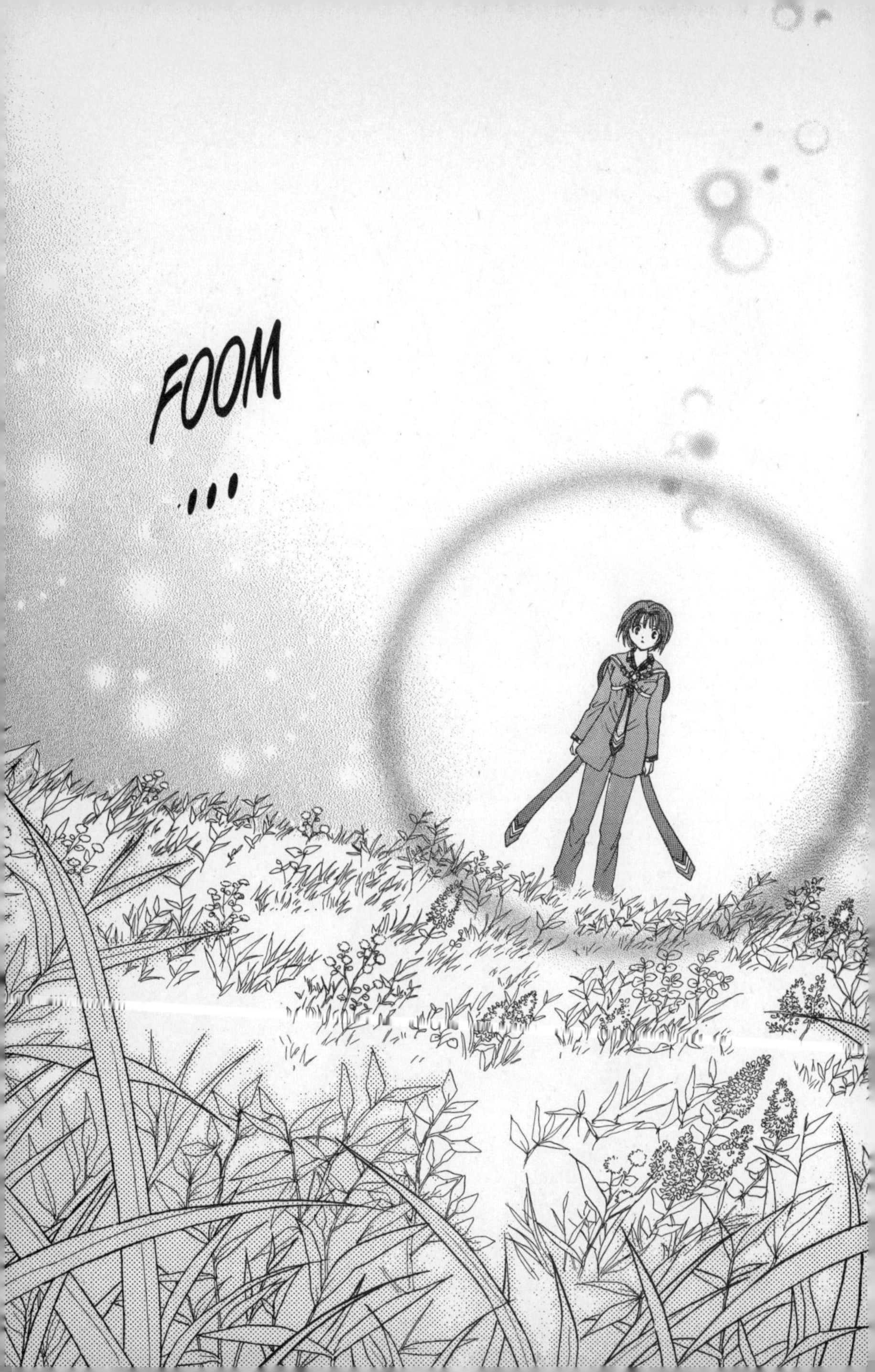
FOOM
...

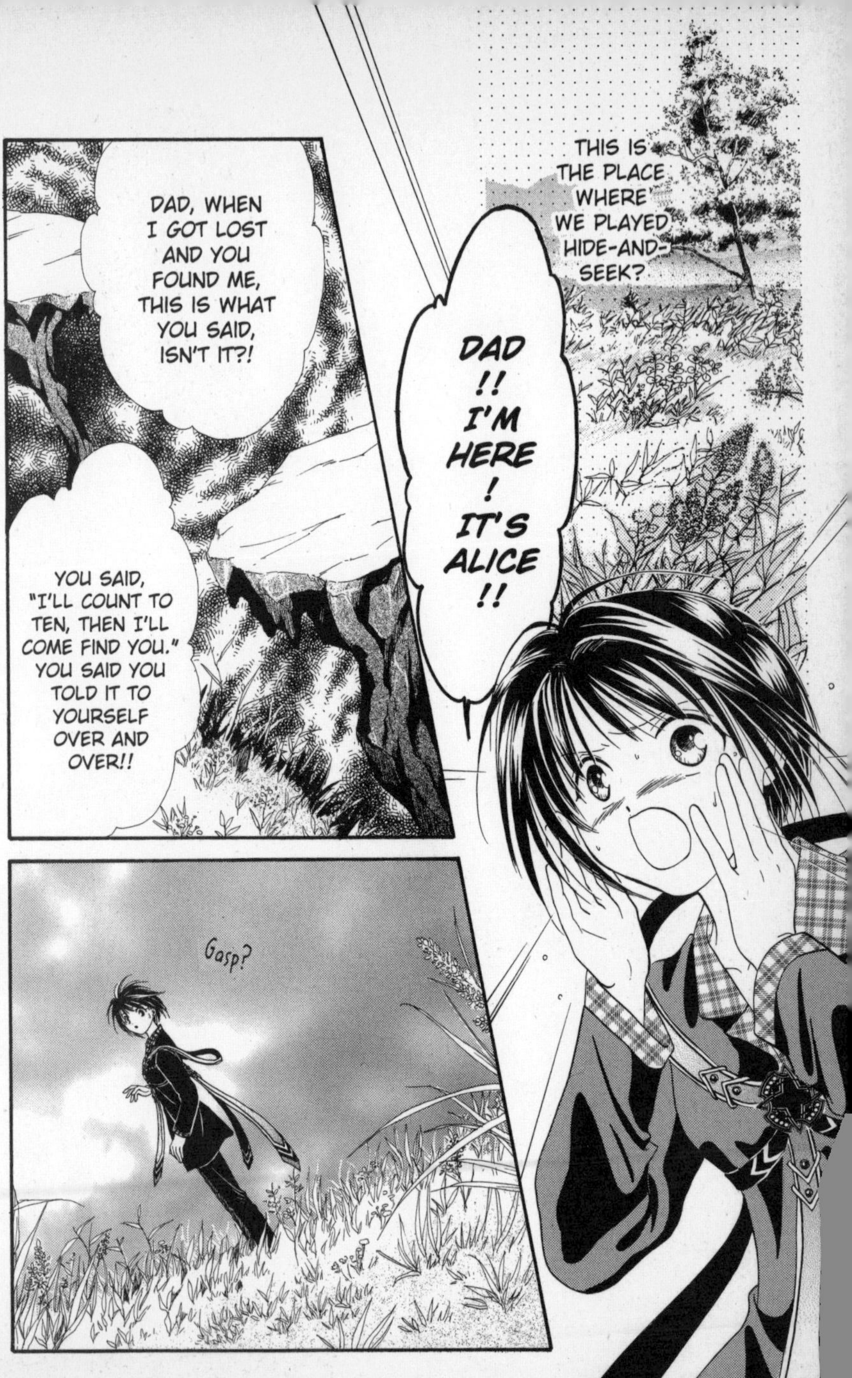
THIS IS THE PLACE WHERE WE PLAYED HIDE-AND-SEEK?
DAD!! I'M HERE! IT'S ALICE!!
DAD, WHEN I GOT LOST AND YOU FOUND ME, THIS IS WHAT YOU SAID, ISN'T IT?!
YOU SAID, "I'LL COUNT TO TEN, THEN I'LL COME FIND YOU." YOU SAID YOU TOLD IT TO YOURSELF OVER AND OVER!!
Gasp?

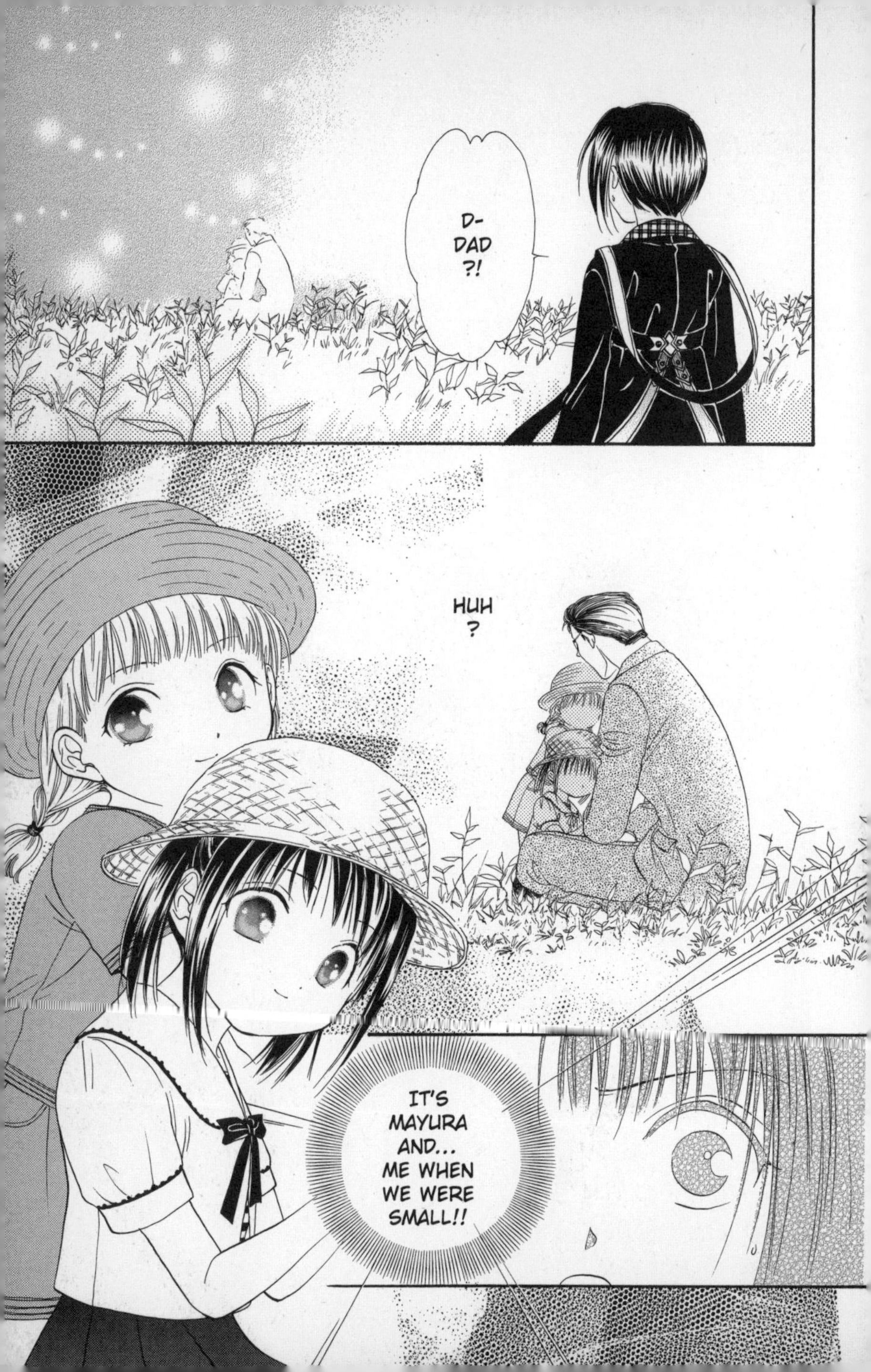
D-DAD?!
HUH?
IT'S MAYURA AND... ME WHEN WE WERE SMALL!!

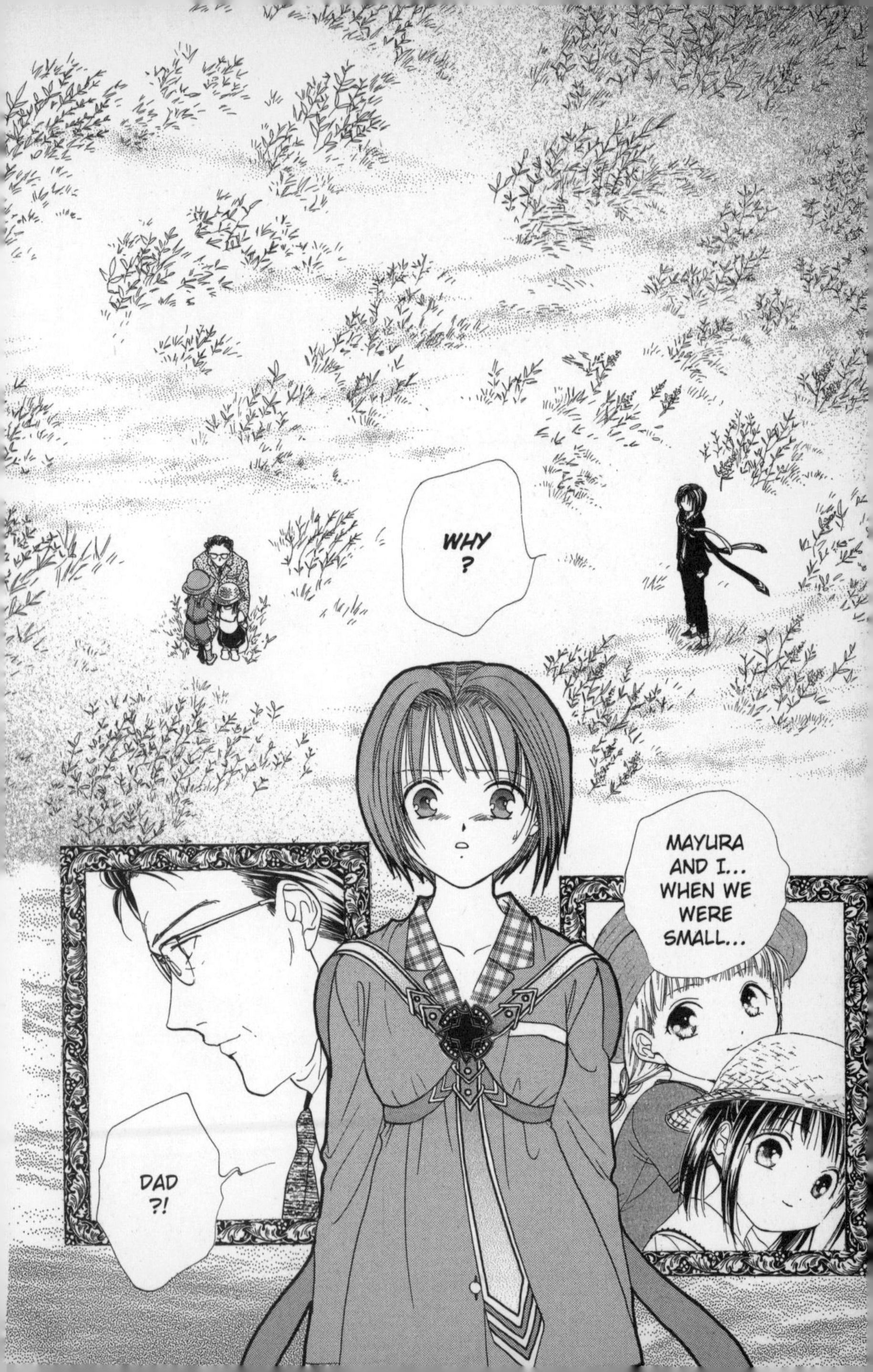
WHY ?
MAYURA AND I... WHEN WE WERE SMALL...
DAD ?!

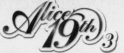

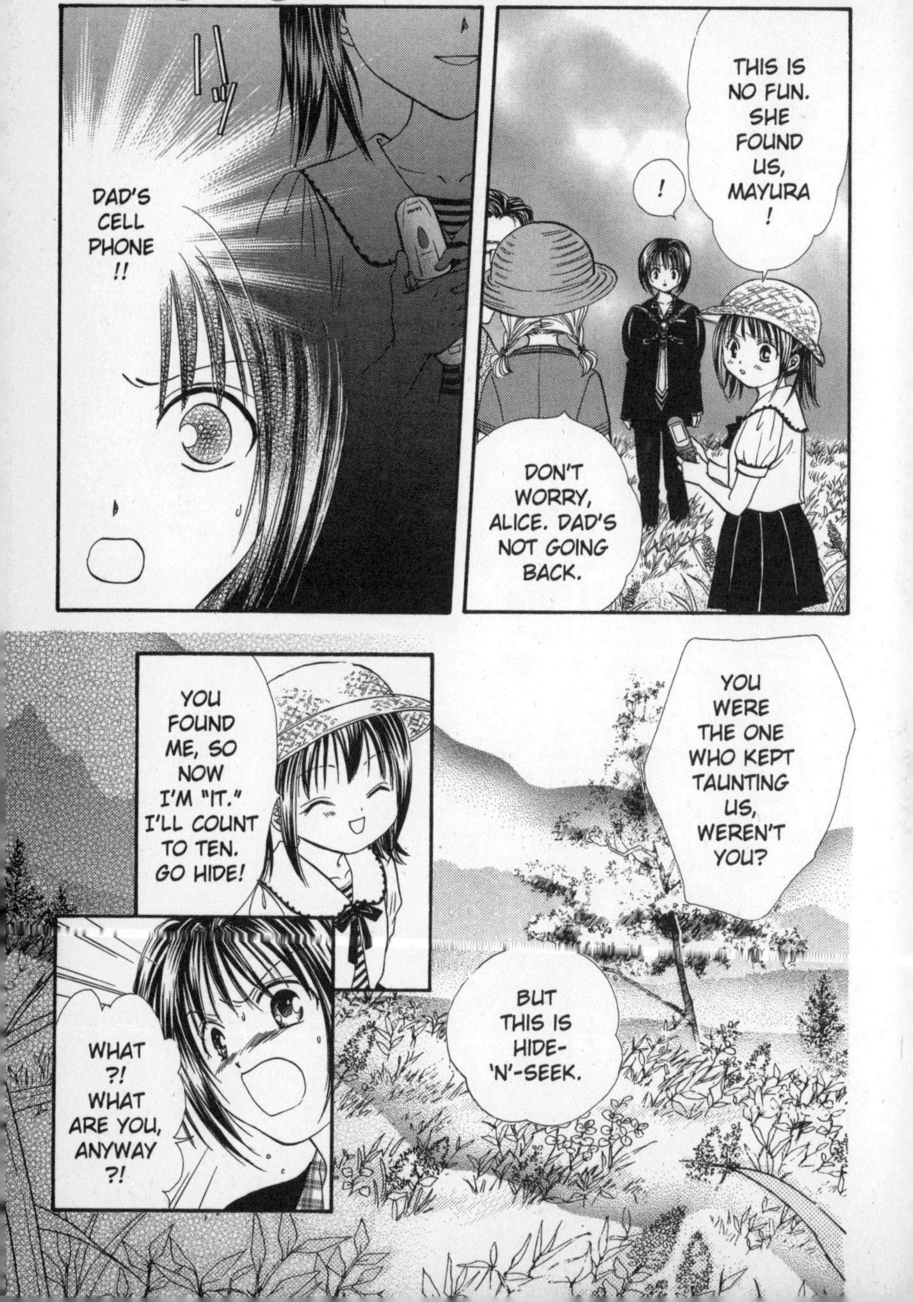
THIS IS NO FUN. SHE FOUND US, MAYURA!
!
DON'T WORRY, ALICE. DAD'S NOT GOING BACK.
DAD'S CELL PHONE!!
YOU WERE THE ONE WHO KEPT TAUNTING US, WEREN'T YOU?
YOU FOUND ME, SO NOW I'M "IT." I'LL COUNT TO TEN. GO HIDE!
BUT THIS IS HIDE-'N'-SEEK.
WHAT?! WHAT ARE YOU, ANYWAY?!

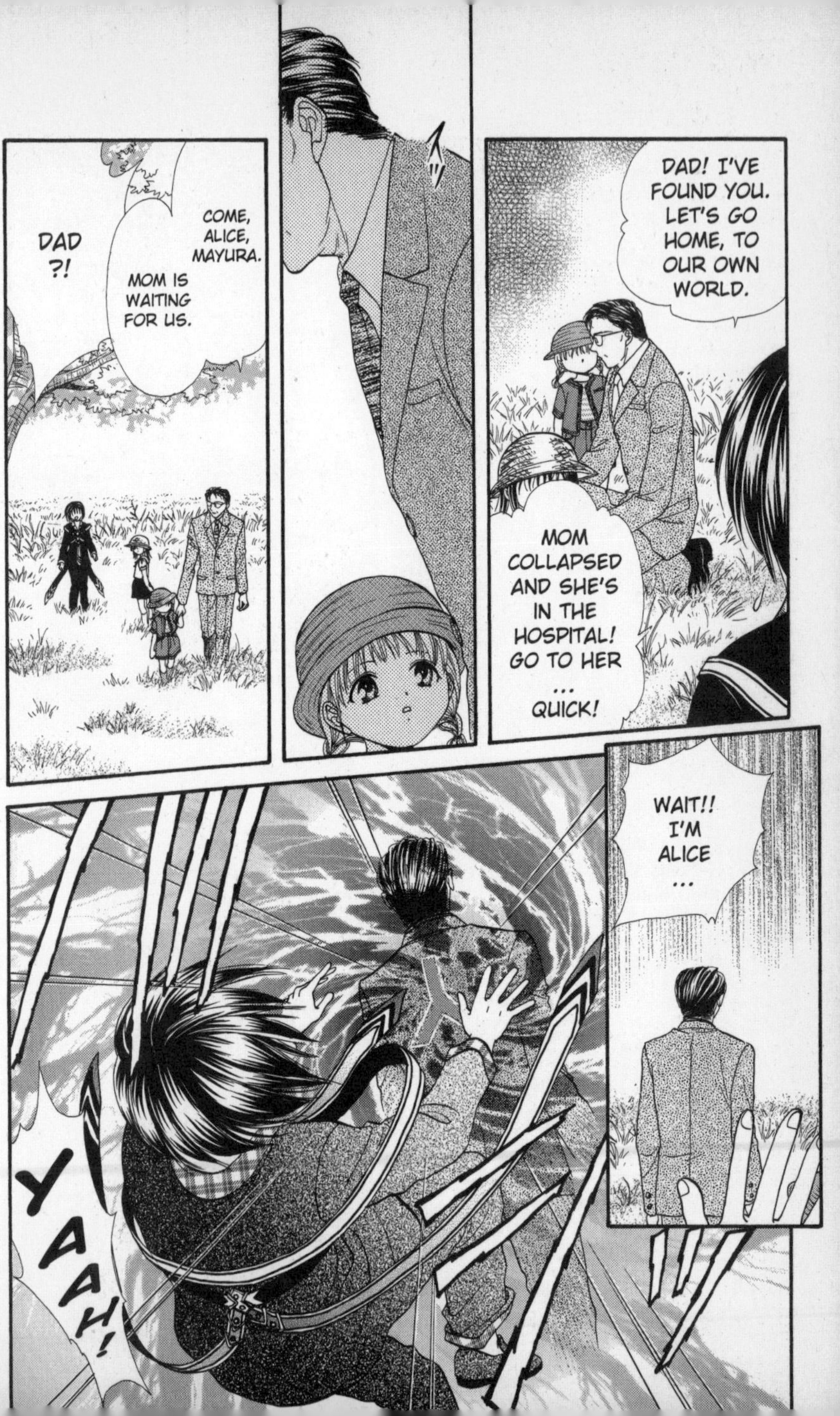
DAD! I'VE FOUND YOU. LET'S GO HOME, TO OUR OWN WORLD.
MOM COLLAPSED AND SHE'S IN THE HOSPITAL! GO TO HER ... QUICK!
COME, ALICE, MAYURA.
MOM IS WAITING FOR US.
DAD ?!
WAIT!! I'M ALICE ...
YAAH!

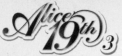

Speaking of music, the soundtrack for Fushigi Yûgi Eikoden OVA is in stores now. Mr. Sakai who wrote the music, helped me with the background music for Ceres, and I liked it so much, I insisted that he do Eikoden, too! I'm very happy. Thank you very much. I especially love the theme song. Now the Fushigi Yûgi six-volume CD Book is difficult to obtain. And Yoko Ueno sang the ending songs. But wow! to my surprise, she sang for the new OVA. ♡♡ The songs in the CD book are seriously good. You'd cry if you played them after watching a drama!! That's how it seems. With a coupon from the Fushigi Yûgi Complete Series, you can get a re-released CD, but that's a collection of the character songs by the voice actors in the CD Book. (Ms. Ueno's songs aren't in it)
But I'd be happy if you listened to and enjoyed these, too.
Also, anyone who wants Fushigi Yûgi products can go to any anime shop. All kinds of new things are out.
Oh...If anyone can't get the complete edition, please contact Shogakukan. I can't supply reprints.
To digress...in celebration of 100,000 hits on my friend's home page. There was a poll for people to vote for the character they most wanted me to draw. (I wonder if I should have?) You can see Nuriko. Until recently, Tôya was the most popular. Well, not that it matters, anyway. (smile) The address: http//homepage2.nifty.com/nankou/
If you send messages, please read the warning! And be considerate, okay?! If the top has changed, I'm sorry.
Well, till Volume 4... ♡
Huh?! It's over already?! I really got into it this time.

I'm tired. I'm sleepy.

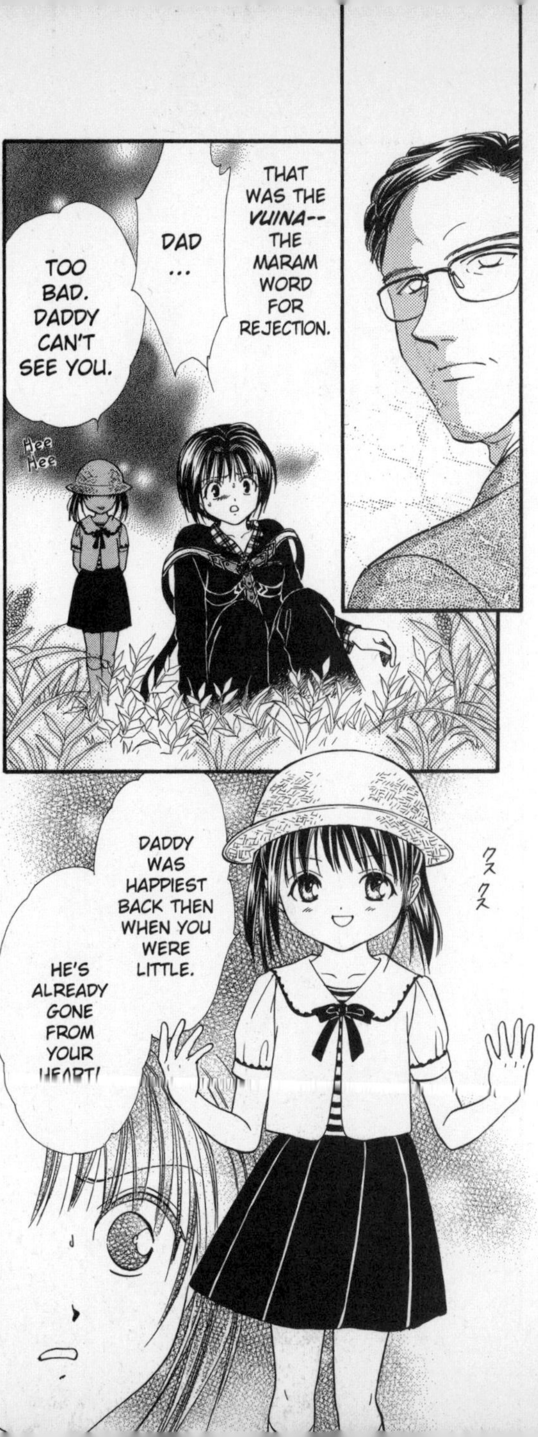
THAT WAS THE *VUINA*-- THE MARAM WORD FOR REJECTION.
DAD ...
TOO BAD. DADDY CAN'T SEE YOU.
Hee Hee
クスクス
DADDY WAS HAPPIEST BACK THEN WHEN YOU WERE LITTLE.
HE'S ALREADY GONE FROM YOUR HEART!

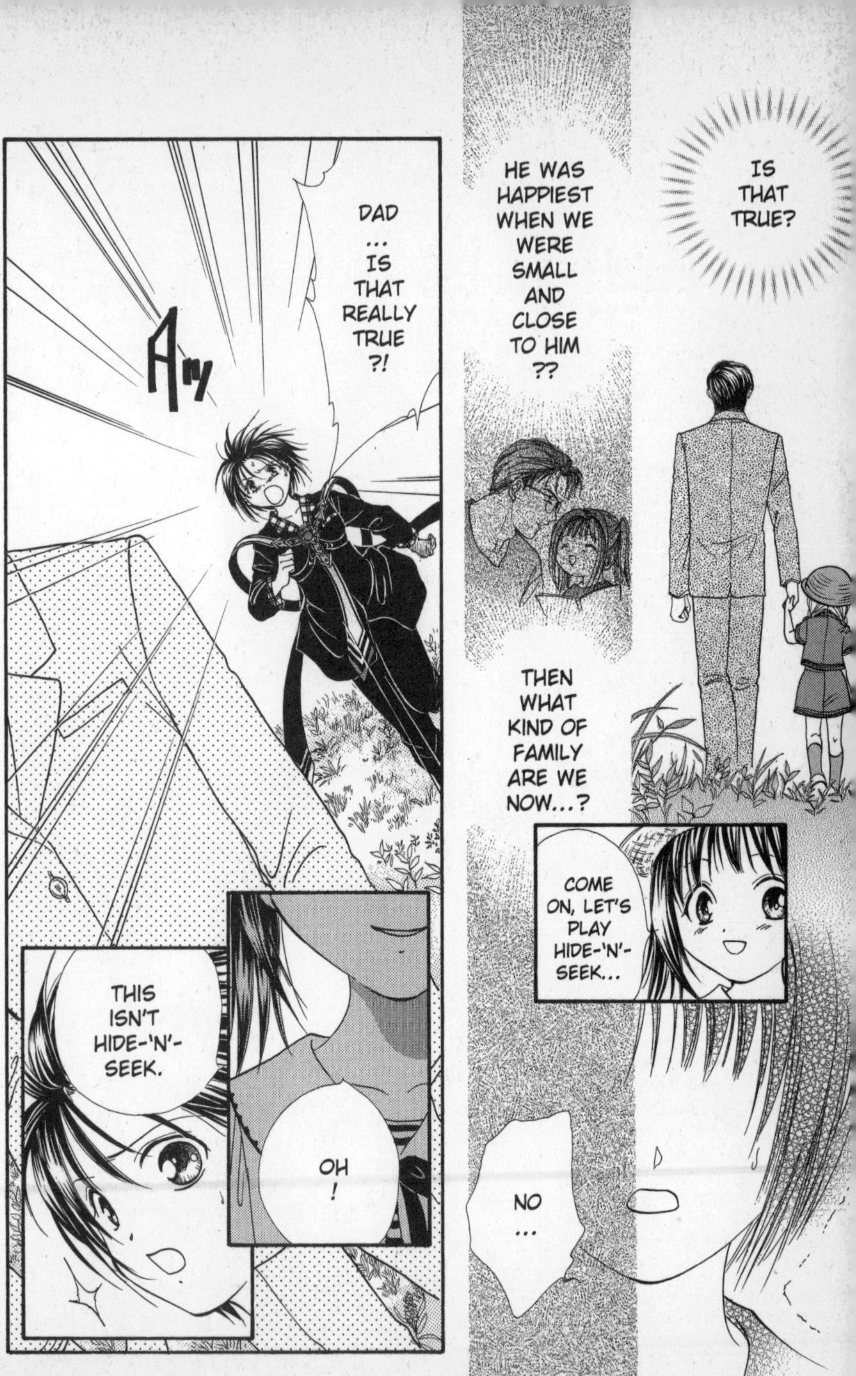
IS THAT TRUE?
HE WAS HAPPIEST WHEN WE WERE SMALL AND CLOSE TO HIM??
THEN WHAT KIND OF FAMILY ARE WE NOW...?
COME ON, LET'S PLAY HIDE-'N'-SEEK...
NO ...
DAD ... IS THAT REALLY TRUE ?!
OH !
THIS ISN'T HIDE-'N'-SEEK.

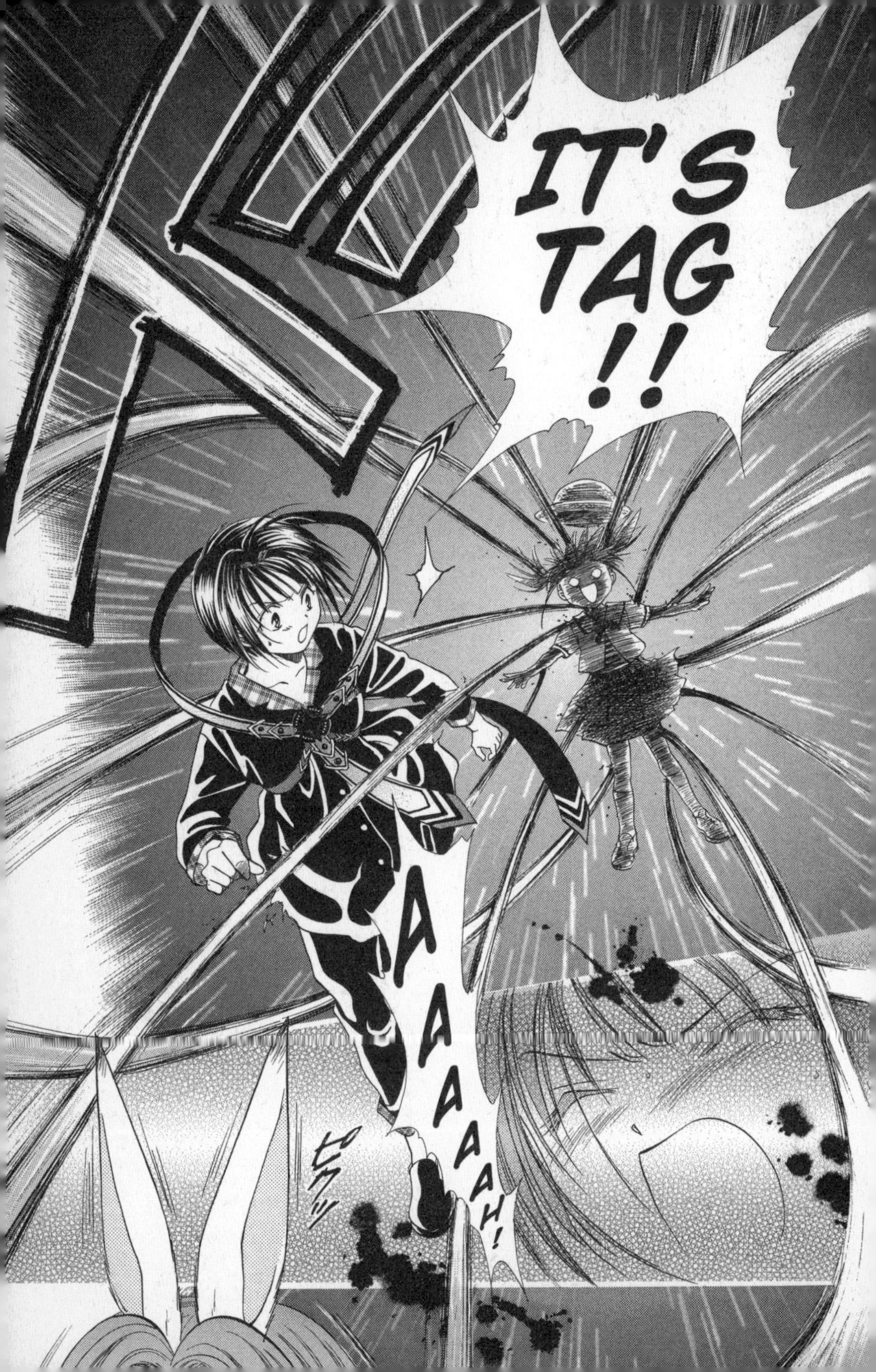
IT'S TAG!!
AAAAAAH!
ビクッ

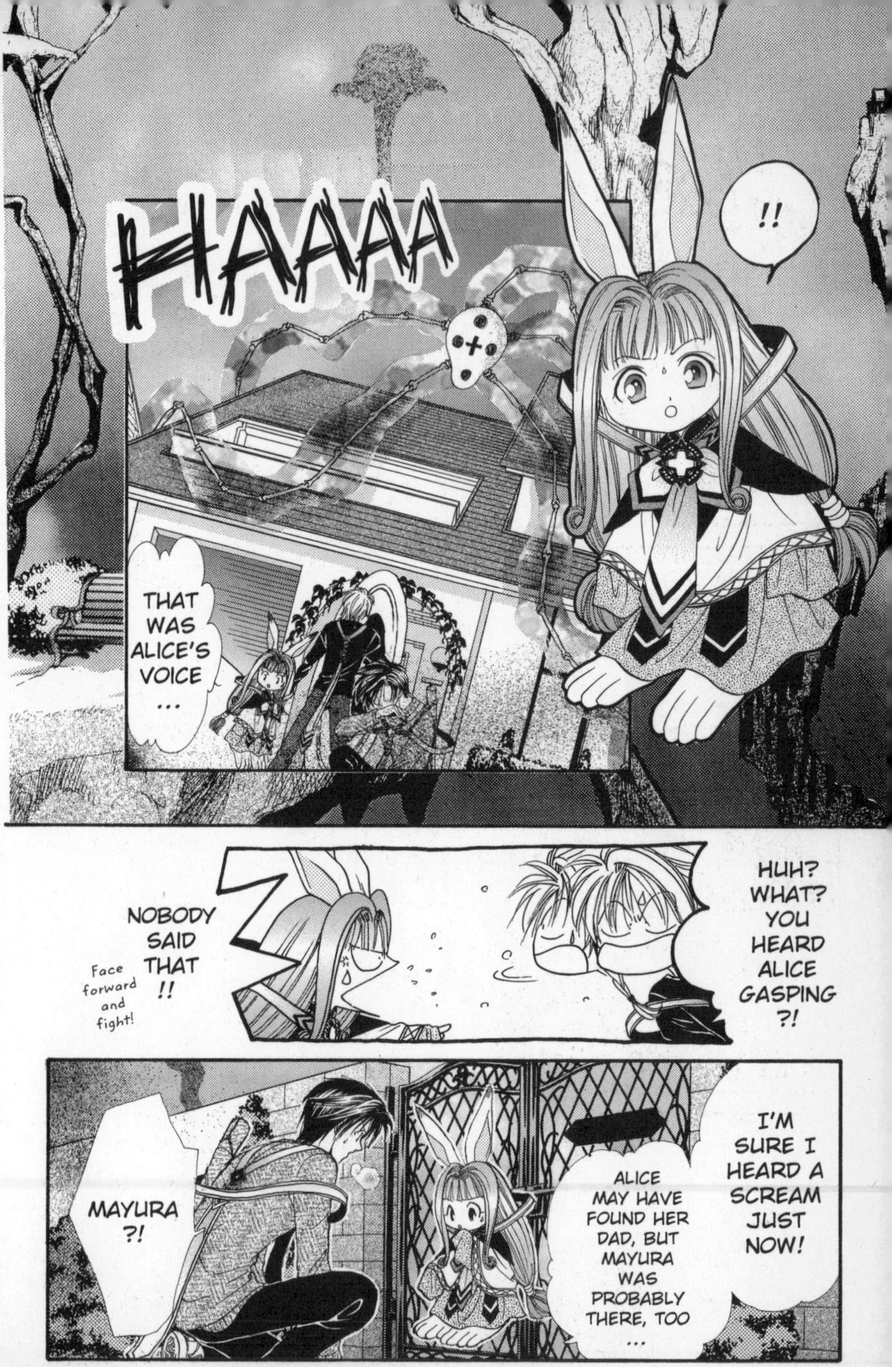
!!
HAAAA
THAT WAS ALICE'S VOICE ...
HUH? WHAT? YOU HEARD ALICE GASPING ?!
NOBODY SAID THAT !!
Face forward and fight!
I'M SURE I HEARD A SCREAM JUST NOW!
ALICE MAY HAVE FOUND HER DAD, BUT MAYURA WAS PROBABLY THERE, TOO ...
MAYURA ?!

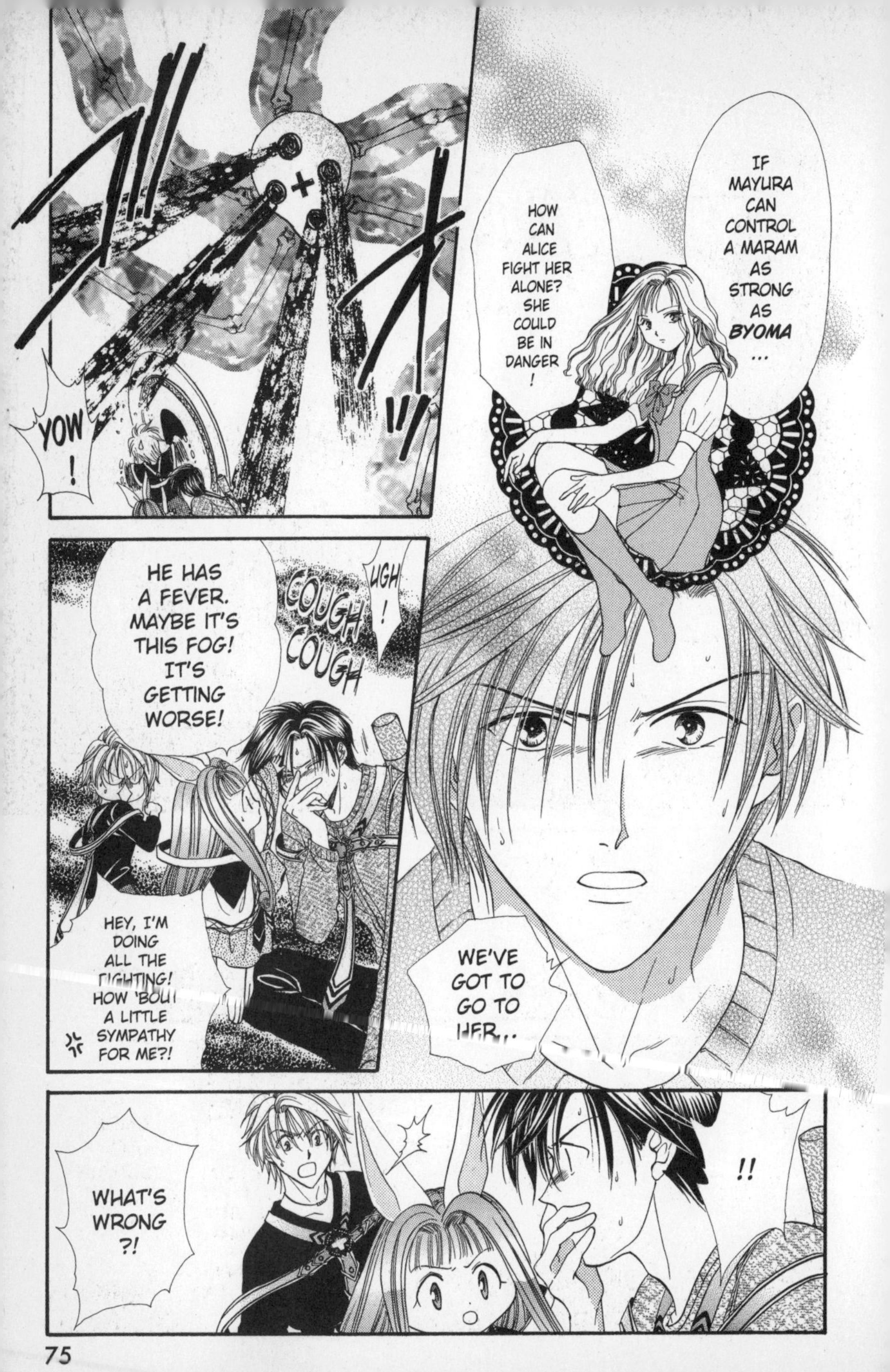
IF MAYURA CAN CONTROL A MARAM AS STRONG AS *BYOMA* ...
HOW CAN ALICE FIGHT HER ALONE? SHE COULD BE IN DANGER!
WE'VE GOT TO GO TO HER...
YOW!
UGH!
COUGH COUGH
HE HAS A FEVER. MAYBE IT'S THIS FOG! IT'S GETTING WORSE!
HEY, I'M DOING ALL THE FIGHTING! HOW 'BOUT A LITTLE SYMPATHY FOR ME?!
!!
WHAT'S WRONG?!

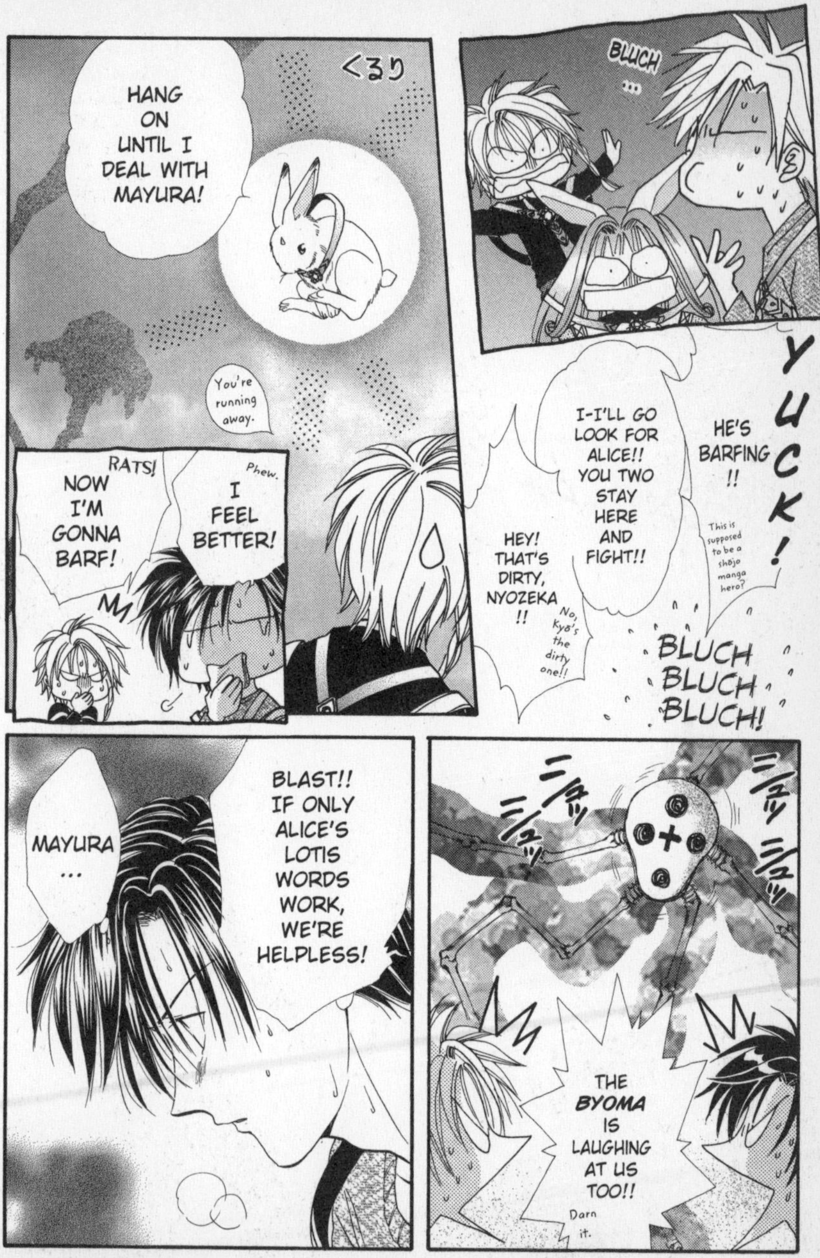
BLUCH ...
YUCK!
HE'S BARFING !!
This is supposed to be a shōjo manga hero?
I-I'LL GO LOOK FOR ALICE!! YOU TWO STAY HERE AND FIGHT!!
HEY! THAT'S DIRTY, NYOZEKA !!
No, Kyō's the dirty one!!
BLUCH BLUCH BLUCH!
くるり
HANG ON UNTIL I DEAL WITH MAYURA!
You're running away.
Phew.
I FEEL BETTER!
RATS! NOW I'M GONNA BARF!
THE BYOMA IS LAUGHING AT US TOO!!
Darn it.
MAYURA ...
BLAST!! IF ONLY ALICE'S LOTIS WORDS WORK, WE'RE HELPLESS!

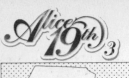

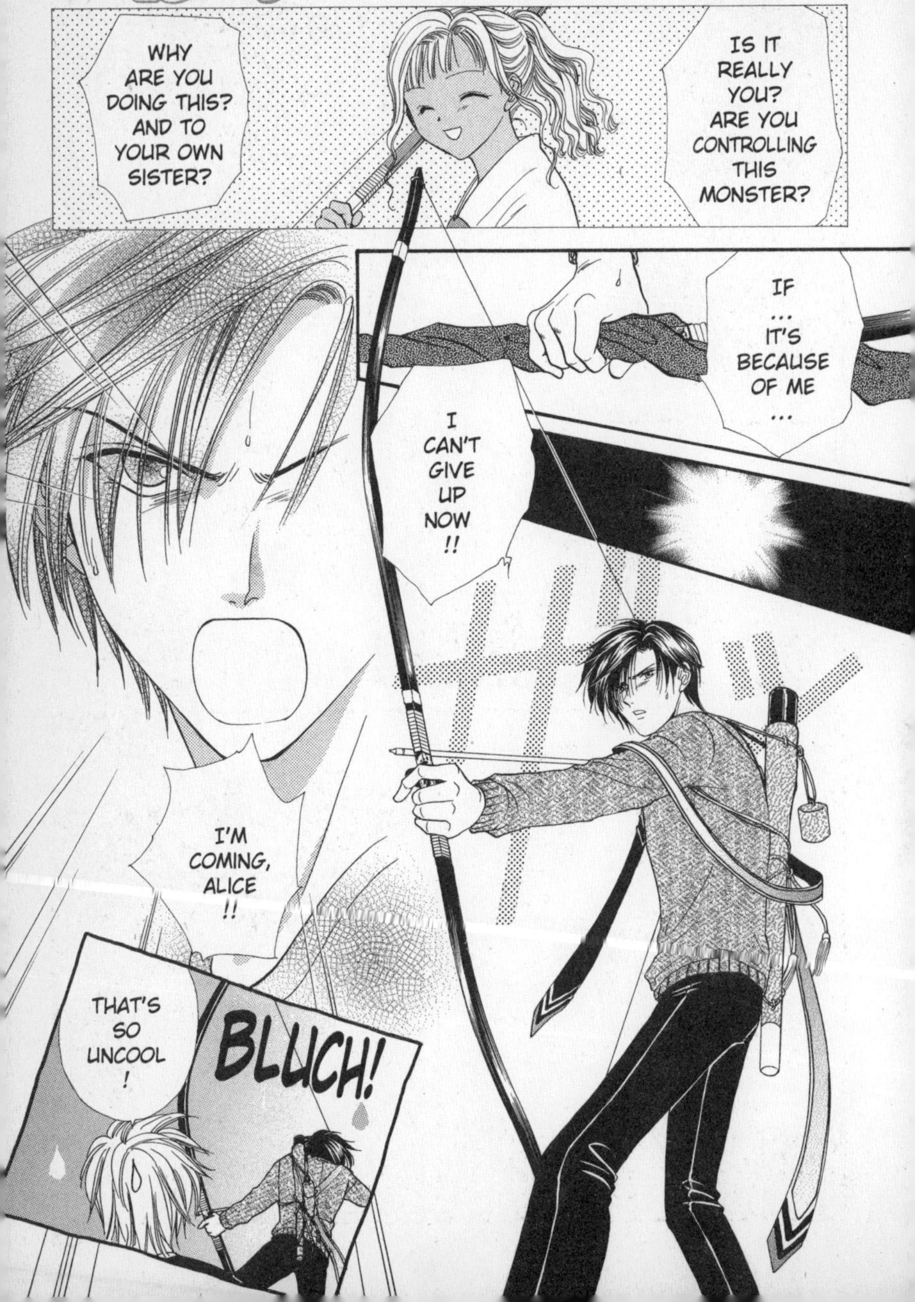
IS IT REALLY YOU? ARE YOU CONTROLLING THIS MONSTER?
WHY ARE YOU DOING THIS? AND TO YOUR OWN SISTER?
IF ... IT'S BECAUSE OF ME ...
I CAN'T GIVE UP NOW !!
I'M COMING, ALICE !!
BLUCH!
THAT'S SO UNCOOL !

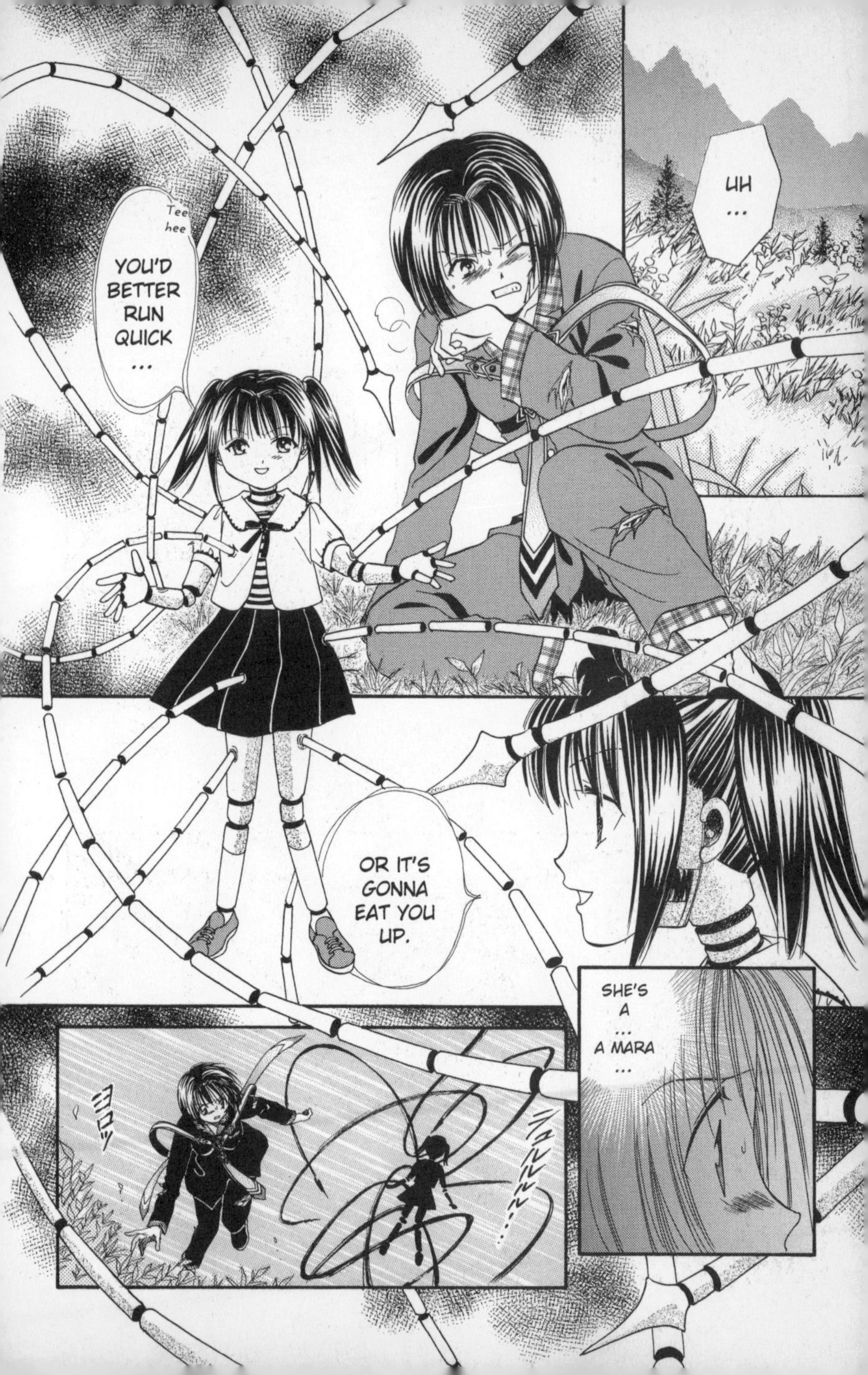
UH ...
Tee hee
YOU'D BETTER RUN QUICK ...
OR IT'S GONNA EAT YOU UP.
SHE'S A ... A MARA ...

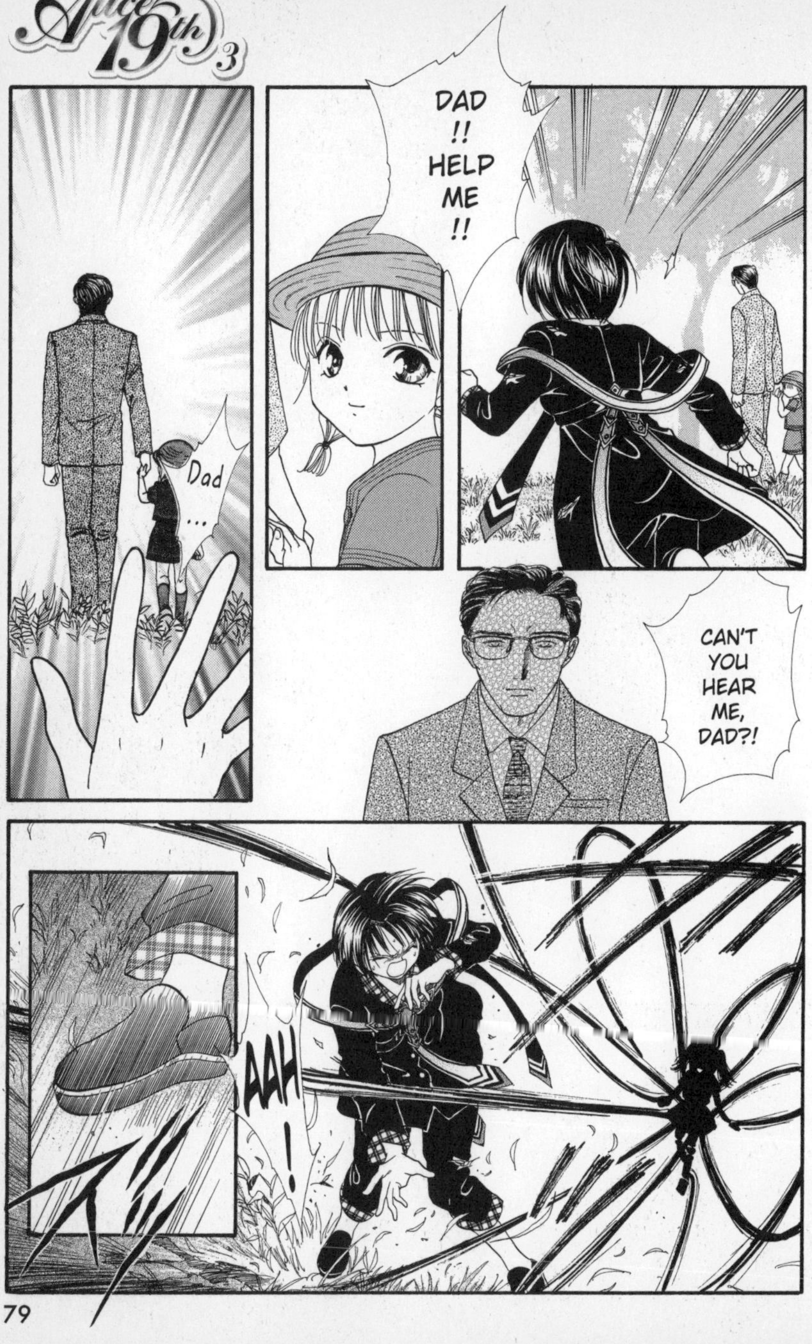
DAD !! HELP ME !!
CAN'T YOU HEAR ME, DAD?!
Dad ...
AAH !

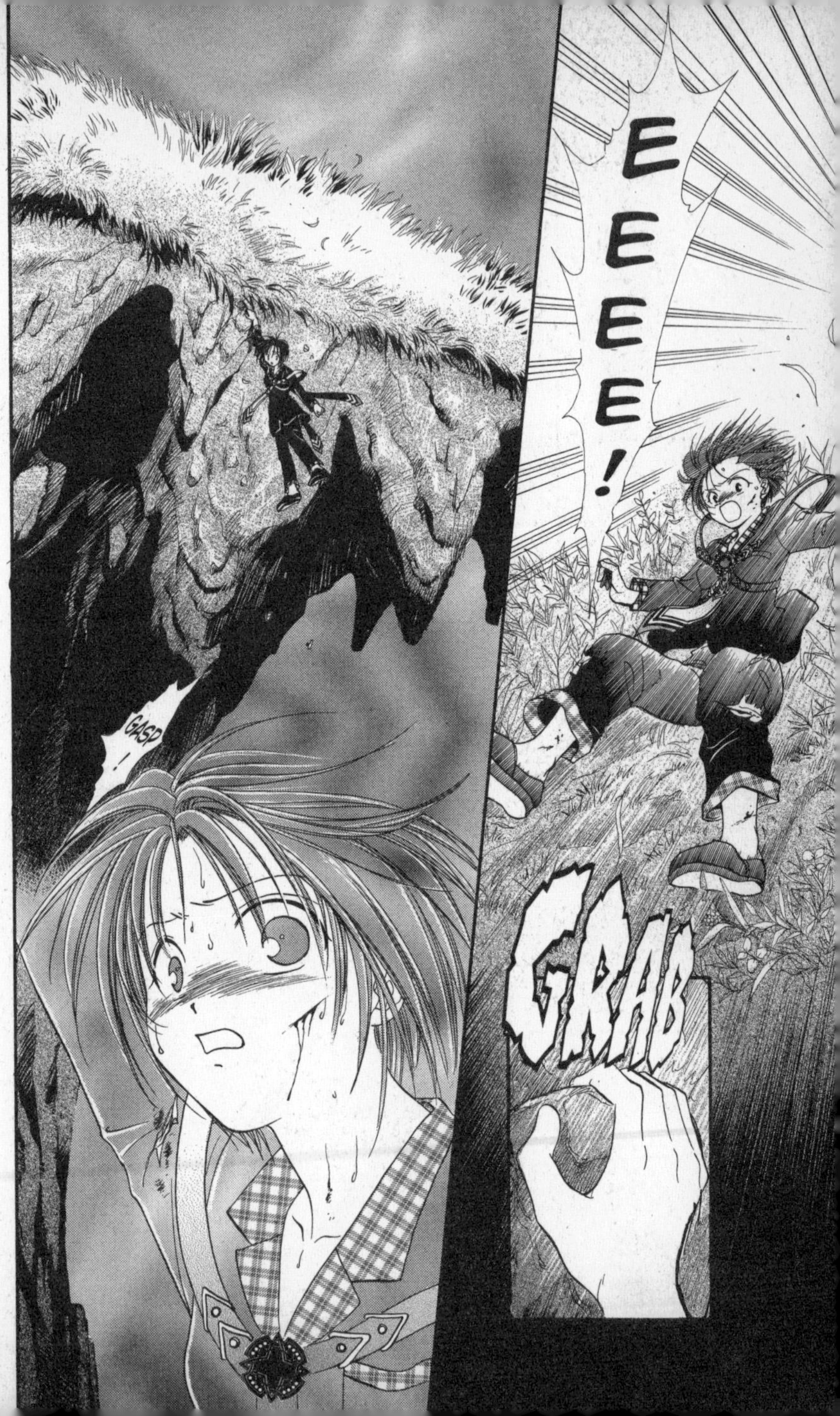
EEEE!
GRAB
GASP!

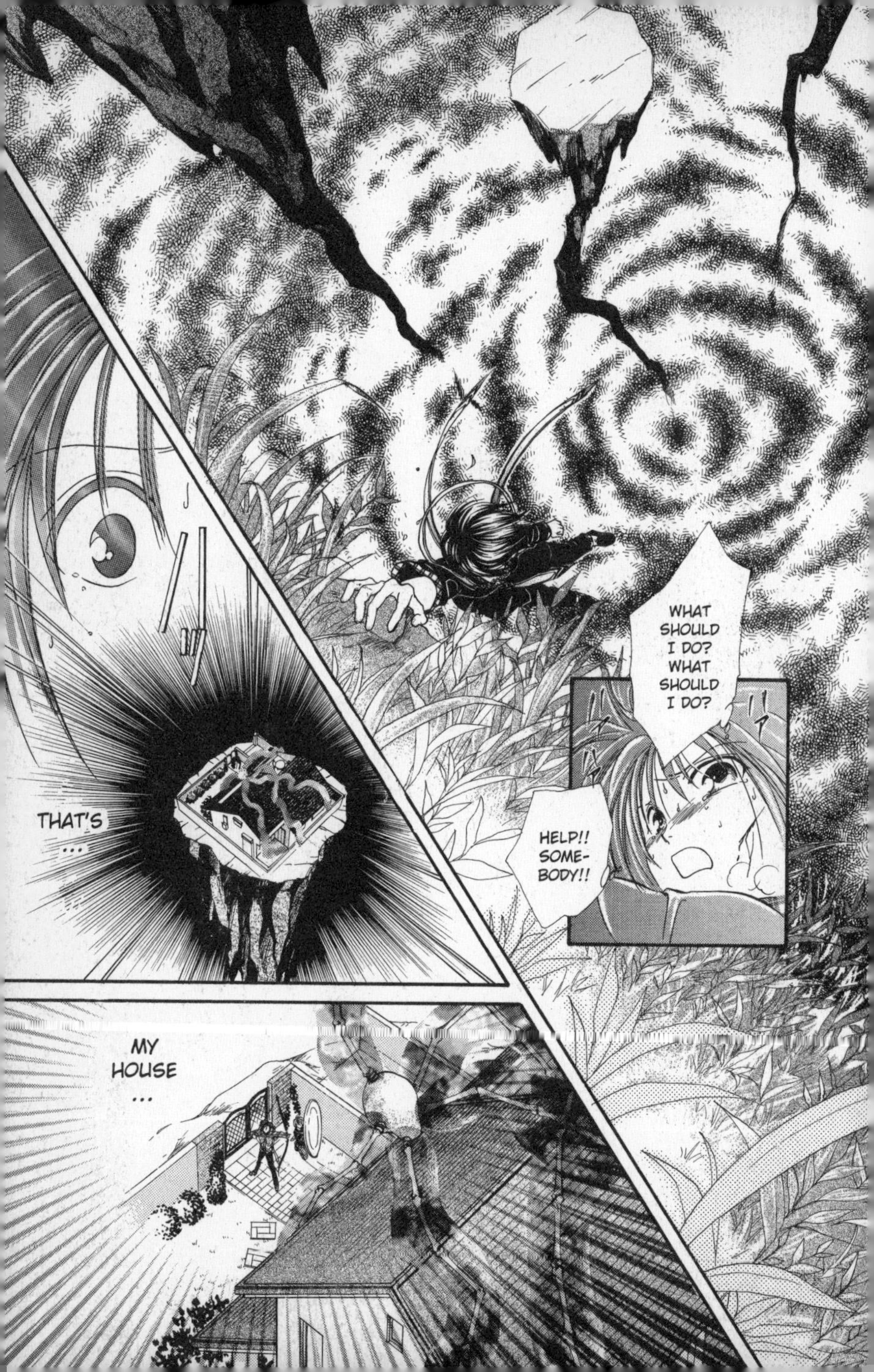
WHAT SHOULD I DO? WHAT SHOULD I DO?
HELP!! SOMEBODY!!
THAT'S ...
MY HOUSE ...

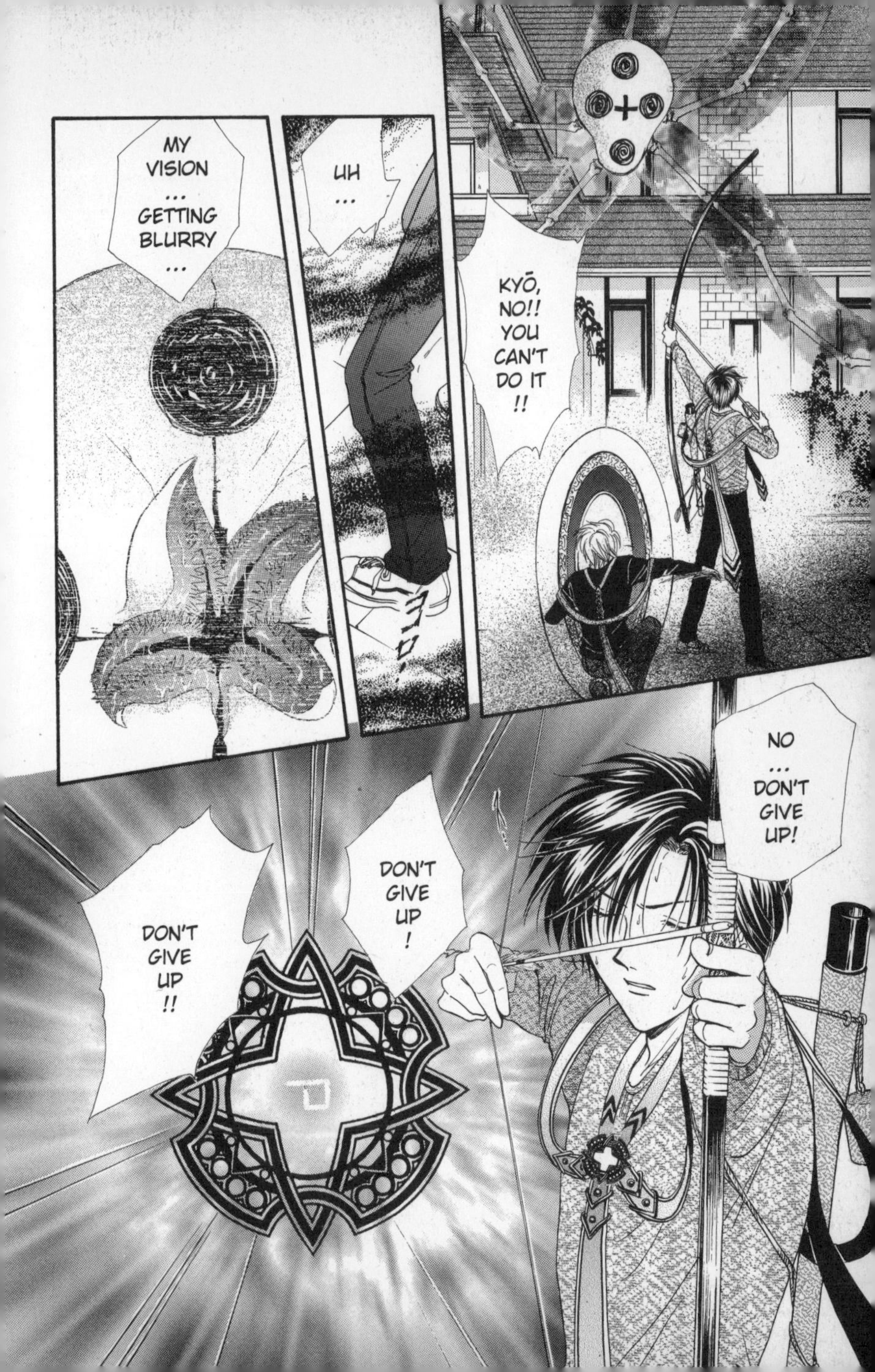
KYŌ, NO!! YOU CAN'T DO IT !!
UH ...
MY VISION ... GETTING BLURRY ...
NO ... DON'T GIVE UP!
DON'T GIVE UP !
DON'T GIVE UP !!

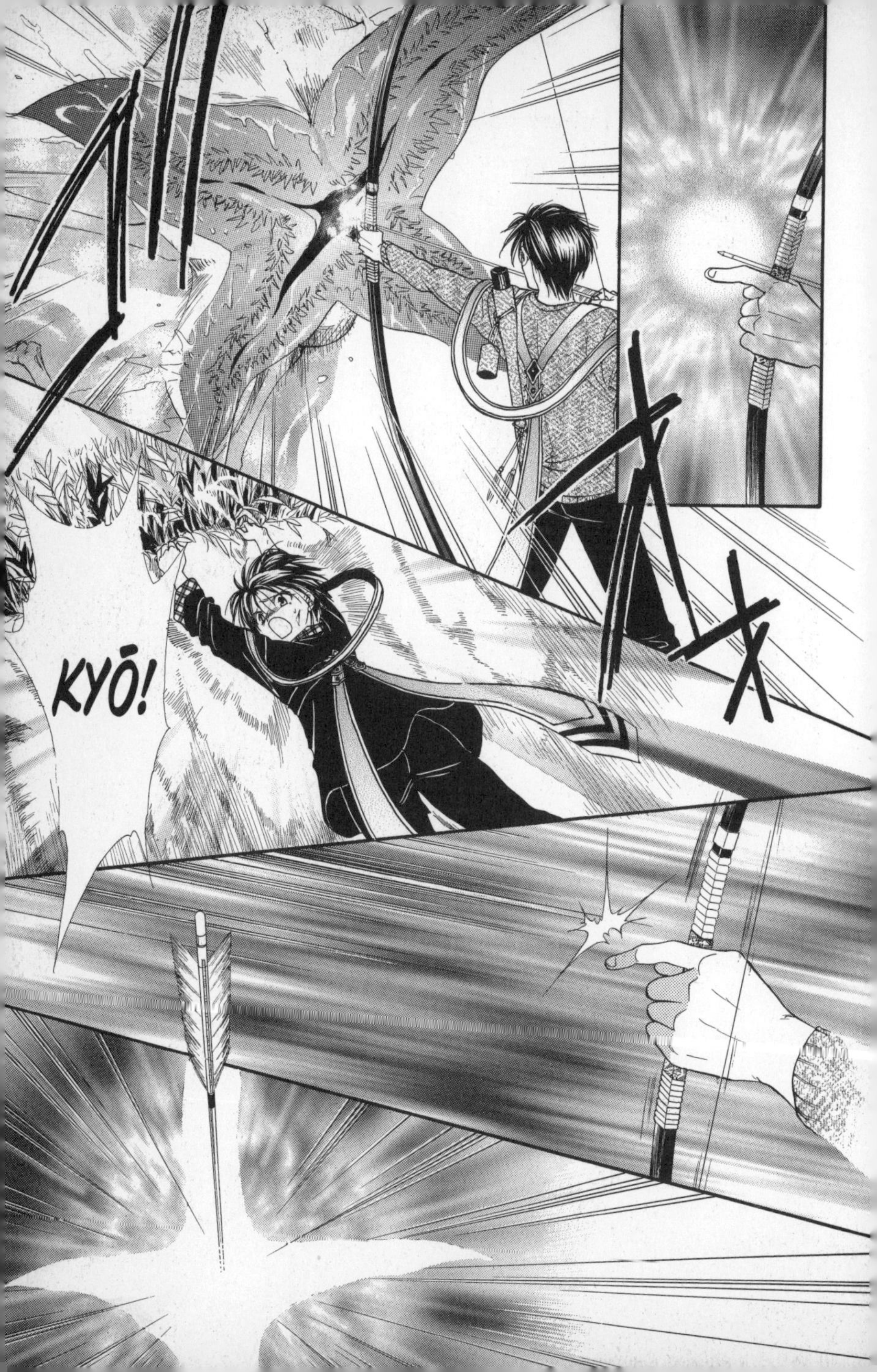
KYŌ!

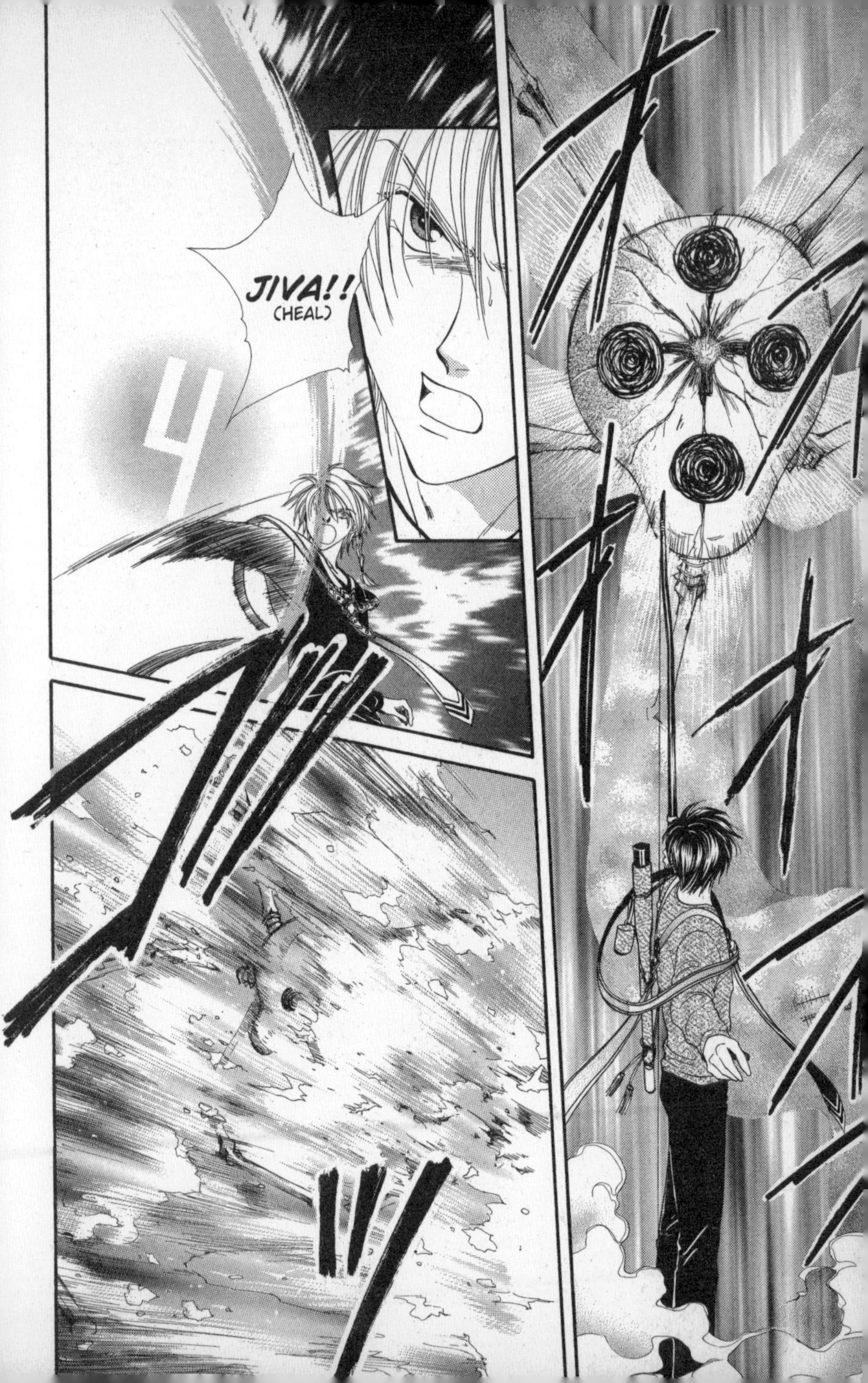
JIVA!!
(HEAL)

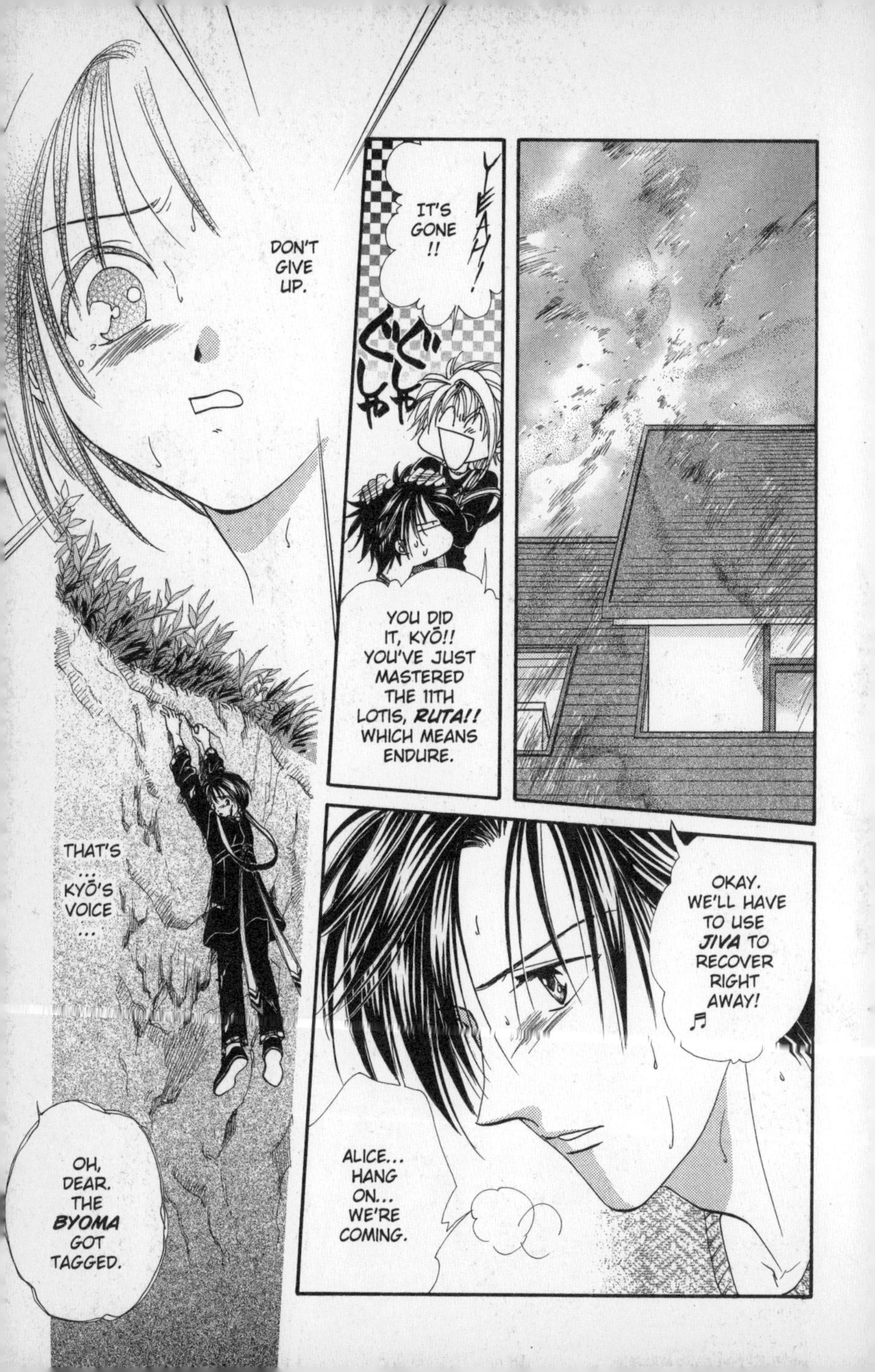
YEAH!
IT'S GONE !!
ぐしゃぐしゃ
YOU DID IT, KYŌ!! YOU'VE JUST MASTERED THE 11TH LOTIS, *RUTA!!* WHICH MEANS ENDURE.
OKAY. WE'LL HAVE TO USE *JIVA* TO RECOVER RIGHT AWAY! ♫
ALICE... HANG ON... WE'RE COMING.
DON'T GIVE UP.
THAT'S ... KYŌ'S VOICE ...
OH, DEAR. THE *BYOMA* GOT TAGGED.

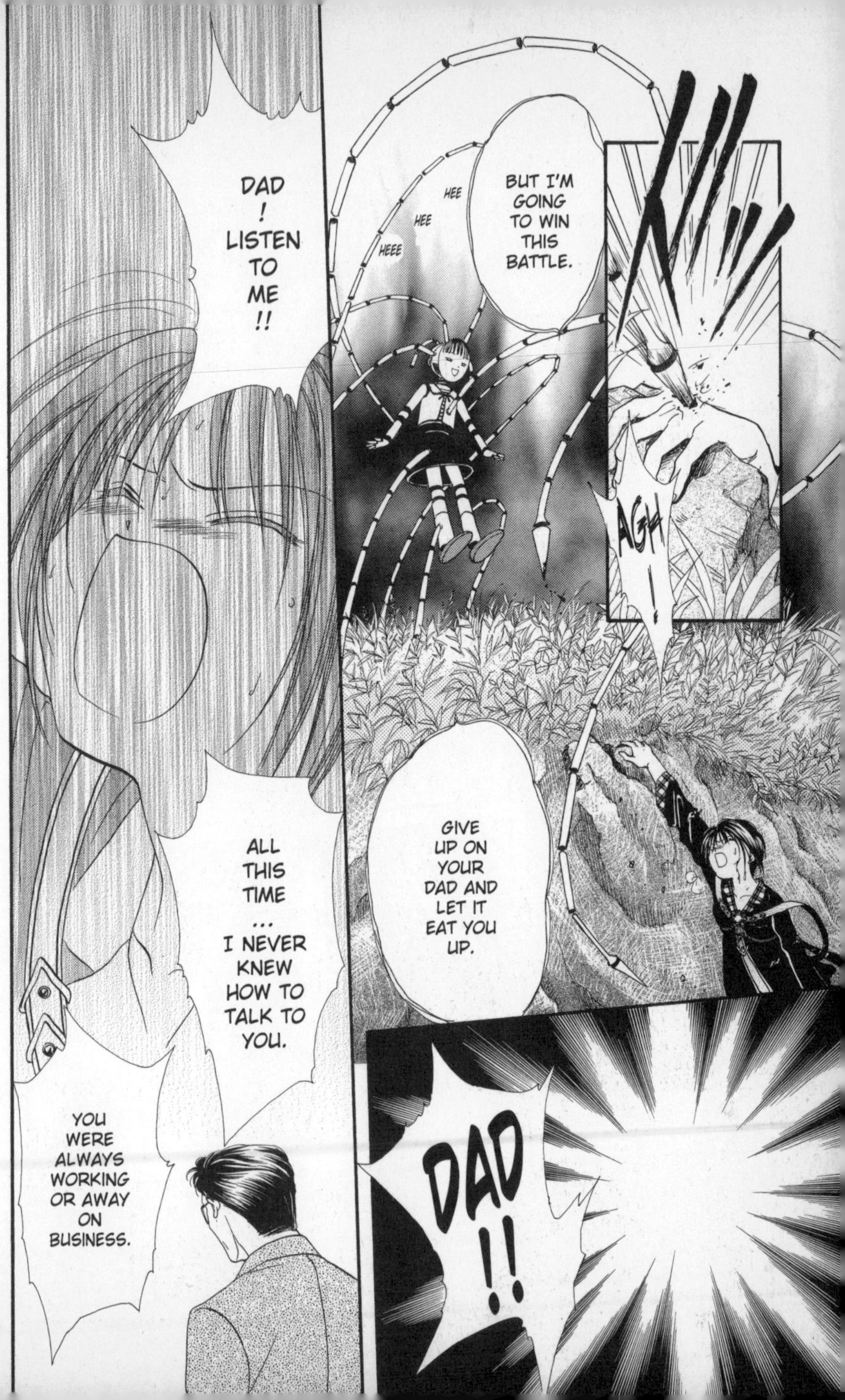
AGH!
BUT I'M GOING TO WIN THIS BATTLE.
HEE
HEE
HEEE
GIVE UP ON YOUR DAD AND LET IT EAT YOU UP.
DAD!!
DAD! LISTEN TO ME!!
ALL THIS TIME... I NEVER KNEW HOW TO TALK TO YOU.
YOU WERE ALWAYS WORKING OR AWAY ON BUSINESS.

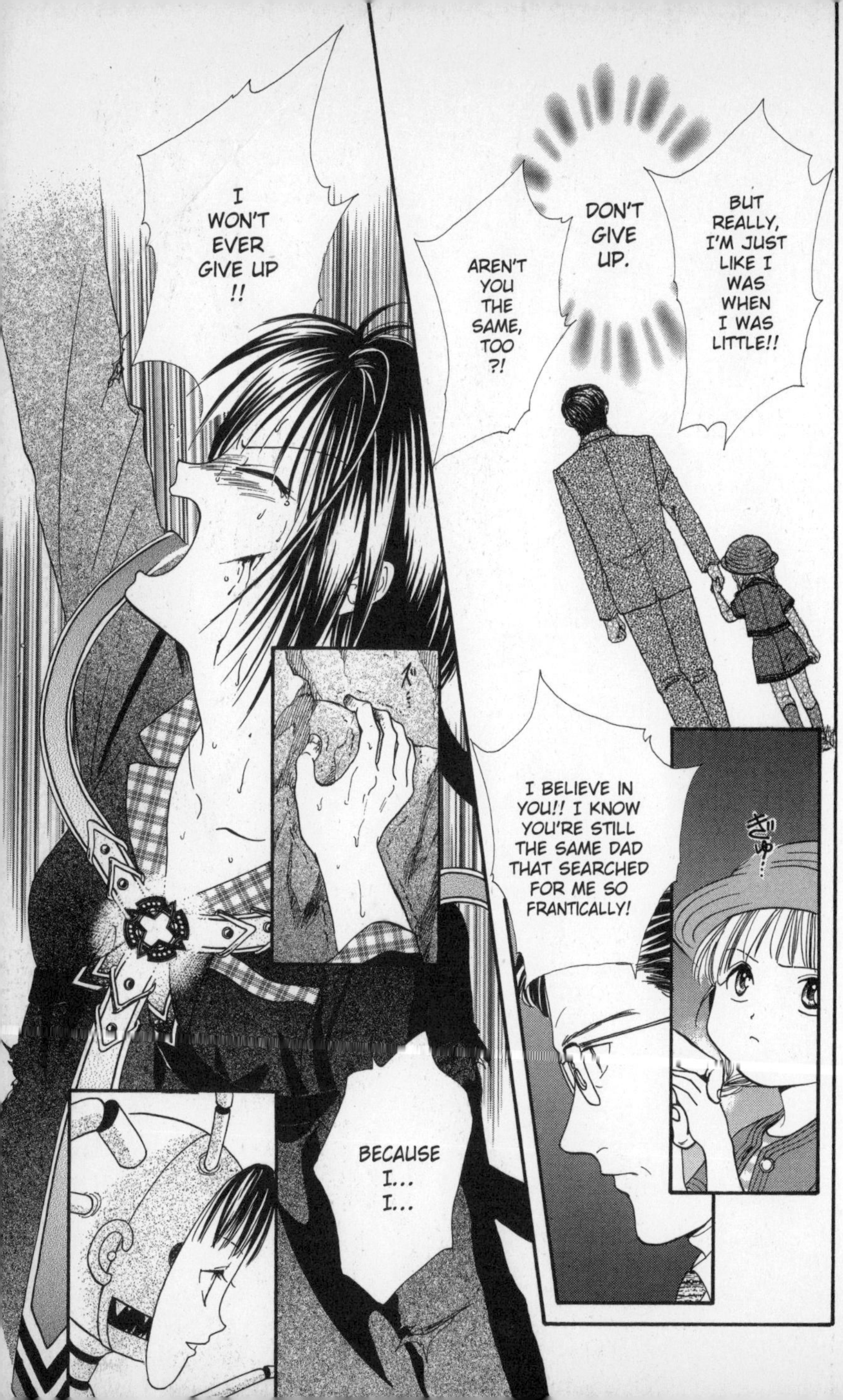
BUT REALLY, I'M JUST LIKE I WAS WHEN I WAS LITTLE!!
DON'T GIVE UP.
AREN'T YOU THE SAME, TOO?!
I BELIEVE IN YOU!! I KNOW YOU'RE STILL THE SAME DAD THAT SEARCHED FOR ME SO FRANTICALLY!
ぎゅ…
I WON'T EVER GIVE UP!!
BECAUSE I... I...

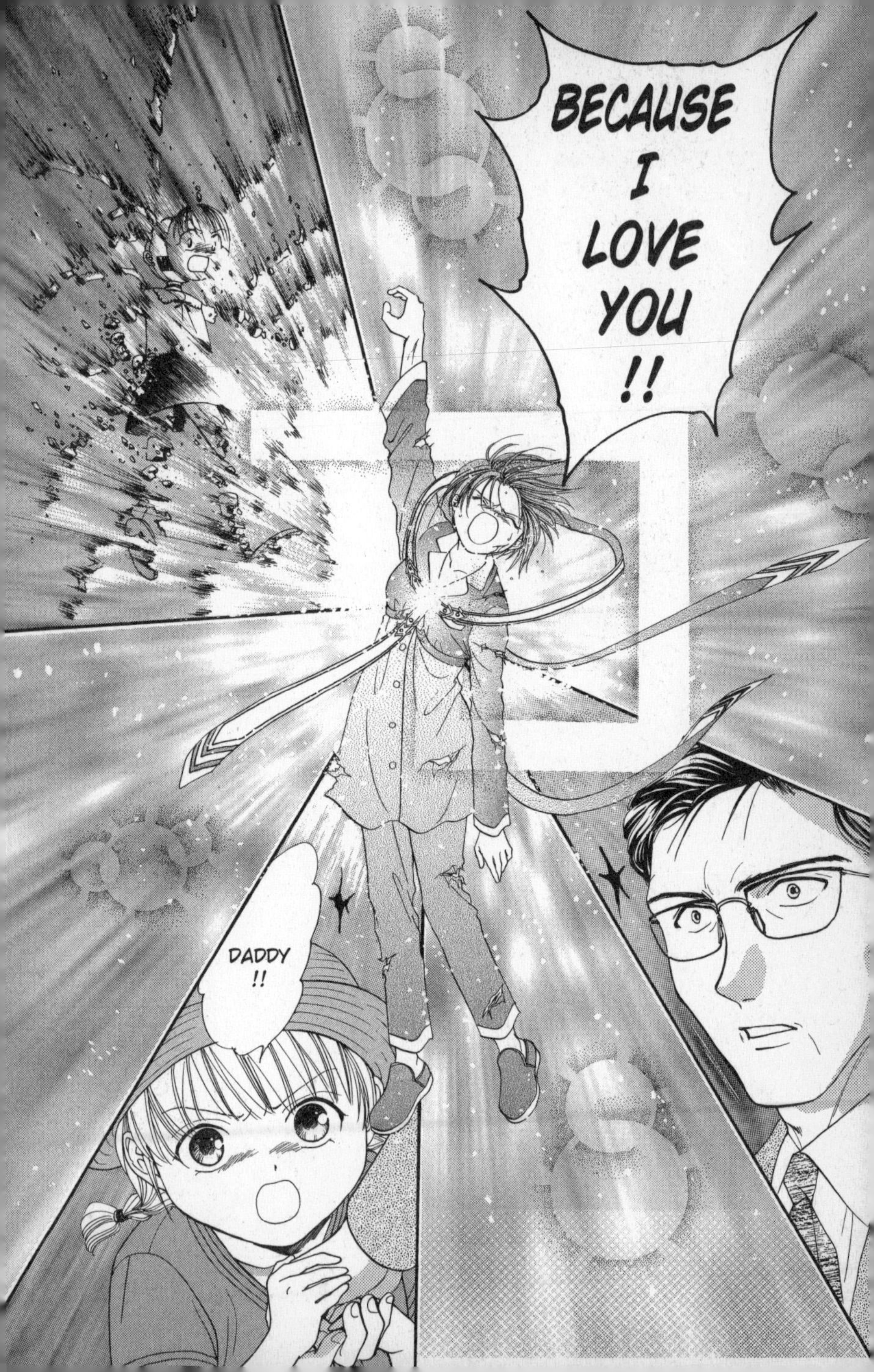
BECAUSE I LOVE YOU !!
DADDY !!

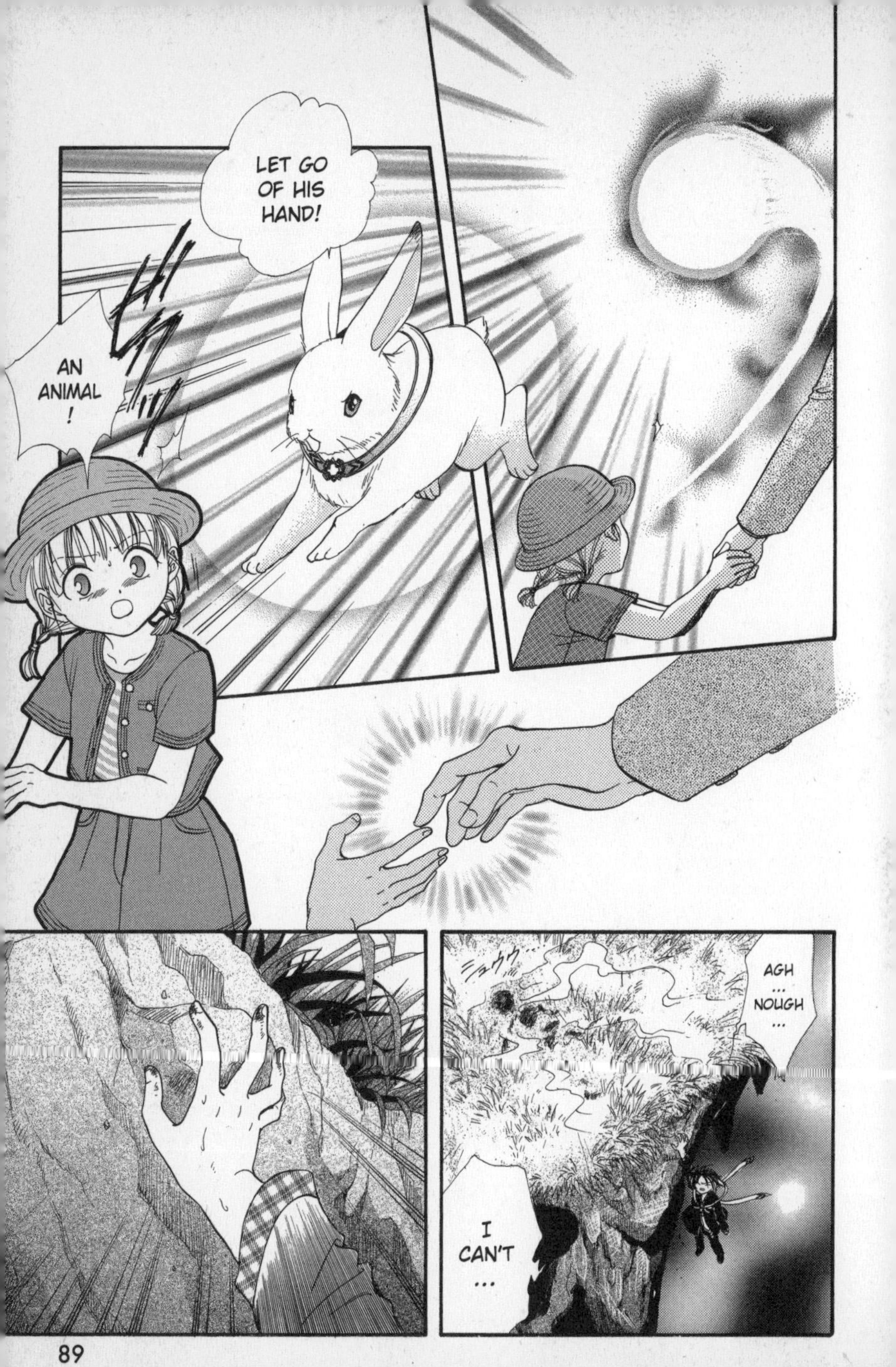
LET GO OF HIS HAND!
AN ANIMAL!
AGH ... NOUGH ...
I CAN'T ...

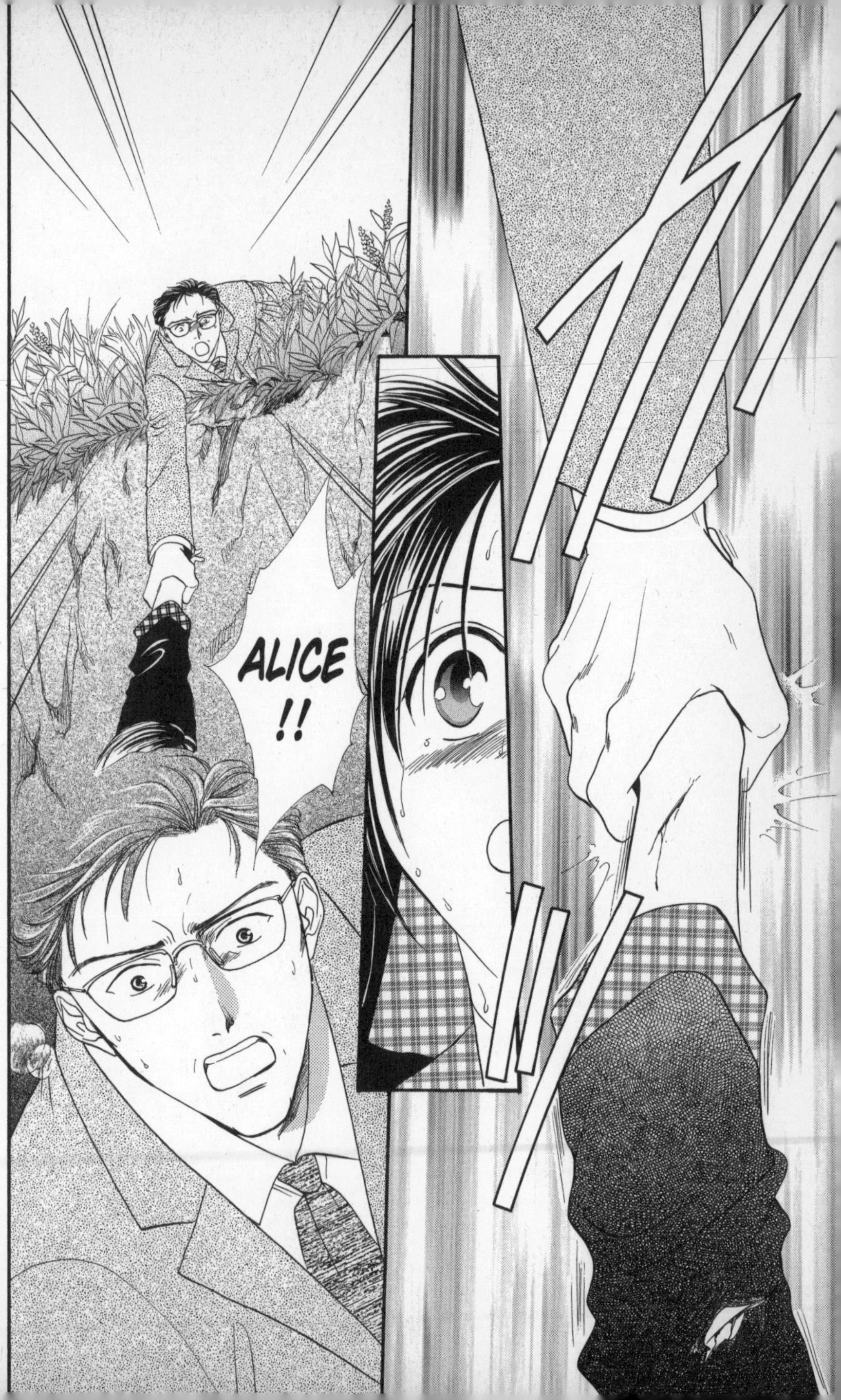
ALICE
!!

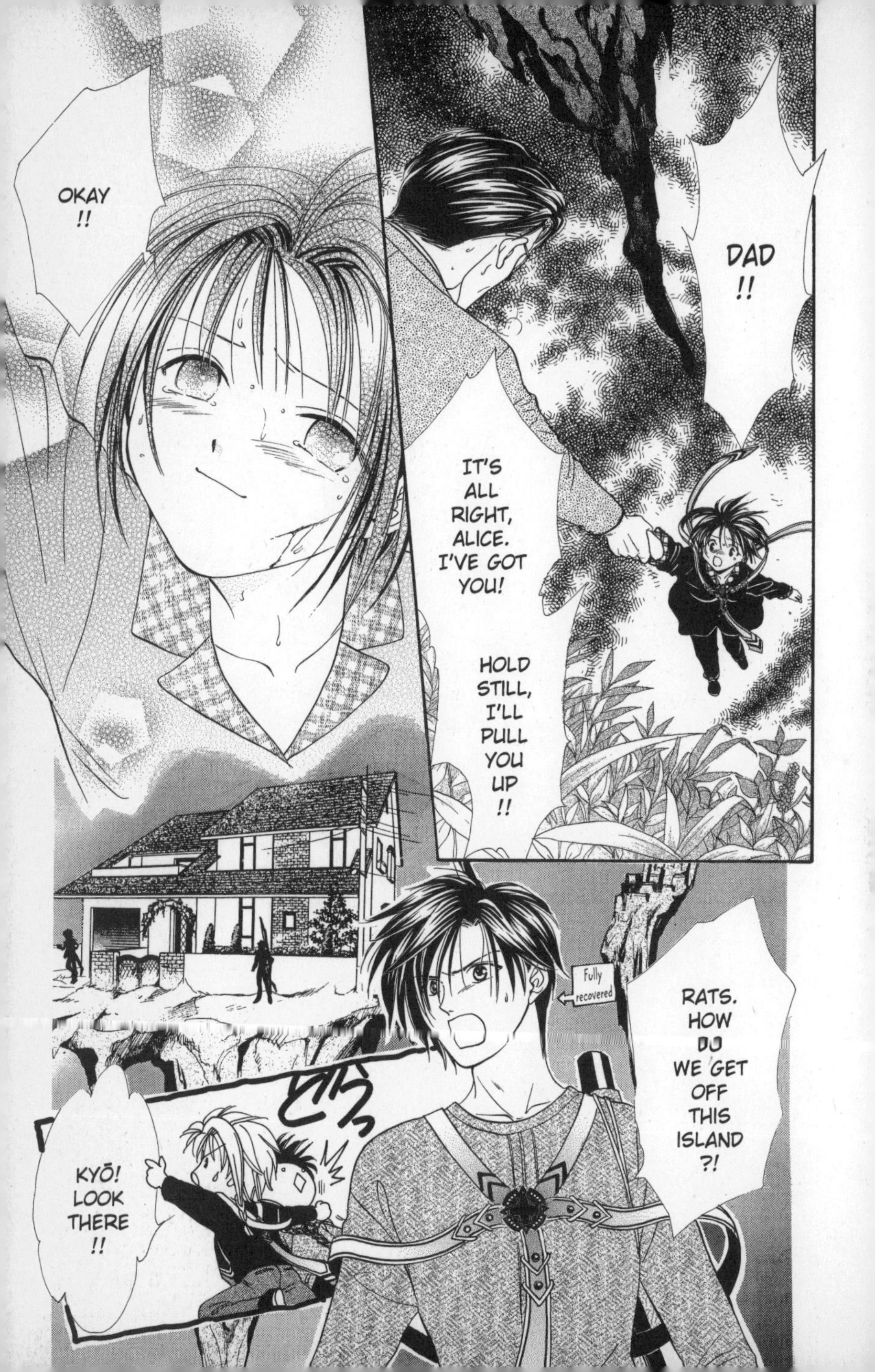
DAD !!
IT'S ALL RIGHT, ALICE. I'VE GOT YOU!
HOLD STILL, I'LL PULL YOU UP !!
OKAY !!
Fully recovered
RATS. HOW DO WE GET OFF THIS ISLAND ?!
KYŌ! LOOK THERE !!

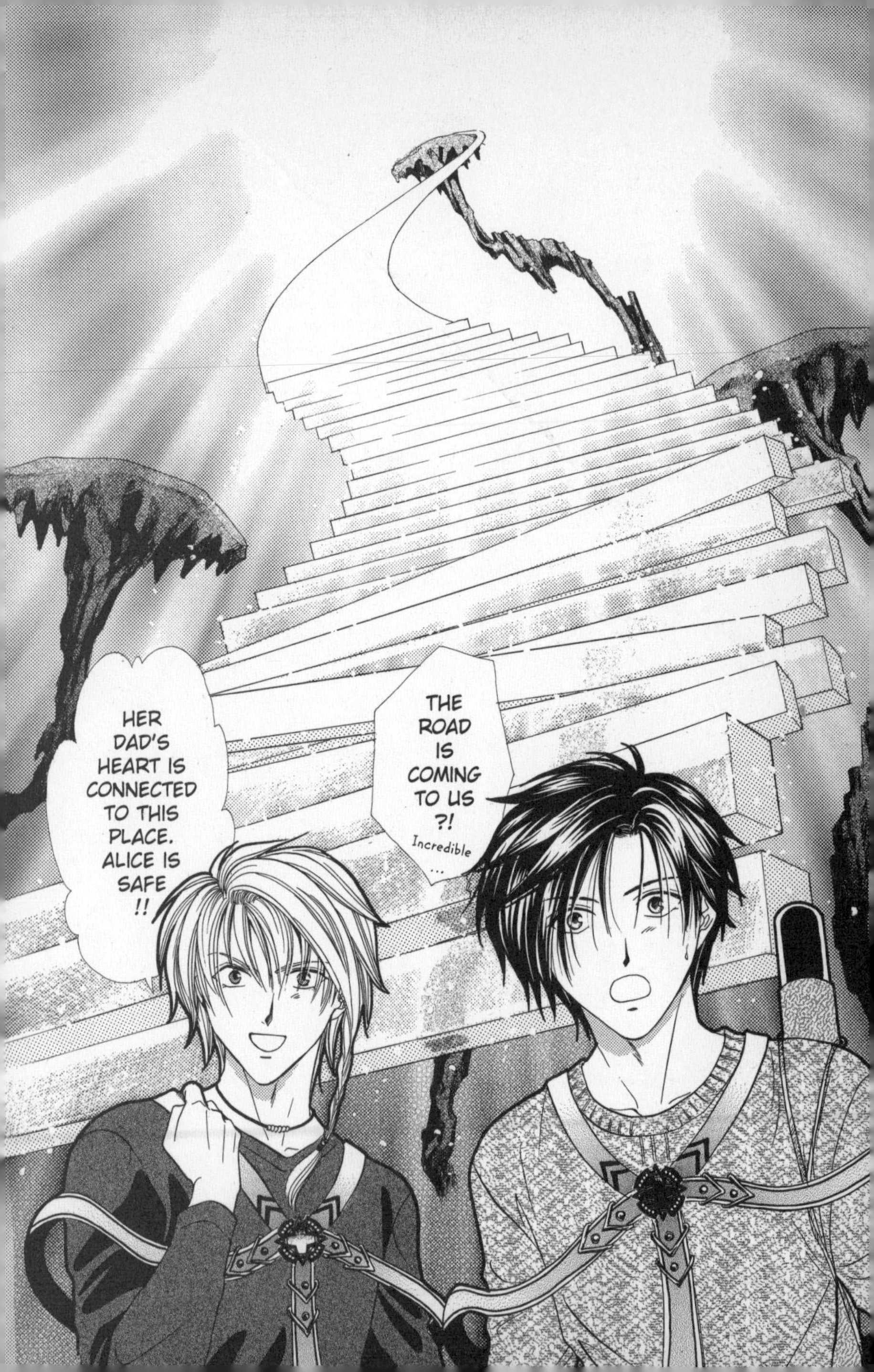
THE ROAD IS COMING TO US ?!
Incredible ...
HER DAD'S HEART IS CONNECTED TO THIS PLACE. ALICE IS SAFE !!

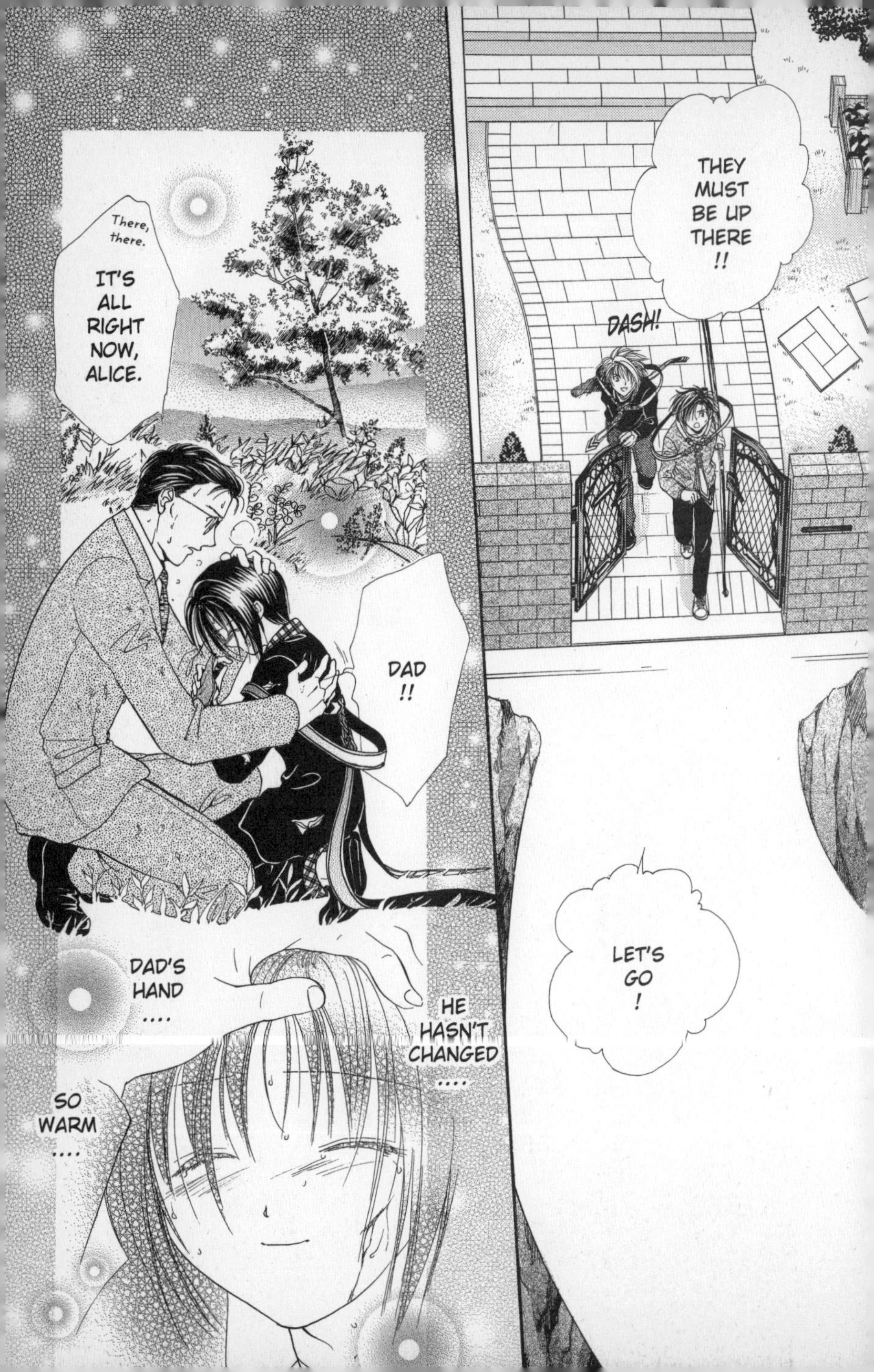
THEY MUST BE UP THERE !!
DASH!
LET'S GO !
There, there.
IT'S ALL RIGHT NOW, ALICE.
DAD !!
DAD'S HAND ....
HE HASN'T CHANGED ....
SO WARM ....

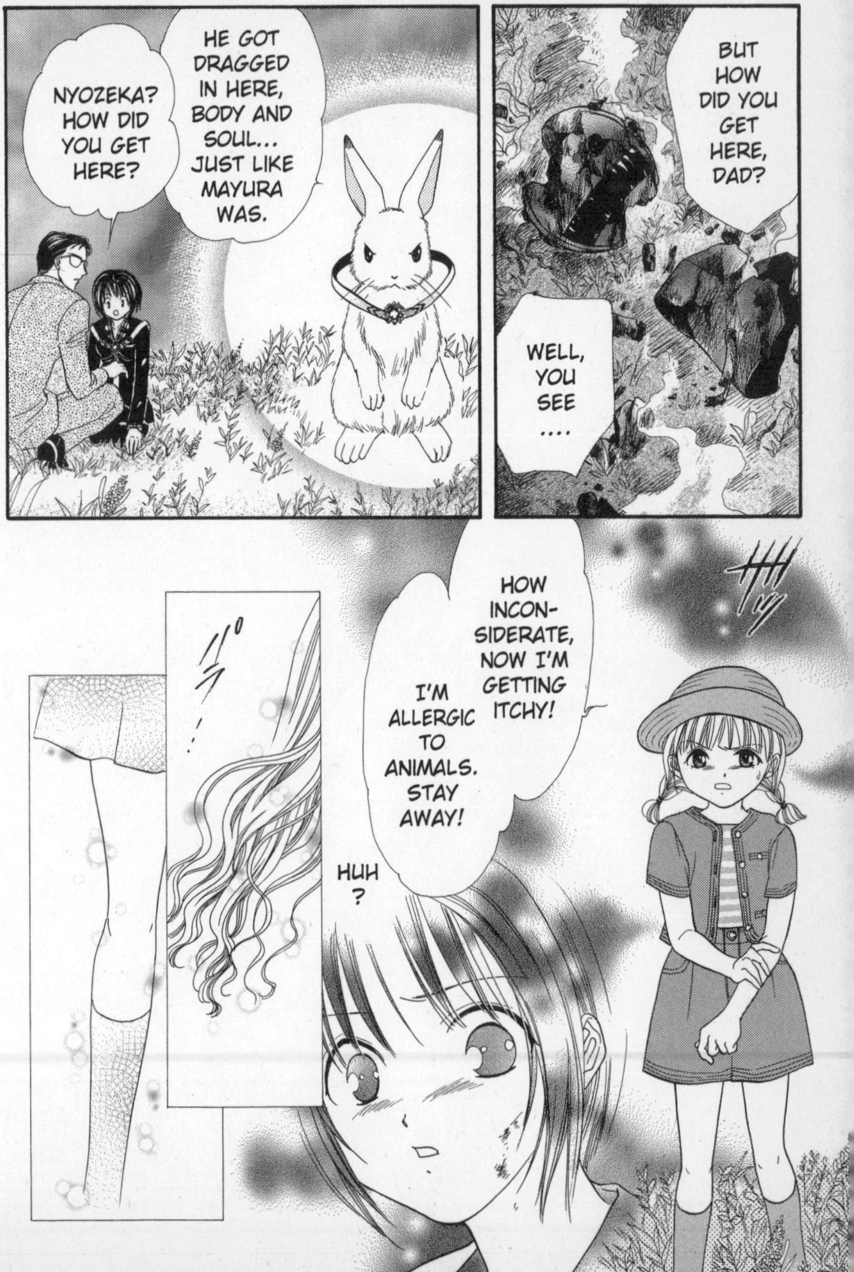
BUT HOW DID YOU GET HERE, DAD?
WELL, YOU SEE....
NYOZEKA? HOW DID YOU GET HERE?
HE GOT DRAGGED IN HERE, BODY AND SOUL... JUST LIKE MAYURA WAS.
HOW INCON-SIDERATE, NOW I'M GETTING ITCHY!
I'M ALLERGIC TO ANIMALS. STAY AWAY!
HUH?

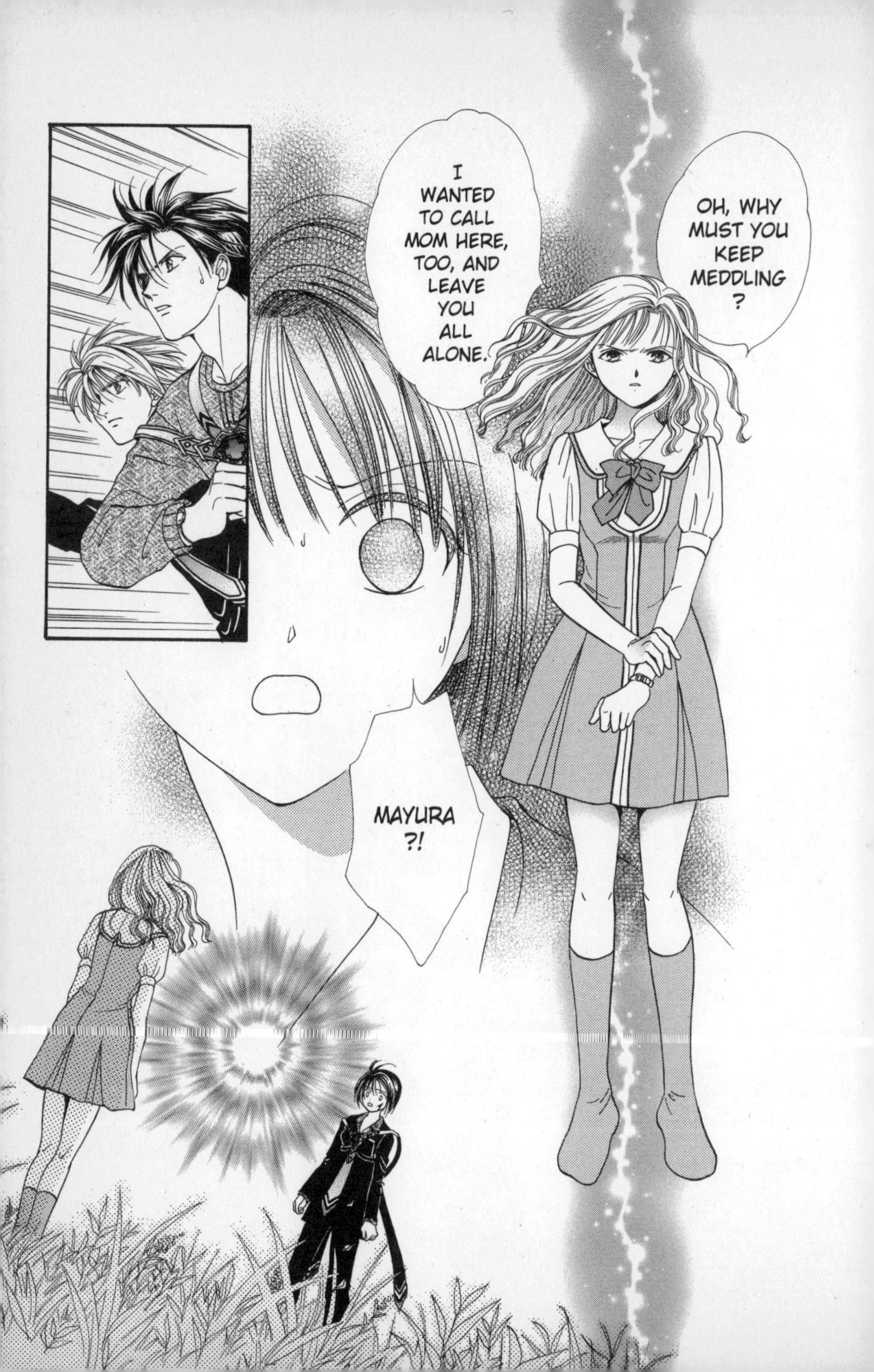
OH, WHY MUST YOU KEEP MEDDLING?
I WANTED TO CALL MOM HERE, TOO, AND LEAVE YOU ALL ALONE.
MAYURA?!

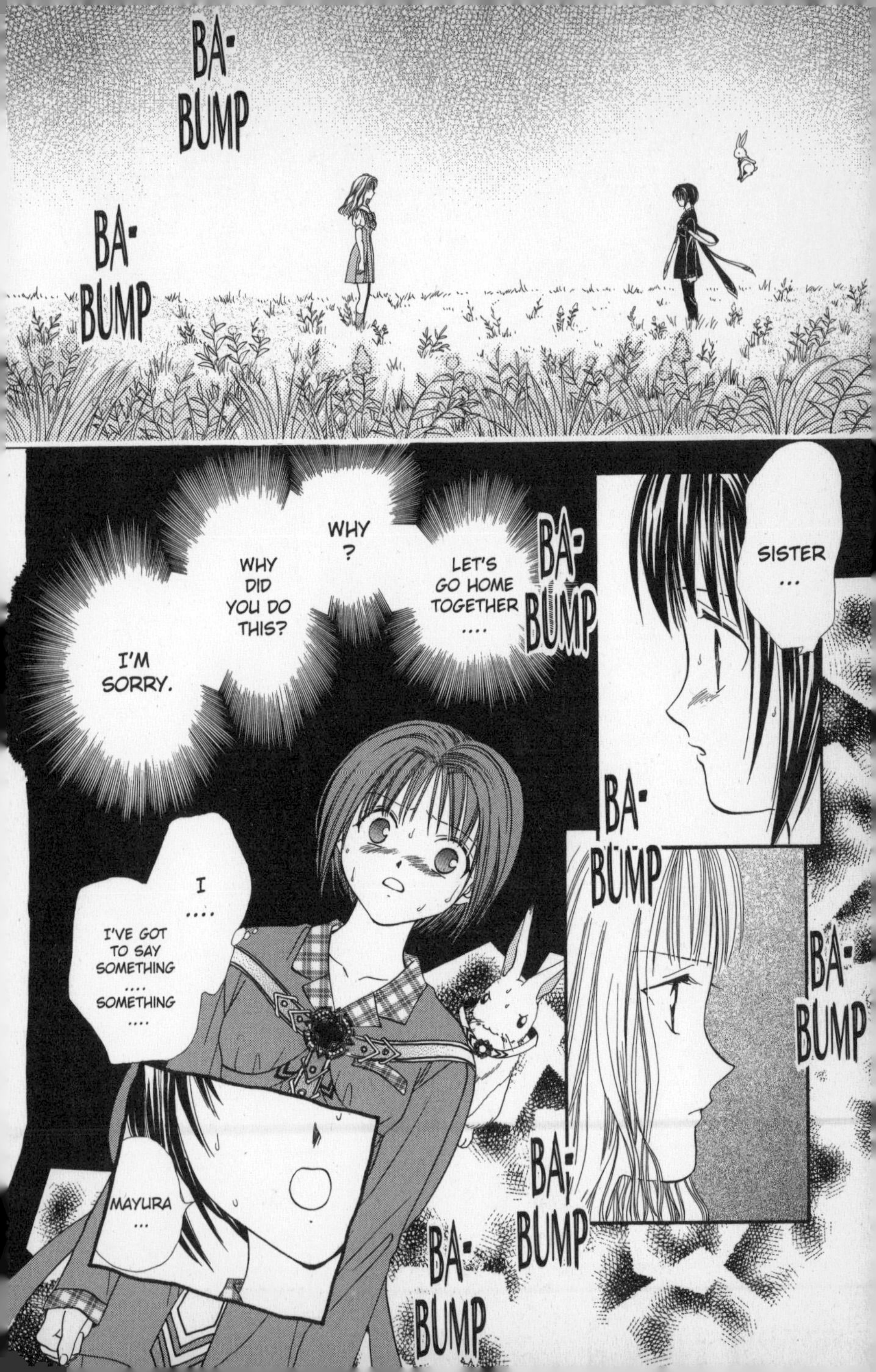
BA-BUMP
BA-BUMP
SISTER ...
BA-BUMP
LET'S GO HOME TOGETHER ....
WHY ?
WHY DID YOU DO THIS?
I'M SORRY.
BA-BUMP
BA-BUMP
BA-BUMP
I ....
I'VE GOT TO SAY SOMETHING .... SOMETHING ....
BA-BUMP
MAYURA ...
BA-BUMP

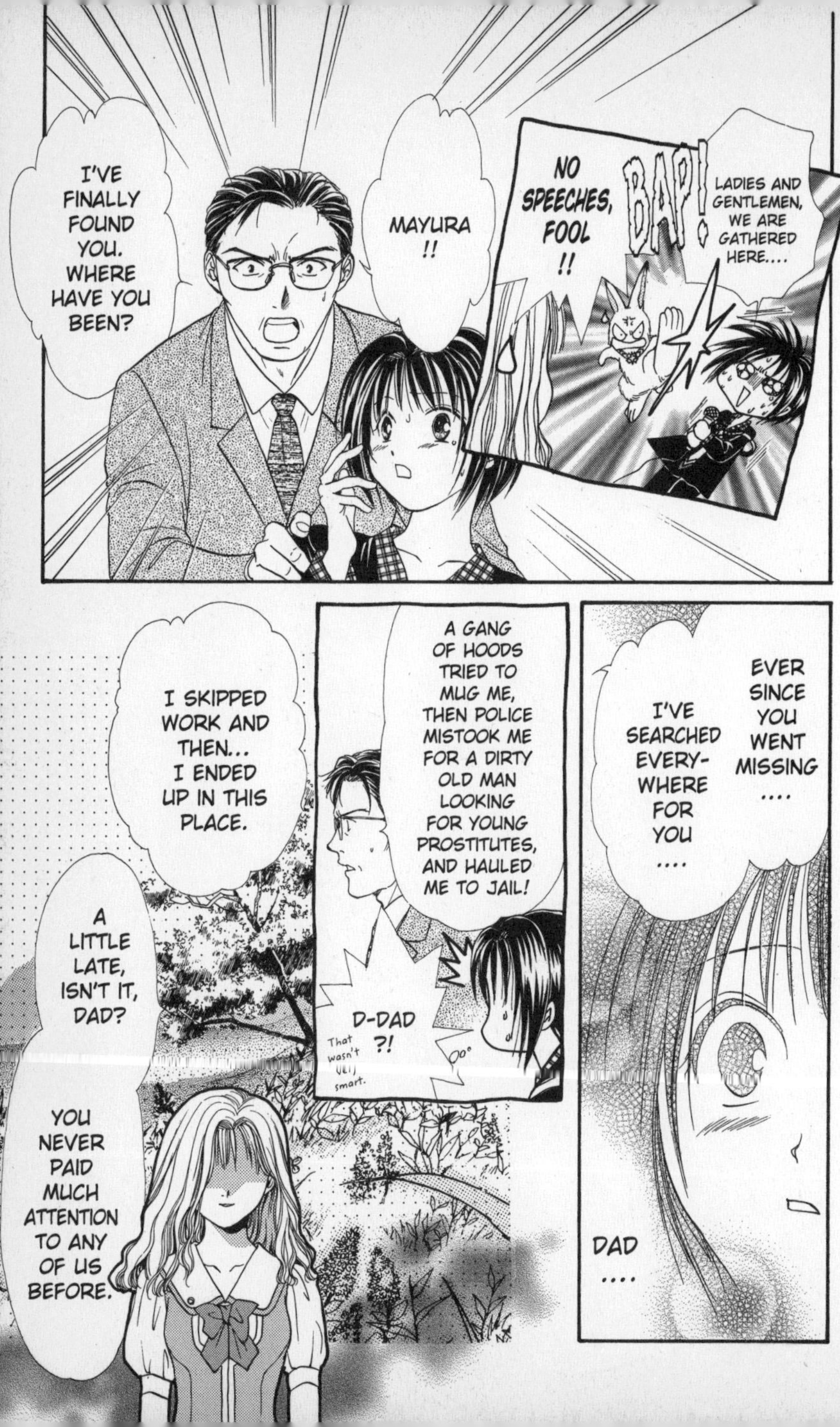
LADIES AND GENTLEMEN, WE ARE GATHERED HERE....
BAP!
NO SPEECHES, FOOL !!
MAYURA !!
I'VE FINALLY FOUND YOU. WHERE HAVE YOU BEEN?
EVER SINCE YOU WENT MISSING ....
I'VE SEARCHED EVERY-WHERE FOR YOU ....
DAD ....
A GANG OF HOODS TRIED TO MUG ME, THEN POLICE MISTOOK ME FOR A DIRTY OLD MAN LOOKING FOR YOUNG PROSTITUTES, AND HAULED ME TO JAIL!
D-DAD ?!
That wasn't very smart.
I SKIPPED WORK AND THEN... I ENDED UP IN THIS PLACE.
A LITTLE LATE, ISN'T IT, DAD?
YOU NEVER PAID MUCH ATTENTION TO ANY OF US BEFORE.

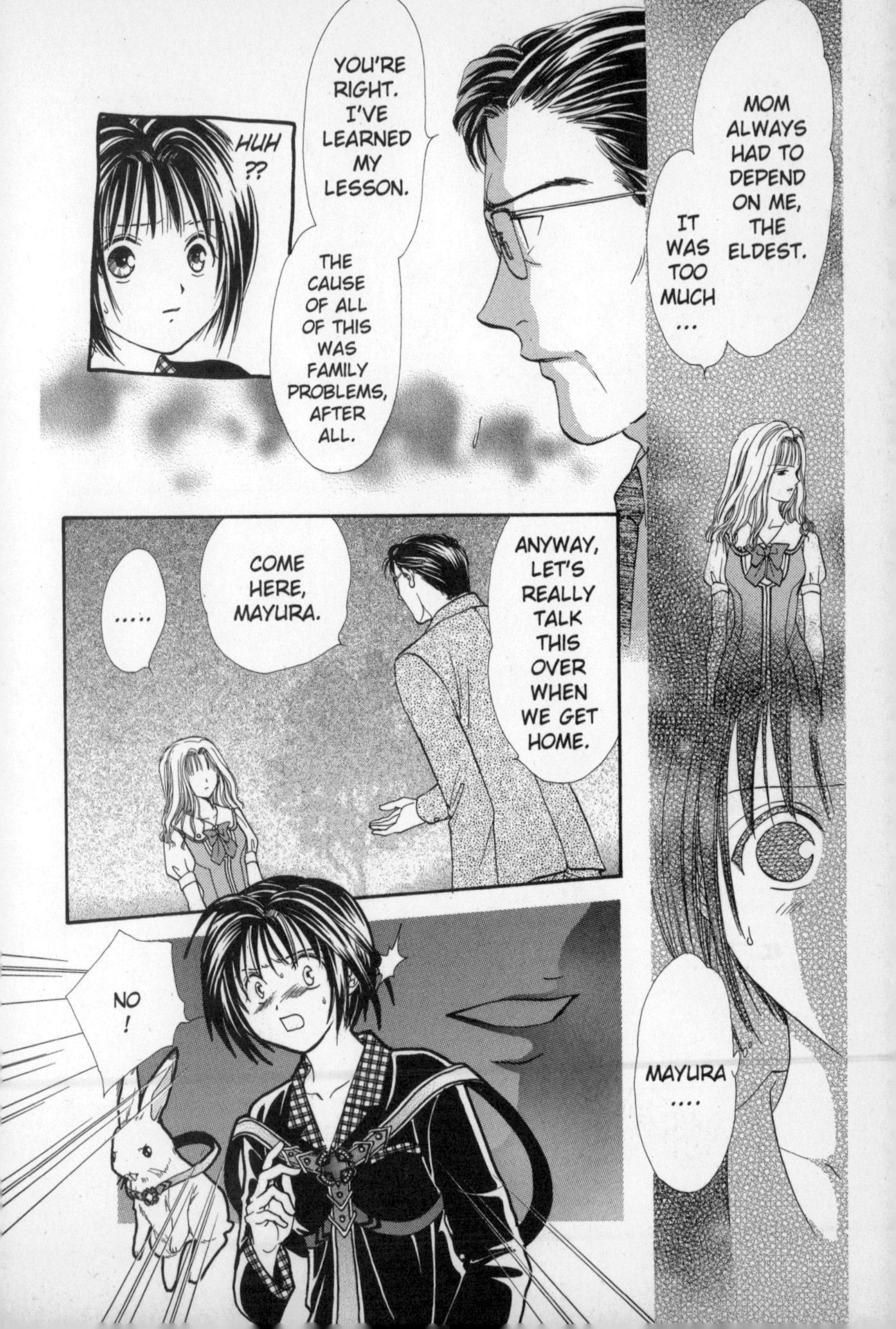
MOM ALWAYS HAD TO DEPEND ON ME, THE ELDEST.
IT WAS TOO MUCH ...
MAYURA ....
YOU'RE RIGHT. I'VE LEARNED MY LESSON.
THE CAUSE OF ALL OF THIS WAS FAMILY PROBLEMS, AFTER ALL.
HUH ??
ANYWAY, LET'S REALLY TALK THIS OVER WHEN WE GET HOME.
COME HERE, MAYURA.
.....
NO !

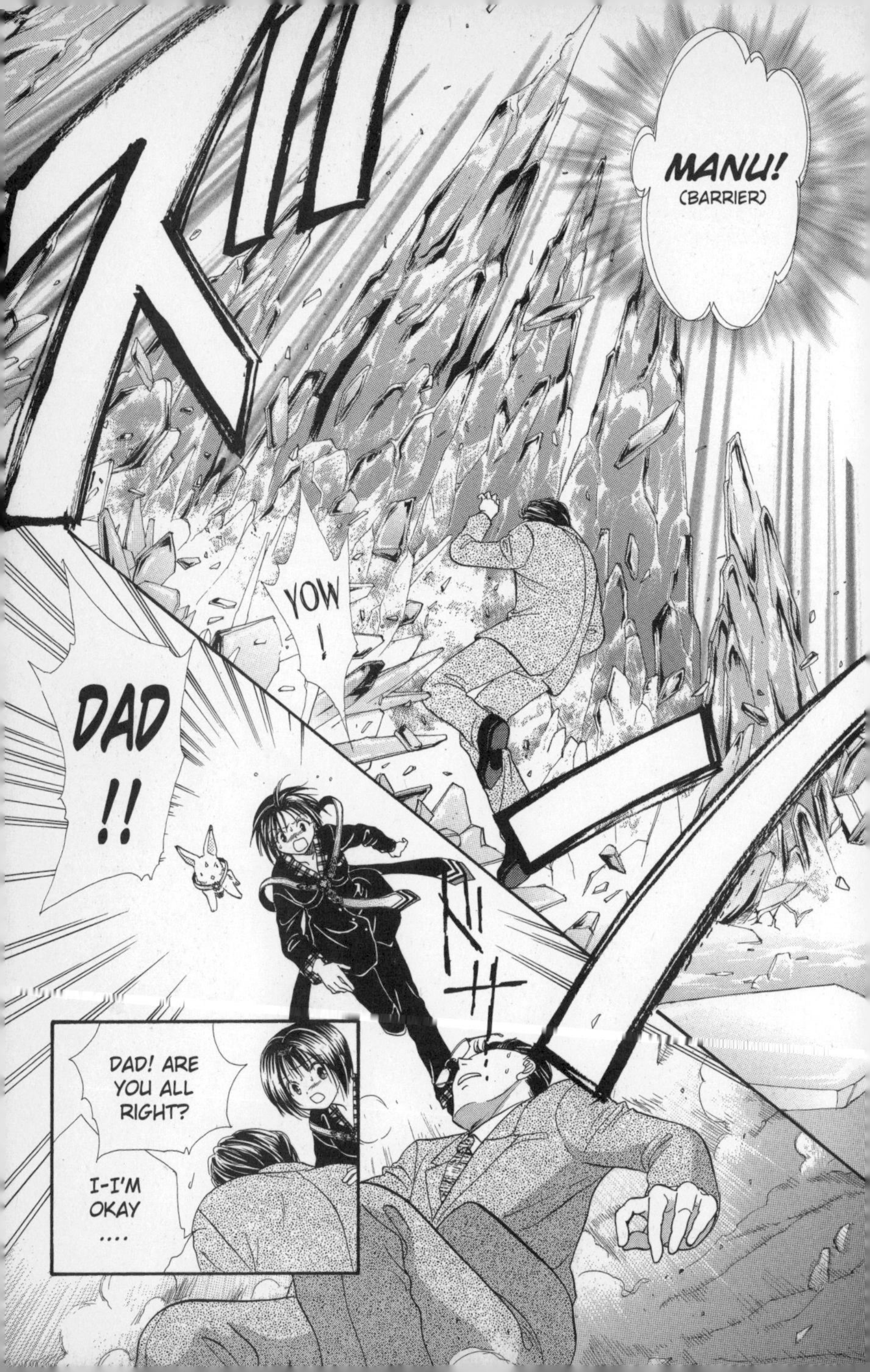
MANU!
(BARRIER)
YOW!
DAD!!
DAD! ARE YOU ALL RIGHT?
I-I'M OKAY ....

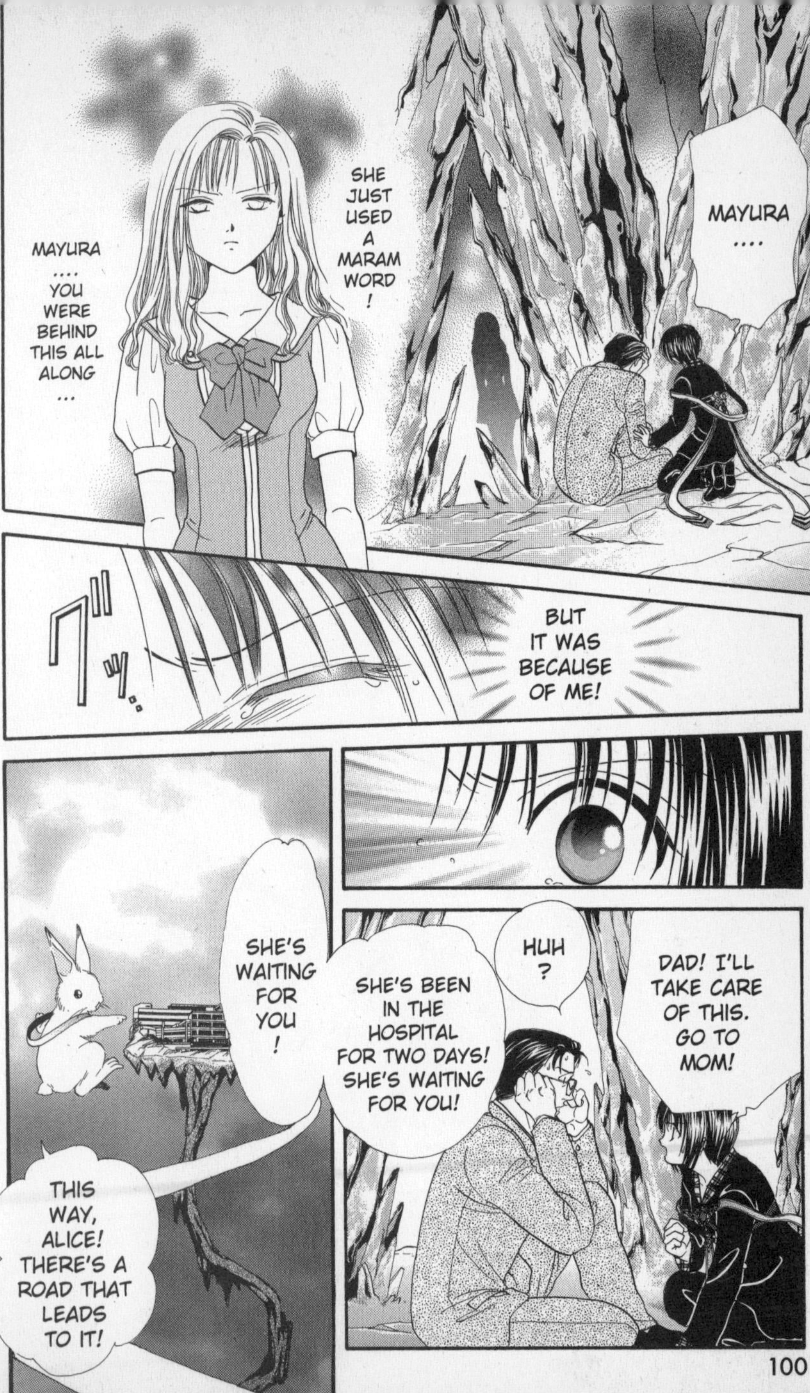
MAYURA ....
SHE JUST USED A MARAM WORD!
MAYURA .... YOU WERE BEHIND THIS ALL ALONG ...
BUT IT WAS BECAUSE OF ME!
DAD! I'LL TAKE CARE OF THIS. GO TO MOM!
HUH?
SHE'S BEEN IN THE HOSPITAL FOR TWO DAYS! SHE'S WAITING FOR YOU!
SHE'S WAITING FOR YOU!
THIS WAY, ALICE! THERE'S A ROAD THAT LEADS TO IT!

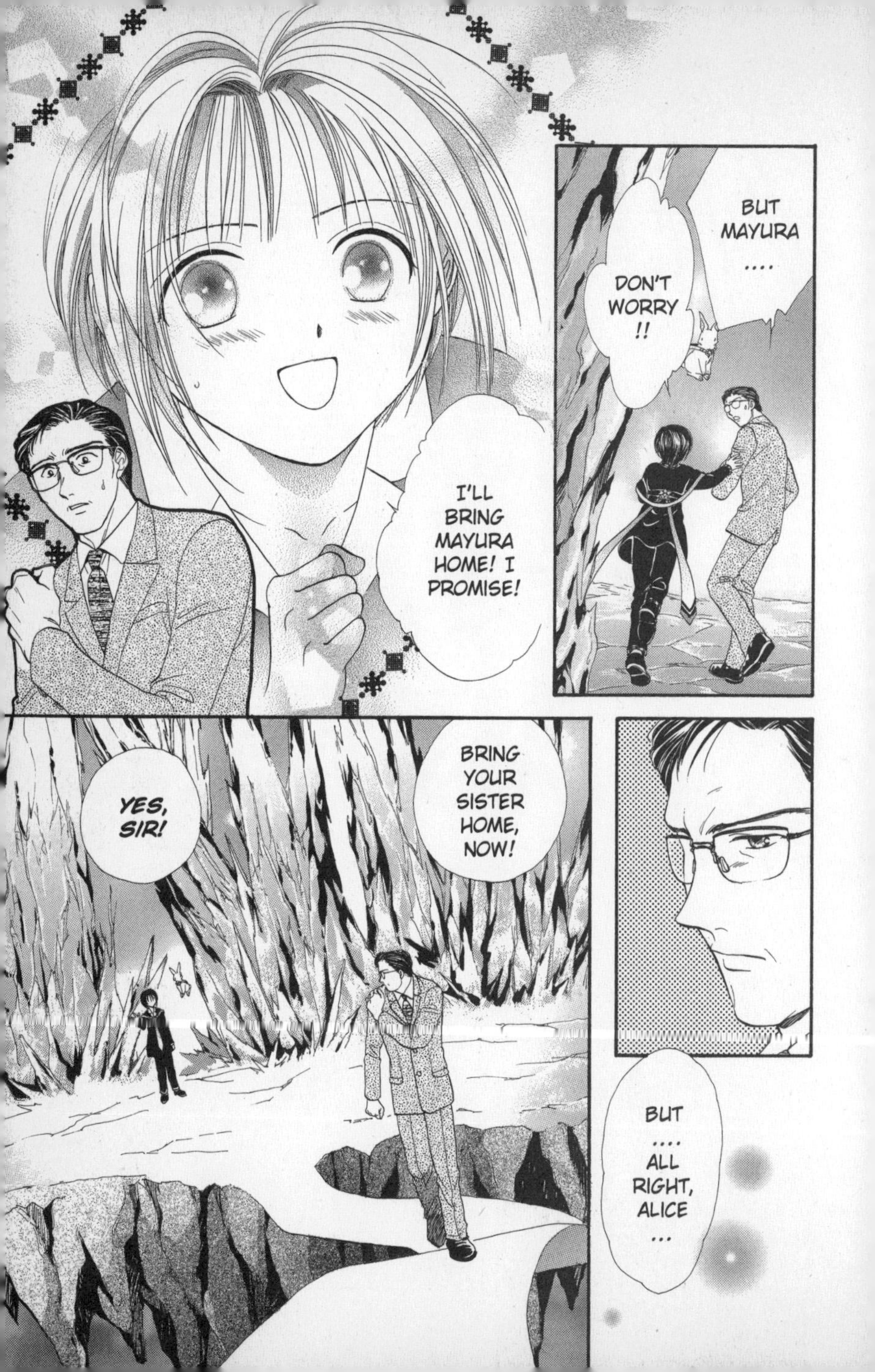
BUT MAYURA ....
DON'T WORRY !!
I'LL BRING MAYURA HOME! I PROMISE!
BUT .... ALL RIGHT, ALICE ...
BRING YOUR SISTER HOME, NOW!
YES, SIR!

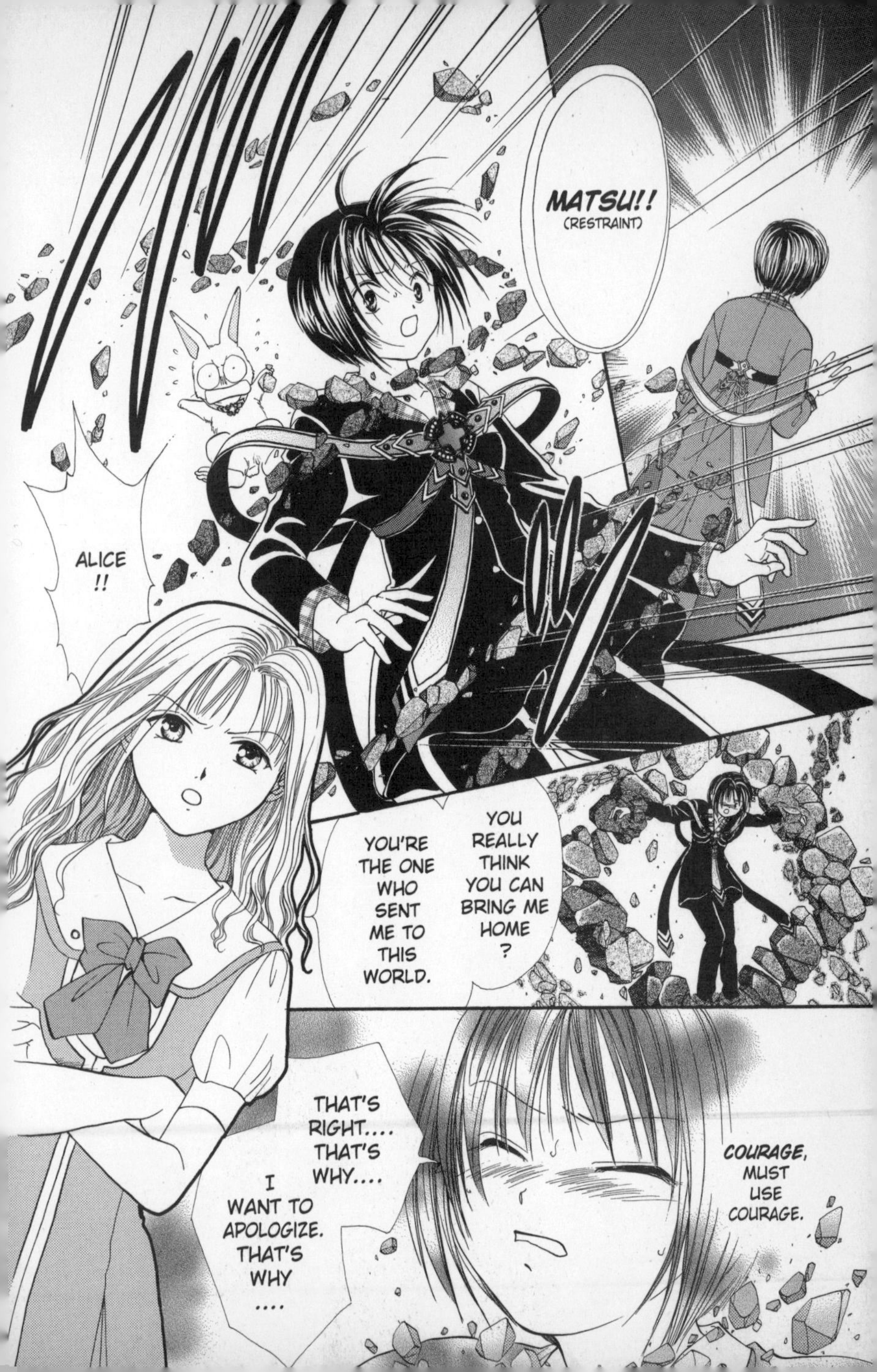
MATSU!!
(RESTRAINT)
ALICE !!
YOU REALLY THINK YOU CAN BRING ME HOME ?
YOU'RE THE ONE WHO SENT ME TO THIS WORLD.
COURAGE, MUST USE COURAGE.
THAT'S RIGHT.... THAT'S WHY....
I WANT TO APOLOGIZE. THAT'S WHY ....

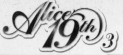

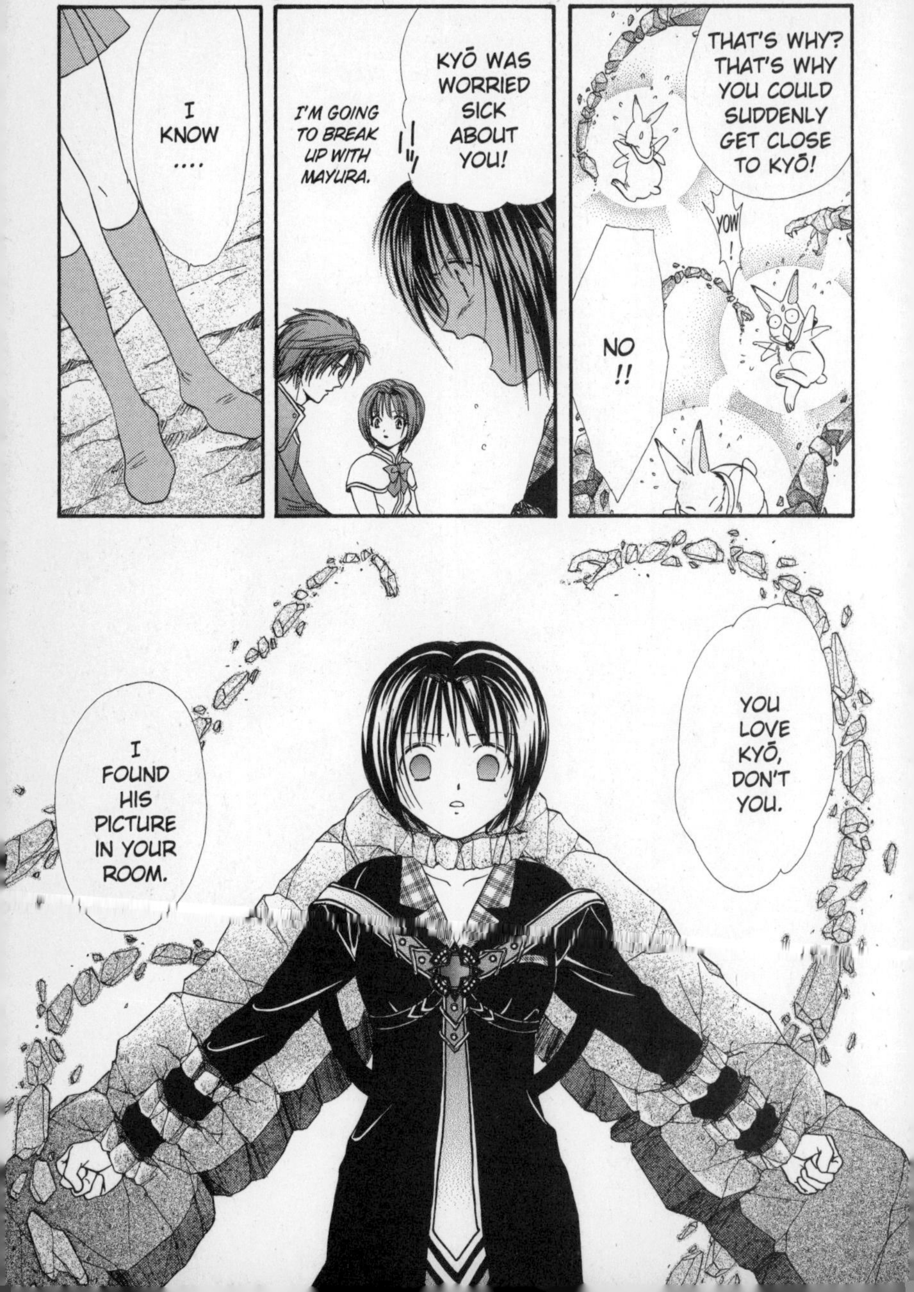
THAT'S WHY? THAT'S WHY YOU COULD SUDDENLY GET CLOSE TO KYŌ!
YOW!
NO!!
KYŌ WAS WORRIED SICK ABOUT YOU!
I'M GOING TO BREAK UP WITH MAYURA.
I KNOW ....
YOU LOVE KYŌ, DON'T YOU.
I FOUND HIS PICTURE IN YOUR ROOM.

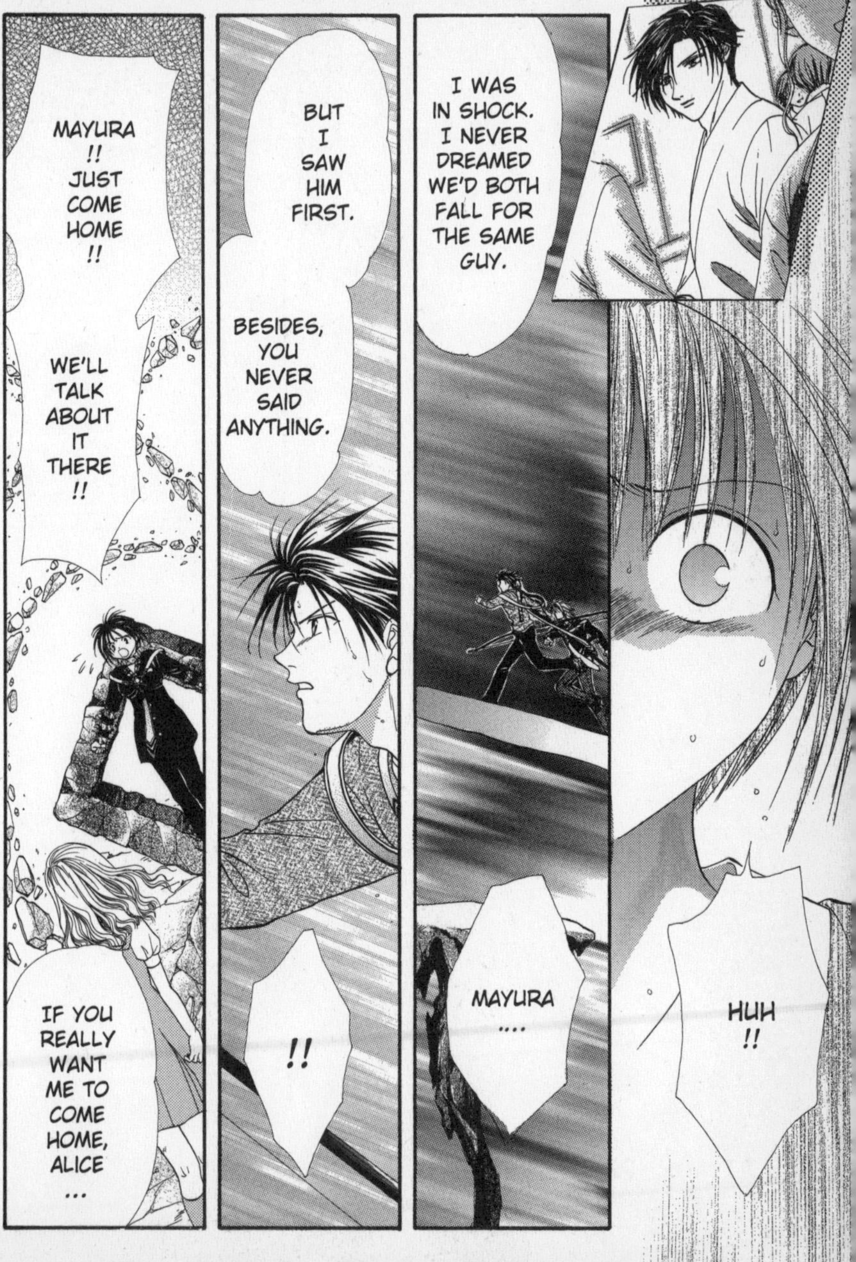
HUH !!
I WAS IN SHOCK. I NEVER DREAMED WE'D BOTH FALL FOR THE SAME GUY.
MAYURA ...
BUT I SAW HIM FIRST.
BESIDES, YOU NEVER SAID ANYTHING.
!!
MAYURA !! JUST COME HOME !!
WE'LL TALK ABOUT IT THERE !!
IF YOU REALLY WANT ME TO COME HOME, ALICE ...

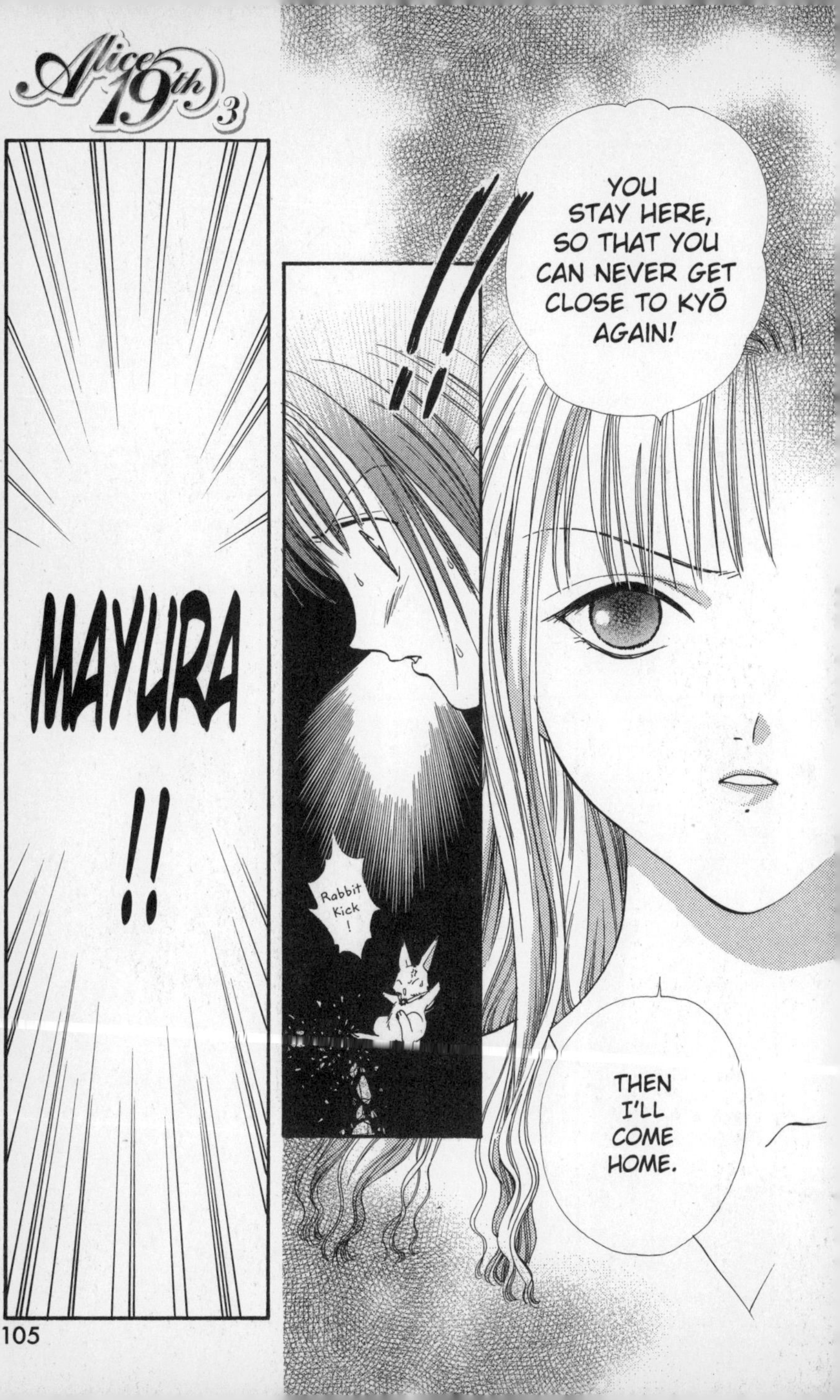
YOU STAY HERE, SO THAT YOU CAN NEVER GET CLOSE TO KYŌ AGAIN!
THEN I'LL COME HOME.
!!
Rabbit Kick!
MAYURA !!

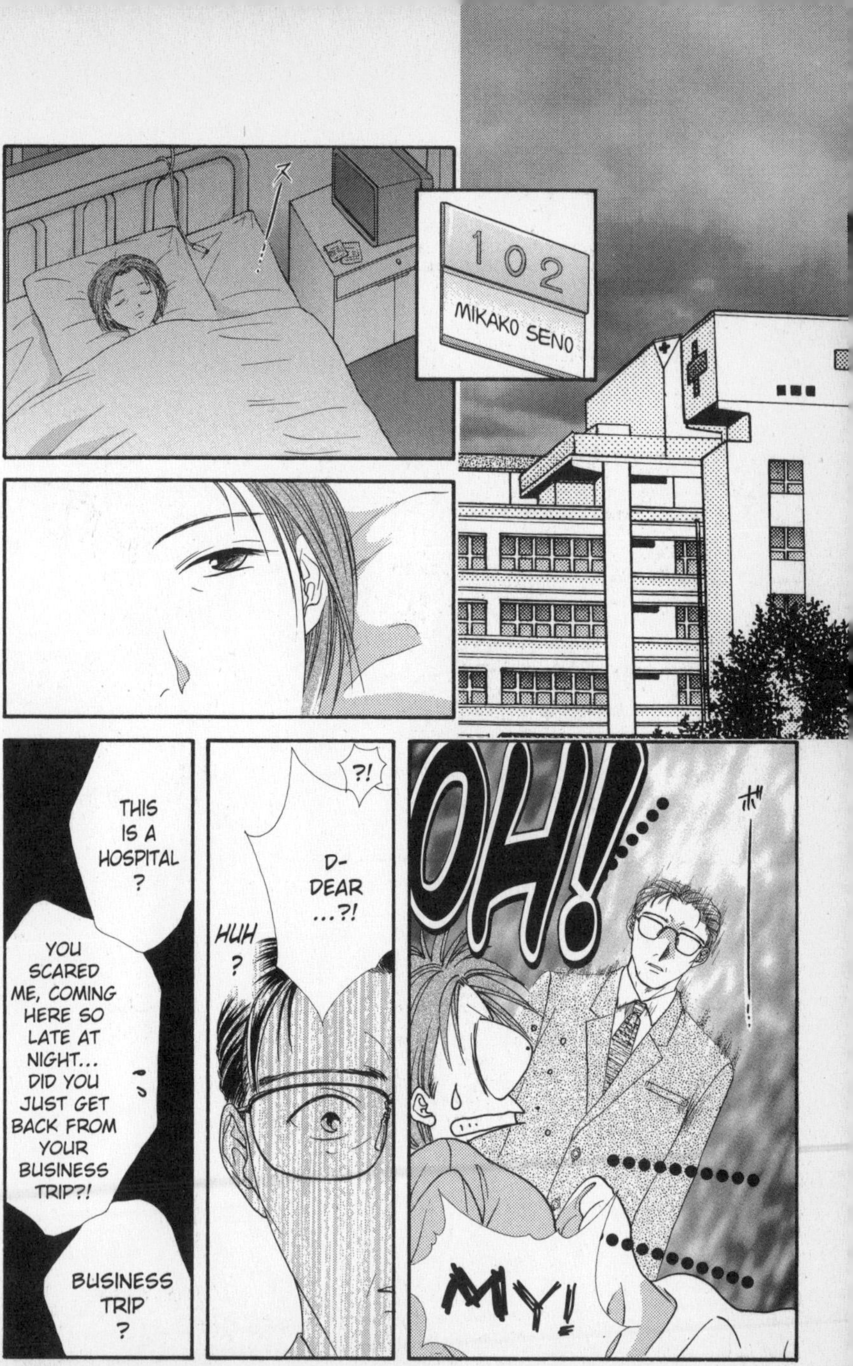

102
MIKAKO SENO
ス…
OH!
ボ…
MY!
?!
D-DEAR...?!
HUH?
THIS IS A HOSPITAL?
YOU SCARED ME, COMING HERE SO LATE AT NIGHT... DID YOU JUST GET BACK FROM YOUR BUSINESS TRIP?!
BUSINESS TRIP?

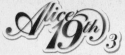

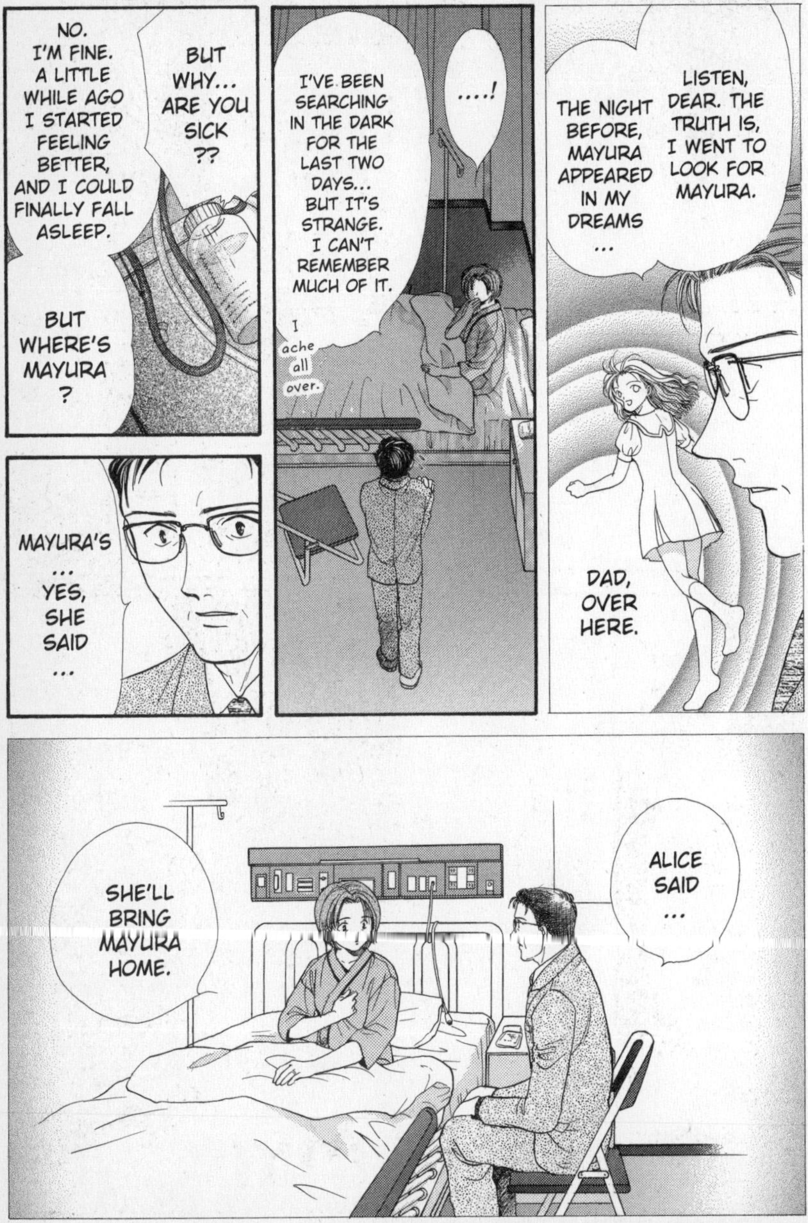
LISTEN, DEAR. THE TRUTH IS, I WENT TO LOOK FOR MAYURA.
THE NIGHT BEFORE, MAYURA APPEARED IN MY DREAMS ...
DAD, OVER HERE.
....!
I'VE BEEN SEARCHING IN THE DARK FOR THE LAST TWO DAYS... BUT IT'S STRANGE. I CAN'T REMEMBER MUCH OF IT.
I ache all over.
BUT WHY... ARE YOU SICK ??
NO. I'M FINE. A LITTLE WHILE AGO I STARTED FEELING BETTER, AND I COULD FINALLY FALL ASLEEP.
BUT WHERE'S MAYURA ?
MAYURA'S ... YES, SHE SAID ...
ALICE SAID ...
SHE'LL BRING MAYURA HOME.

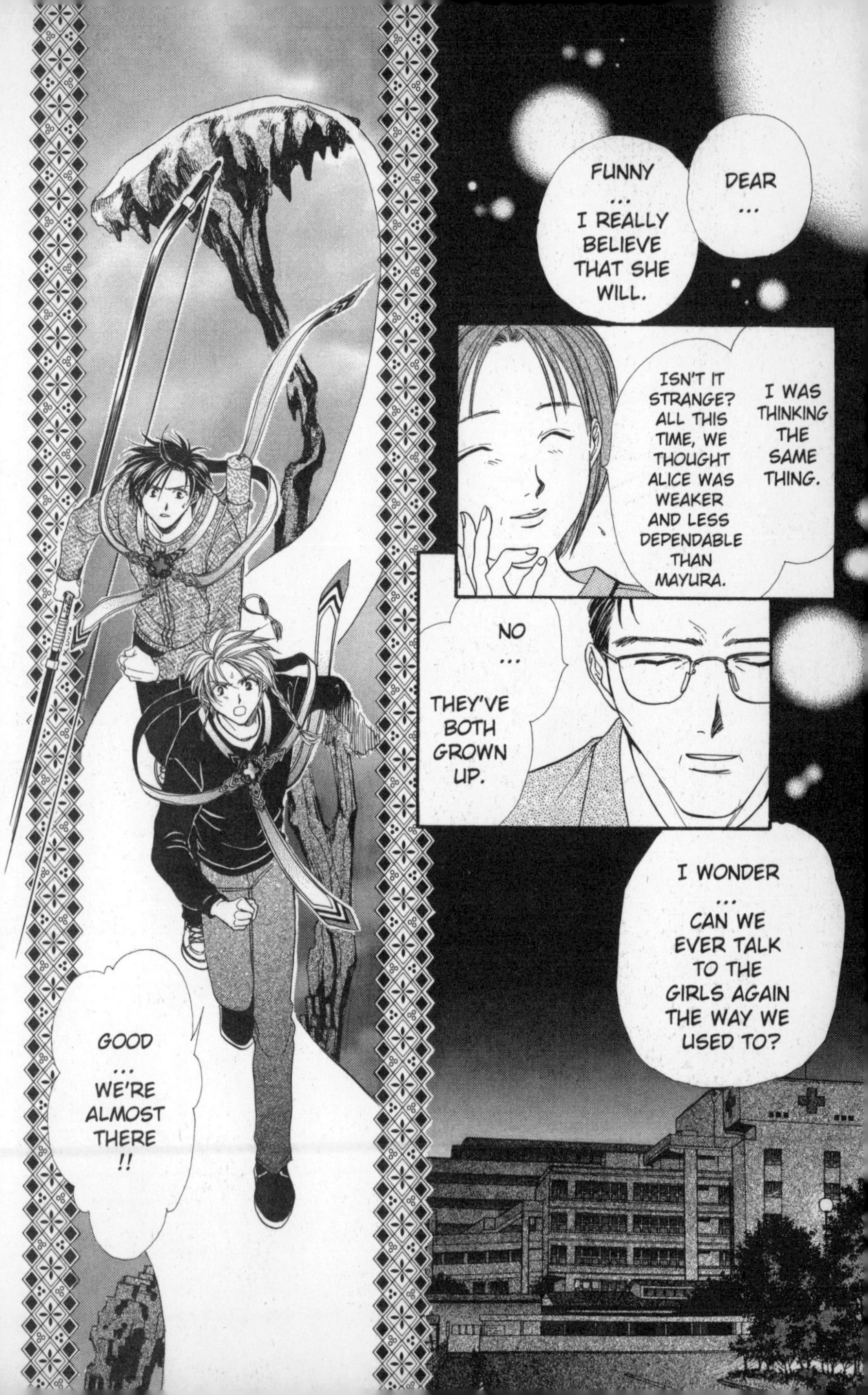
DEAR ...
FUNNY ... I REALLY BELIEVE THAT SHE WILL.
I WAS THINKING THE SAME THING.
ISN'T IT STRANGE? ALL THIS TIME, WE THOUGHT ALICE WAS WEAKER AND LESS DEPENDABLE THAN MAYURA.
NO ... THEY'VE BOTH GROWN UP.
I WONDER ... CAN WE EVER TALK TO THE GIRLS AGAIN THE WAY WE USED TO?
GOOD ... WE'RE ALMOST THERE !!

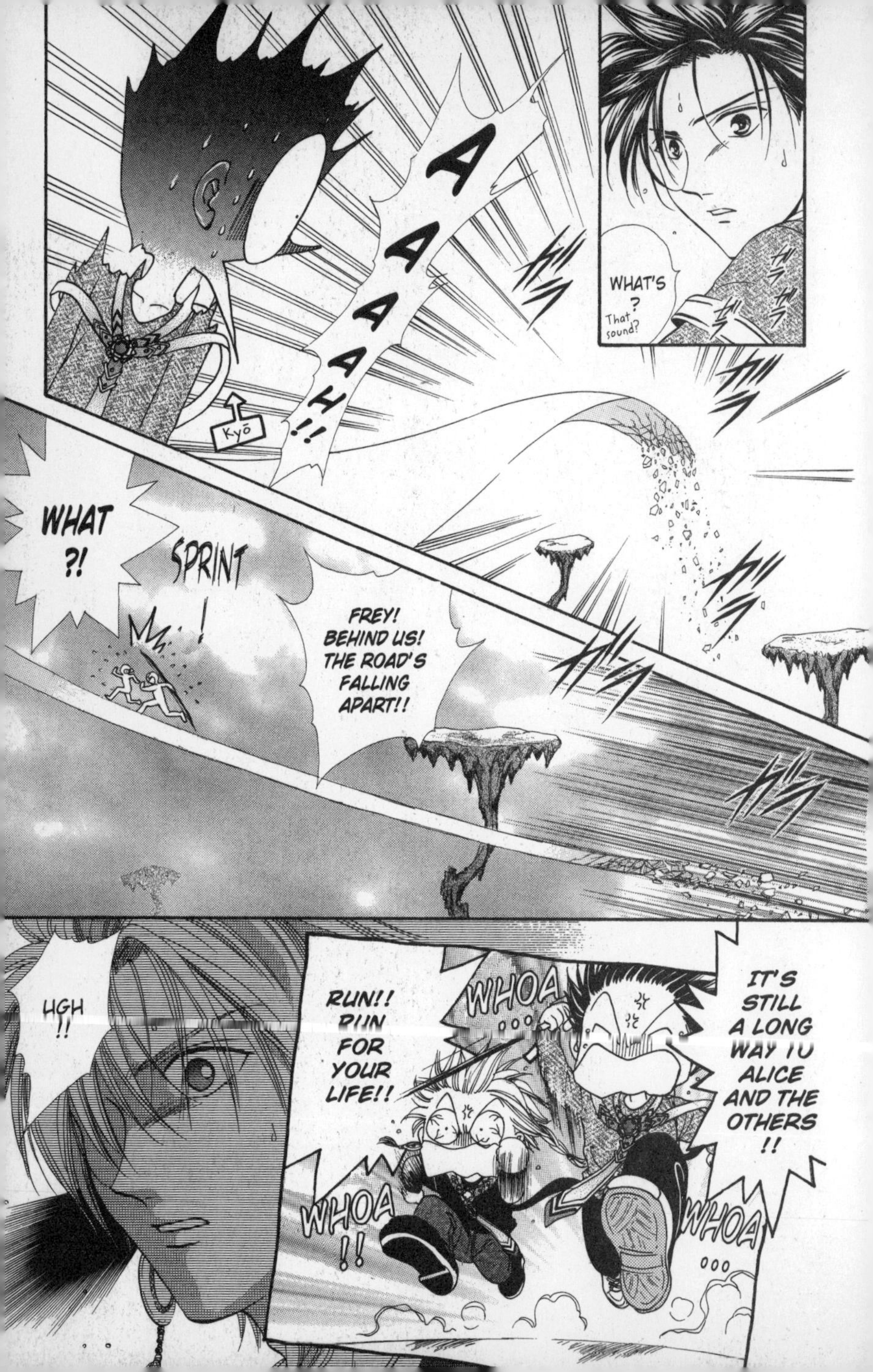
WHAT'S ?
That sound?
AAAAAH!!
Kyō
FREY! BEHIND US! THE ROAD'S FALLING APART!!
SPRINT !
WHAT ?!
IT'S STILL A LONG WAY TO ALICE AND THE OTHERS !!
WHOA ...
RUN!! RUN FOR YOUR LIFE!!
WHOA ...
WHOA !!
UGH !!

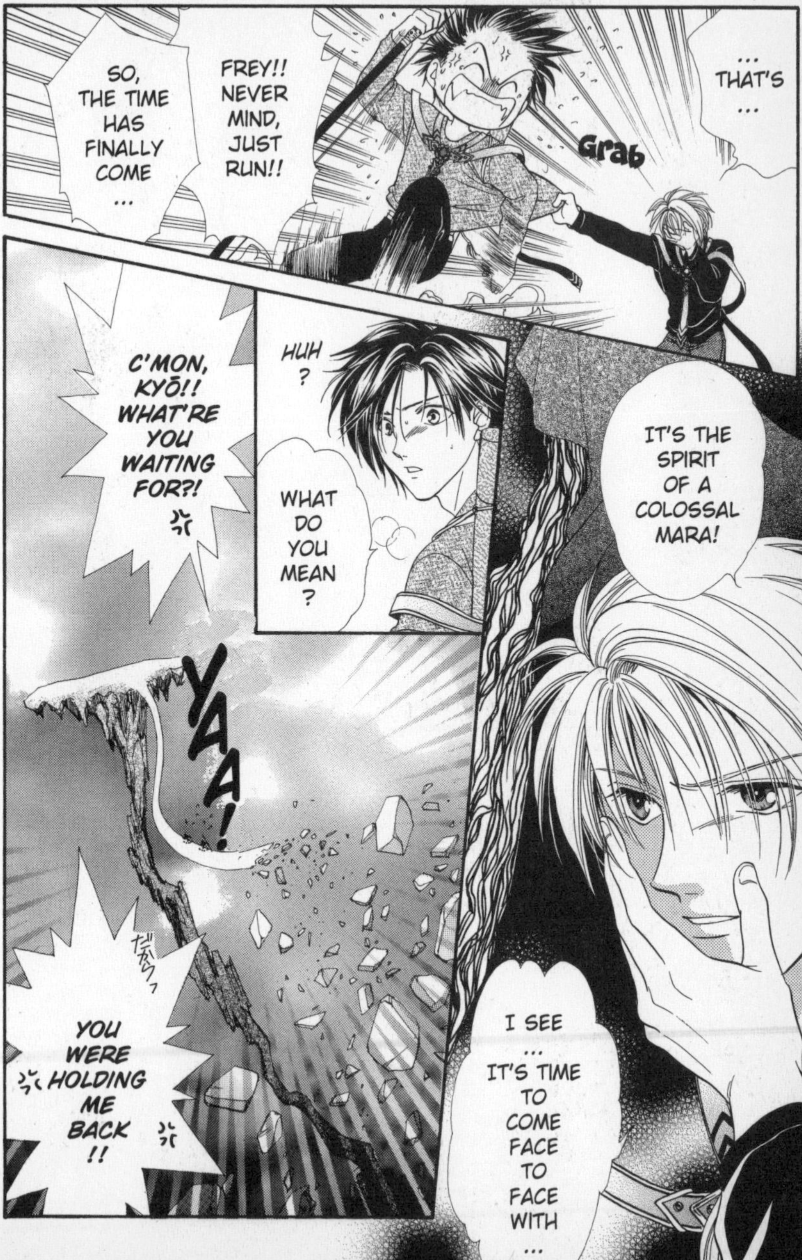
... THAT'S ...
Grab
FREY!! NEVER MIND, JUST RUN!!
SO, THE TIME HAS FINALLY COME ...
IT'S THE SPIRIT OF A COLOSSAL MARA!
I SEE ... IT'S TIME TO COME FACE TO FACE WITH ...
HUH ?
WHAT DO YOU MEAN ?
C'MON, KYŌ!! WHAT'RE YOU WAITING FOR?!
YAAA!
YOU WERE HOLDING ME BACK !!

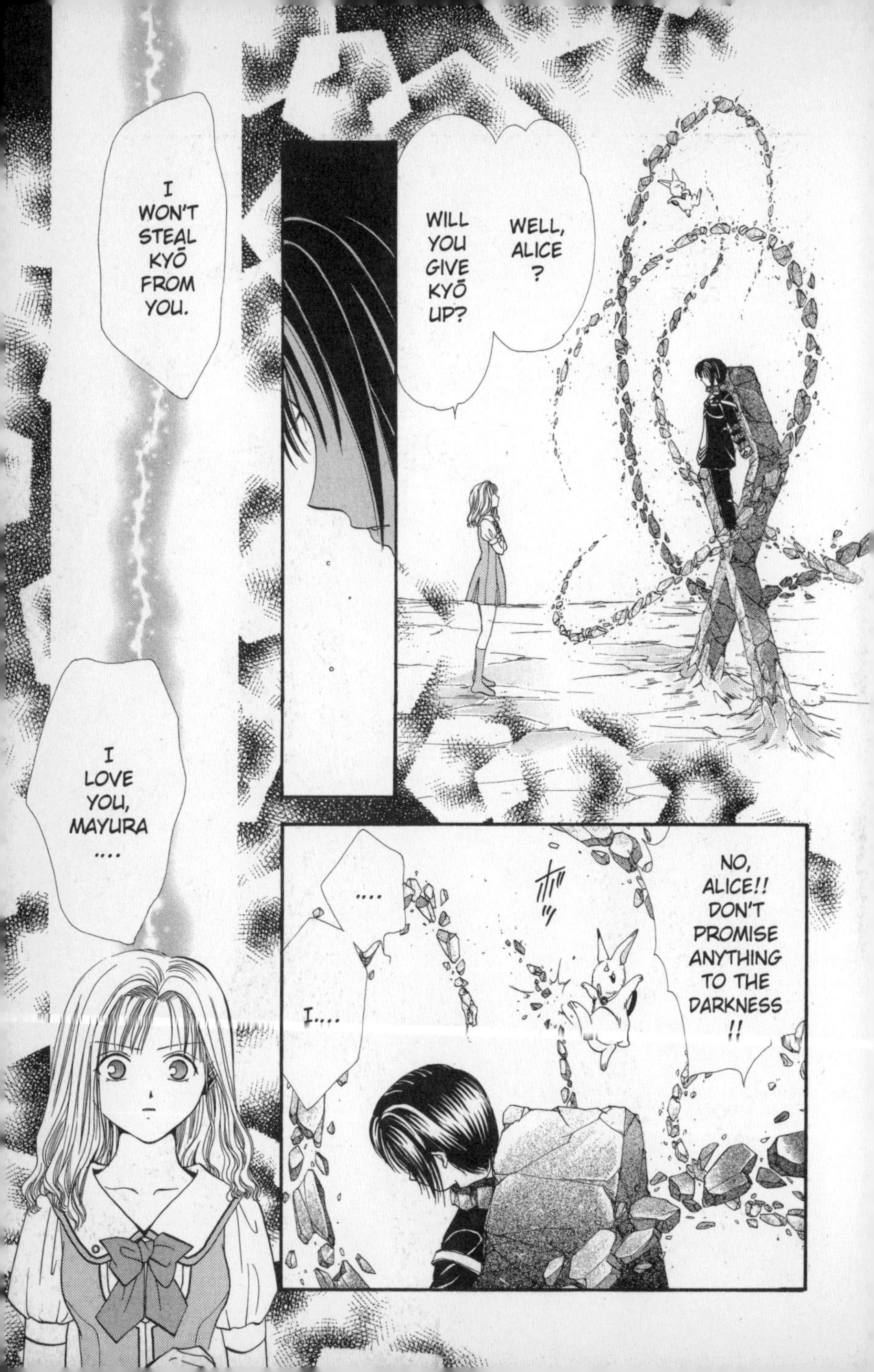
WELL, ALICE? WILL YOU GIVE KYŌ UP?
NO, ALICE!! DON'T PROMISE ANYTHING TO THE DARKNESS!!
....
I....
I WON'T STEAL KYŌ FROM YOU.
I LOVE YOU, MAYURA ....

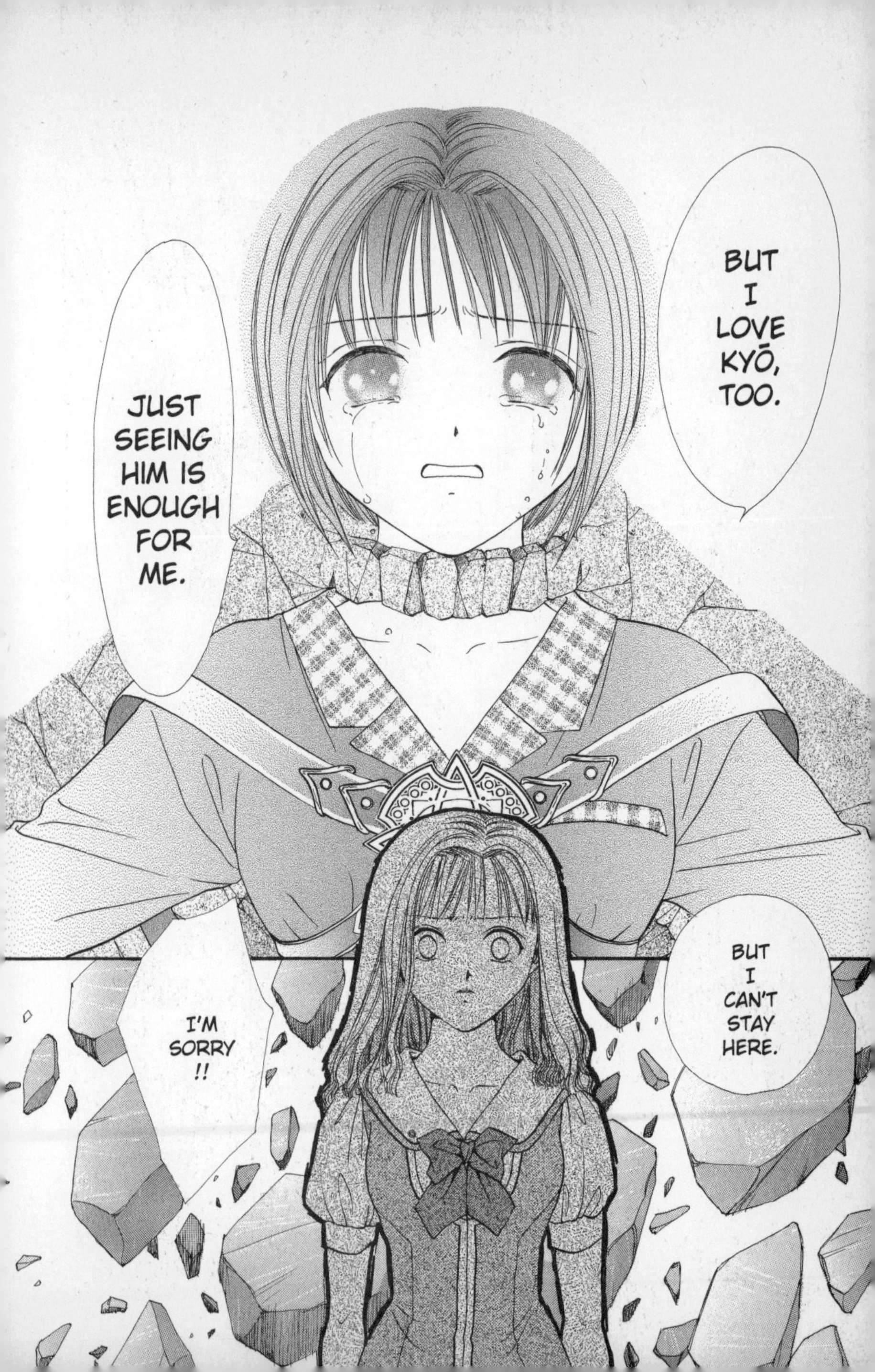
BUT I LOVE KYŌ, TOO.
JUST SEEING HIM IS ENOUGH FOR ME.
BUT I CAN'T STAY HERE.
I'M SORRY !!

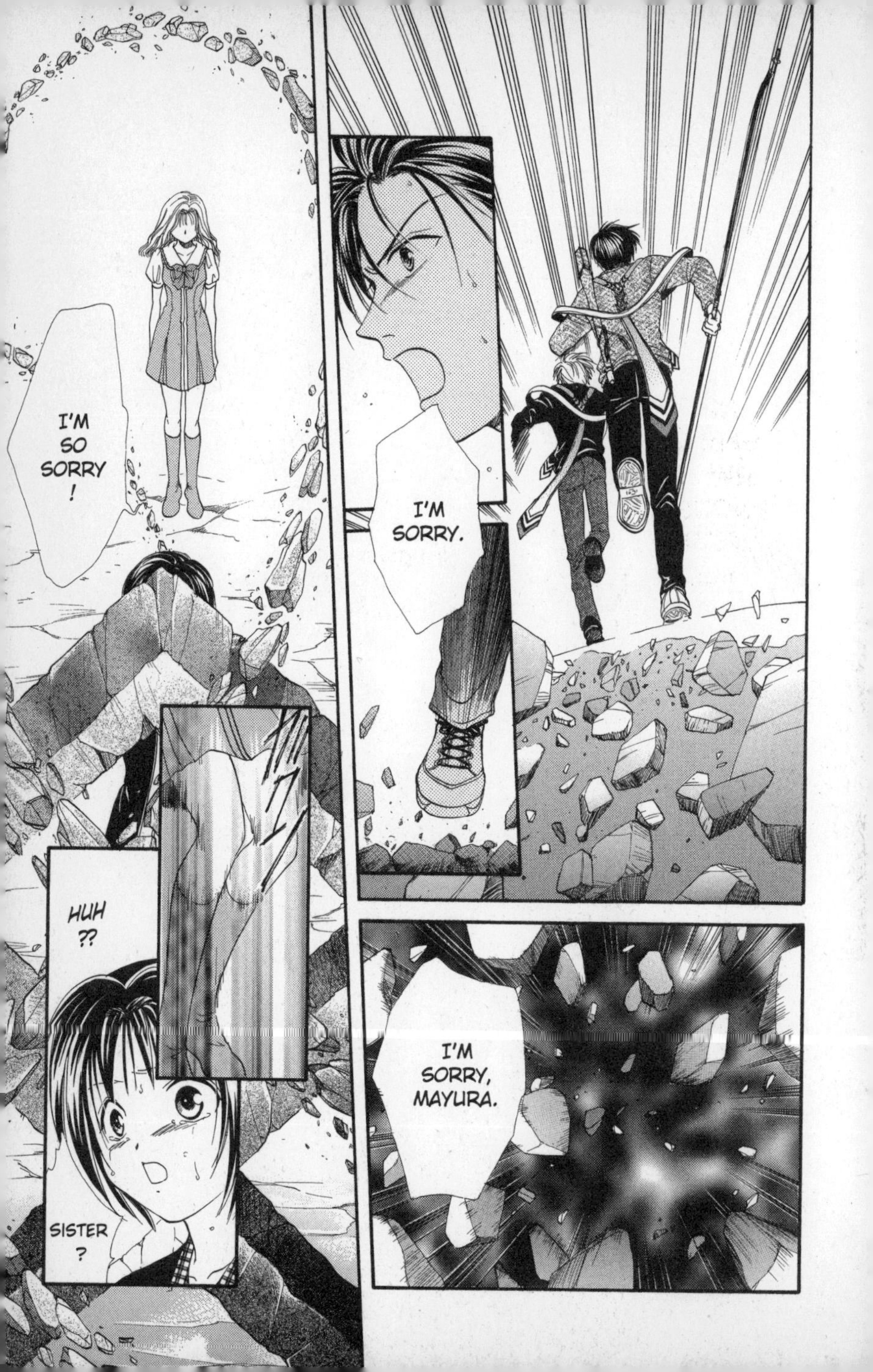
I'M SORRY.
I'M SORRY, MAYURA.
I'M SO SORRY!
HUH??
SISTER?

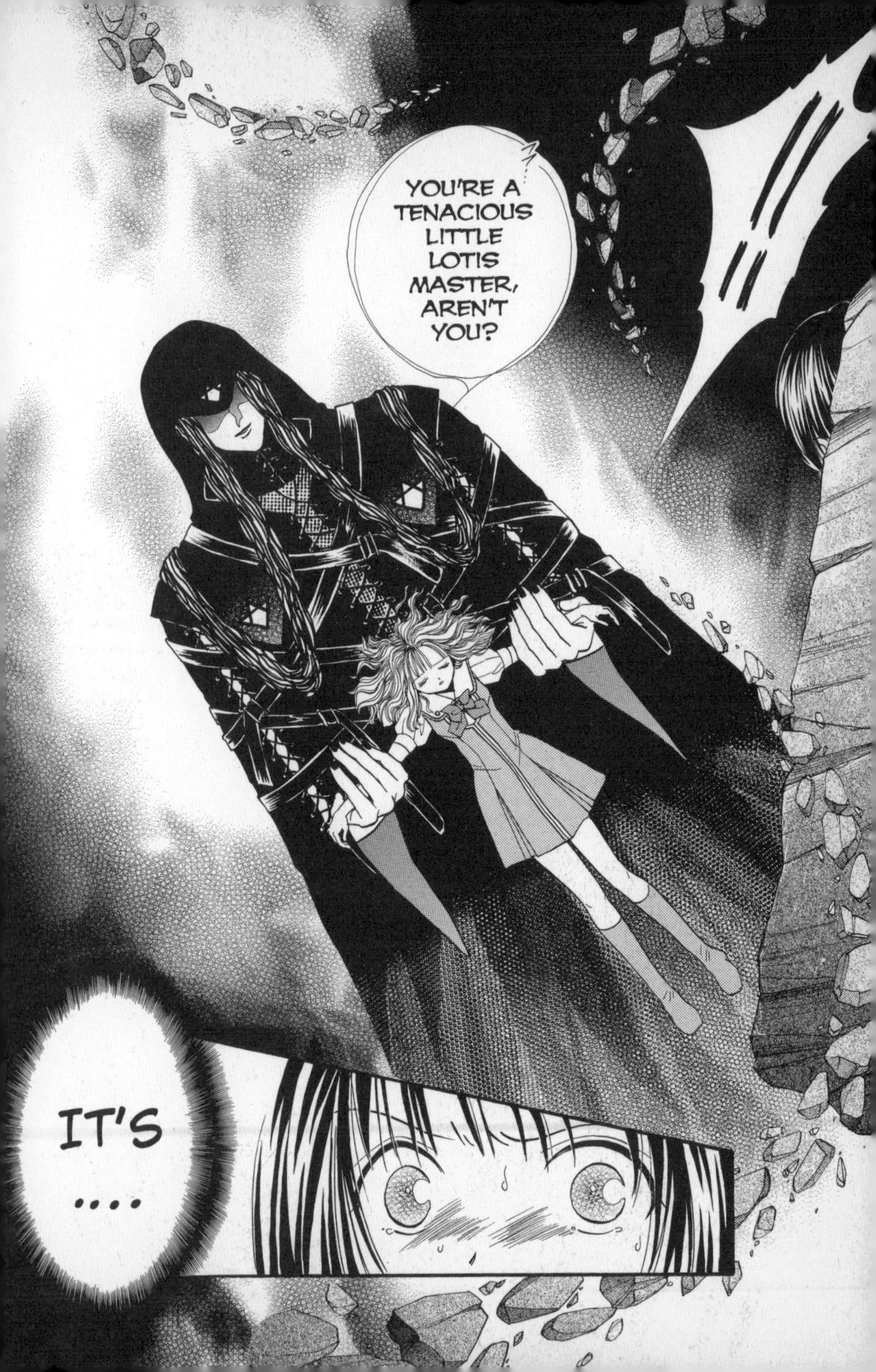
YOU'RE A TENACIOUS LITTLE LOTIS MASTER, AREN'T YOU?
IT'S ....

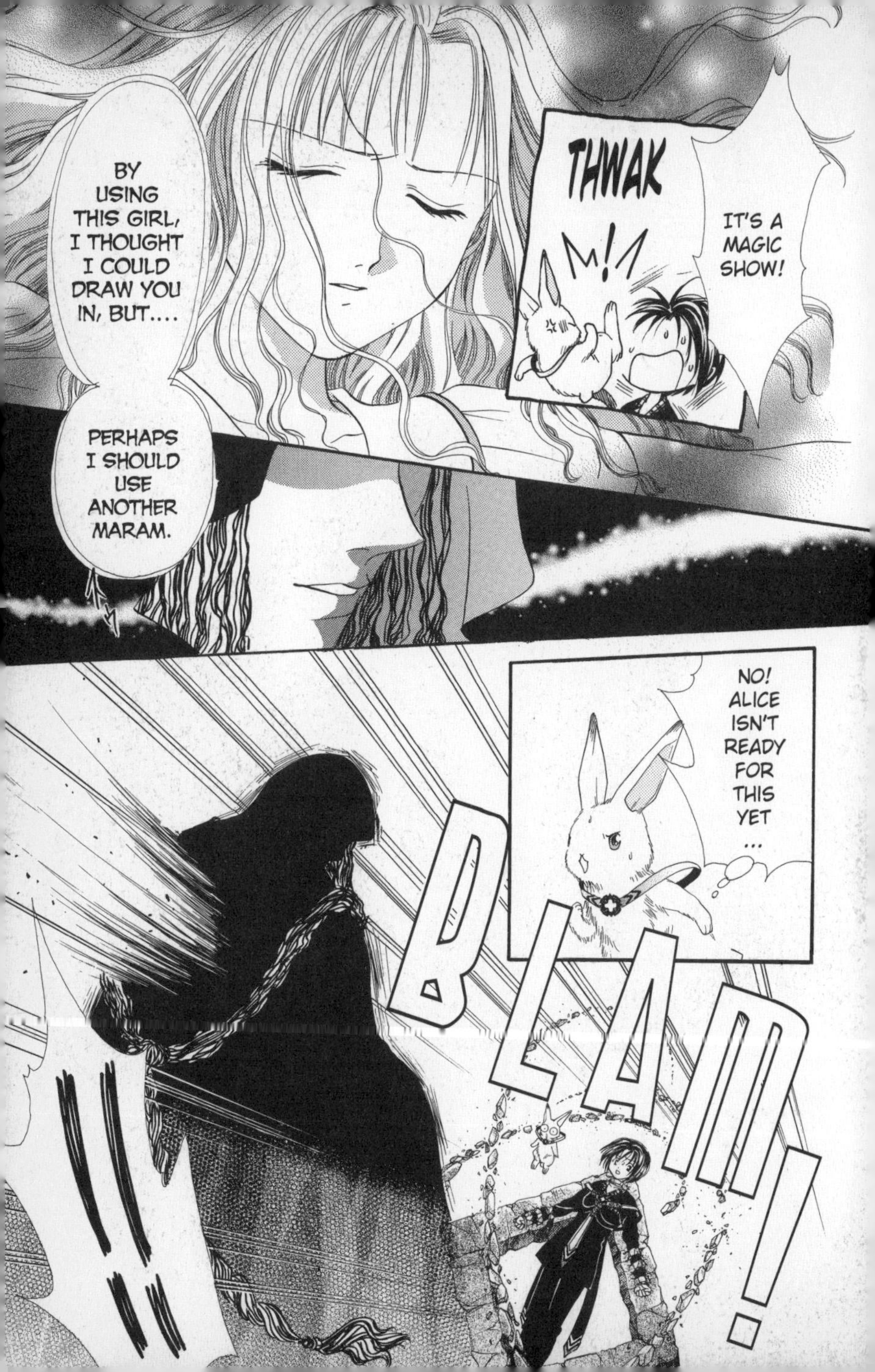
IT'S A MAGIC SHOW!
THWAK
BY USING THIS GIRL, I THOUGHT I COULD DRAW YOU IN, BUT....
PERHAPS I SHOULD USE ANOTHER MARAM.
NO! ALICE ISN'T READY FOR THIS YET ...
BLAM!

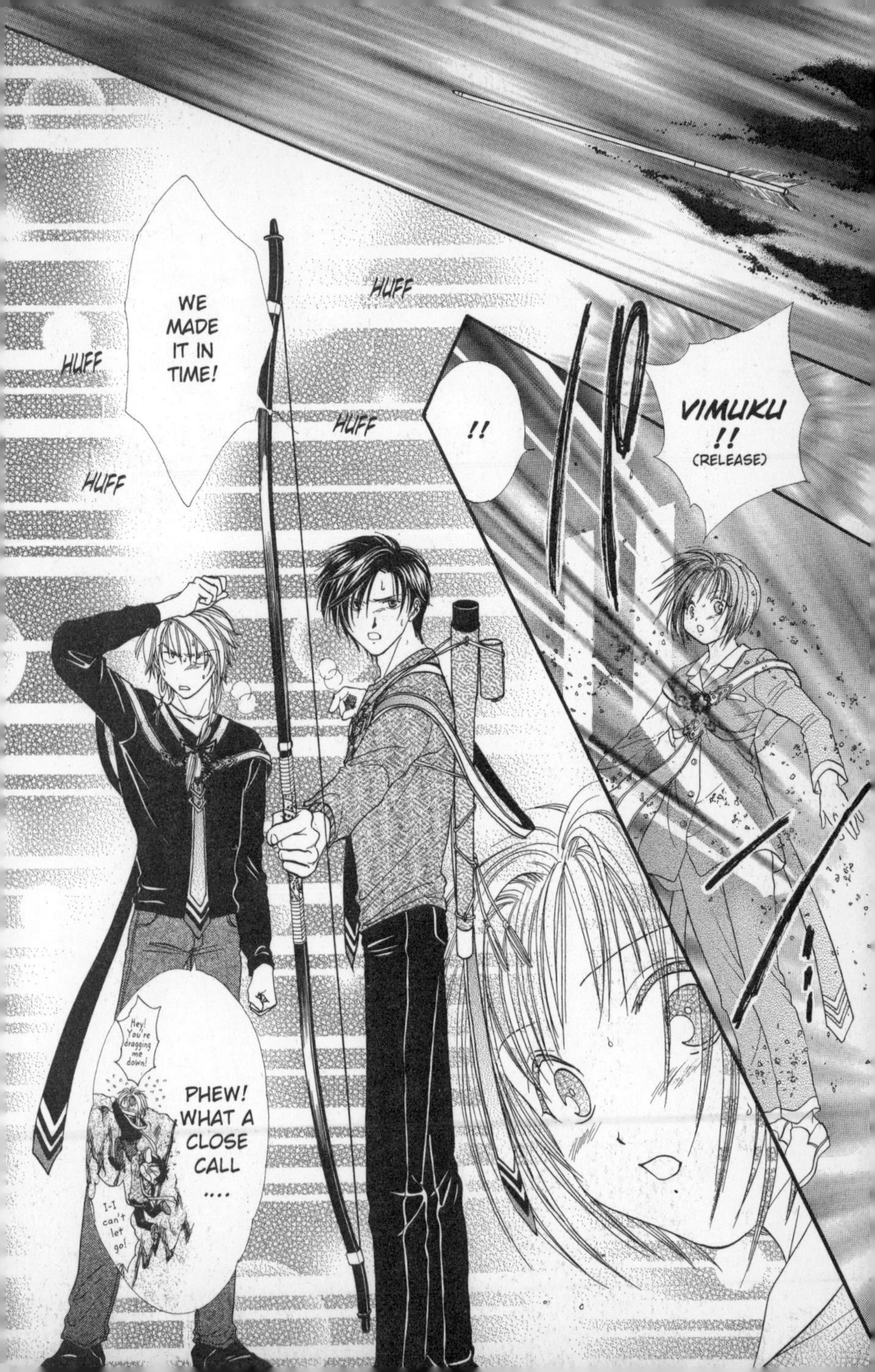
VIMUKU !! (RELEASE)
!!
HUFF
HUFF
WE MADE IT IN TIME!
HUFF
HUFF
PHEW! WHAT A CLOSE CALL ....
Hey! You're dragging me down!
I-I can't let go!

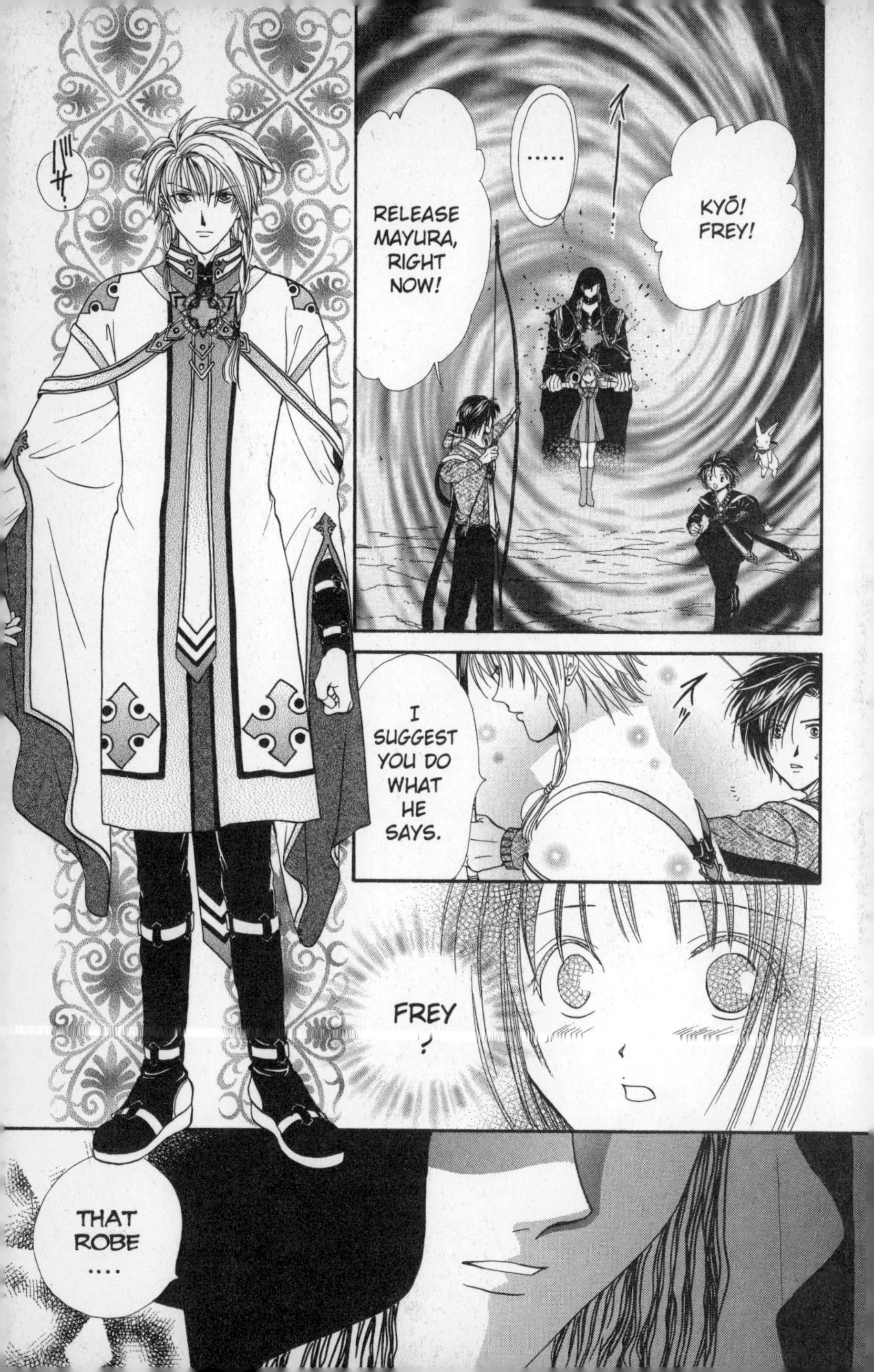
KYŌ! FREY!
......
RELEASE MAYURA, RIGHT NOW!
I SUGGEST YOU DO WHAT HE SAYS.
FREY?
THAT ROBE ....

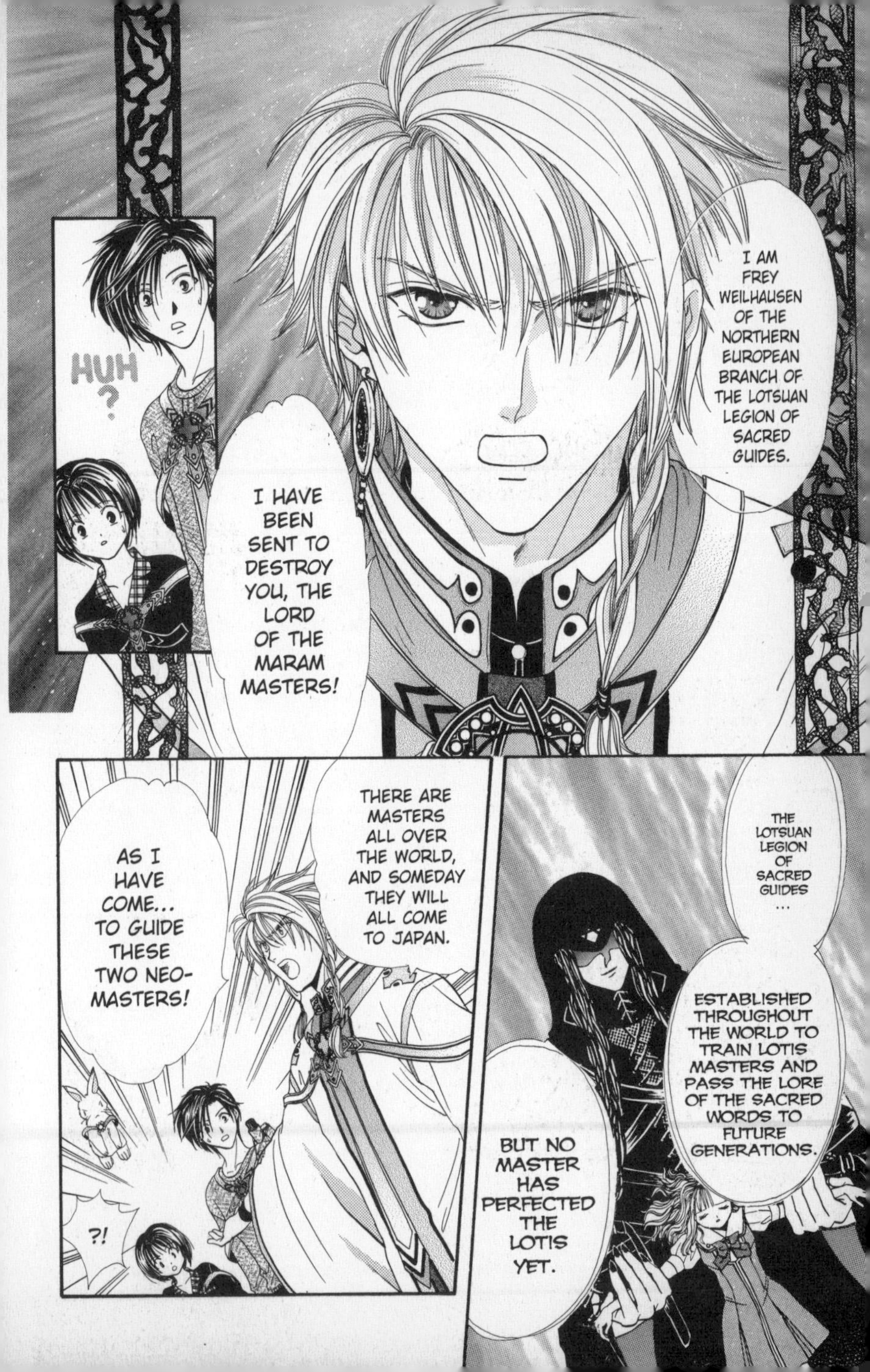
I AM FREY WEILHAUSEN OF THE NORTHERN EUROPEAN BRANCH OF THE LOTSUAN LEGION OF SACRED GUIDES.
I HAVE BEEN SENT TO DESTROY YOU, THE LORD OF THE MARAM MASTERS!
HUH ?
THE LOTSUAN LEGION OF SACRED GUIDES ...
ESTABLISHED THROUGHOUT THE WORLD TO TRAIN LOTIS MASTERS AND PASS THE LORE OF THE SACRED WORDS TO FUTURE GENERATIONS.
BUT NO MASTER HAS PERFECTED THE LOTIS YET.
THERE ARE MASTERS ALL OVER THE WORLD, AND SOMEDAY THEY WILL ALL COME TO JAPAN.
AS I HAVE COME... TO GUIDE THESE TWO NEO-MASTERS!
?!

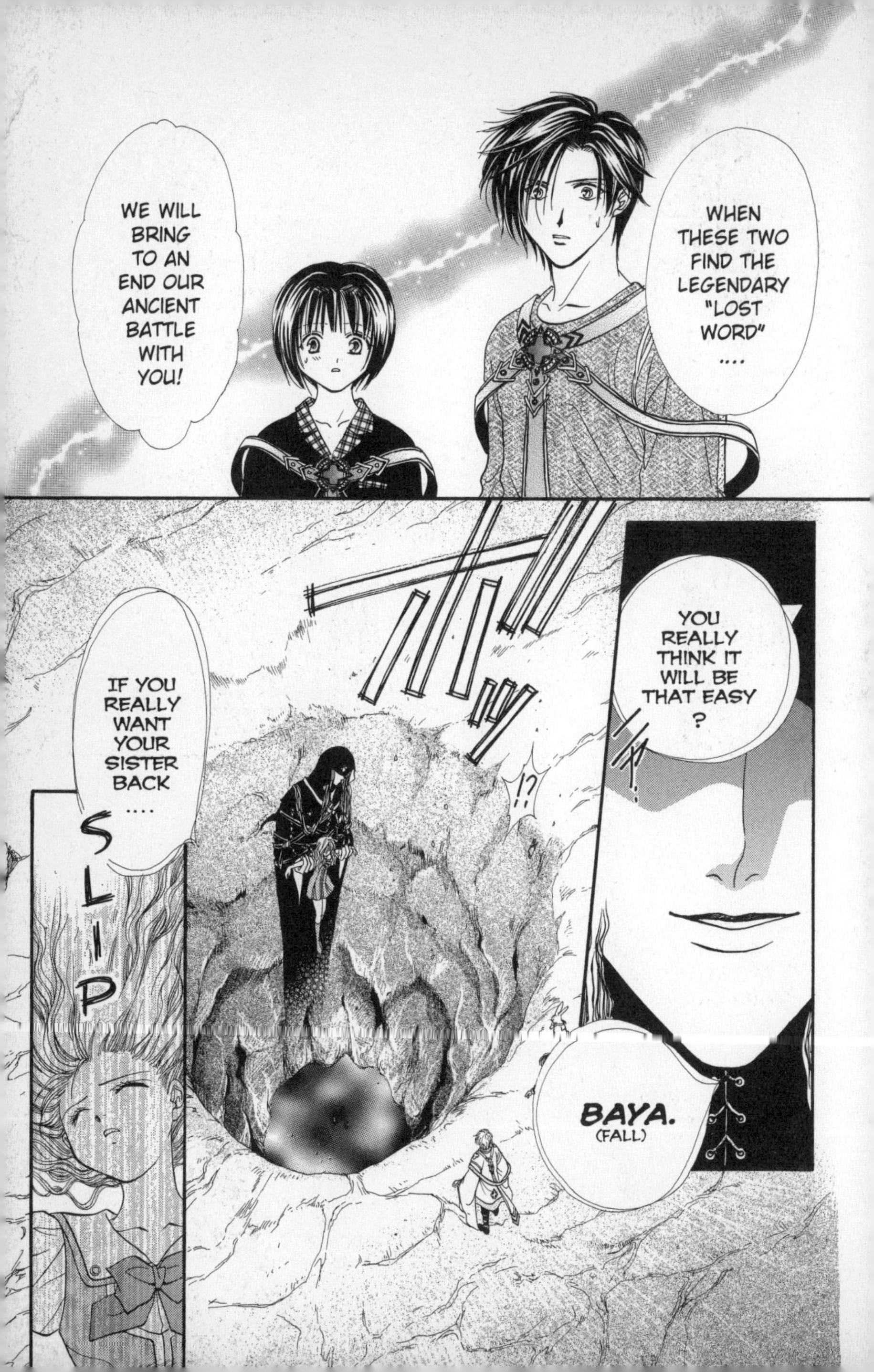
WHEN THESE TWO FIND THE LEGENDARY "LOST WORD" ....
WE WILL BRING TO AN END OUR ANCIENT BATTLE WITH YOU!
YOU REALLY THINK IT WILL BE THAT EASY ?
!?
IF YOU REALLY WANT YOUR SISTER BACK ....
BAYA.
(FALL)
SLIP

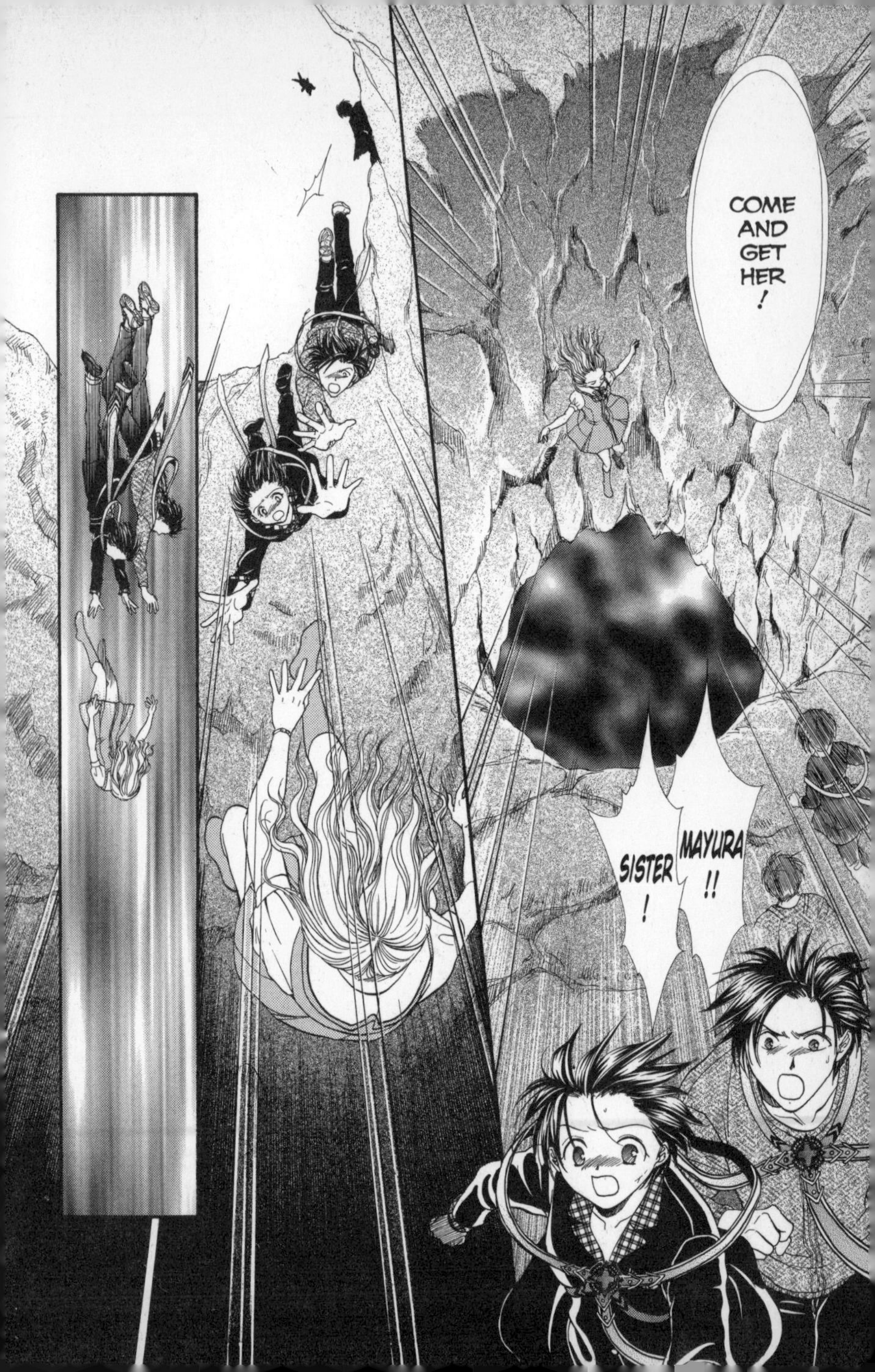
COME AND GET HER!
MAYURA!!
SISTER!

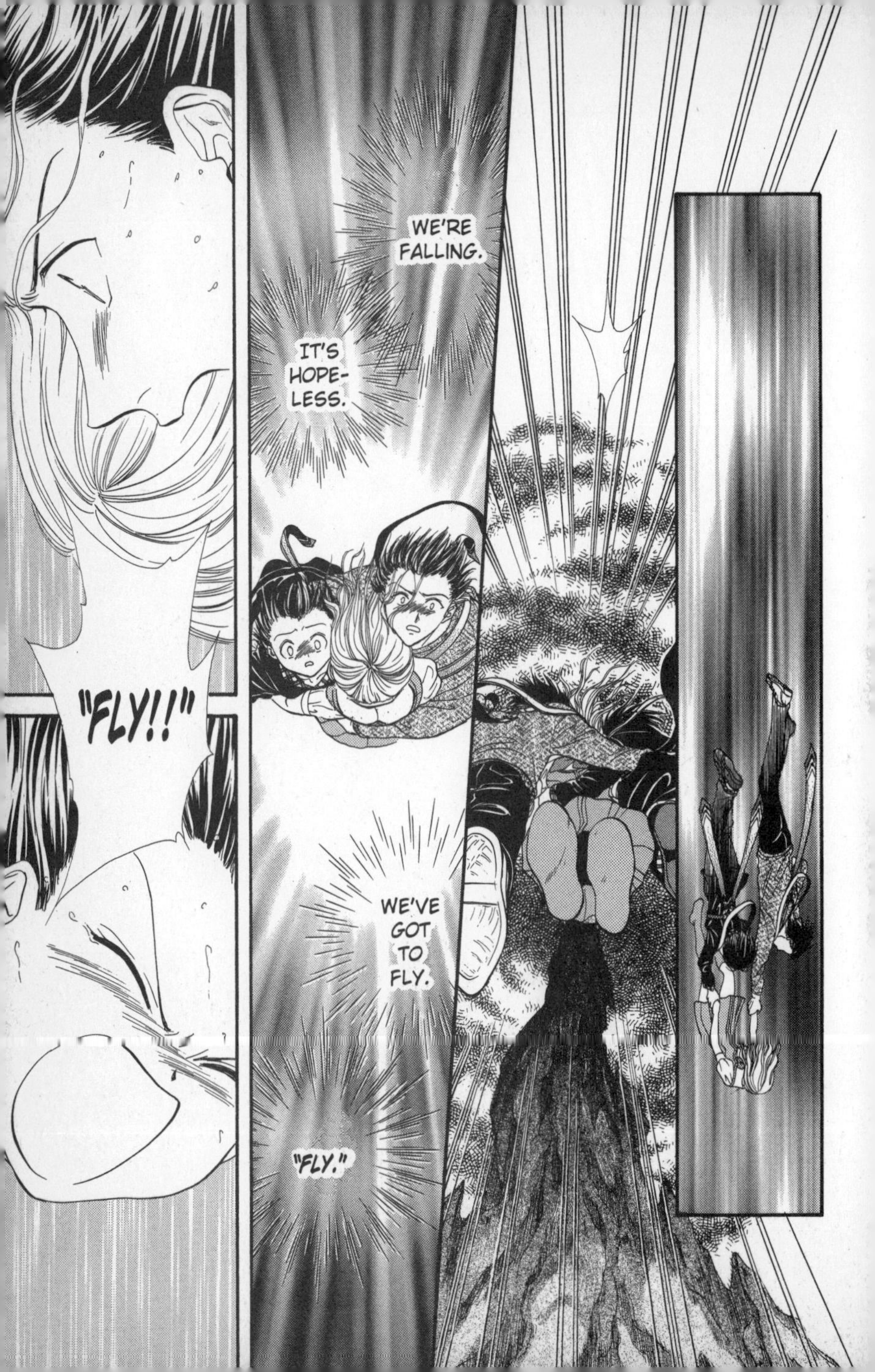
WE'RE FALLING.
IT'S HOPE-LESS.
WE'VE GOT TO FLY.
"FLY."
"FLY!!"

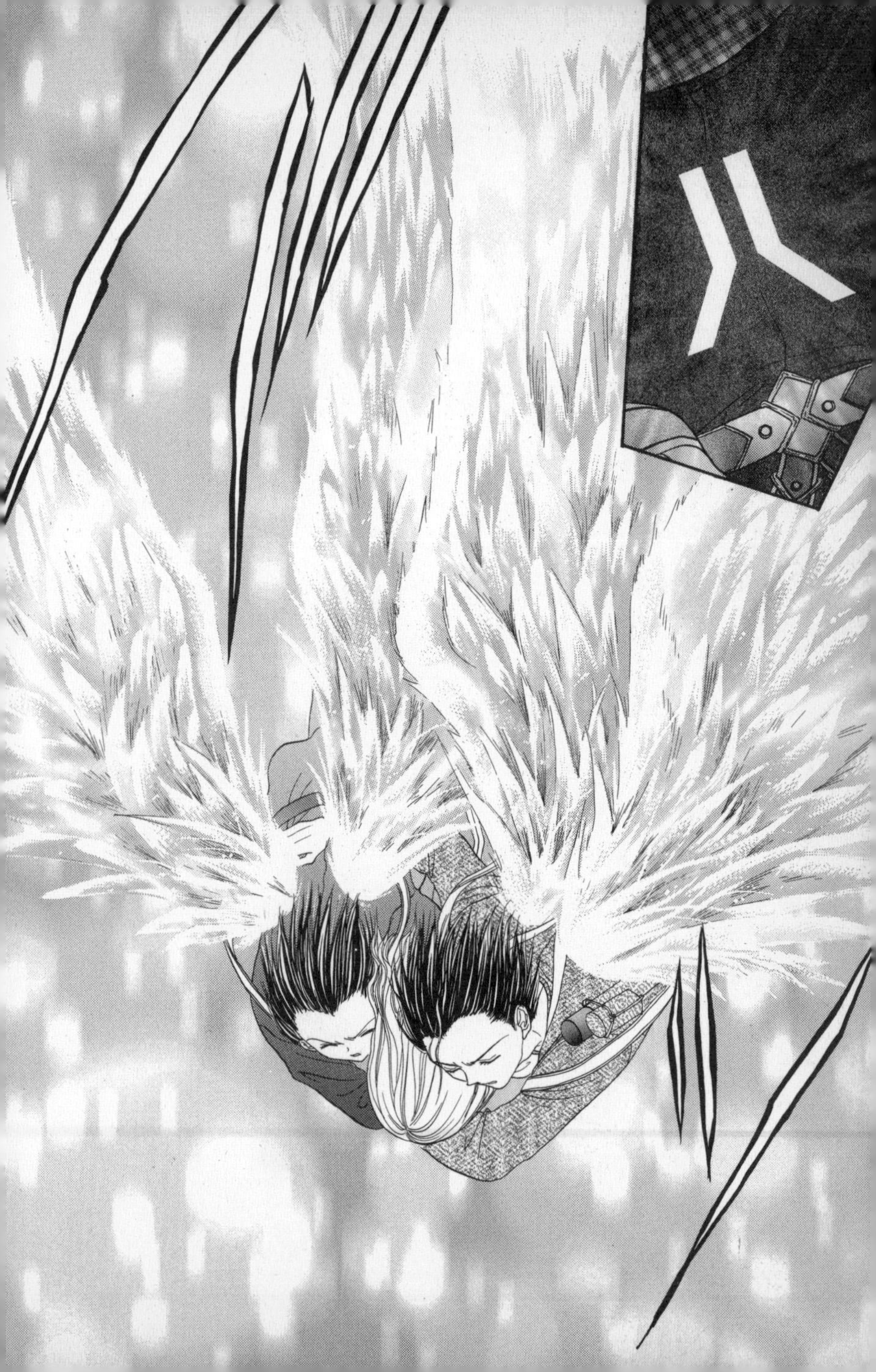

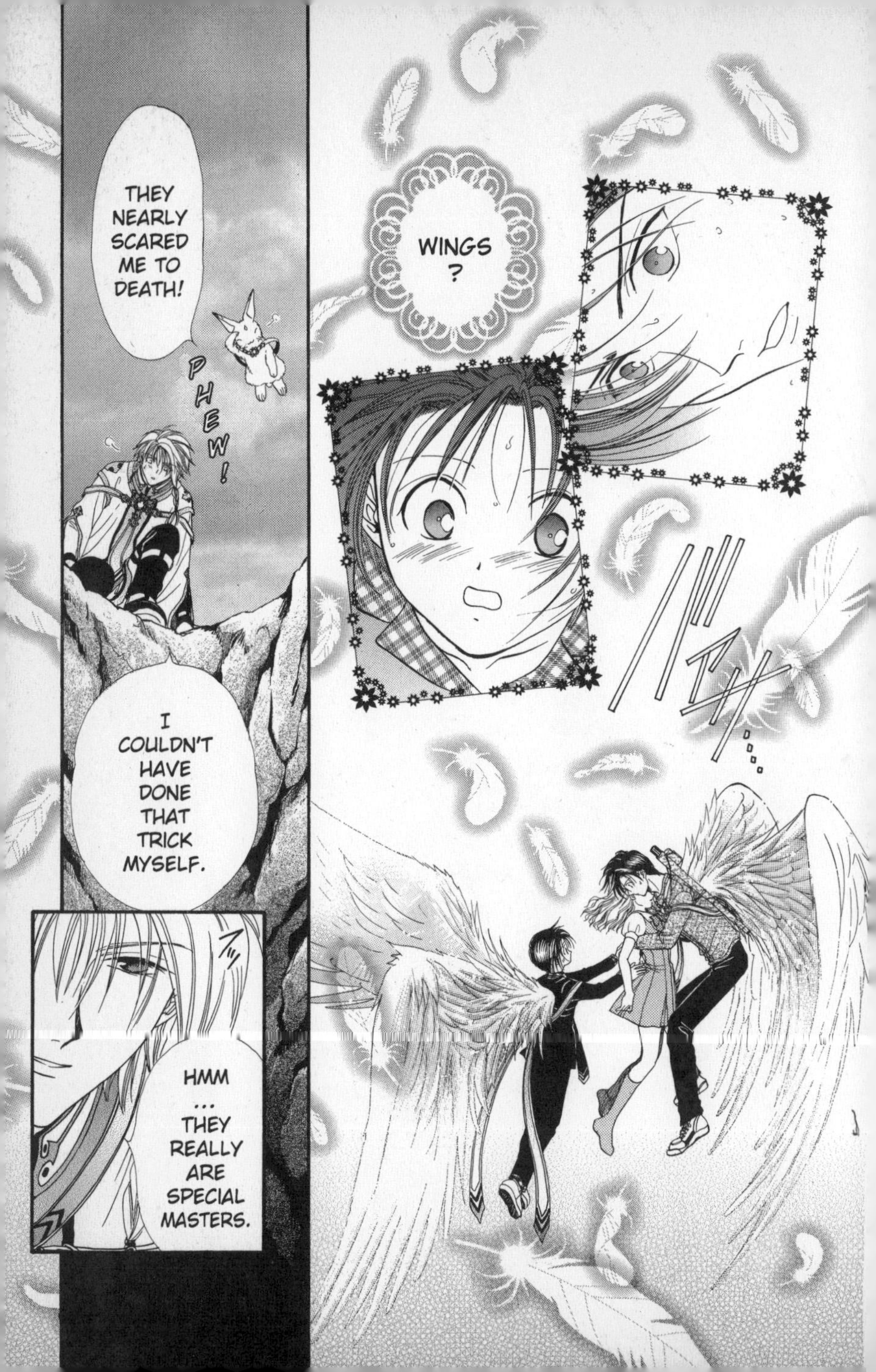
WINGS ?
THEY NEARLY SCARED ME TO DEATH!
PHEW!
I COULDN'T HAVE DONE THAT TRICK MYSELF.
HMM ... THEY REALLY ARE SPECIAL MASTERS.

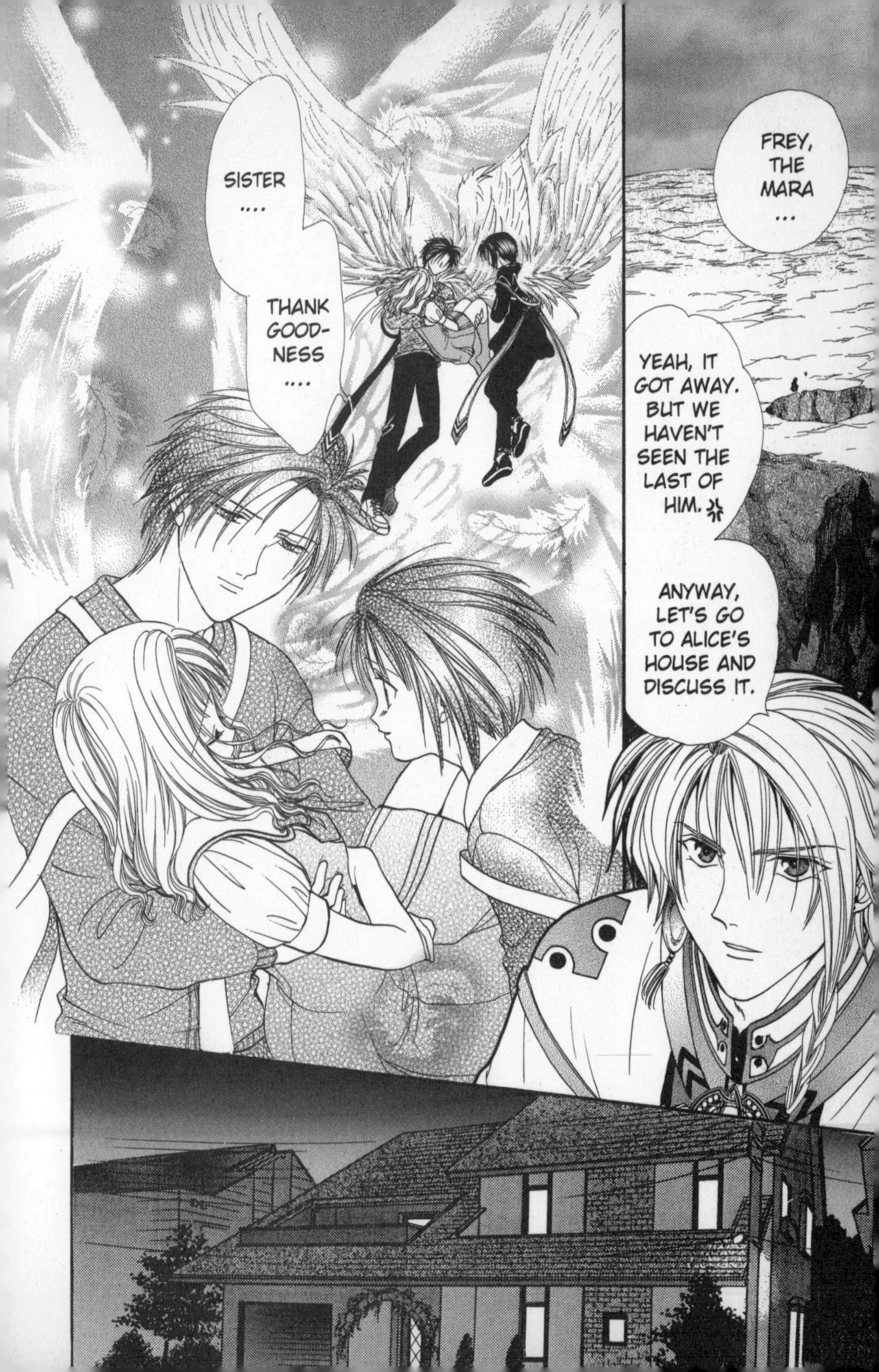
FREY, THE MARA ...
YEAH, IT GOT AWAY. BUT WE HAVEN'T SEEN THE LAST OF HIM.
ANYWAY, LET'S GO TO ALICE'S HOUSE AND DISCUSS IT.
SISTER ....
THANK GOOD-NESS ....

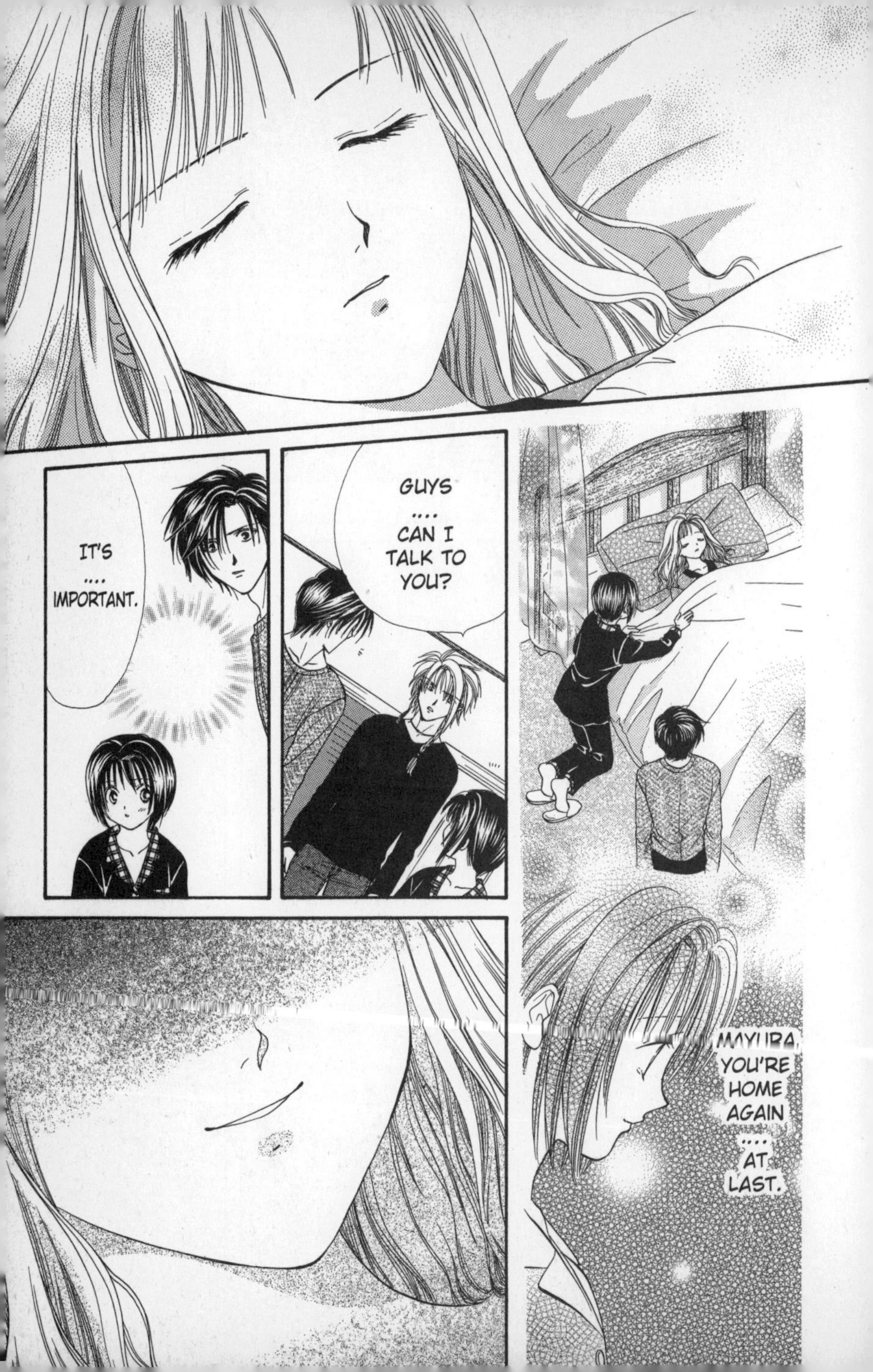
GUYS .... CAN I TALK TO YOU?
IT'S .... IMPORTANT.
MAYURA, YOU'RE HOME AGAIN .... AT LAST.

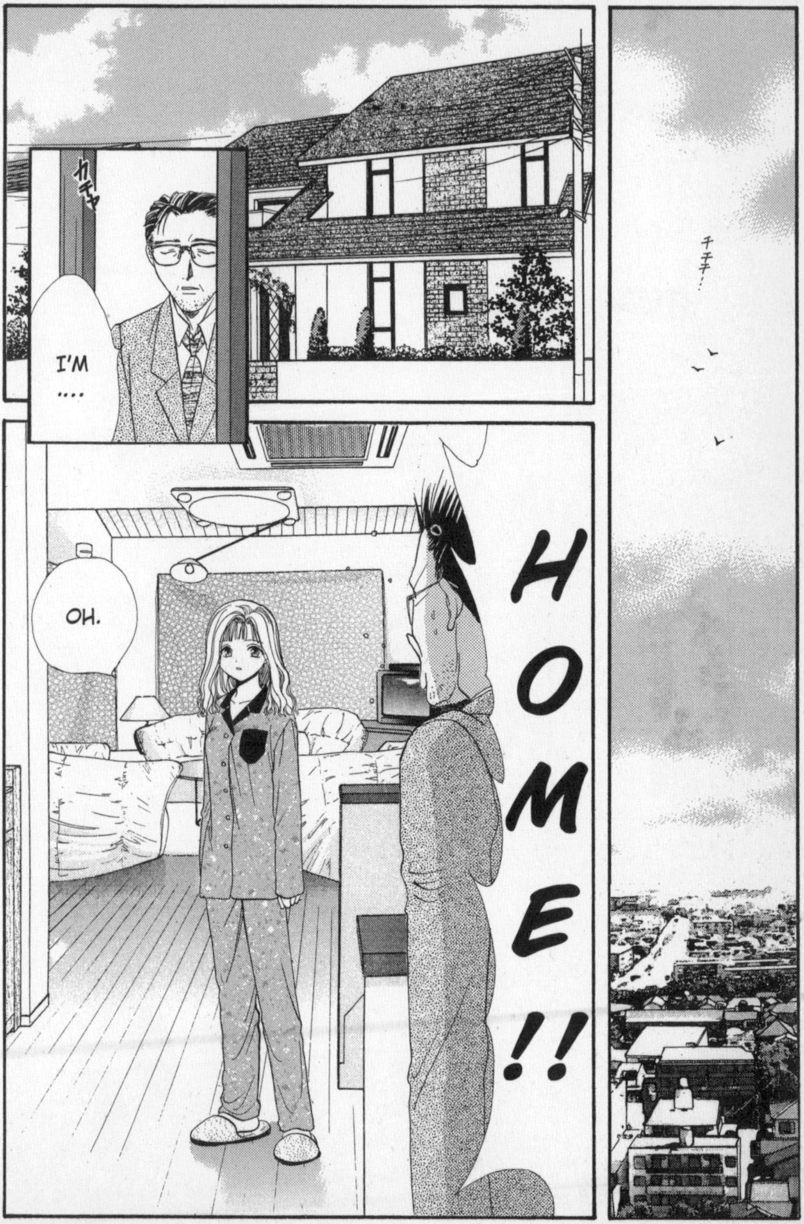
チチチ…
カチャ
I'M ....
HOME!!
OH.

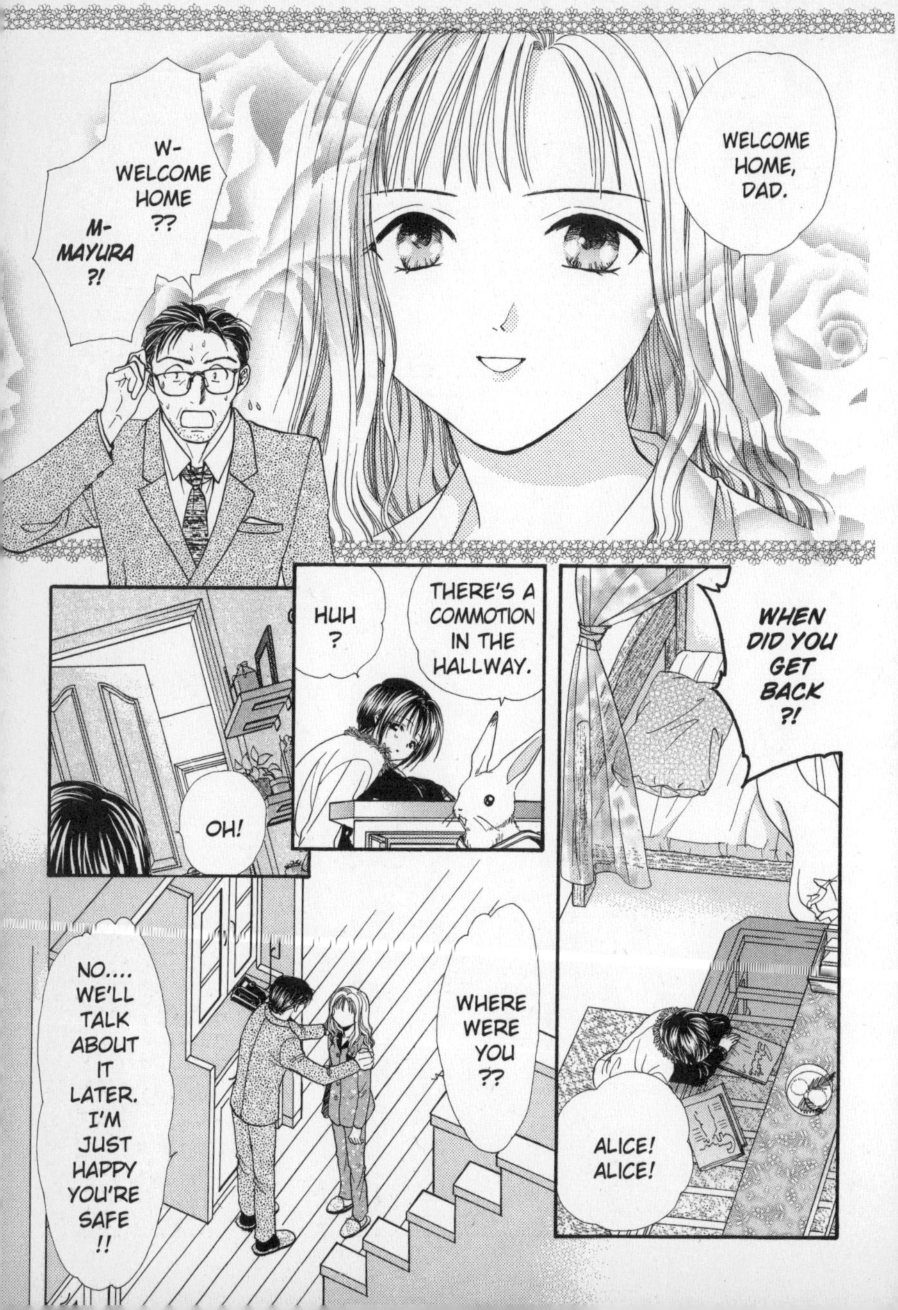
WELCOME HOME, DAD.
W- WELCOME HOME ??
M- MAYURA ?!
WHEN DID YOU GET BACK ?!
ALICE! ALICE!
THERE'S A COMMOTION IN THE HALLWAY.
HUH ?
OH!
WHERE WERE YOU ??
NO.... WE'LL TALK ABOUT IT LATER. I'M JUST HAPPY YOU'RE SAFE !!

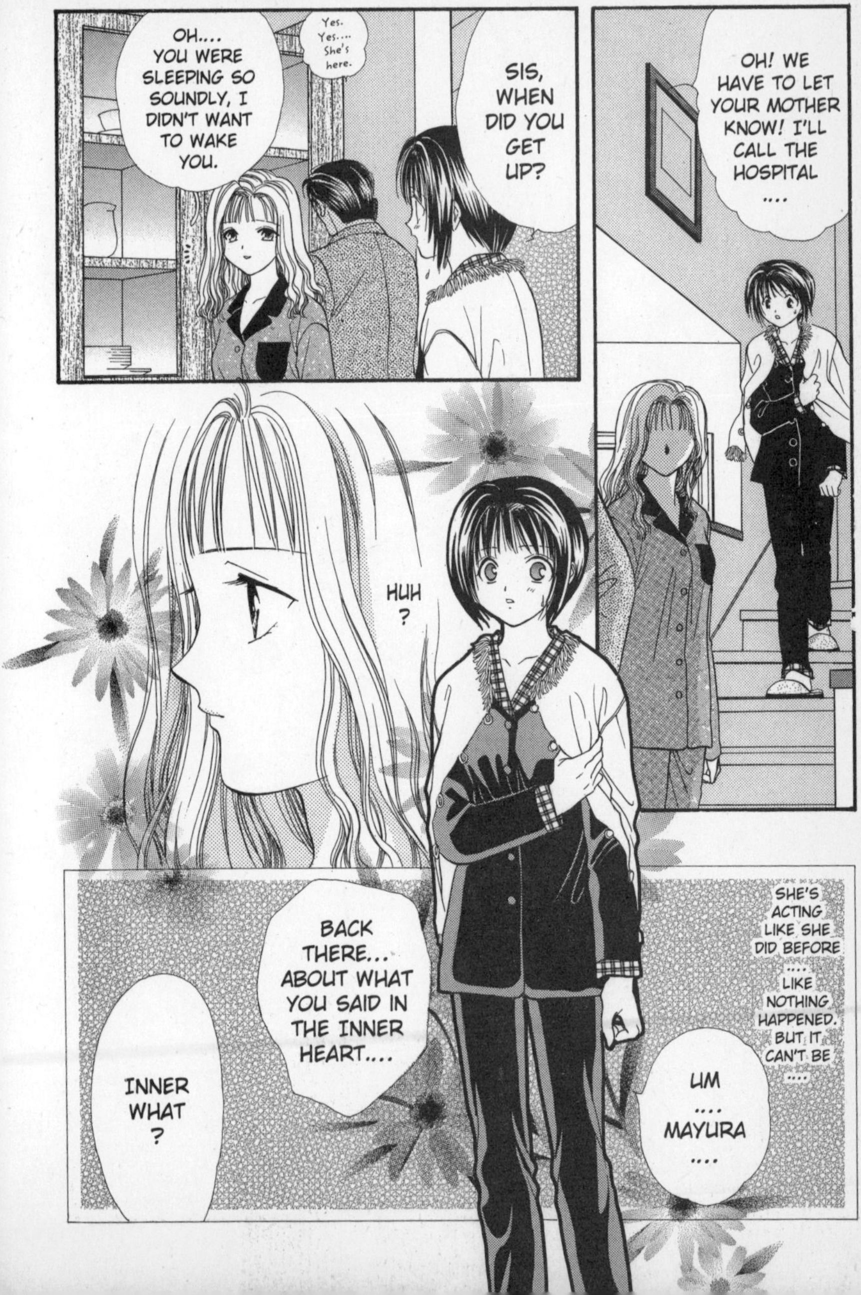
OH! WE HAVE TO LET YOUR MOTHER KNOW! I'LL CALL THE HOSPITAL ....
SIS, WHEN DID YOU GET UP?
Yes. Yes.... She's here.
OH.... YOU WERE SLEEPING SO SOUNDLY, I DIDN'T WANT TO WAKE YOU.
HUH ?
SHE'S ACTING LIKE SHE DID BEFORE .... LIKE NOTHING HAPPENED. BUT IT CAN'T BE ....
UM .... MAYURA ....
BACK THERE... ABOUT WHAT YOU SAID IN THE INNER HEART....
INNER WHAT ?

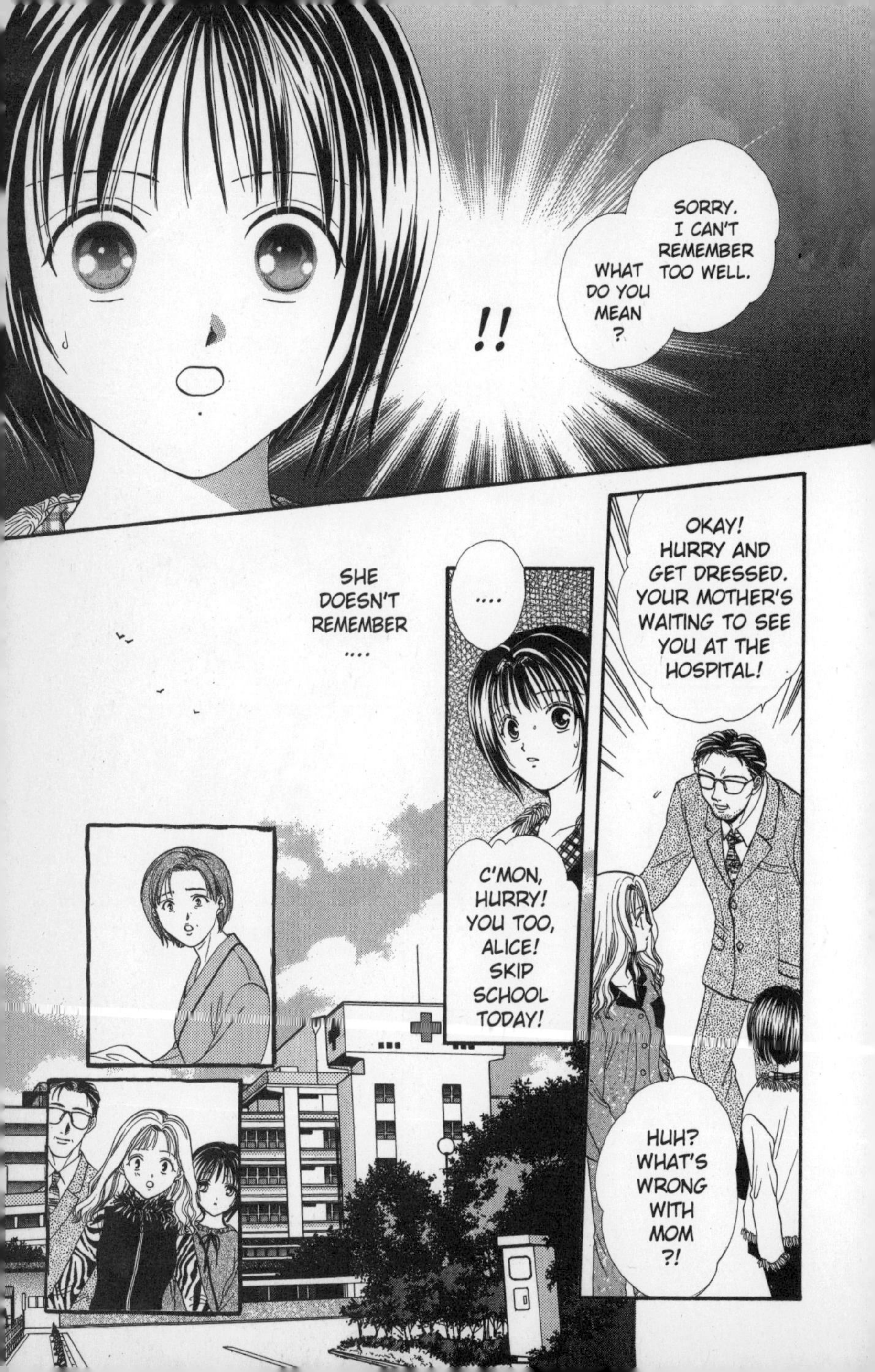
SORRY. I CAN'T REMEMBER TOO WELL.
WHAT DO YOU MEAN?
!!
OKAY! HURRY AND GET DRESSED. YOUR MOTHER'S WAITING TO SEE YOU AT THE HOSPITAL!
HUH? WHAT'S WRONG WITH MOM?!
....
C'MON, HURRY! YOU TOO, ALICE! SKIP SCHOOL TODAY!
SHE DOESN'T REMEMBER ....

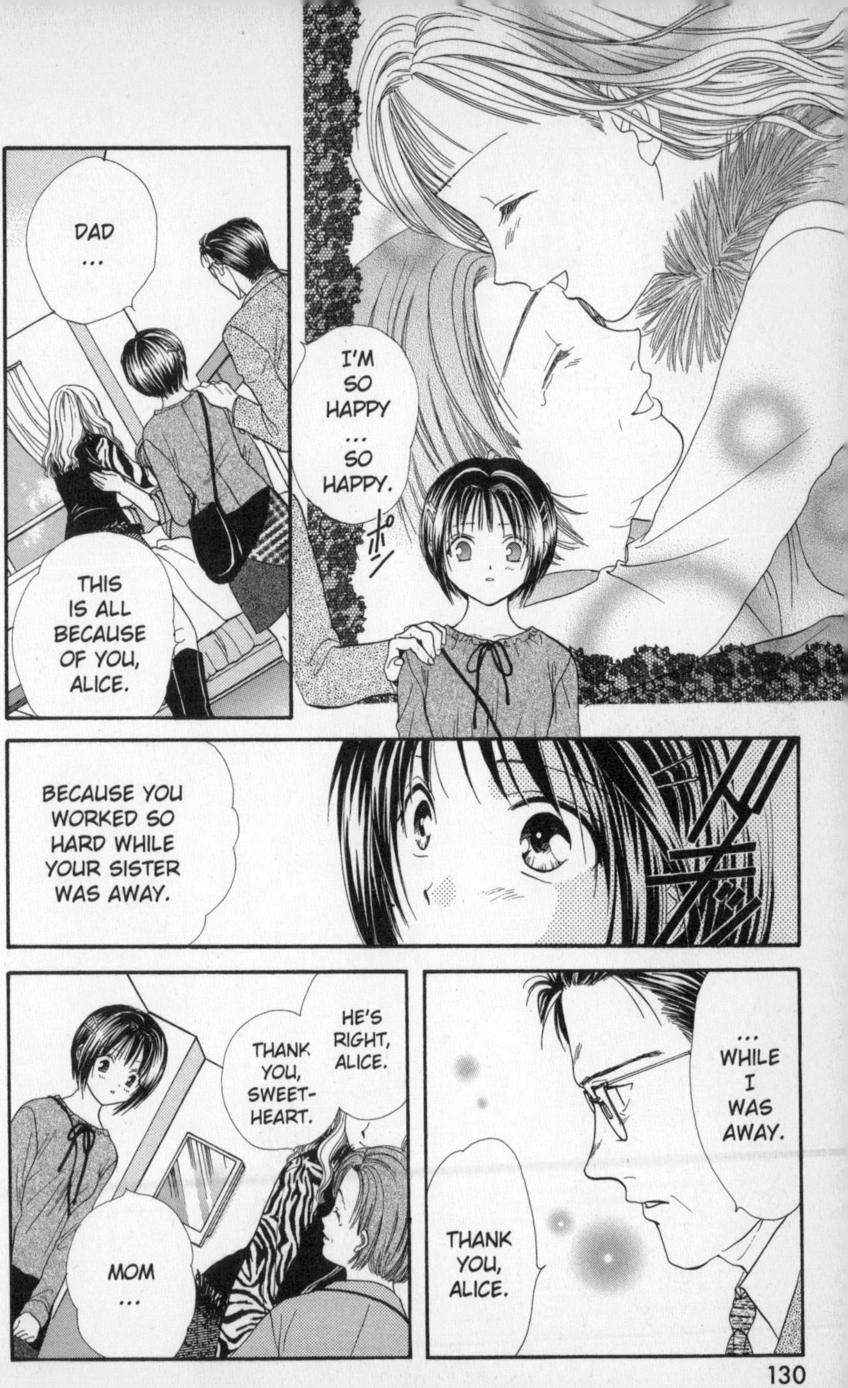
I'M SO HAPPY ... SO HAPPY.
ポ
DAD ...
THIS IS ALL BECAUSE OF YOU, ALICE.
BECAUSE YOU WORKED SO HARD WHILE YOUR SISTER WAS AWAY.
... WHILE I WAS AWAY.
THANK YOU, ALICE.
HE'S RIGHT, ALICE.
THANK YOU, SWEET-HEART.
MOM ...

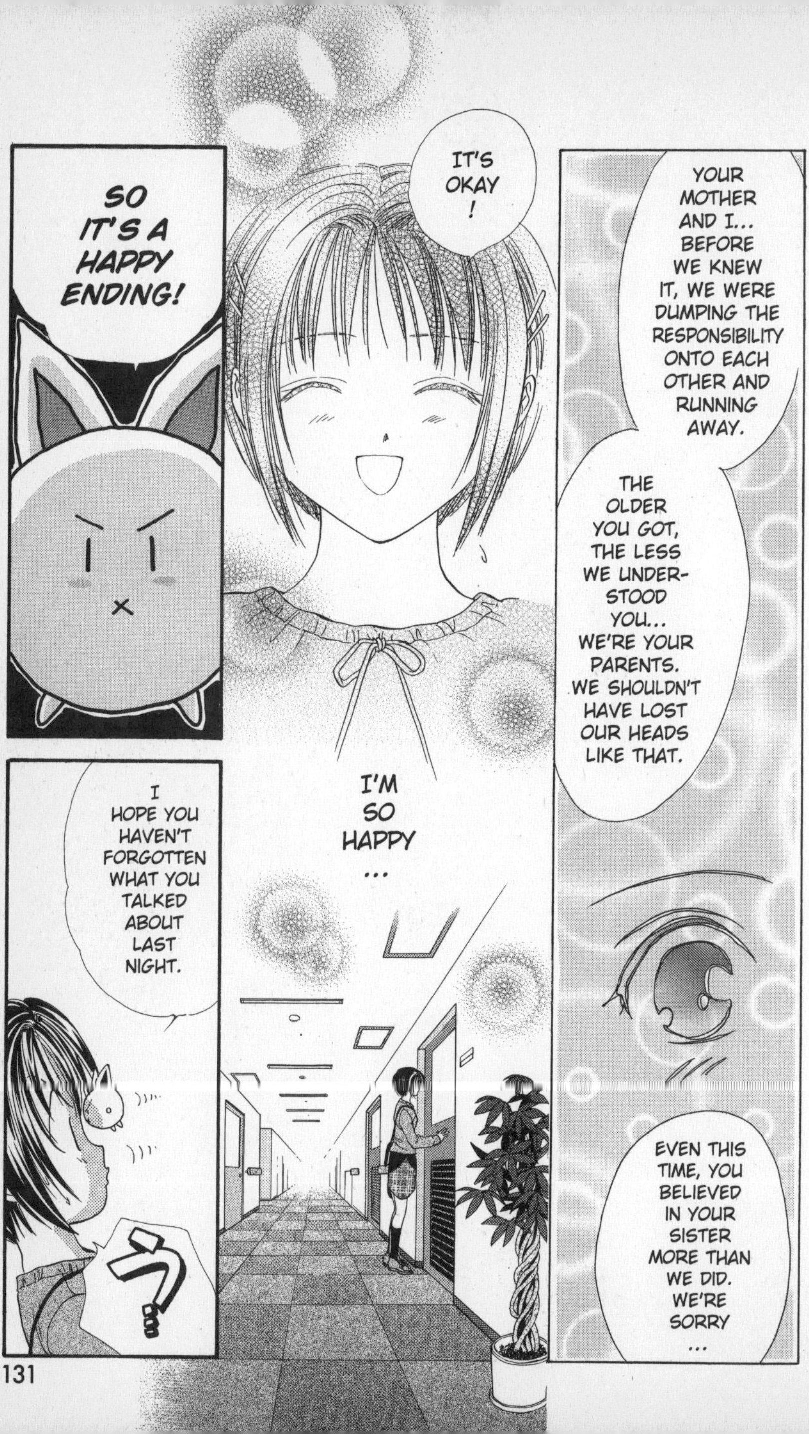
YOUR MOTHER AND I... BEFORE WE KNEW IT, WE WERE DUMPING THE RESPONSIBILITY ONTO EACH OTHER AND RUNNING AWAY.
THE OLDER YOU GOT, THE LESS WE UNDER-STOOD YOU... WE'RE YOUR PARENTS. WE SHOULDN'T HAVE LOST OUR HEADS LIKE THAT.
EVEN THIS TIME, YOU BELIEVED IN YOUR SISTER MORE THAN WE DID. WE'RE SORRY...
IT'S OKAY!
I'M SO HAPPY...
SO IT'S A HAPPY ENDING!
I HOPE YOU HAVEN'T FORGOTTEN WHAT YOU TALKED ABOUT LAST NIGHT.

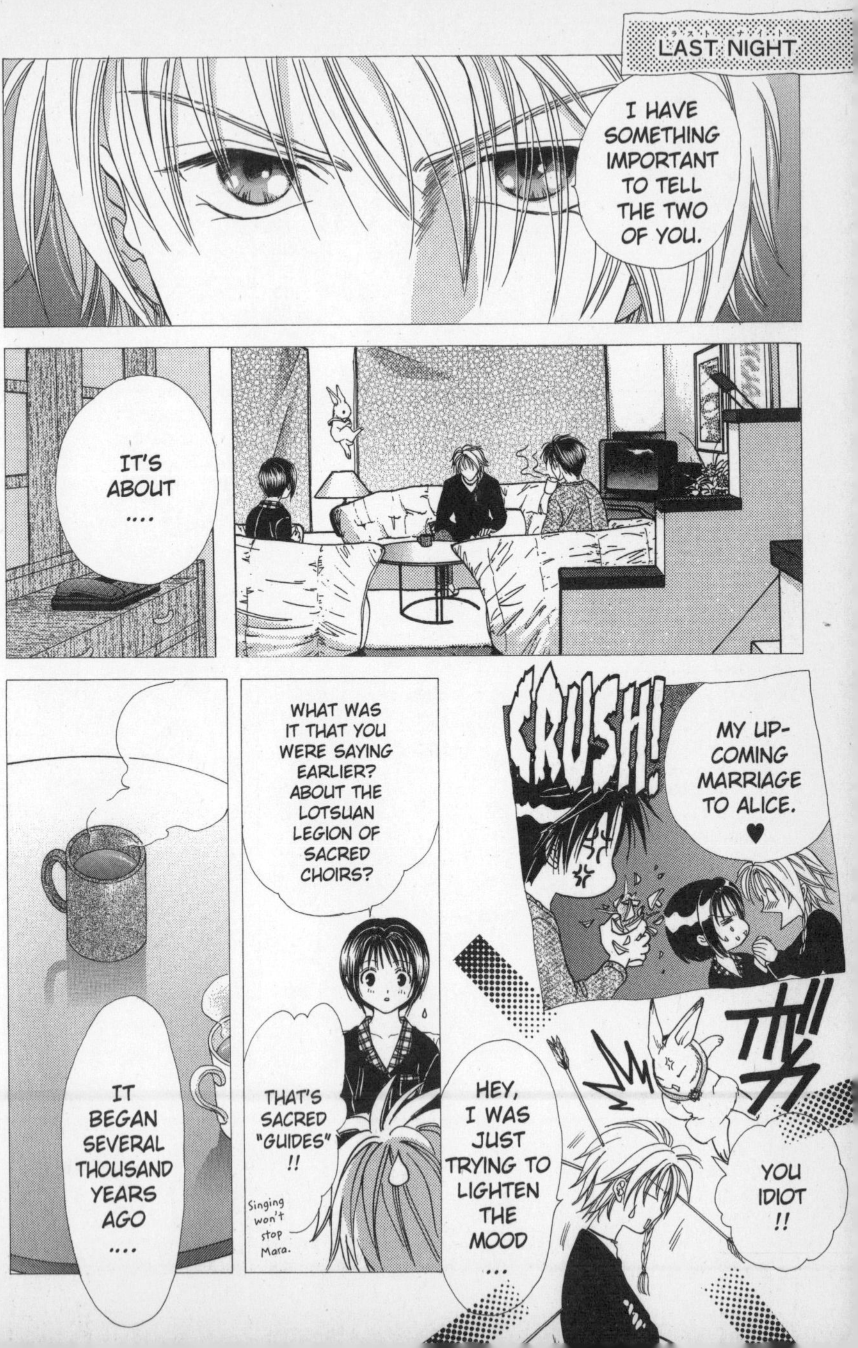
LAST NIGHT
I HAVE SOMETHING IMPORTANT TO TELL THE TWO OF YOU.
IT'S ABOUT ....
CRUSH!
MY UP-COMING MARRIAGE TO ALICE. ♥
ガッ
YOU IDIOT !!
HEY, I WAS JUST TRYING TO LIGHTEN THE MOOD ...
WHAT WAS IT THAT YOU WERE SAYING EARLIER? ABOUT THE LOTSUAN LEGION OF SACRED CHOIRS?
THAT'S SACRED "GUIDES" !!
Singing won't stop Mara.
IT BEGAN SEVERAL THOUSAND YEARS AGO ....

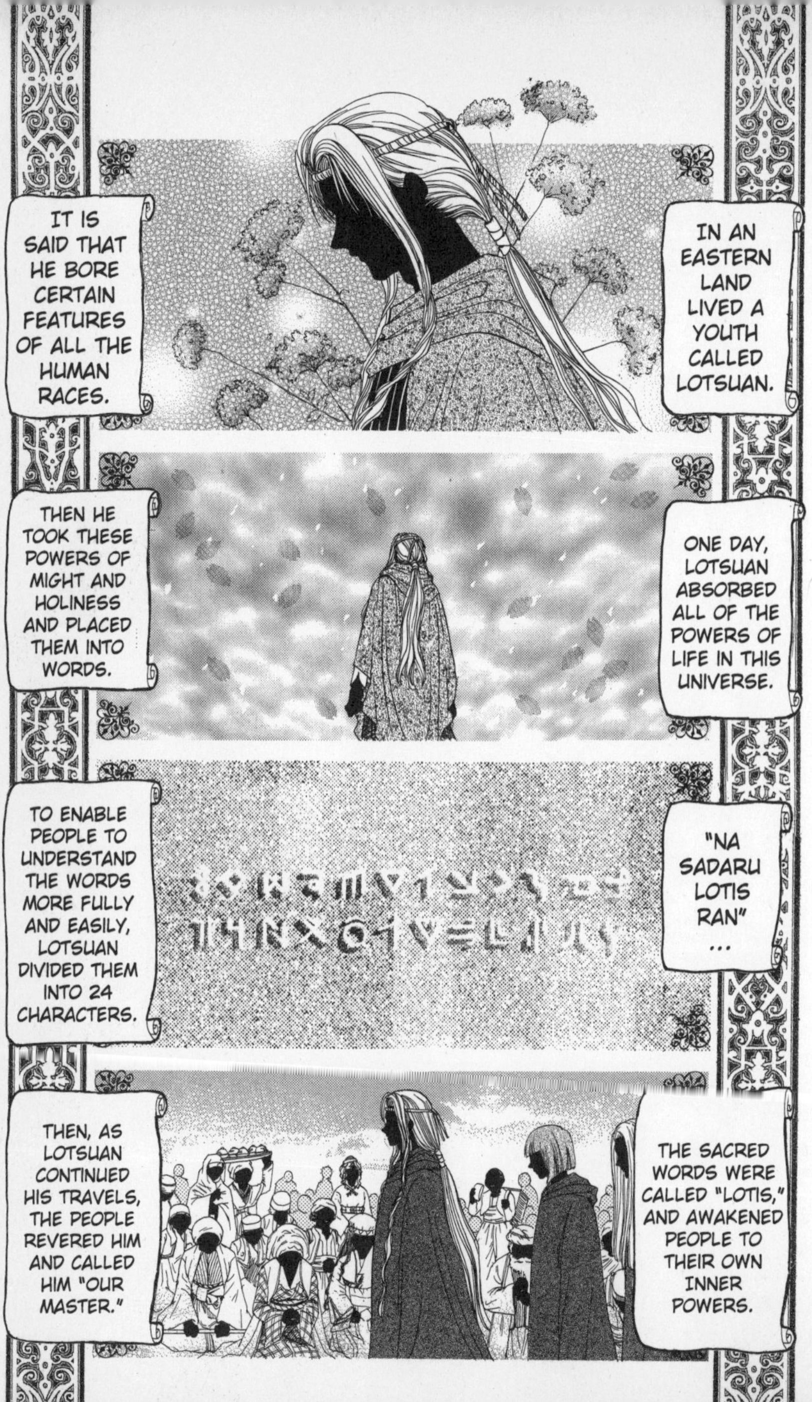
IN AN EASTERN LAND LIVED A YOUTH CALLED LOTSUAN.
IT IS SAID THAT HE BORE CERTAIN FEATURES OF ALL THE HUMAN RACES.
ONE DAY, LOTSUAN ABSORBED ALL OF THE POWERS OF LIFE IN THIS UNIVERSE.
THEN HE TOOK THESE POWERS OF MIGHT AND HOLINESS AND PLACED THEM INTO WORDS.
"NA SADARU LOTIS RAN" ...
TO ENABLE PEOPLE TO UNDERSTAND THE WORDS MORE FULLY AND EASILY, LOTSUAN DIVIDED THEM INTO 24 CHARACTERS.
THE SACRED WORDS WERE CALLED "LOTIS," AND AWAKENED PEOPLE TO THEIR OWN INNER POWERS.
THEN, AS LOTSUAN CONTINUED HIS TRAVELS, THE PEOPLE REVERED HIM AND CALLED HIM "OUR MASTER."

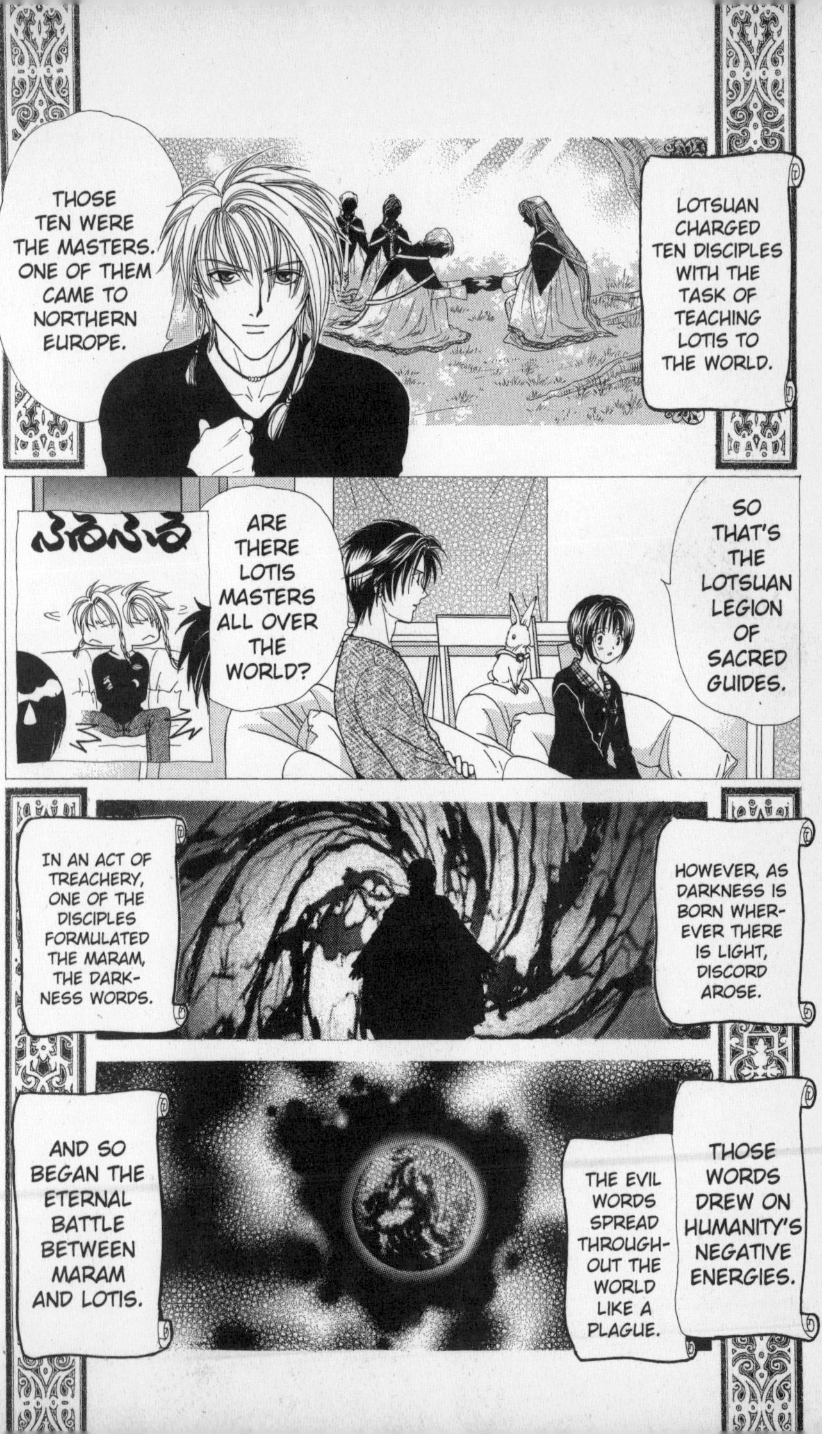
LOTSUAN CHARGED TEN DISCIPLES WITH THE TASK OF TEACHING LOTIS TO THE WORLD.
THOSE TEN WERE THE MASTERS. ONE OF THEM CAME TO NORTHERN EUROPE.
SO THAT'S THE LOTSUAN LEGION OF SACRED GUIDES.
ARE THERE LOTIS MASTERS ALL OVER THE WORLD?
ふるふる
HOWEVER, AS DARKNESS IS BORN WHER-EVER THERE IS LIGHT, DISCORD AROSE.
IN AN ACT OF TREACHERY, ONE OF THE DISCIPLES FORMULATED THE MARAM, THE DARK-NESS WORDS.
THOSE WORDS DREW ON HUMANITY'S NEGATIVE ENERGIES.
THE EVIL WORDS SPREAD THROUGH-OUT THE WORLD LIKE A PLAGUE.
AND SO BEGAN THE ETERNAL BATTLE BETWEEN MARAM AND LOTIS.

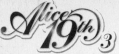

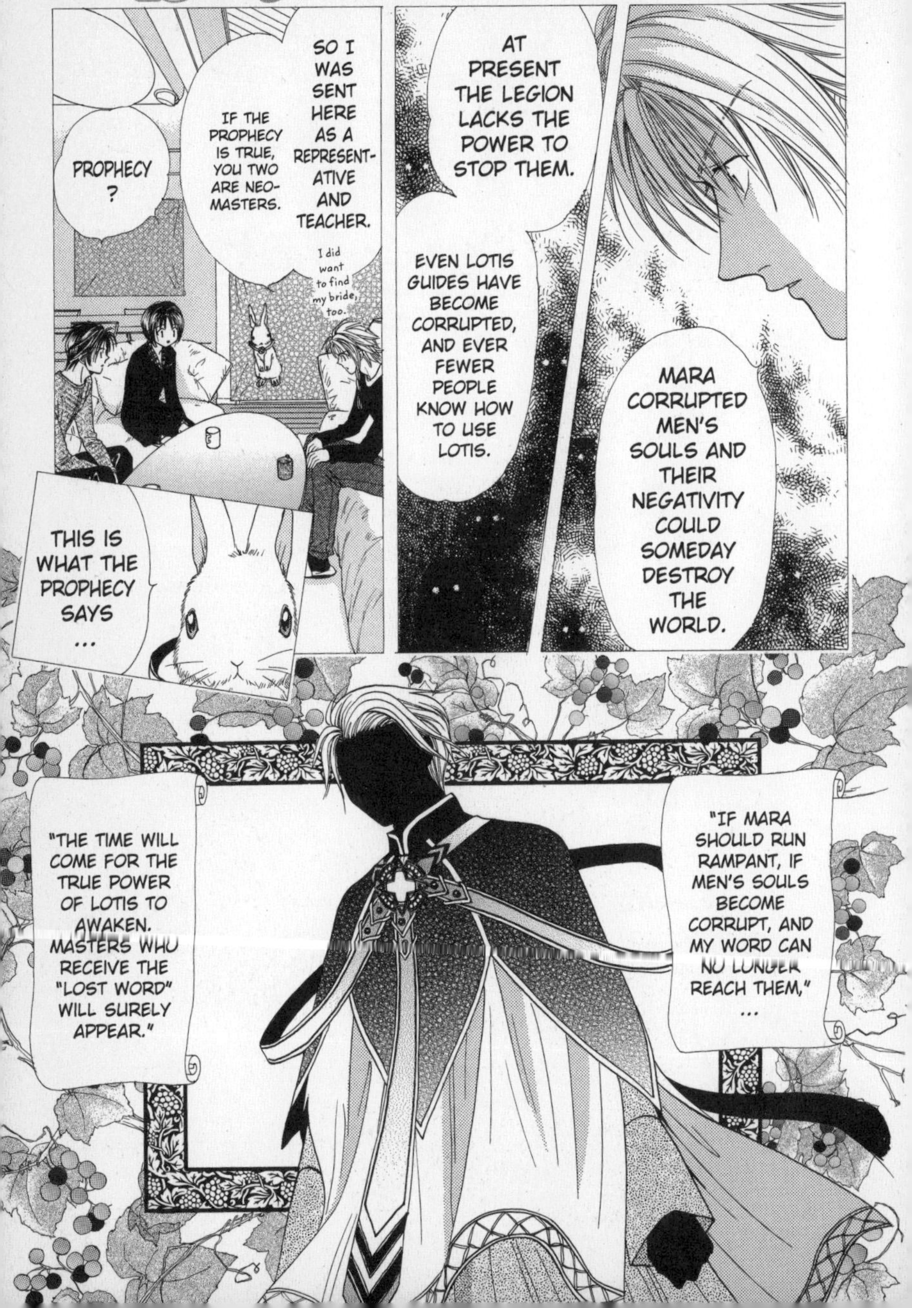
MARA CORRUPTED MEN'S SOULS AND THEIR NEGATIVITY COULD SOMEDAY DESTROY THE WORLD.
AT PRESENT THE LEGION LACKS THE POWER TO STOP THEM.
EVEN LOTIS GUIDES HAVE BECOME CORRUPTED, AND EVER FEWER PEOPLE KNOW HOW TO USE LOTIS.
SO I WAS SENT HERE AS A REPRESENTATIVE AND TEACHER.
IF THE PROPHECY IS TRUE, YOU TWO ARE NEO-MASTERS.
PROPHECY?
I did want to find my bride, too.
THIS IS WHAT THE PROPHECY SAYS ...
"IF MARA SHOULD RUN RAMPANT, IF MEN'S SOULS BECOME CORRUPT, AND MY WORD CAN NO LONGER REACH THEM," ...
"THE TIME WILL COME FOR THE TRUE POWER OF LOTIS TO AWAKEN. MASTERS WHO RECEIVE THE "LOST WORD" WILL SURELY APPEAR."

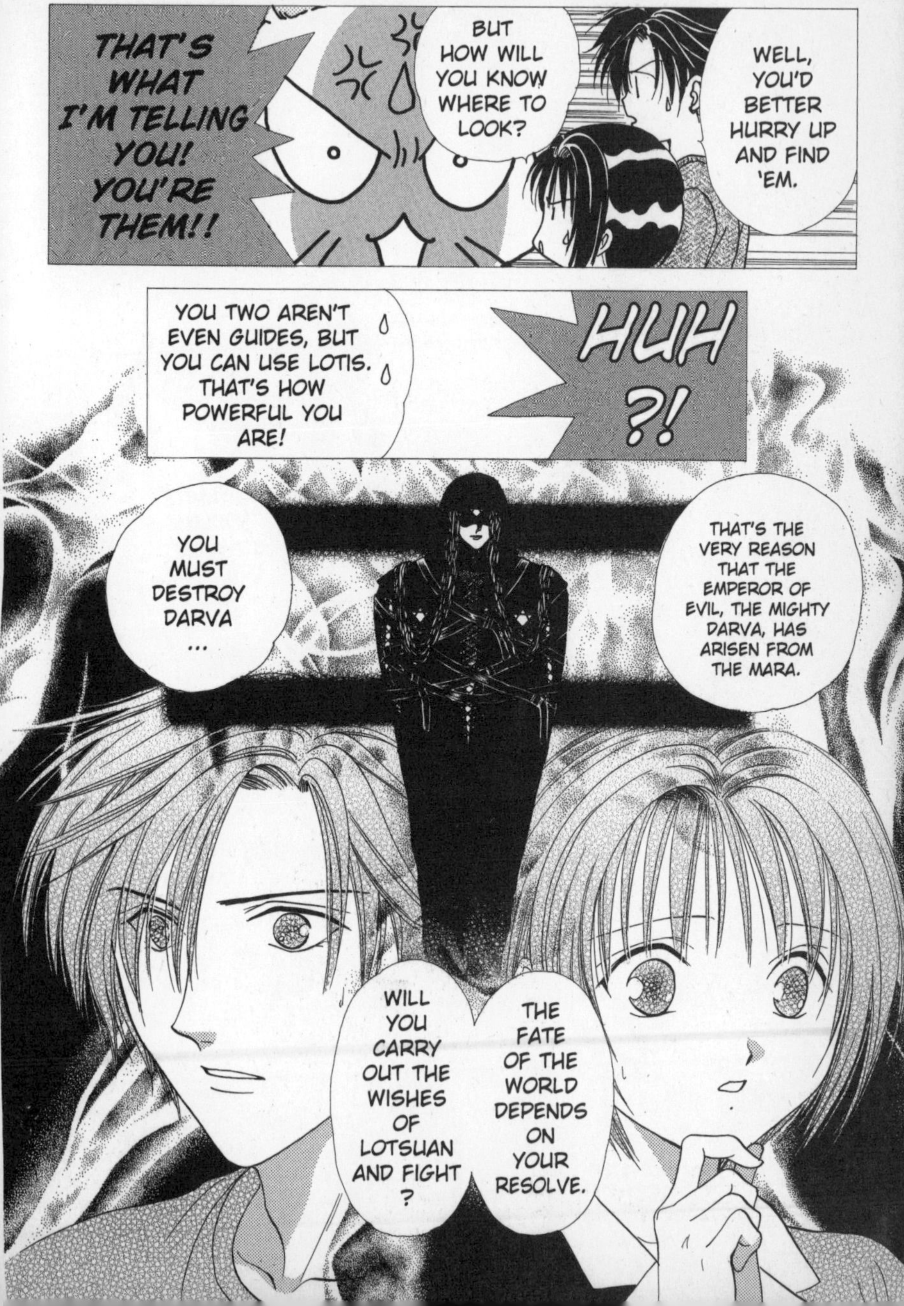
WELL, YOU'D BETTER HURRY UP AND FIND 'EM.
BUT HOW WILL YOU KNOW WHERE TO LOOK?
THAT'S WHAT I'M TELLING YOU! YOU'RE THEM!!
HUH ?!
YOU TWO AREN'T EVEN GUIDES, BUT YOU CAN USE LOTIS. THAT'S HOW POWERFUL YOU ARE!
THAT'S THE VERY REASON THAT THE EMPEROR OF EVIL, THE MIGHTY DARVA, HAS ARISEN FROM THE MARA.
YOU MUST DESTROY DARVA ...
THE FATE OF THE WORLD DEPENDS ON YOUR RESOLVE.
WILL YOU CARRY OUT THE WISHES OF LOTSUAN AND FIGHT ?

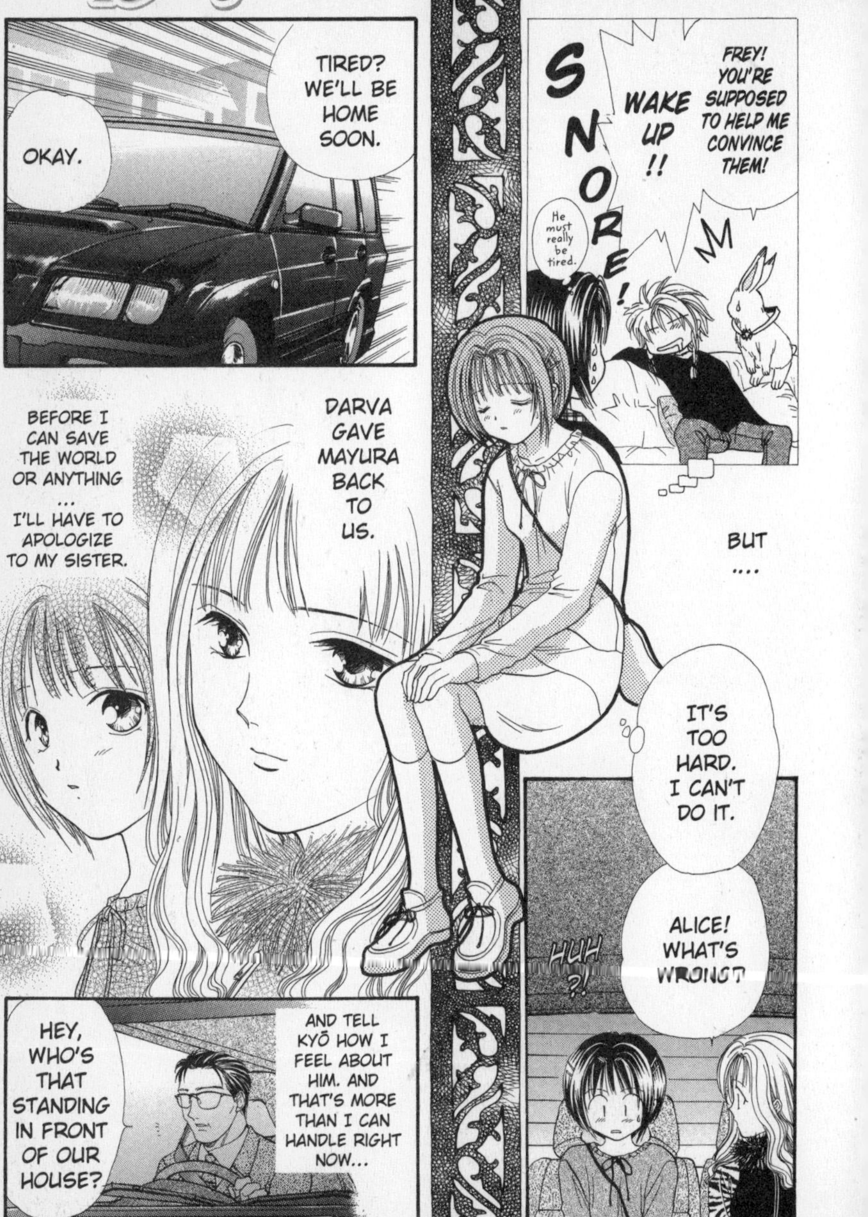
FREY! YOU'RE SUPPOSED TO HELP ME CONVINCE THEM!
WAKE UP!!
SNORE!
He must really be tired.
BUT ....
IT'S TOO HARD. I CAN'T DO IT.
ALICE! WHAT'S WRONG?
HUH?!
TIRED? WE'LL BE HOME SOON.
OKAY.
DARVA GAVE MAYURA BACK TO US.
BEFORE I CAN SAVE THE WORLD OR ANYTHING ... I'LL HAVE TO APOLOGIZE TO MY SISTER.
AND TELL KYŌ HOW I FEEL ABOUT HIM. AND THAT'S MORE THAN I CAN HANDLE RIGHT NOW...
HEY, WHO'S THAT STANDING IN FRONT OF OUR HOUSE?

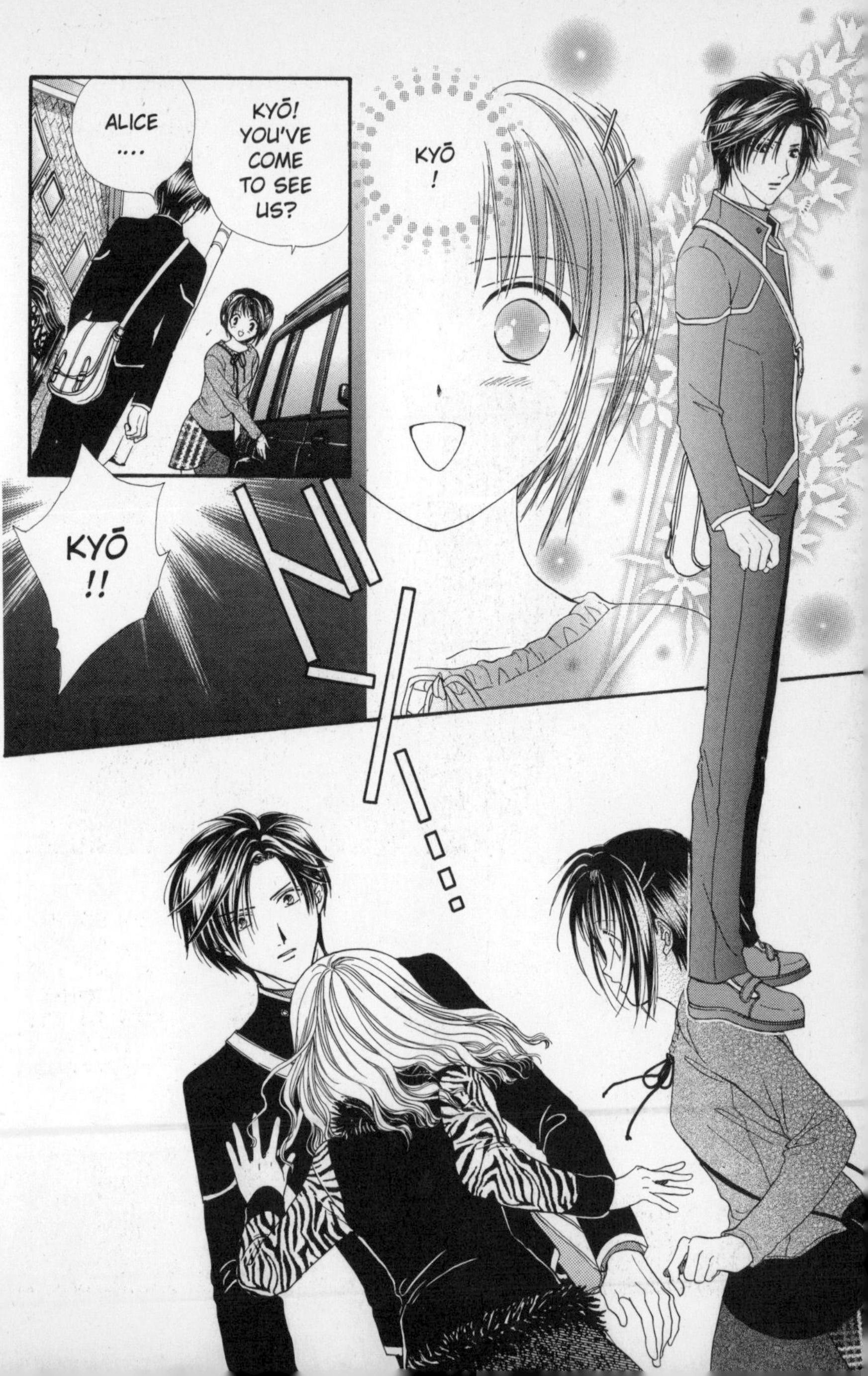
KYŌ !
KYŌ! YOU'VE COME TO SEE US?
ALICE ....
KYŌ !!

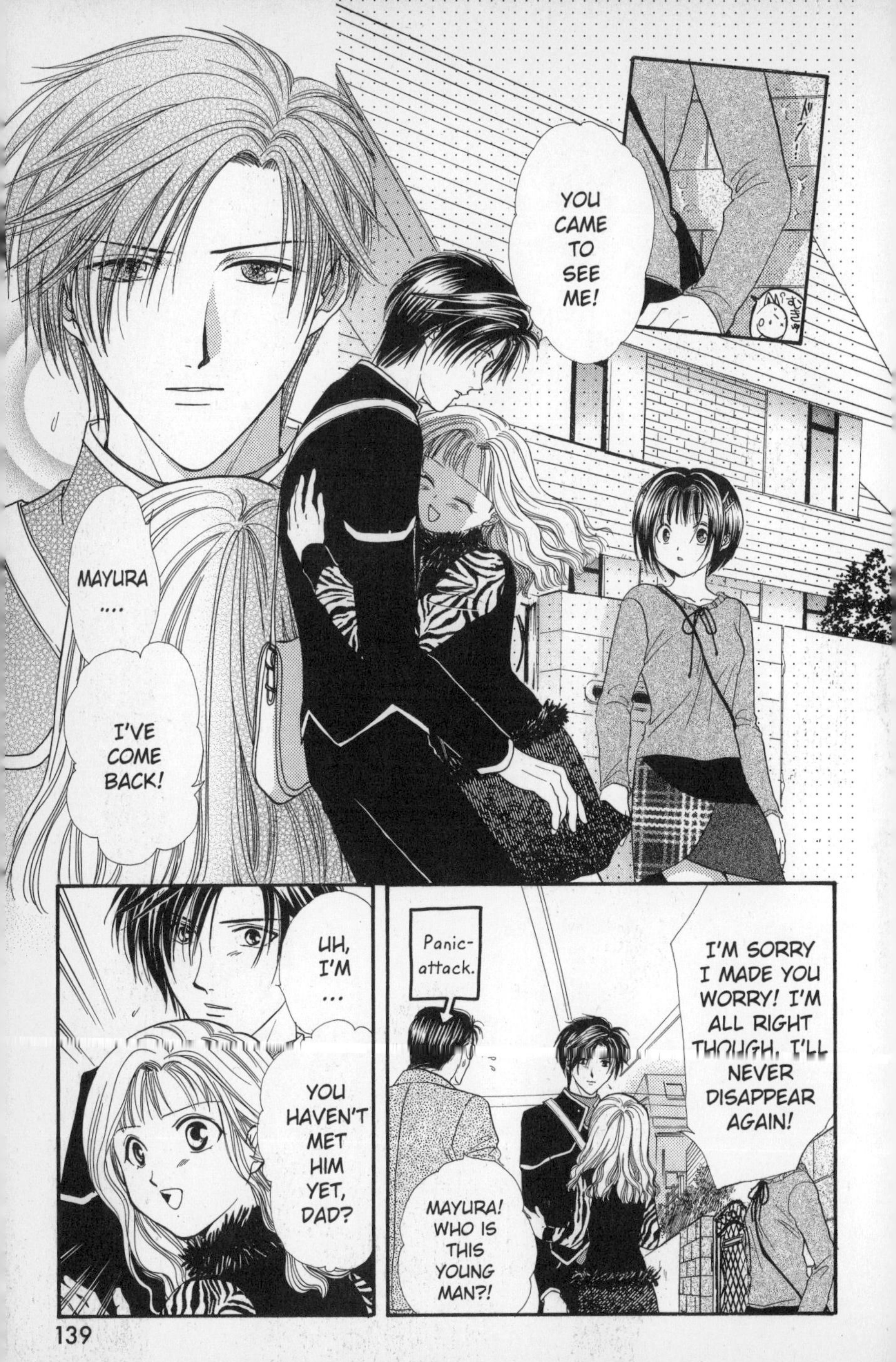
YOU CAME TO SEE ME!
MAYURA ....
I'VE COME BACK!
I'M SORRY I MADE YOU WORRY! I'M ALL RIGHT THOUGH. I'LL NEVER DISAPPEAR AGAIN!
Panic-attack.
MAYURA! WHO IS THIS YOUNG MAN?!
UH, I'M ...
YOU HAVEN'T MET HIM YET, DAD?

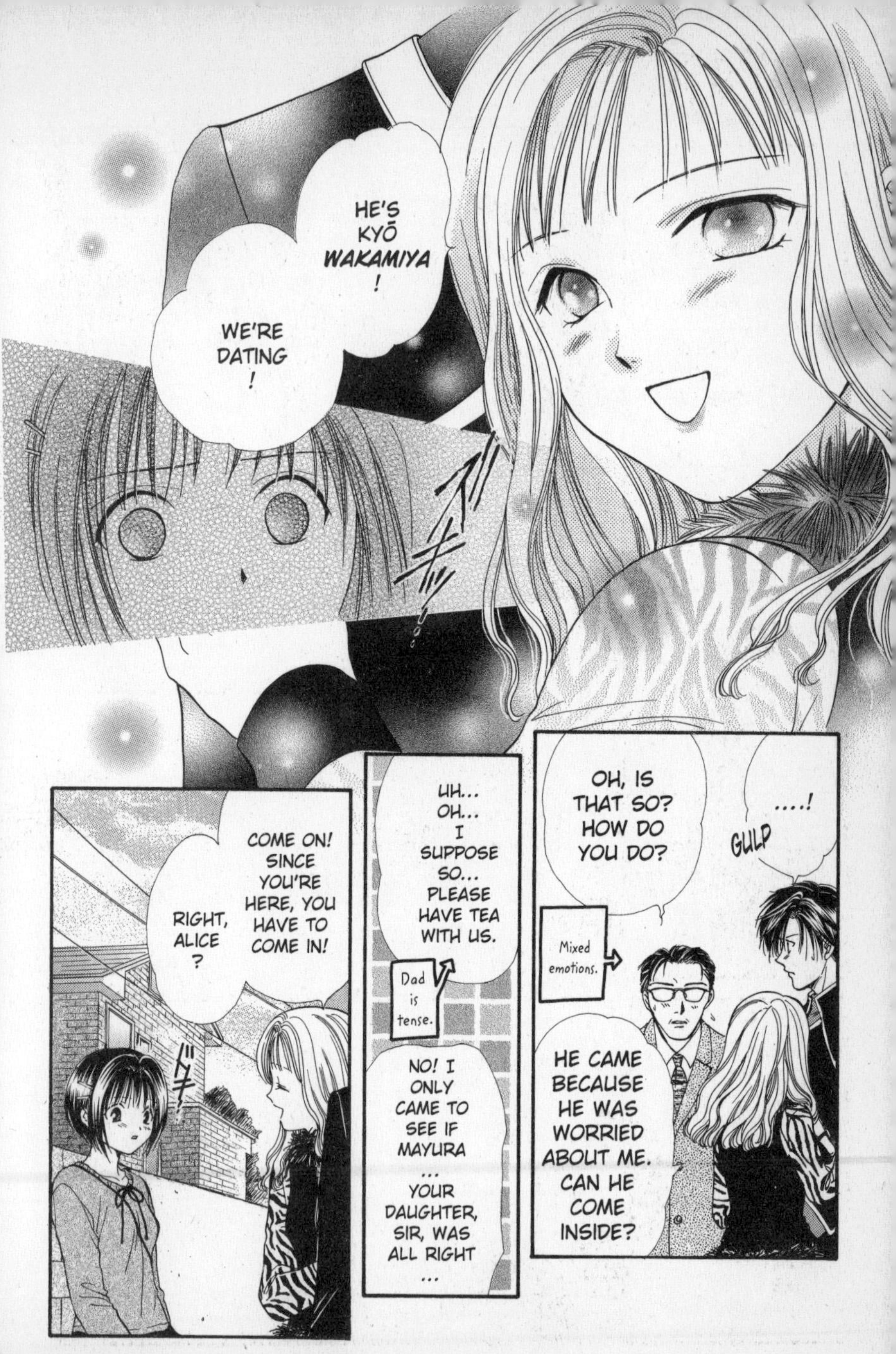
HE'S KYŌ WAKAMIYA!
WE'RE DATING!
....!
GULP
OH, IS THAT SO? HOW DO YOU DO?
Mixed emotions.
HE CAME BECAUSE HE WAS WORRIED ABOUT ME. CAN HE COME INSIDE?
UH... OH... I SUPPOSE SO... PLEASE HAVE TEA WITH US.
Dad is tense.
NO! I ONLY CAME TO SEE IF MAYURA... YOUR DAUGHTER, SIR, WAS ALL RIGHT...
COME ON! SINCE YOU'RE HERE, YOU HAVE TO COME IN!
RIGHT, ALICE?

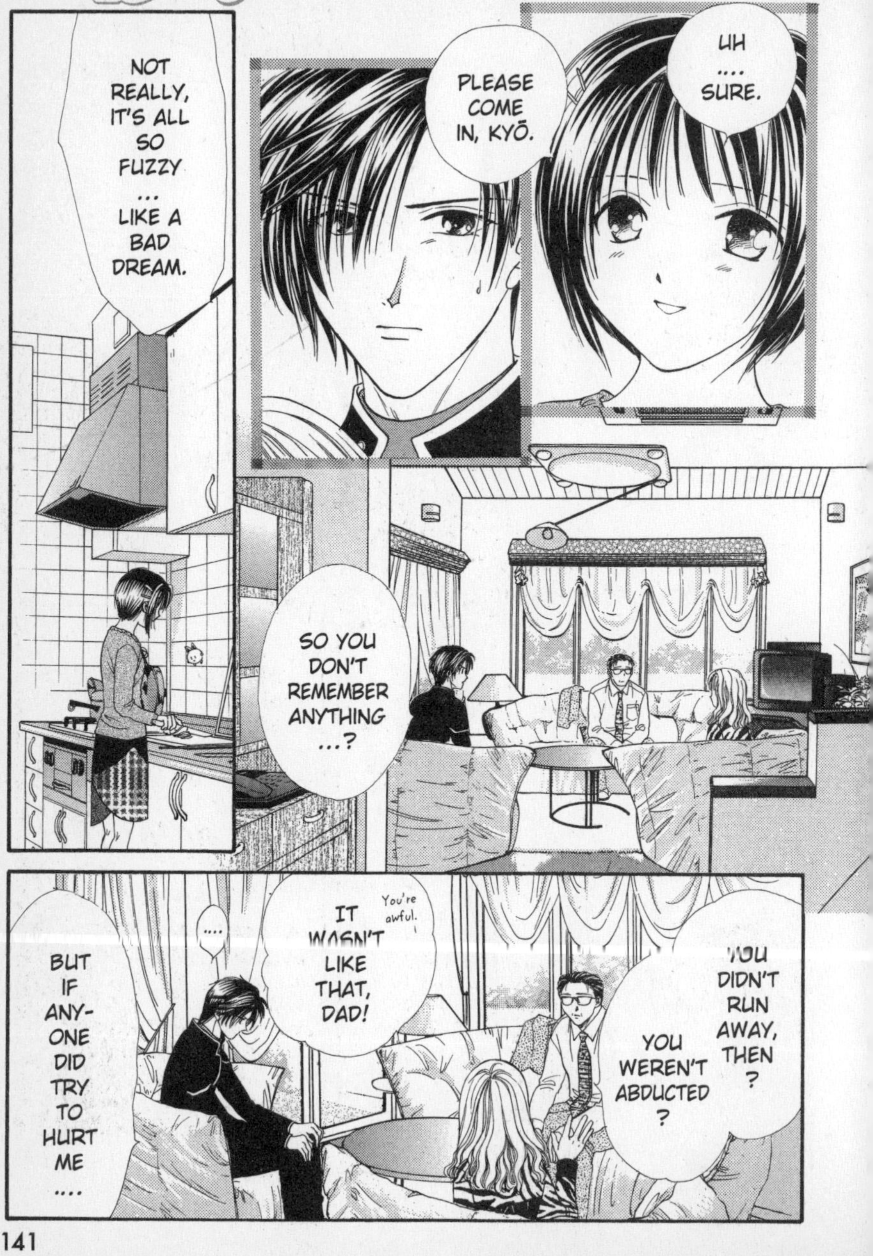
UH .... SURE.
PLEASE COME IN, KYŌ.
SO YOU DON'T REMEMBER ANYTHING ...?
NOT REALLY, IT'S ALL SO FUZZY ... LIKE A BAD DREAM.
YOU DIDN'T RUN AWAY, THEN ?
YOU WEREN'T ABDUCTED ?
IT WASN'T LIKE THAT, DAD!
You're awful.
....
BUT IF ANY-ONE DID TRY TO HURT ME ....

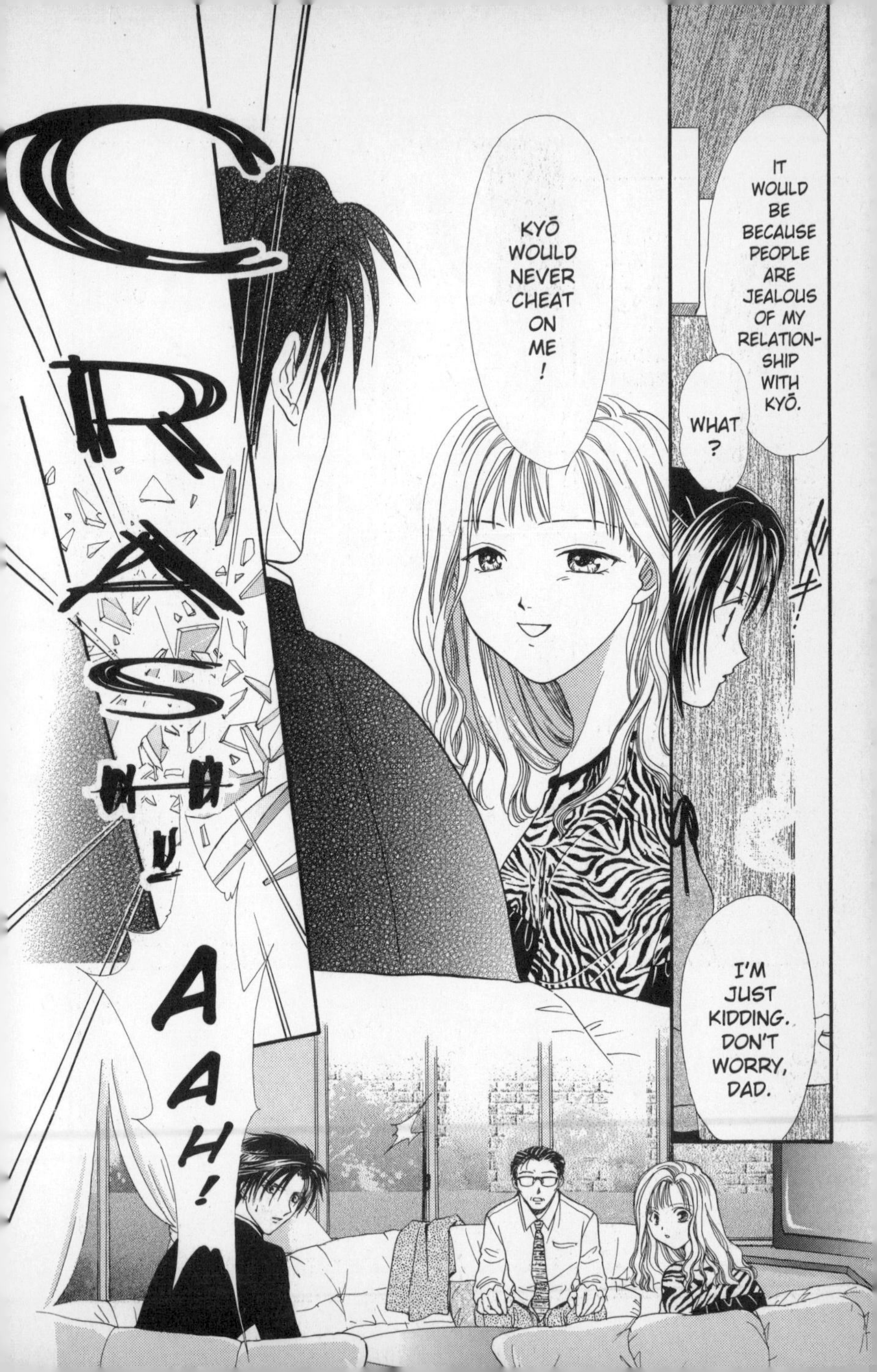
IT WOULD BE BECAUSE PEOPLE ARE JEALOUS OF MY RELATION-SHIP WITH KYŌ.
WHAT?
I'M JUST KIDDING. DON'T WORRY, DAD.
KYŌ WOULD NEVER CHEAT ON ME!
CRASH
AAH!

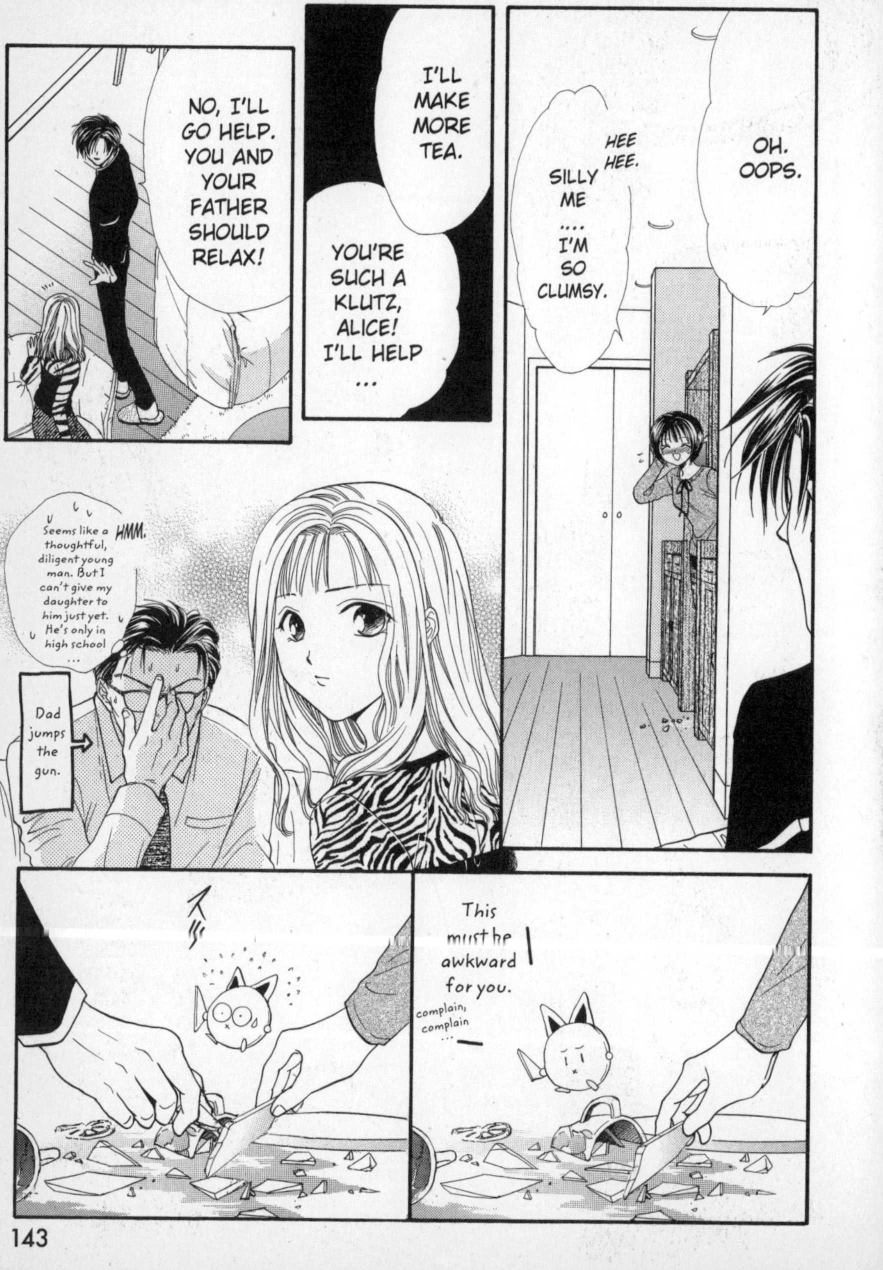
OH. OOPS.
HEE HEE.
SILLY ME .... I'M SO CLUMSY.
I'LL MAKE MORE TEA.
YOU'RE SUCH A KLUTZ, ALICE! I'LL HELP ...
NO, I'LL GO HELP. YOU AND YOUR FATHER SHOULD RELAX!
HMM.
Seems like a thoughtful, diligent young man. But I can't give my daughter to him just yet. He's only in high school ...
Dad jumps the gun.
This must be awkward for you.
complain, complain ...

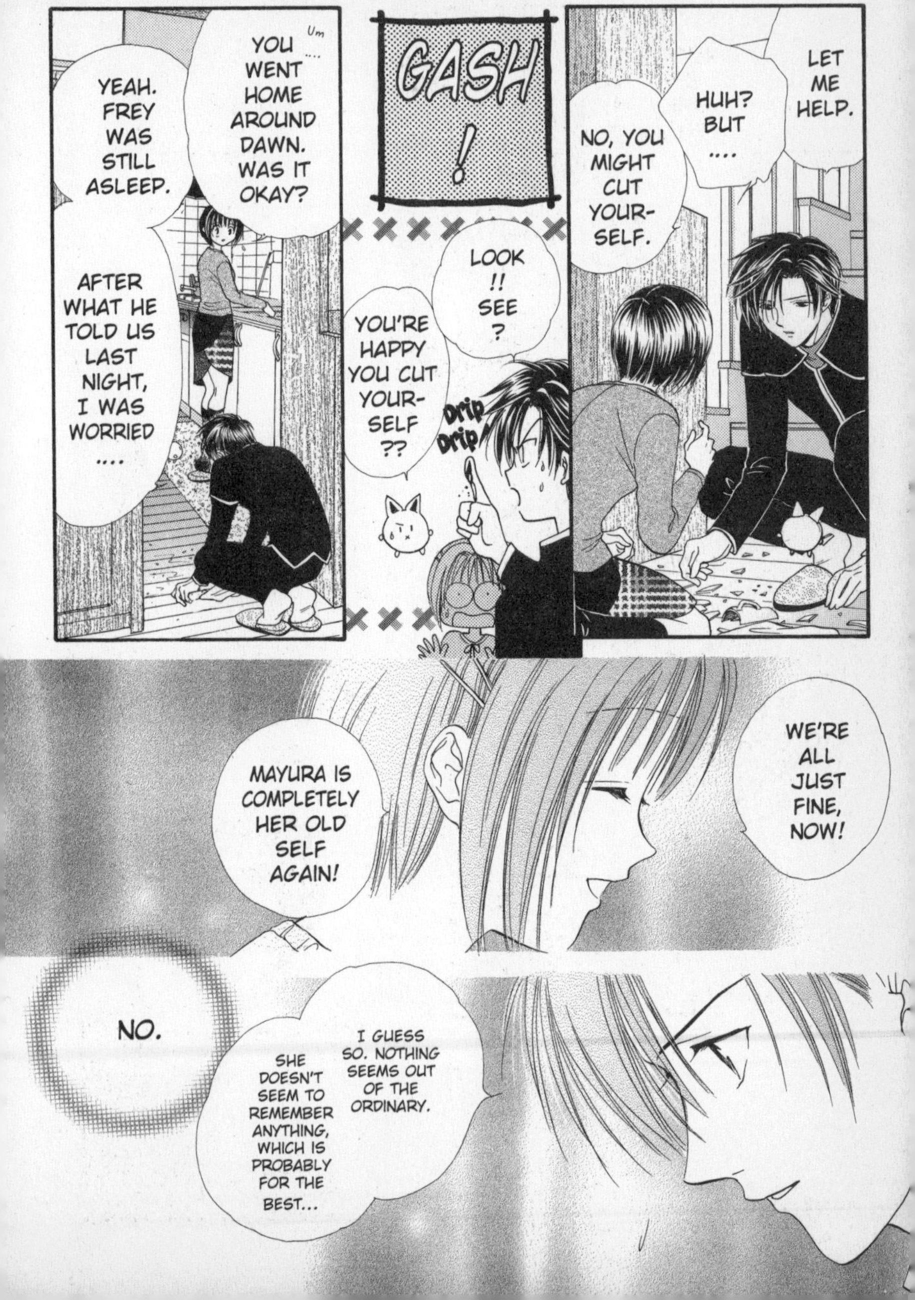
LET ME HELP.
HUH? BUT ....
NO, YOU MIGHT CUT YOURSELF.
GASH!
LOOK!! SEE?
YOU'RE HAPPY YOU CUT YOURSELF??
Drip Drip
Um ....
YOU WENT HOME AROUND DAWN. WAS IT OKAY?
YEAH. FREY WAS STILL ASLEEP.
AFTER WHAT HE TOLD US LAST NIGHT, I WAS WORRIED ....
WE'RE ALL JUST FINE, NOW!
MAYURA IS COMPLETELY HER OLD SELF AGAIN!
I GUESS SO. NOTHING SEEMS OUT OF THE ORDINARY.
SHE DOESN'T SEEM TO REMEMBER ANYTHING, WHICH IS PROBABLY FOR THE BEST...
NO.

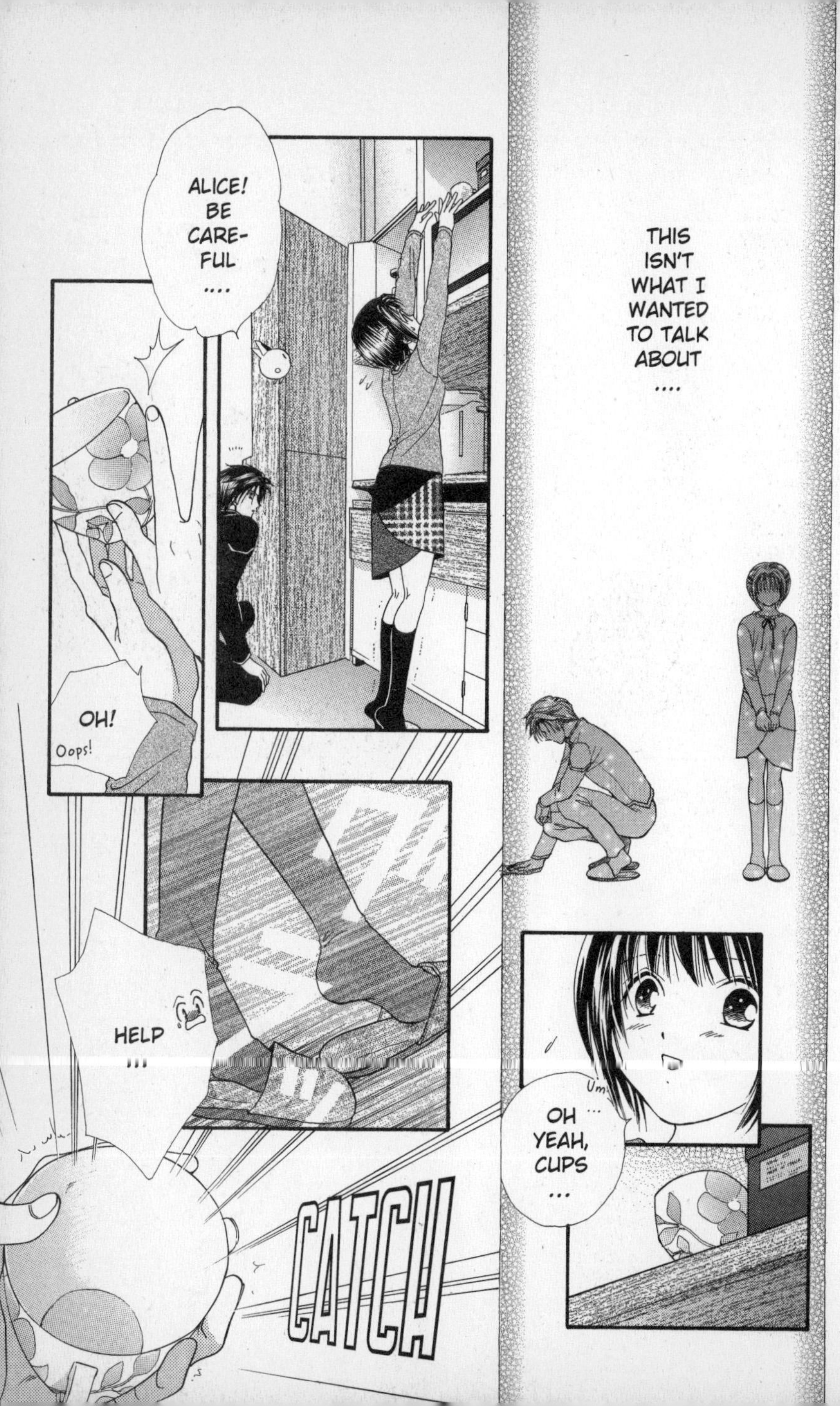
THIS ISN'T WHAT I WANTED TO TALK ABOUT ....
Um ...
OH YEAH, CUPS ...
ALICE! BE CARE-FUL ....
OH!
Oops!
HELP !!!
CATCH

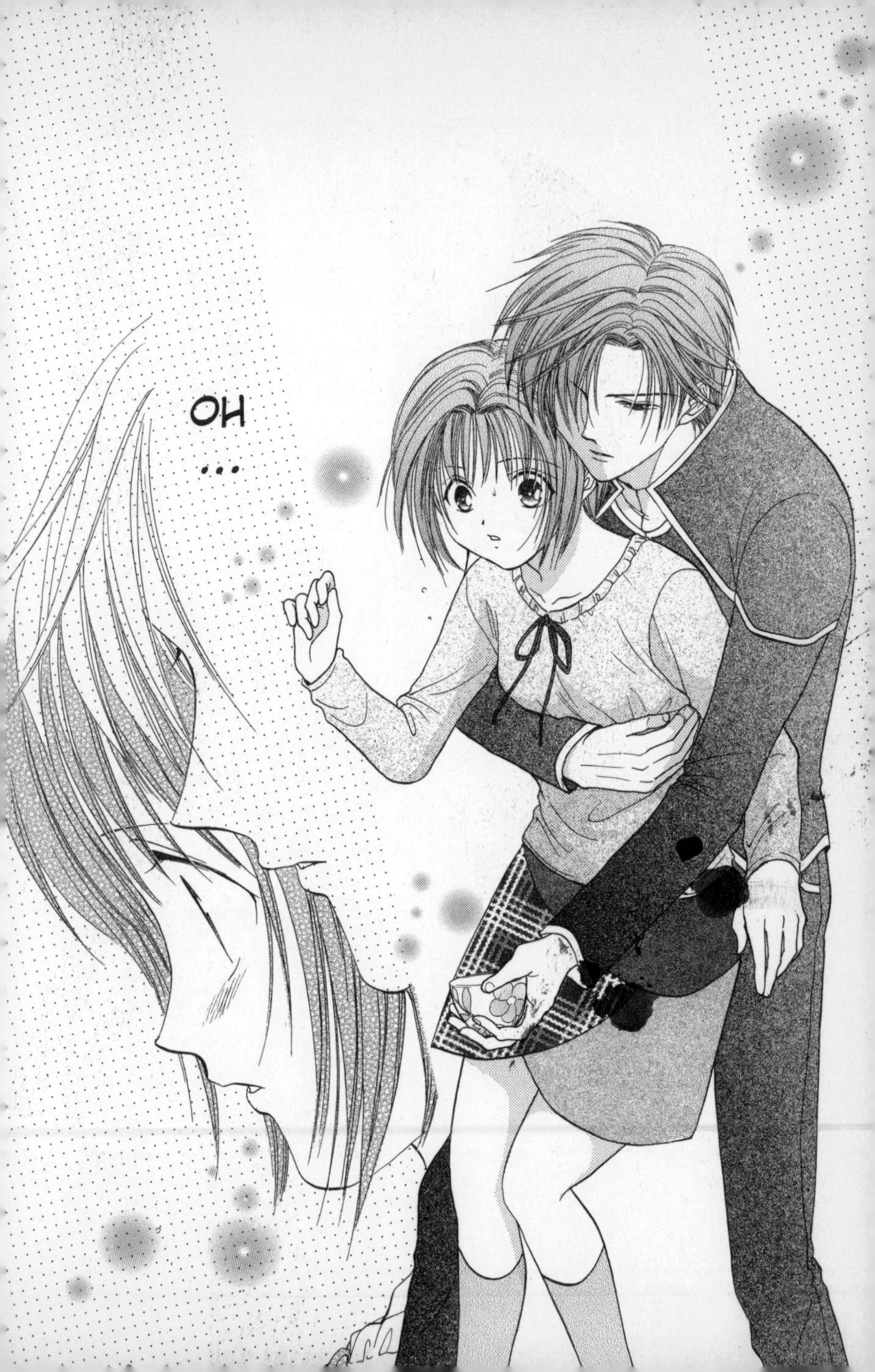
OH
...

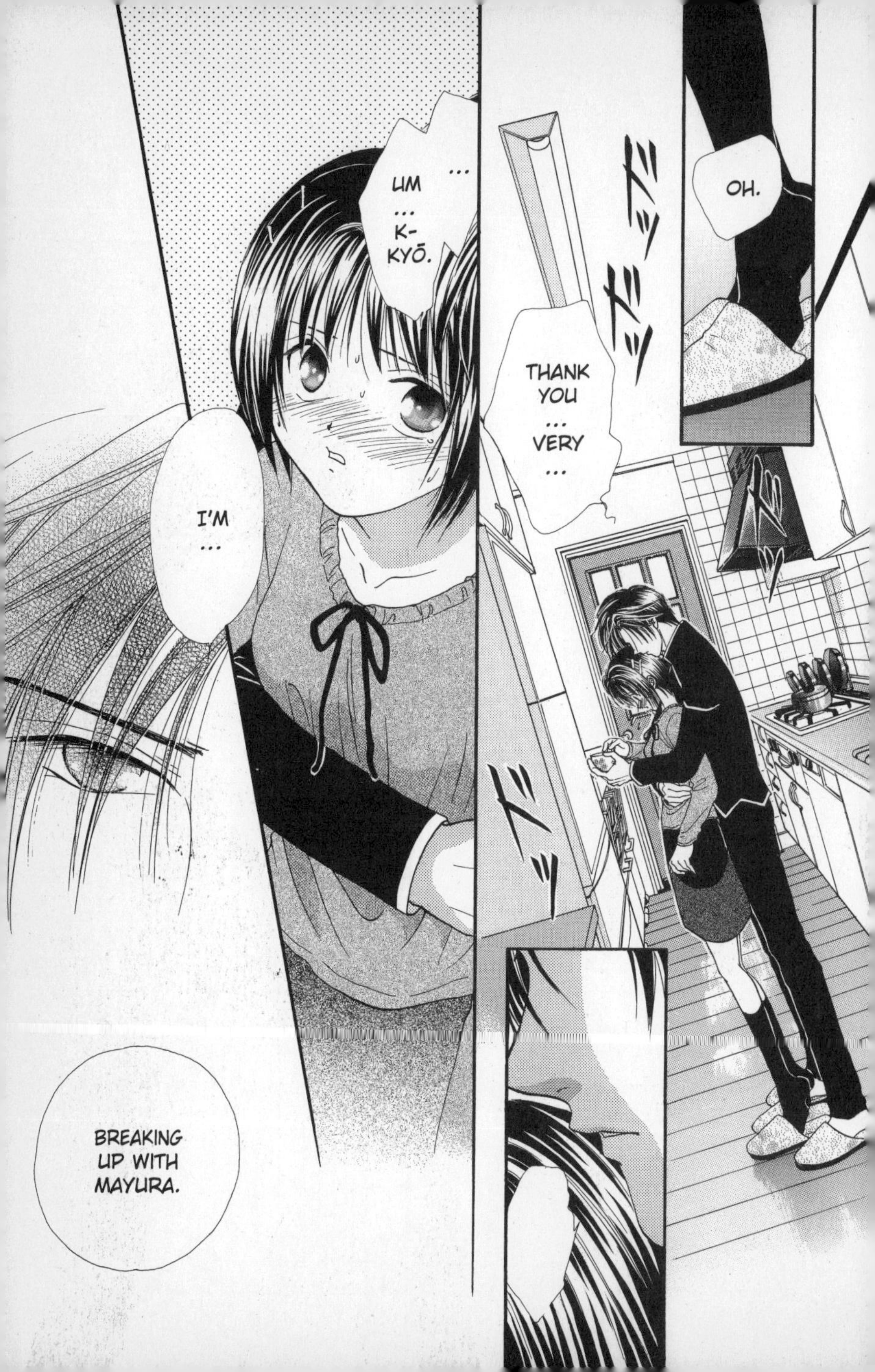
OH.
ドッドッ
THANK YOU ... VERY ...
ドッ
... UM ... K-KYŌ.
I'M ...
BREAKING UP WITH MAYURA.

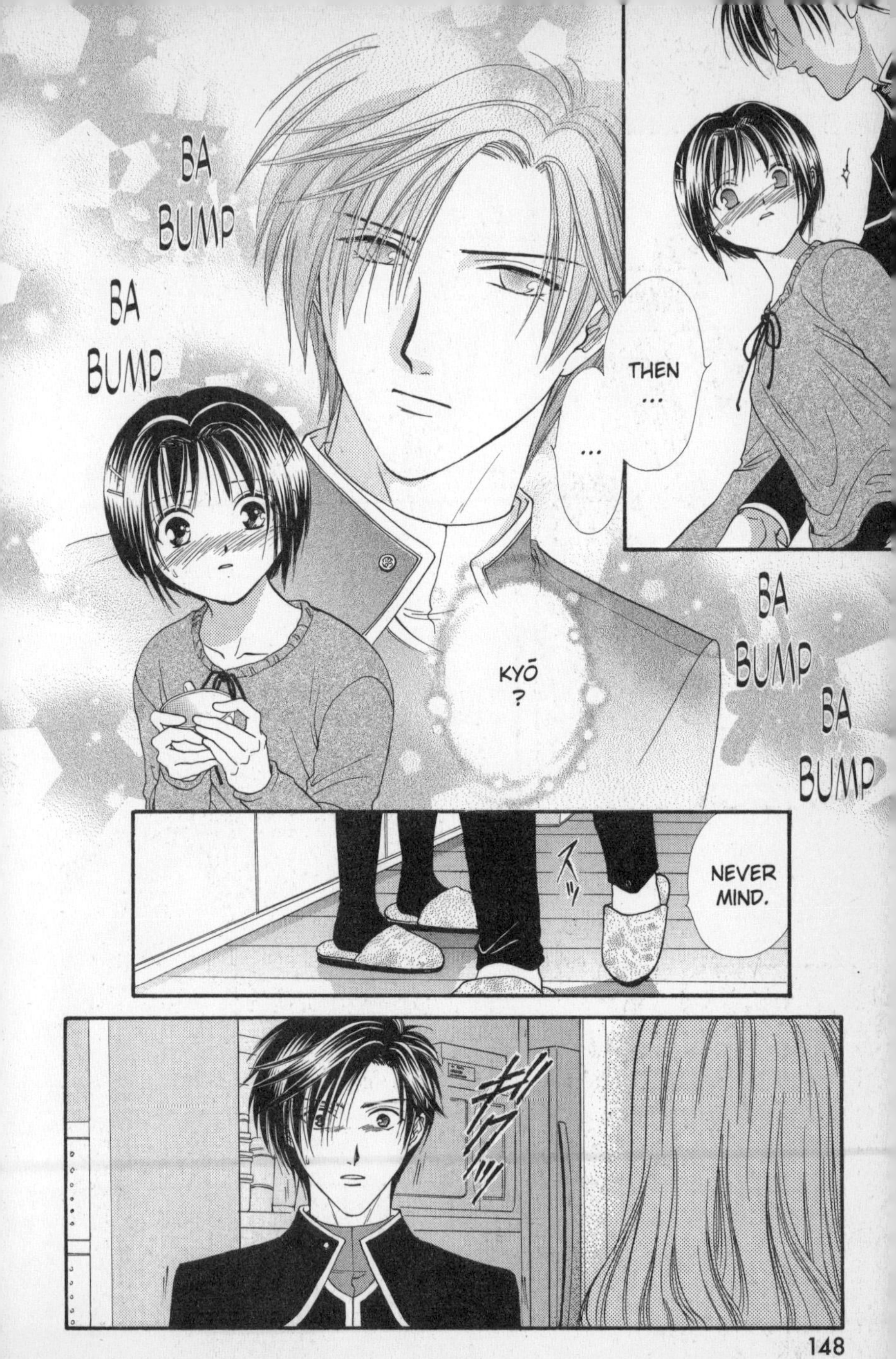
THEN ...
...
BA BUMP
BA BUMP
KYŌ ?
BA BUMP
BA BUMP
NEVER MIND.
ズッ

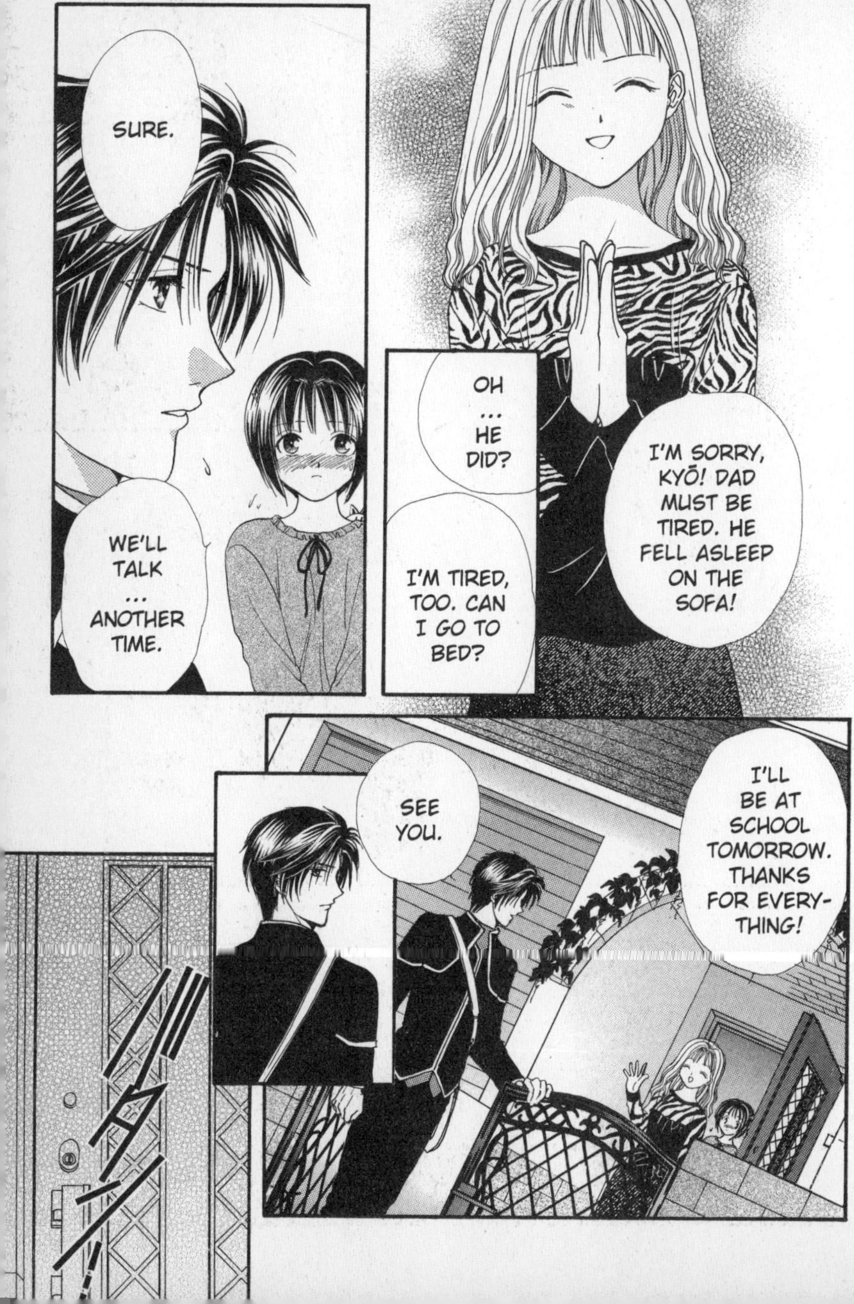
I'M SORRY, KYŌ! DAD MUST BE TIRED. HE FELL ASLEEP ON THE SOFA!
OH ... HE DID?
I'M TIRED, TOO. CAN I GO TO BED?
SURE.
WE'LL TALK ... ANOTHER TIME.
I'LL BE AT SCHOOL TOMORROW. THANKS FOR EVERY-THING!
SEE YOU.

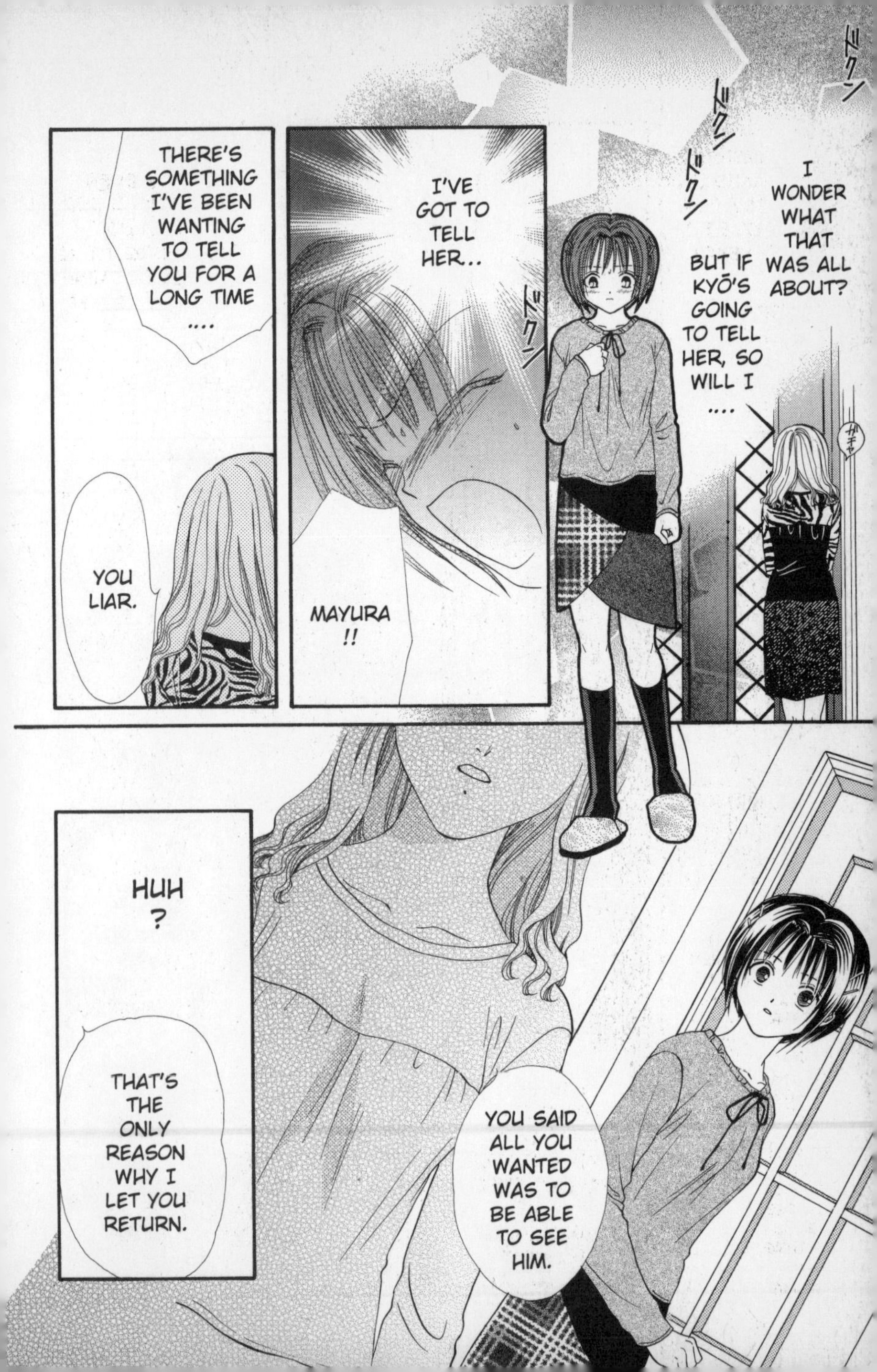
ドクン
ドクン
ドクン
I WONDER WHAT THAT WAS ALL ABOUT?
BUT IF KYŌ'S GOING TO TELL HER, SO WILL I ....
ガチャ
ドクン
I'VE GOT TO TELL HER...
MAYURA !!
THERE'S SOMETHING I'VE BEEN WANTING TO TELL YOU FOR A LONG TIME ....
YOU LIAR.
HUH ?
YOU SAID ALL YOU WANTED WAS TO BE ABLE TO SEE HIM.
THAT'S THE ONLY REASON WHY I LET YOU RETURN.

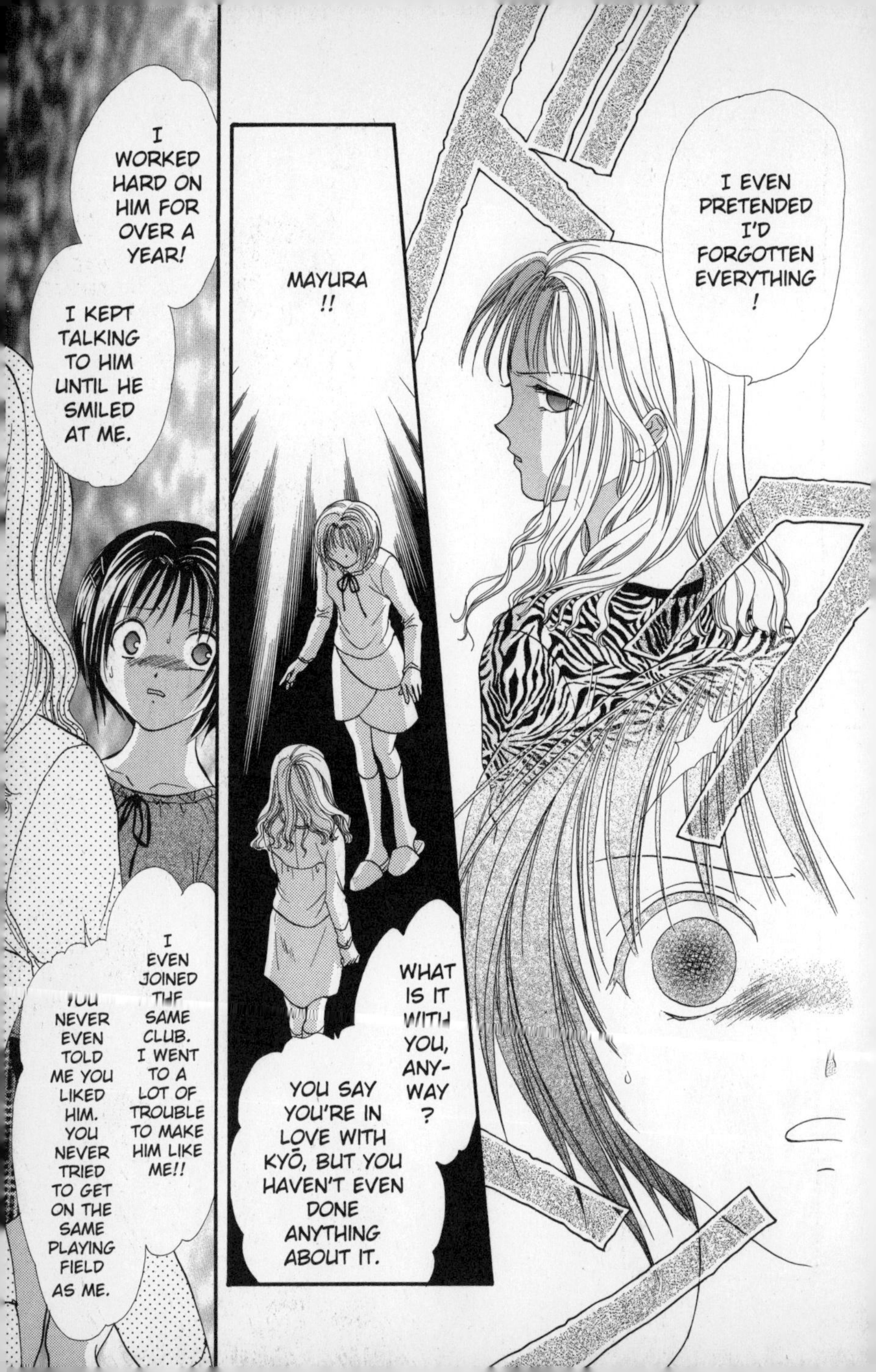
I EVEN PRETENDED I'D FORGOTTEN EVERYTHING!
MAYURA!!
WHAT IS IT WITH YOU, ANYWAY?
YOU SAY YOU'RE IN LOVE WITH KYŌ, BUT YOU HAVEN'T EVEN DONE ANYTHING ABOUT IT.
I WORKED HARD ON HIM FOR OVER A YEAR!
I KEPT TALKING TO HIM UNTIL HE SMILED AT ME.
I EVEN JOINED THE SAME CLUB. I WENT TO A LOT OF TROUBLE TO MAKE HIM LIKE ME!!
YOU NEVER EVEN TOLD ME YOU LIKED HIM. YOU NEVER TRIED TO GET ON THE SAME PLAYING FIELD AS ME.

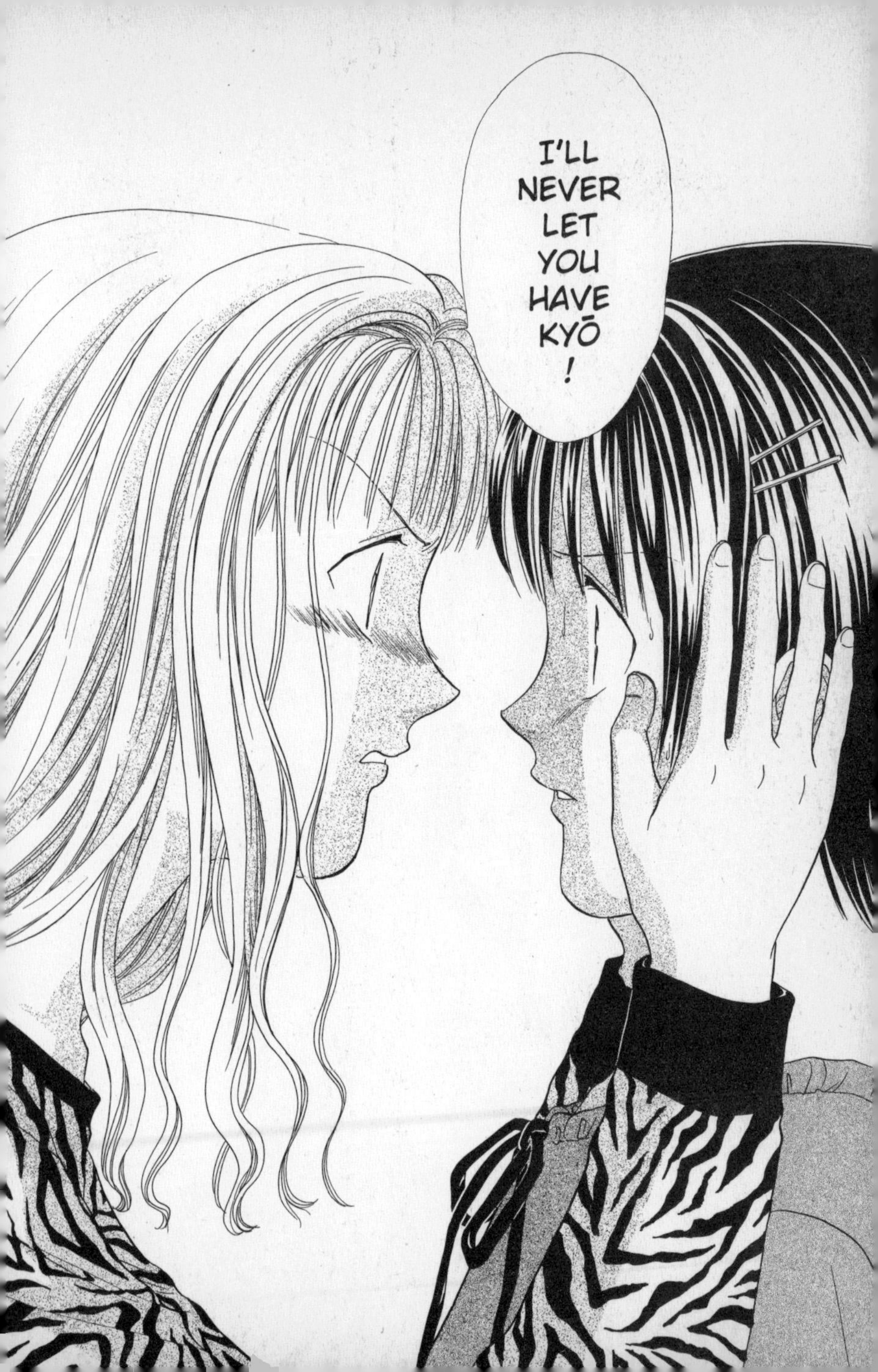
I'LL NEVER LET YOU HAVE KYŌ!

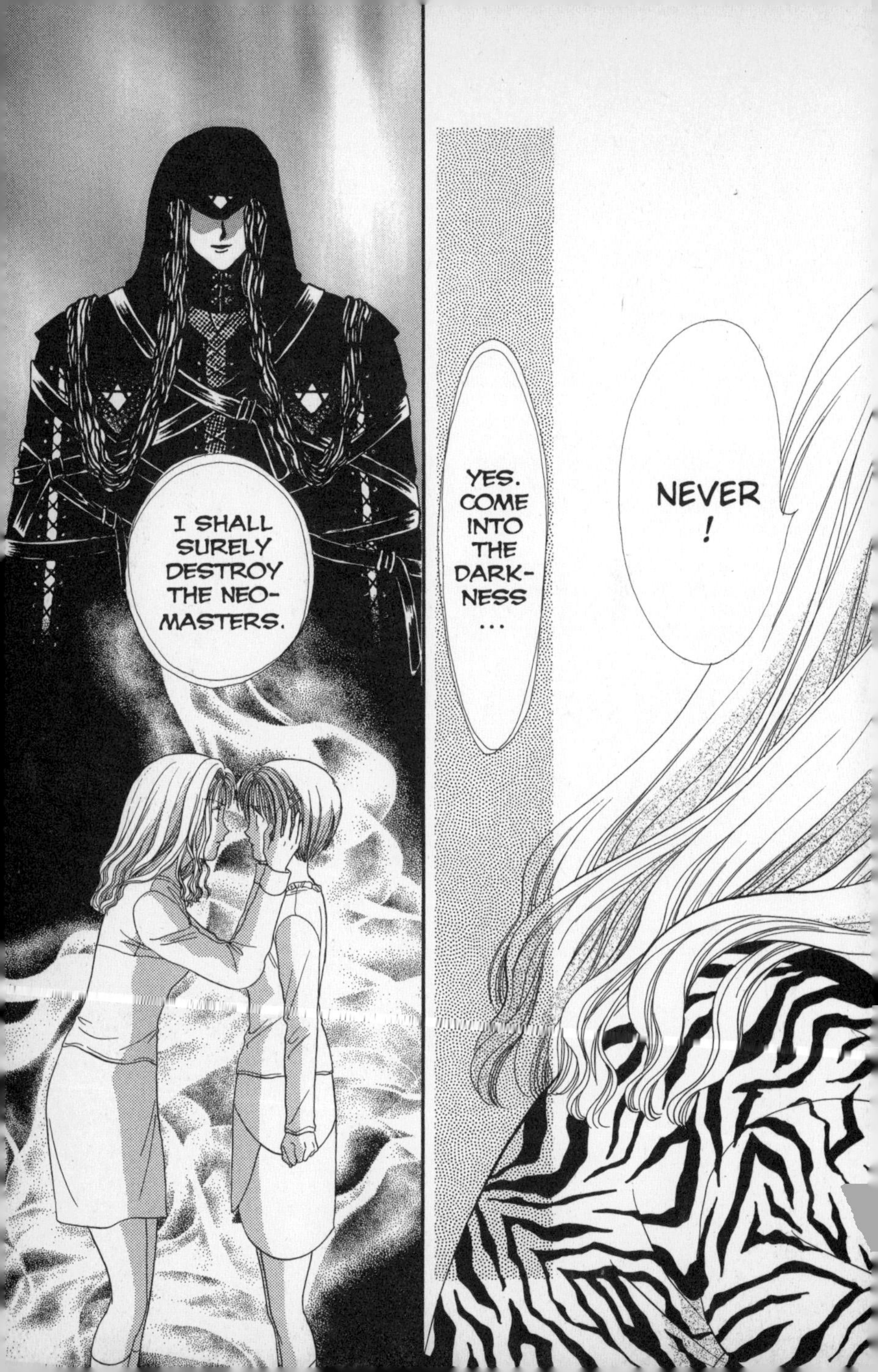
NEVER!
YES. COME INTO THE DARKNESS...
I SHALL SURELY DESTROY THE NEO-MASTERS.

KYŌ WAKAMIYA

❦ 181 CM TALL

❦ TAURUS (5/12)

❦ BLOOD TYPE A

❦ VISION: RIGHT 0.3, LEFT 0.5 USUALLY WEARS CONTACT LENSES.

❦ ELEMENTARY SCHOOL ACTIVITIES: KENDO (JAPANESE FENCING) AND CALLIGRAPHY. JOINED ARCHERY CLUB IN HIGH SCHOOL.

❦ UPRIGHT, HARDWORKING, DEMANDS A LOT OF HIMSELF. USUALLY CALM AND GOOD-HEARTED, BUT PRONE TO EMOTIONAL OUT-BURSTS. AFTER HIS PARENTS PASSED AWAY, HE LIVED WITH A SERIES OF RELATIVES. PERHAPS THIS IS WHY, THOUGH HE TRIES TO BE RESPECTFUL, HE ALWAYS DISTANCES HIMSELF FROM OTHERS.

❦ EXCELS IN ALL SUBJECTS AT SCHOOL.

❦ HOBBY: READING. HABITUALLY TALKS IN 4-CHARACTER COMPOUND WORDS.

❦ UNIQUE SKILL: MAKING WESTERN-STYLE CON-FECTIONS. (FOR HIS AUNT AND UNCLE WITH WHOM HE LIVES)

❦ THOUGH HE HATES VIOLENT BULLIES LIKE HIS DRUNKEN FATHER, KYŌ IS PLAGUED BY FEARS THAT HE WILL BECOME ONE HIMSELF.

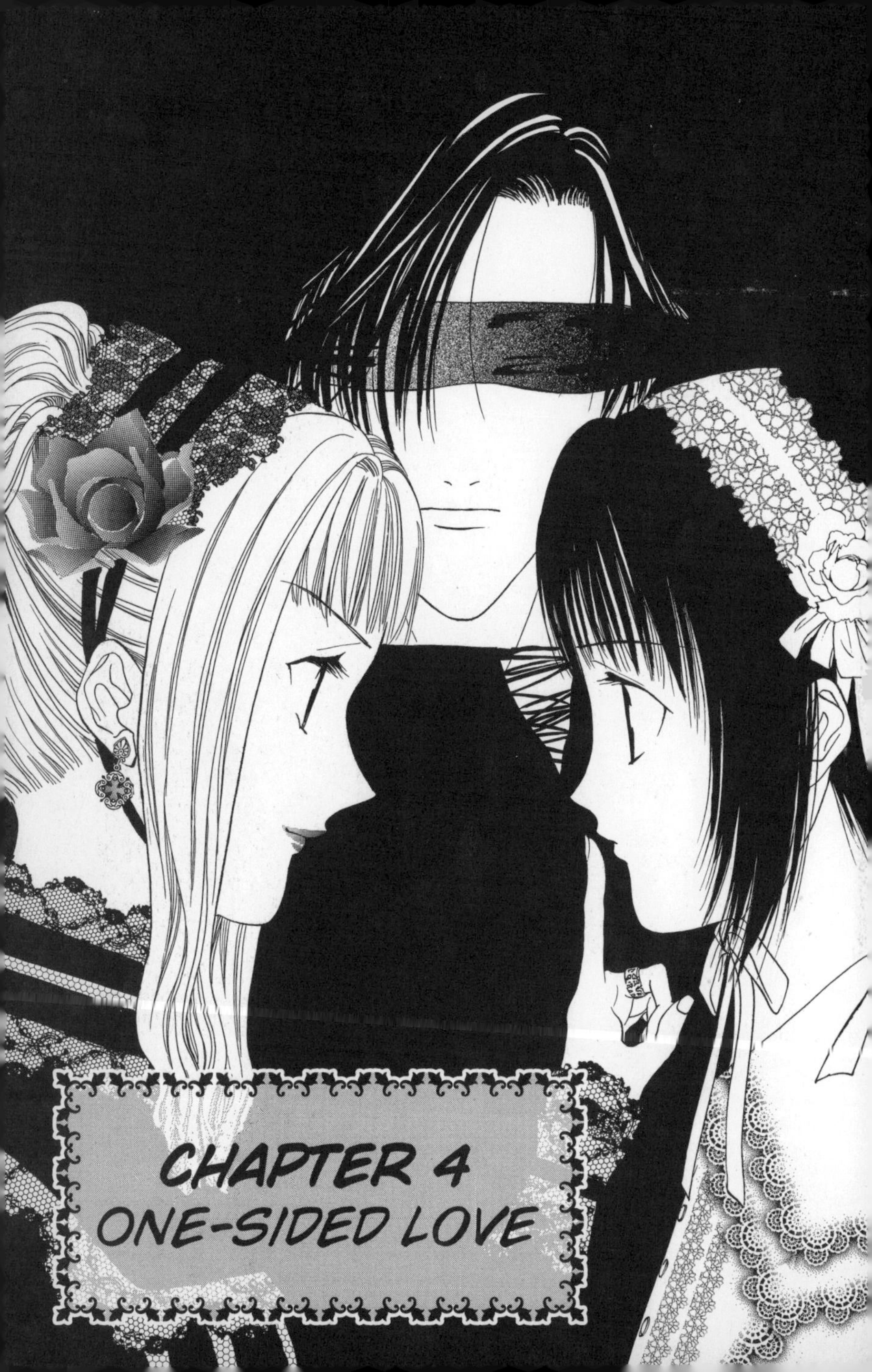
CHAPTER 4
ONE-SIDED LOVE

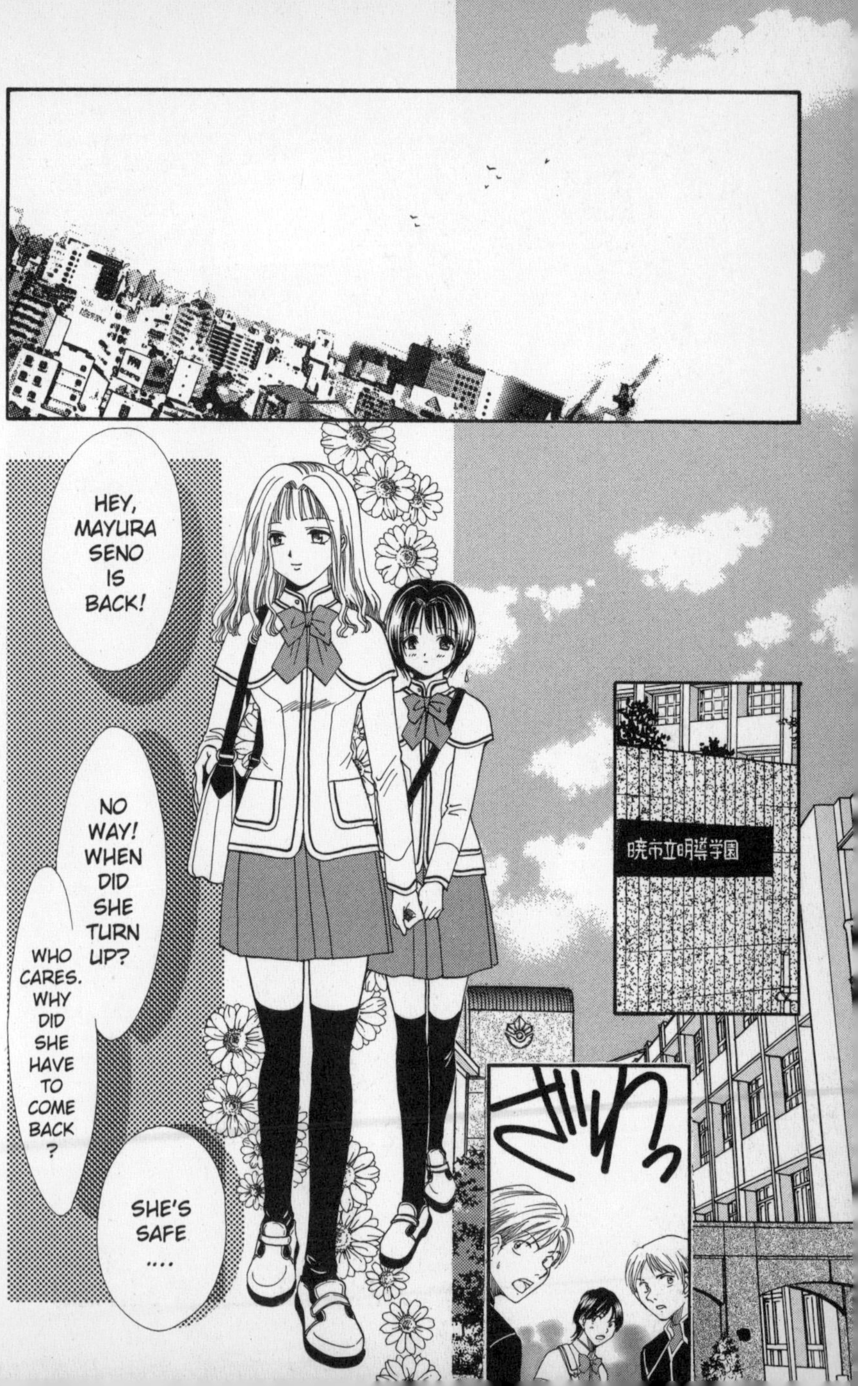

暁市立明導学園
ざわっ
HEY, MAYURA SENO IS BACK!
NO WAY! WHEN DID SHE TURN UP?
WHO CARES. WHY DID SHE HAVE TO COME BACK?
SHE'S SAFE....

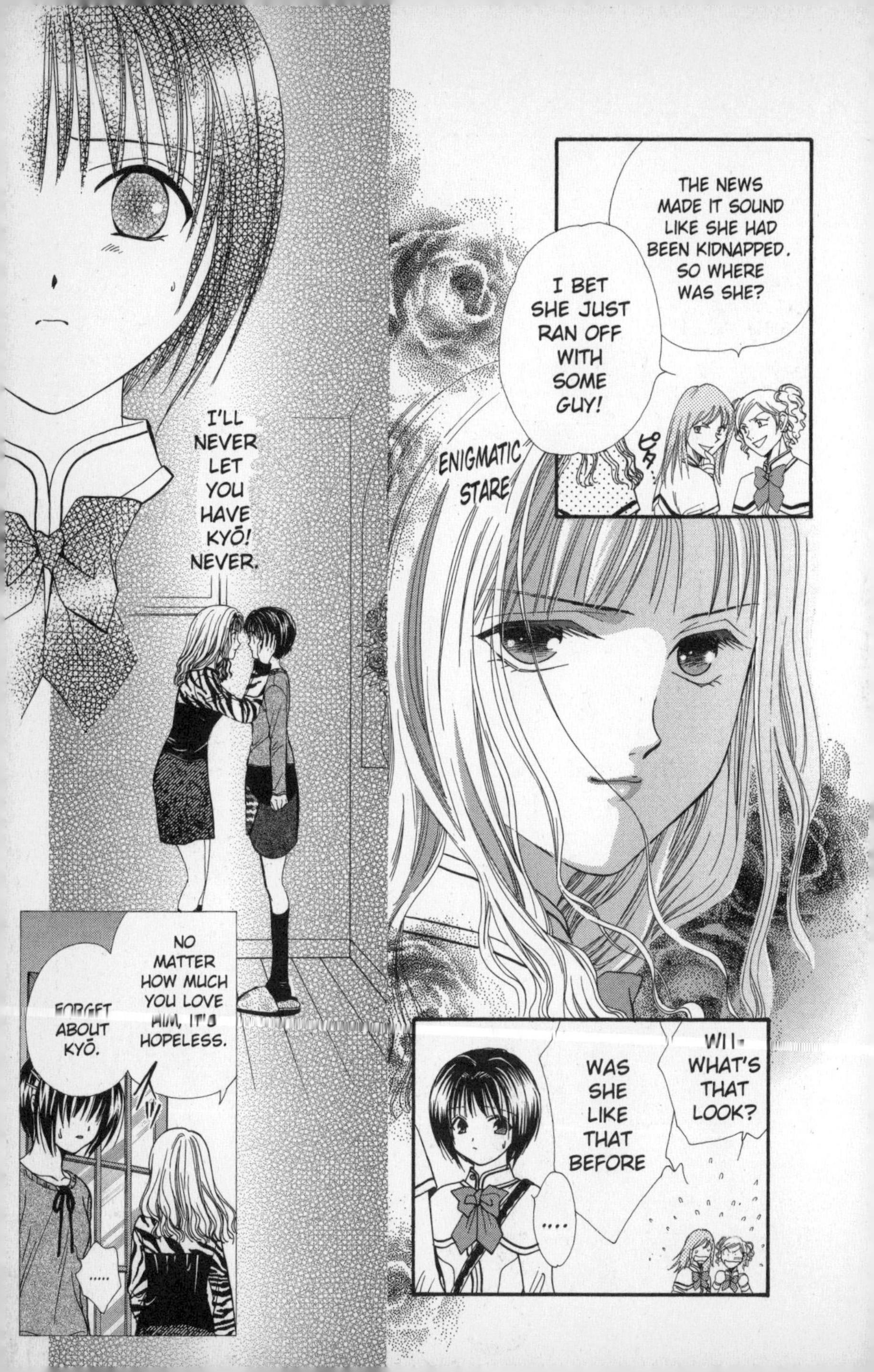
THE NEWS MADE IT SOUND LIKE SHE HAD BEEN KIDNAPPED. SO WHERE WAS SHE?
I BET SHE JUST RAN OFF WITH SOME GUY!
ENIGMATIC STARE
WH- WHAT'S THAT LOOK?
WAS SHE LIKE THAT BEFORE
....
I'LL NEVER LET YOU HAVE KYŌ! NEVER.
NO MATTER HOW MUCH YOU LOVE HIM, IT'S HOPELESS.
FORGET ABOUT KYŌ.
.....

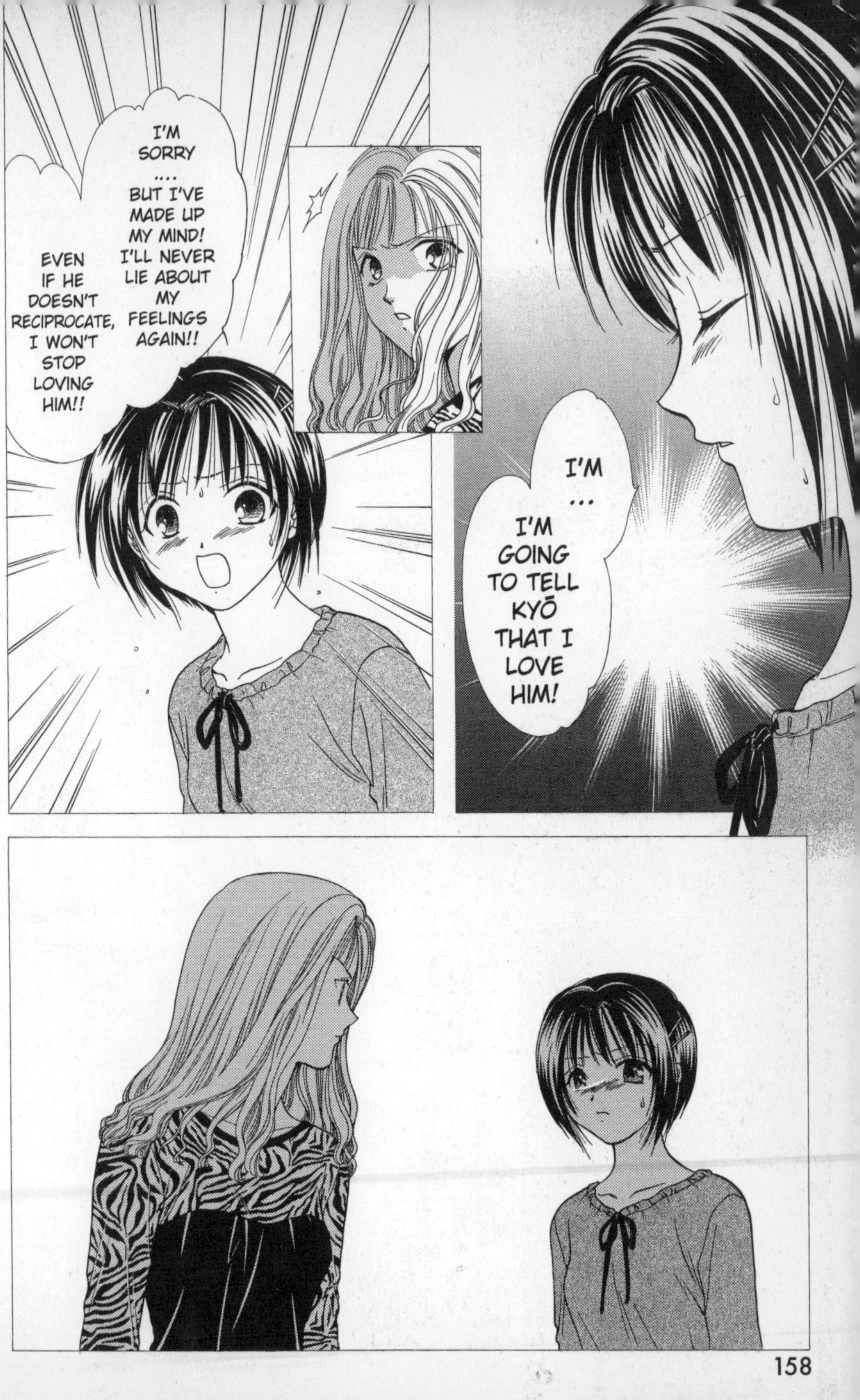
I'M ... I'M GOING TO TELL KYŌ THAT I LOVE HIM!
I'M SORRY .... BUT I'VE MADE UP MY MIND! I'LL NEVER LIE ABOUT MY FEELINGS AGAIN!!
EVEN IF HE DOESN'T RECIPROCATE, I WON'T STOP LOVING HIM!!

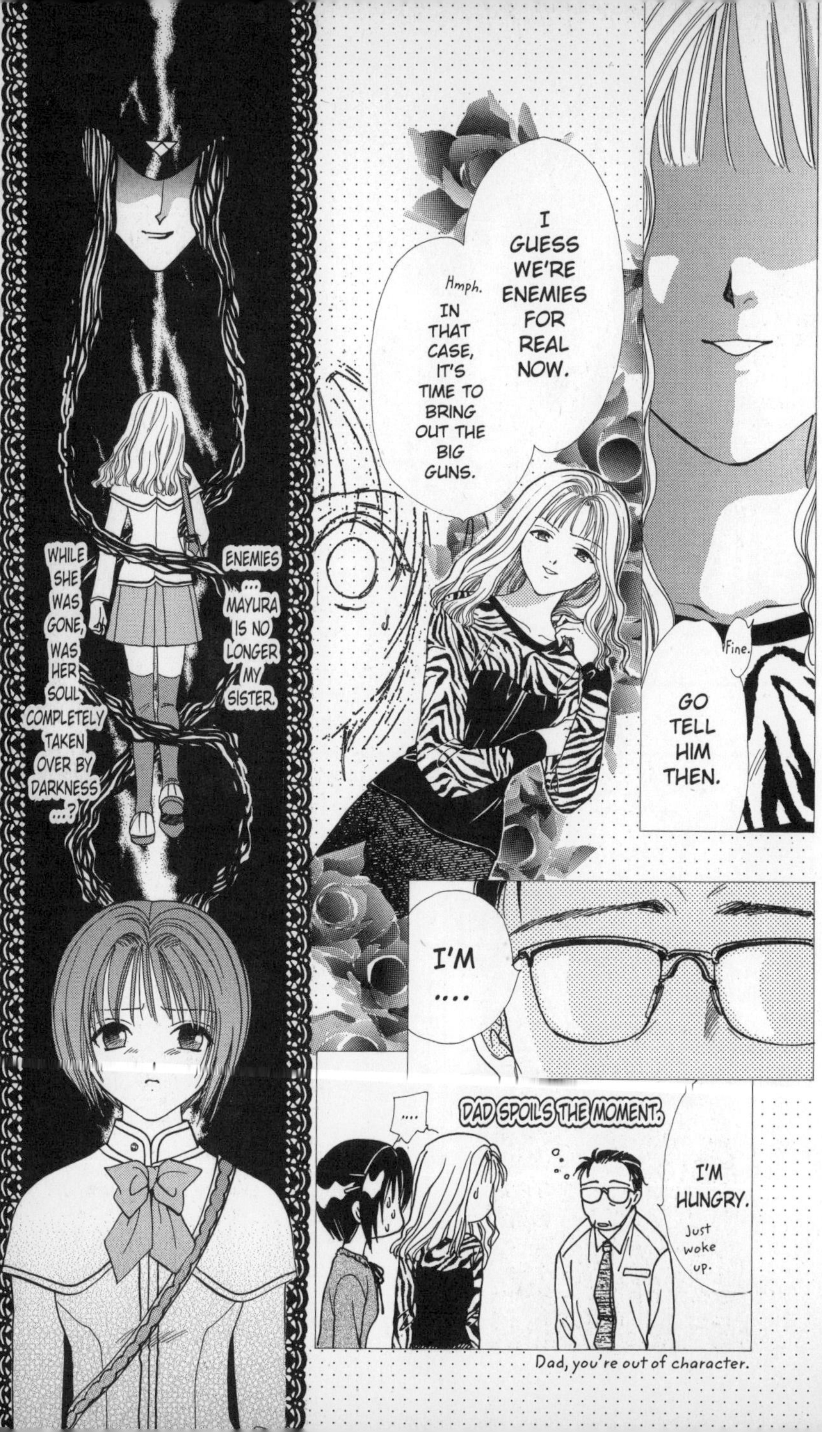
Fine.
GO TELL HIM THEN.
I GUESS WE'RE ENEMIES FOR REAL NOW.
Hmph.
IN THAT CASE, IT'S TIME TO BRING OUT THE BIG GUNS.
I'M ....
DAD SPOILS THE MOMENT.
I'M HUNGRY.
Just woke up.
....
Dad, you're out of character.
ENEMIES ... MAYURA IS NO LONGER MY SISTER.
WHILE SHE WAS GONE, WAS HER SOUL COMPLETELY TAKEN OVER BY DARKNESS ...?

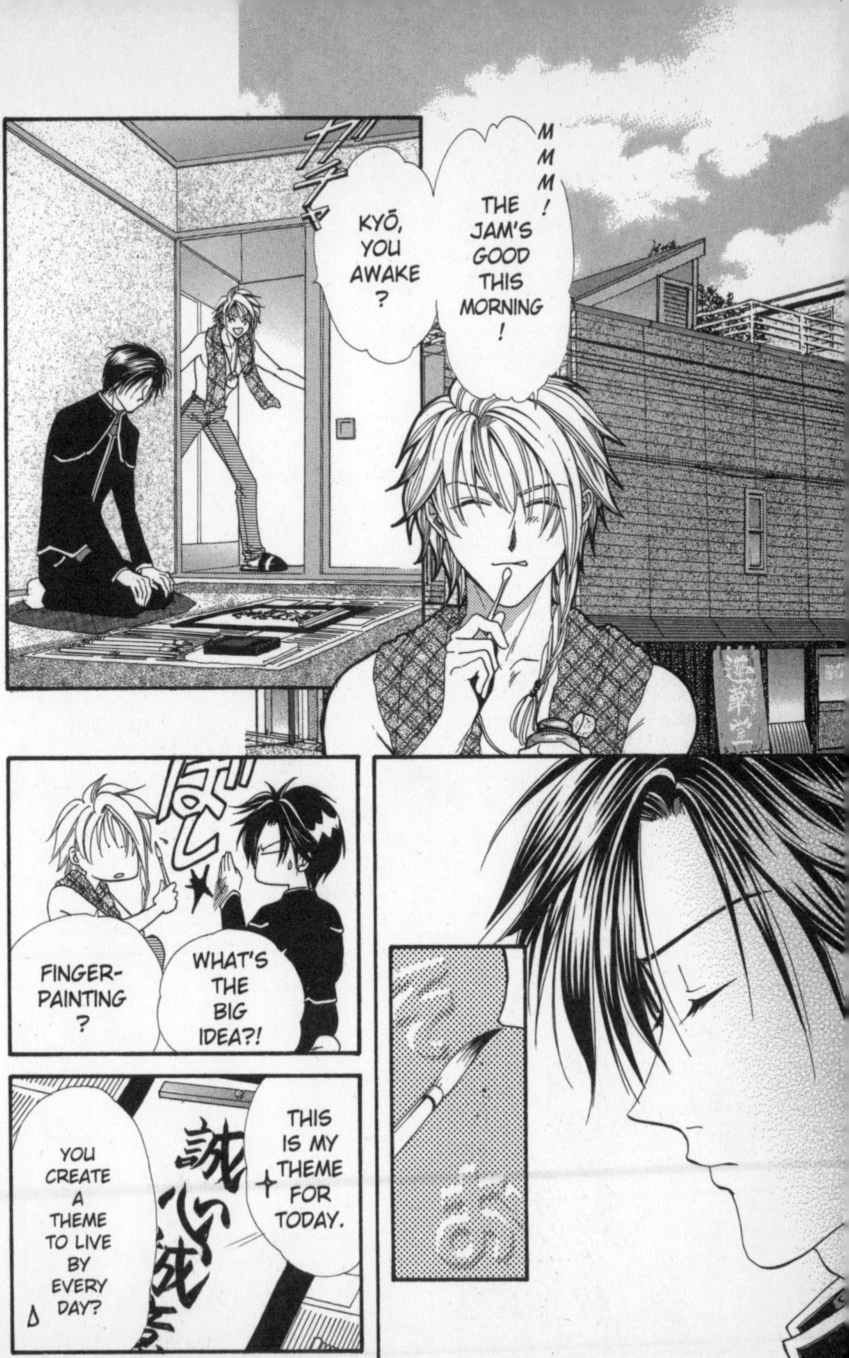
MMM! THE JAM'S GOOD THIS MORNING!
KYŌ, YOU AWAKE?
WHAT'S THE BIG IDEA?!
FINGER-PAINTING?
THIS IS MY THEME FOR TODAY.
YOU CREATE A THEME TO LIVE BY EVERY DAY?

"Heart and Soul"

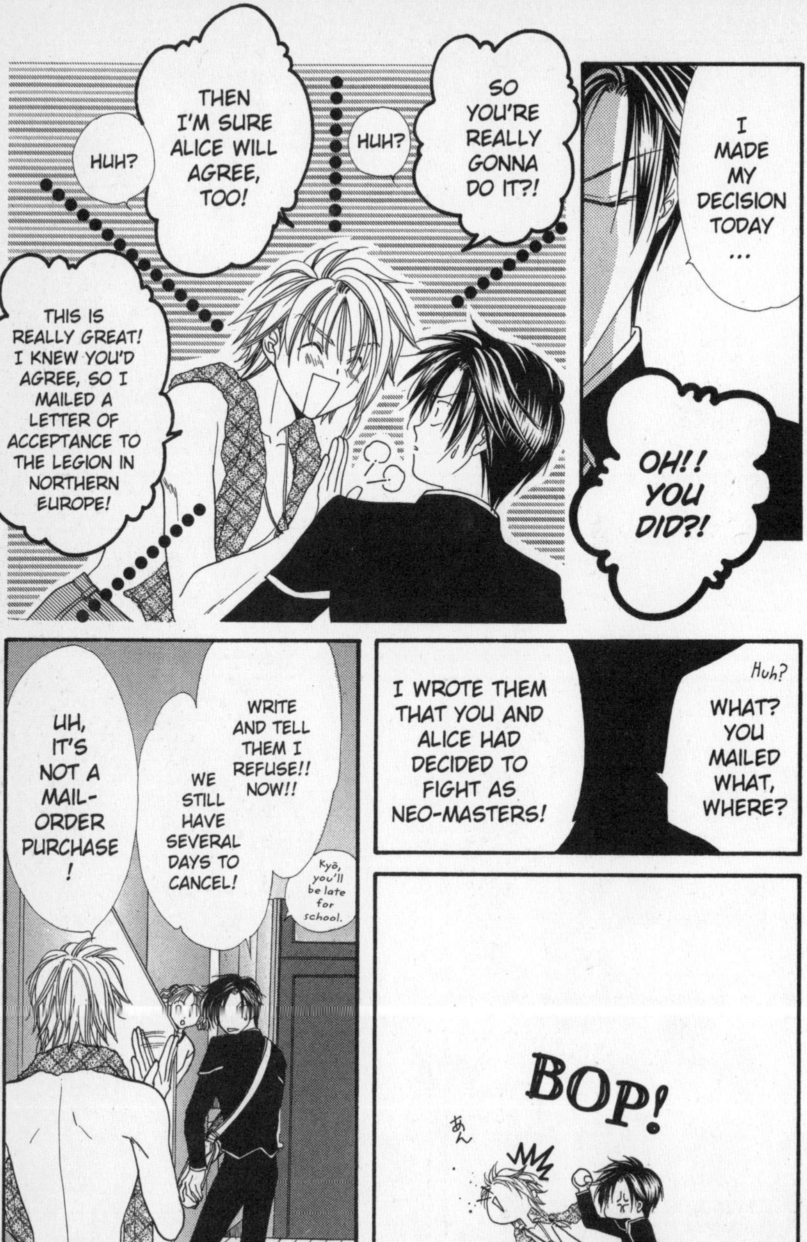
I MADE MY DECISION TODAY...
OH!! YOU DID?!
SO YOU'RE REALLY GONNA DO IT?!
HUH?
THEN I'M SURE ALICE WILL AGREE, TOO!
HUH?
THIS IS REALLY GREAT! I KNEW YOU'D AGREE, SO I MAILED A LETTER OF ACCEPTANCE TO THE LEGION IN NORTHERN EUROPE!
Huh?
WHAT? YOU MAILED WHAT, WHERE?
I WROTE THEM THAT YOU AND ALICE HAD DECIDED TO FIGHT AS NEO-MASTERS!
BOP!
あん
WRITE AND TELL THEM I REFUSE!! NOW!!
UH, IT'S NOT A MAIL-ORDER PURCHASE!
WE STILL HAVE SEVERAL DAYS TO CANCEL!
Kyō, you'll be late for school.

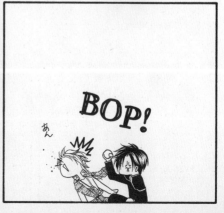

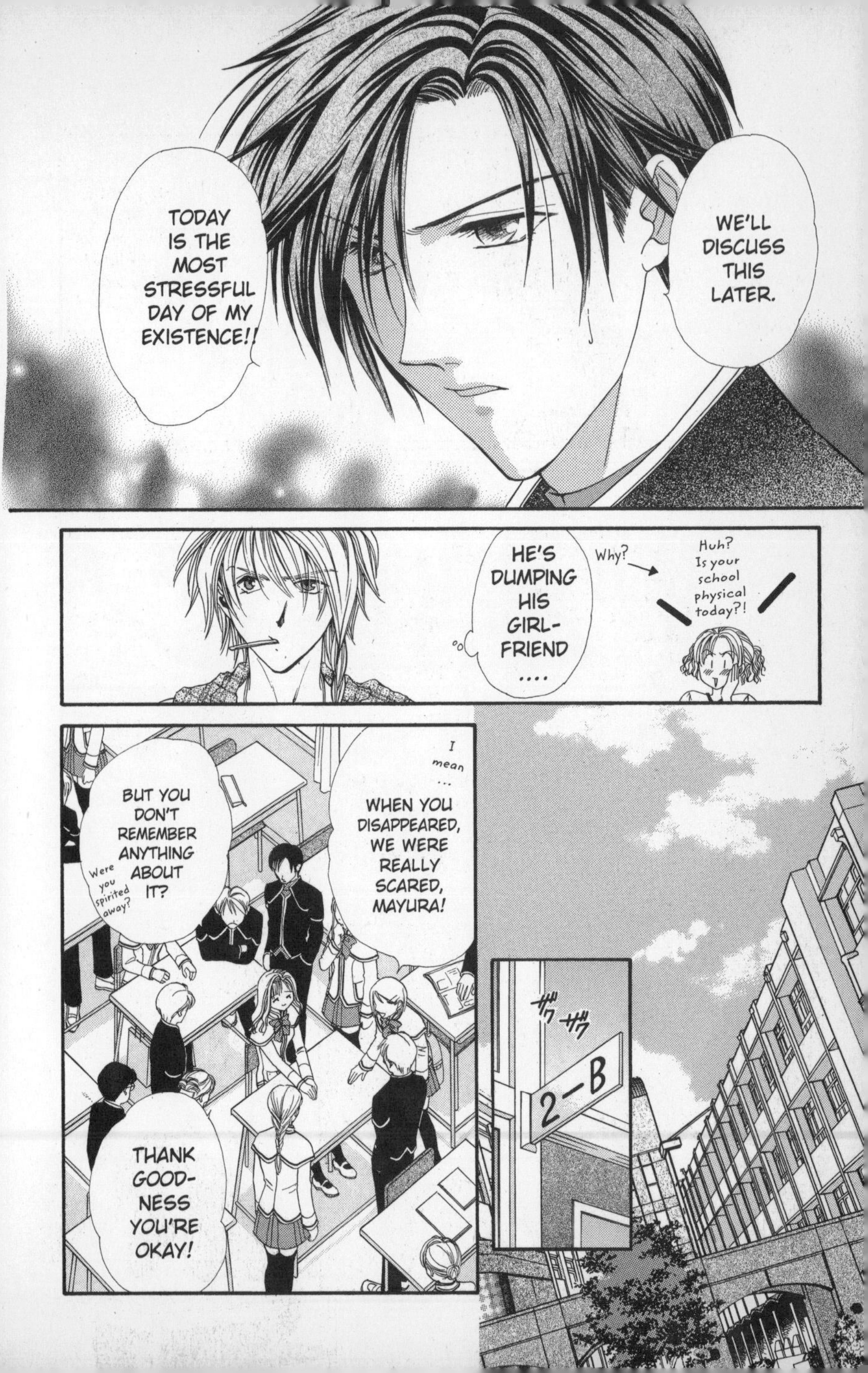
WE'LL DISCUSS THIS LATER.
TODAY IS THE MOST STRESSFUL DAY OF MY EXISTENCE!!
Huh? Is your school physical today?!
Why?
HE'S DUMPING HIS GIRL-FRIEND ....
ザワ ザワ
2-B
I mean ...
WHEN YOU DISAPPEARED, WE WERE REALLY SCARED, MAYURA!
BUT YOU DON'T REMEMBER ANYTHING ABOUT IT?
Were you spirited away?
THANK GOOD-NESS YOU'RE OKAY!

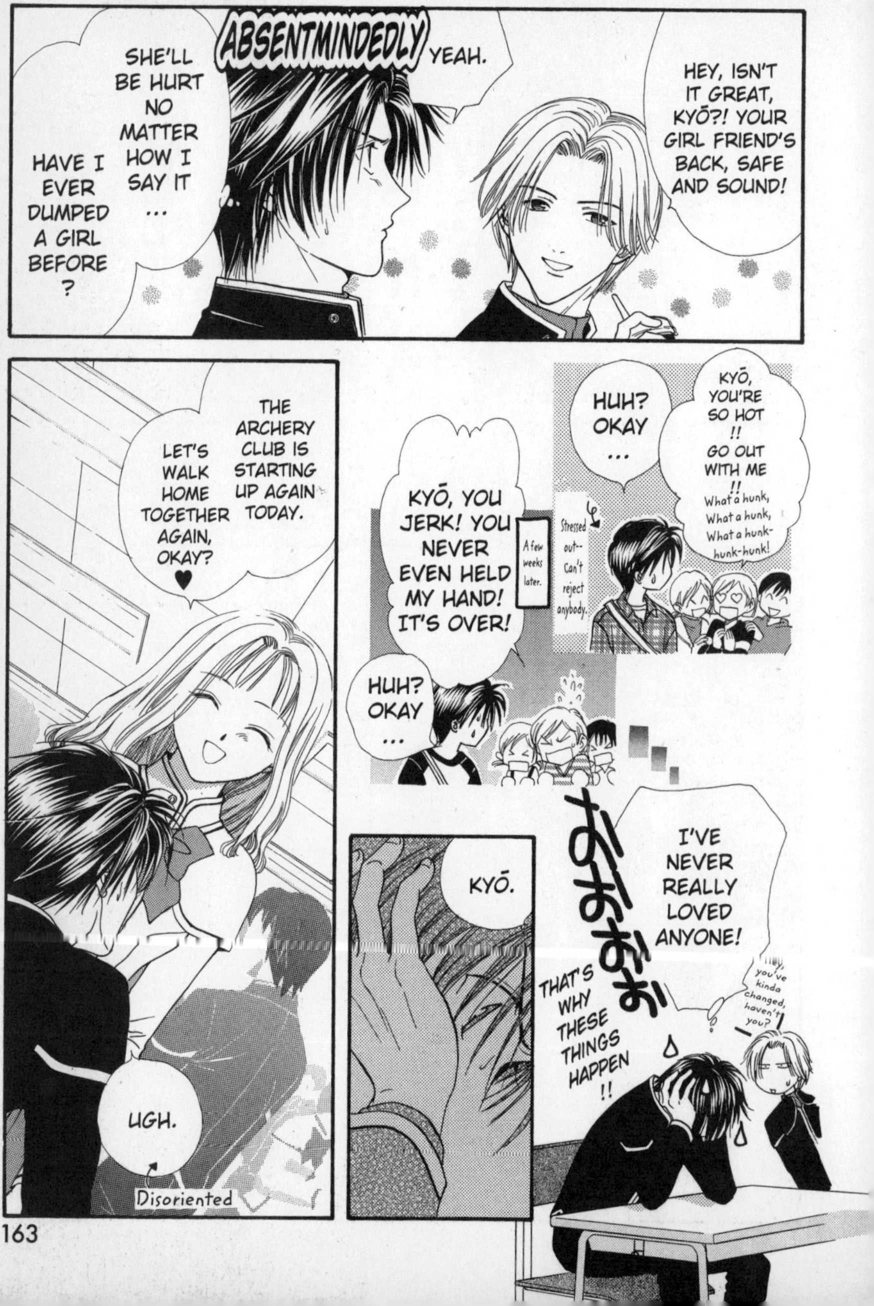
HEY, ISN'T IT GREAT, KYŌ?! YOUR GIRL FRIEND'S BACK, SAFE AND SOUND!
ABSENTMINDEDLY
YEAH.
SHE'LL BE HURT NO MATTER HOW I SAY IT ...
HAVE I EVER DUMPED A GIRL BEFORE?
KYŌ, YOU'RE SO HOT!! GO OUT WITH ME!!
What a hunk, What a hunk, What a hunk-hunk-hunk!
HUH? OKAY ...
Stressed out-- Can't reject anybody.
A few weeks later.
KYŌ, YOU JERK! YOU NEVER EVEN HELD MY HAND! IT'S OVER!
HUH? OKAY ...
I'VE NEVER REALLY LOVED ANYONE!
おおおお
you've kinda changed, haven't you?
THAT'S WHY THESE THINGS HAPPEN!!
KYŌ.
THE ARCHERY CLUB IS STARTING UP AGAIN TODAY.
LET'S WALK HOME TOGETHER AGAIN, OKAY? ♥
UGH.
Disoriented

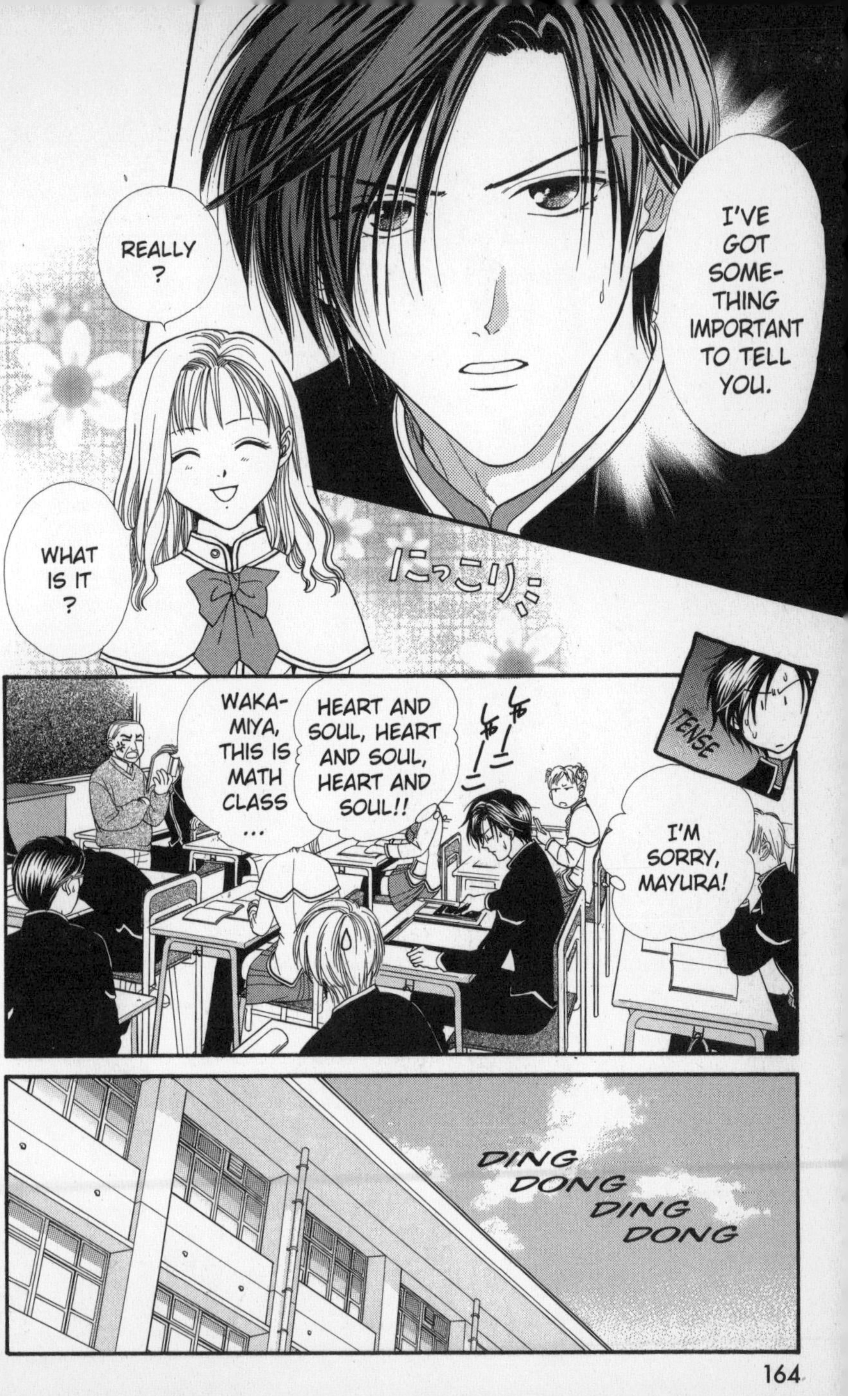
I'VE GOT SOME-THING IMPORTANT TO TELL YOU.
REALLY?
WHAT IS IT?
にっこり
TENSE
I'M SORRY, MAYURA!
HEART AND SOUL, HEART AND SOUL, HEART AND SOUL!!
WAKA-MIYA, THIS IS MATH CLASS...
DING DONG DING DONG

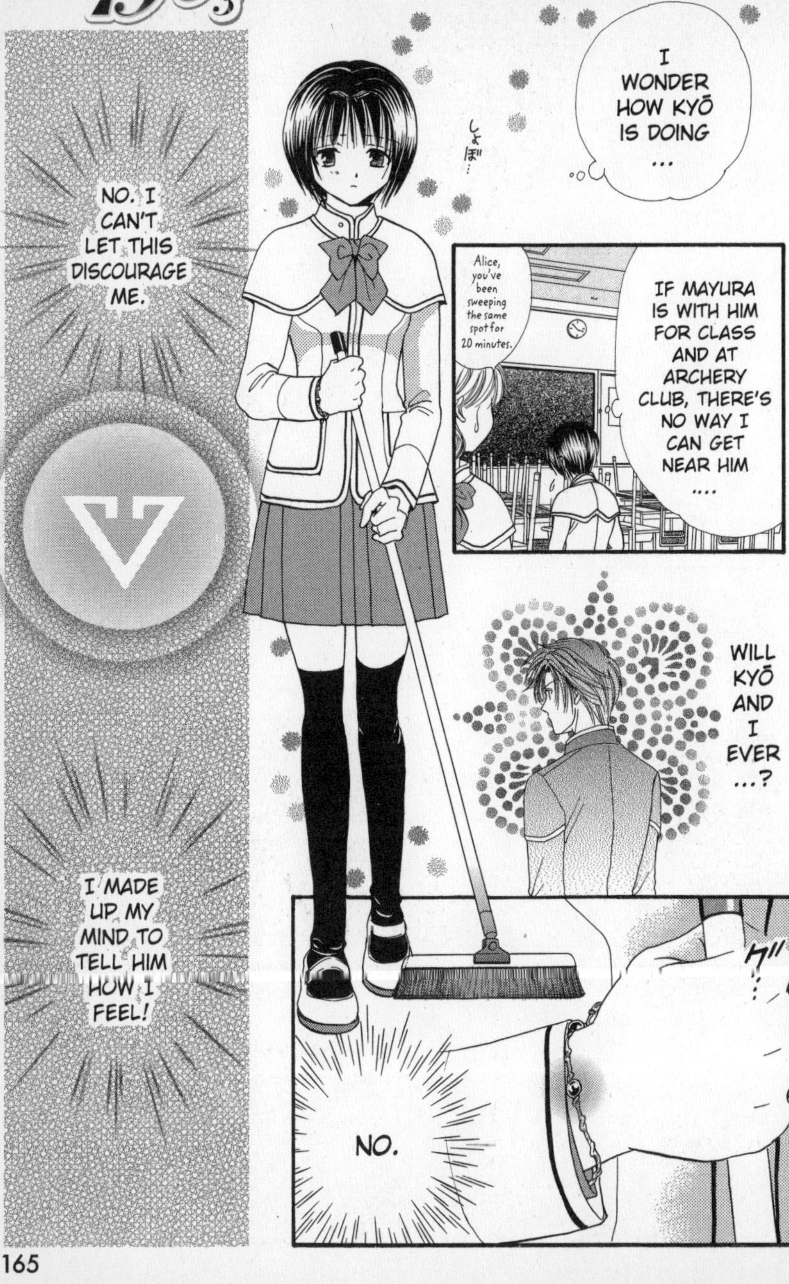
I WONDER HOW KYŌ IS DOING ...
しょぼ…
IF MAYURA IS WITH HIM FOR CLASS AND AT ARCHERY CLUB, THERE'S NO WAY I CAN GET NEAR HIM ....
Alice, you've been sweeping the same spot for 20 minutes.
WILL KYŌ AND I EVER ...?
グッ…
NO.
NO. I CAN'T LET THIS DISCOURAGE ME.
I MADE UP MY MIND TO TELL HIM HOW I FEEL!

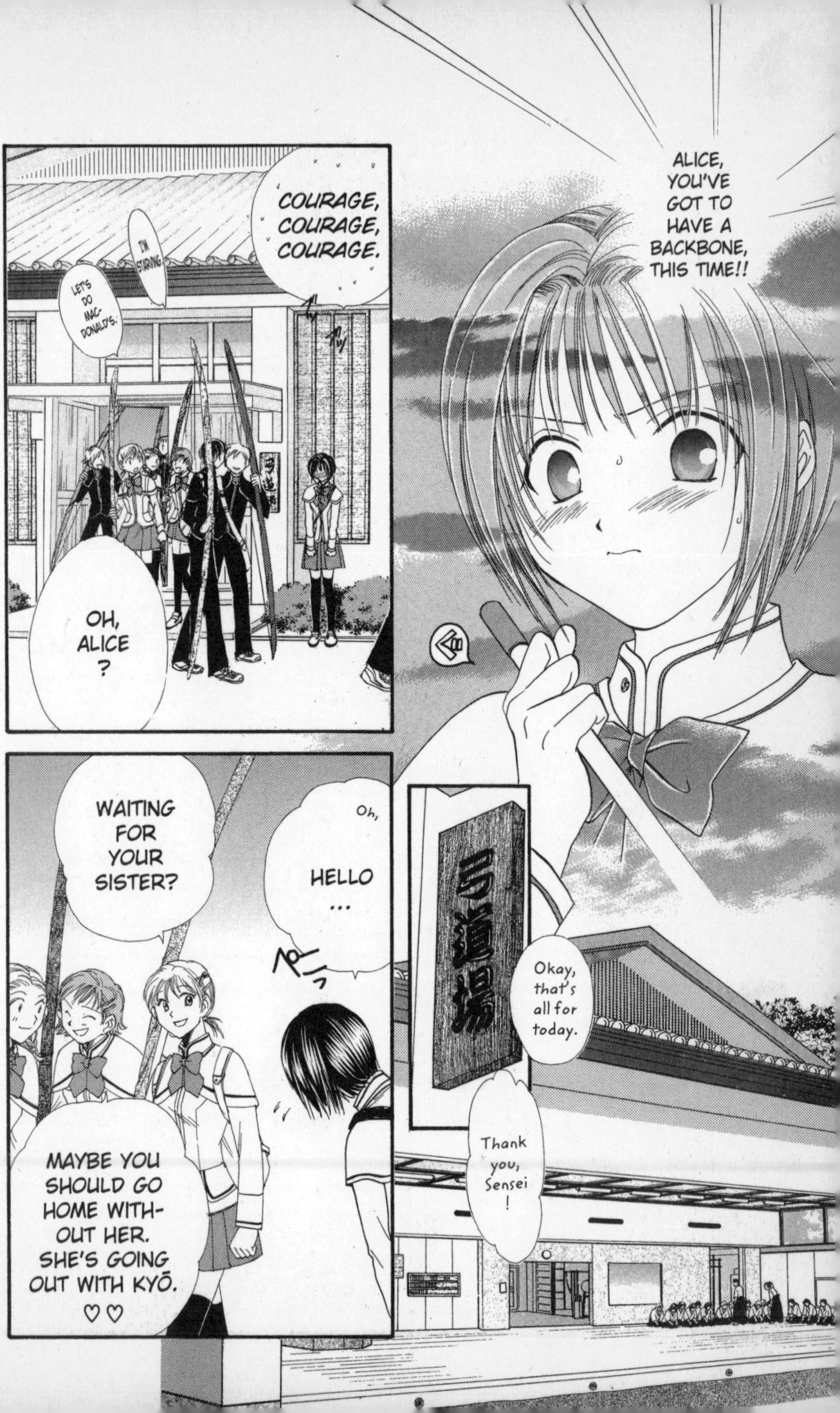
ALICE, YOU'VE GOT TO HAVE A BACKBONE, THIS TIME!!
Okay, that's all for today.
Thank you, Sensei!
COURAGE, COURAGE, COURAGE.
I'M STARVING.
LET'S DO MAC-DONALD'S.
OH, ALICE?
Oh, HELLO...
WAITING FOR YOUR SISTER?
MAYBE YOU SHOULD GO HOME WITH-OUT HER. SHE'S GOING OUT WITH KYŌ. ♡♡

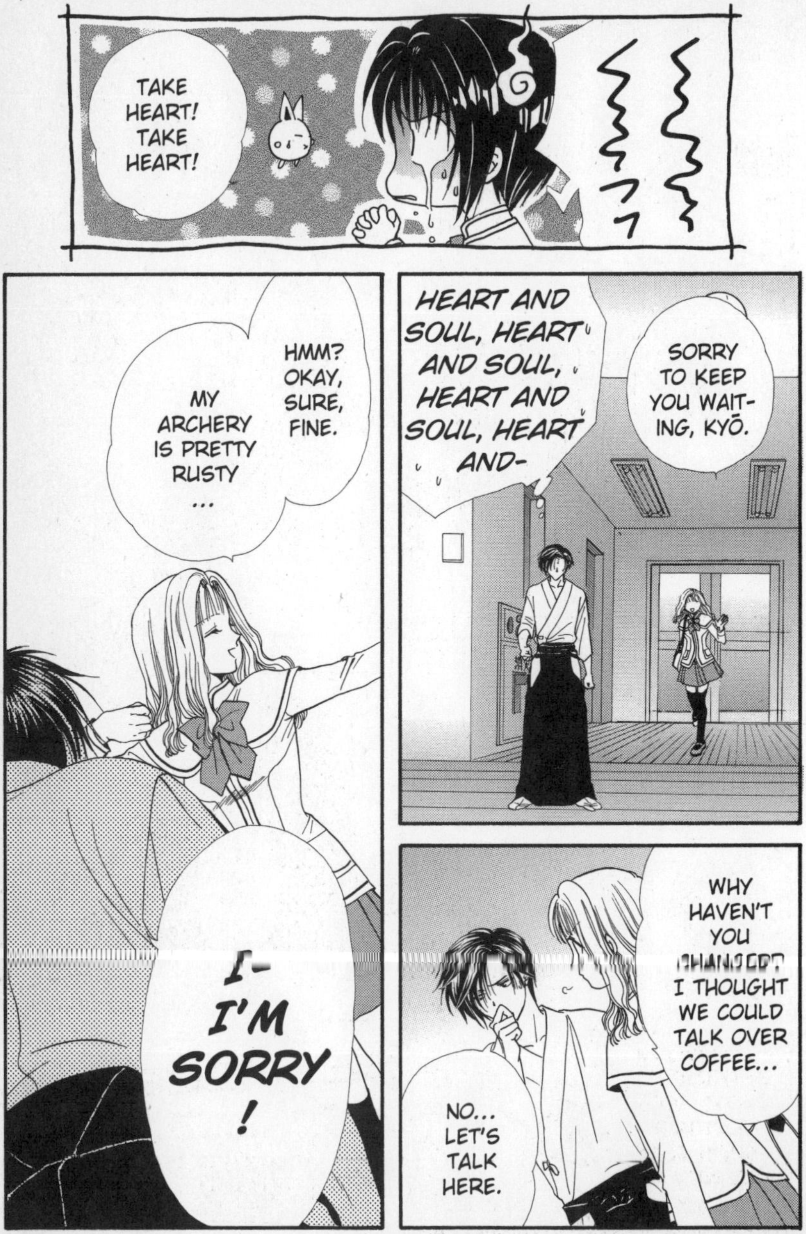
TAKE HEART! TAKE HEART!
SORRY TO KEEP YOU WAIT-ING, KYŌ.
HEART AND SOUL, HEART AND SOUL, HEART AND SOUL, HEART AND-
WHY HAVEN'T YOU CHANGED? I THOUGHT WE COULD TALK OVER COFFEE...
NO... LET'S TALK HERE.
HMM? OKAY, SURE, FINE.
MY ARCHERY IS PRETTY RUSTY ...
I- I'M SORRY!

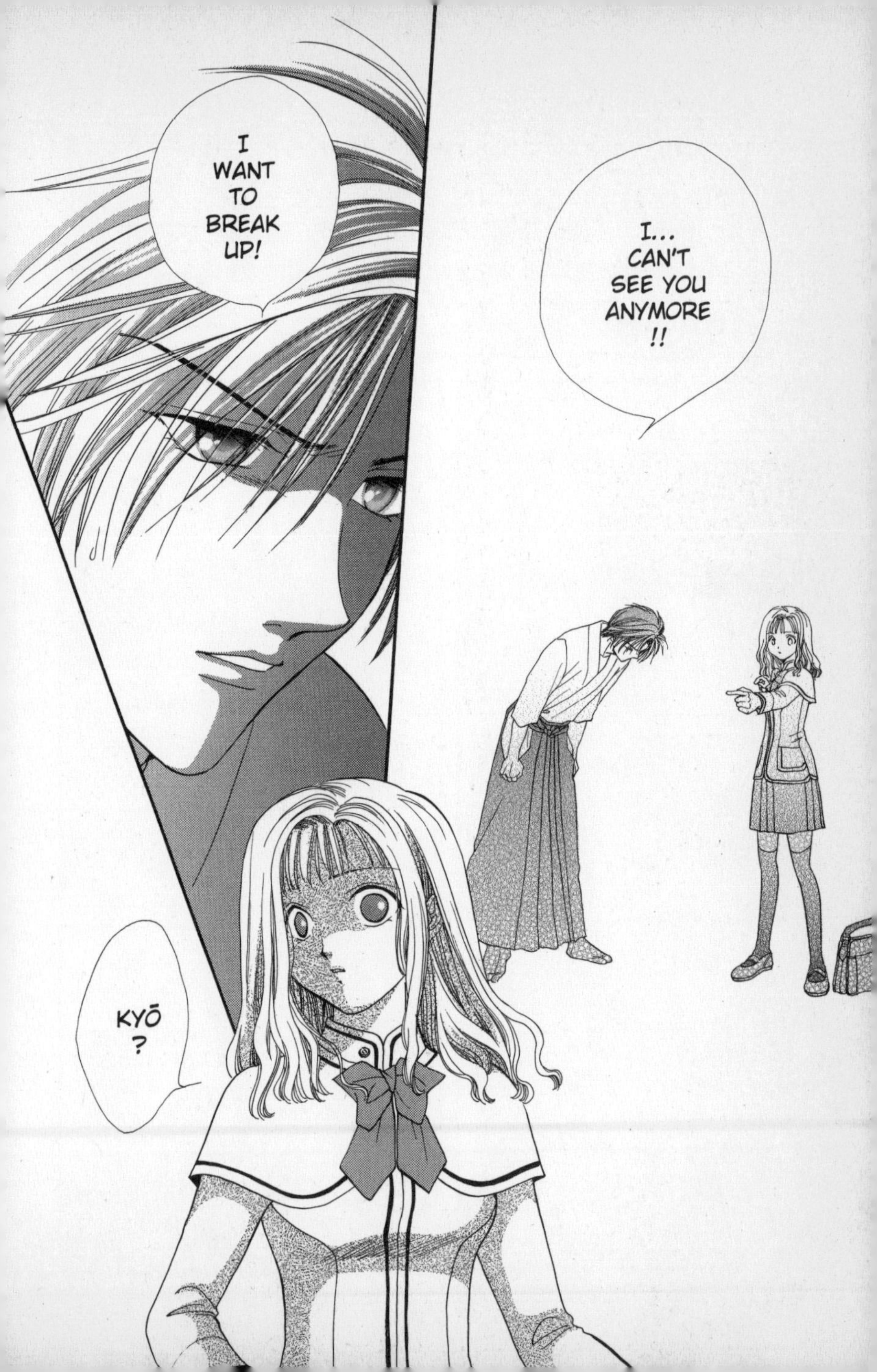
I... CAN'T SEE YOU ANYMORE!!
I WANT TO BREAK UP!
KYŌ?

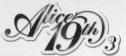

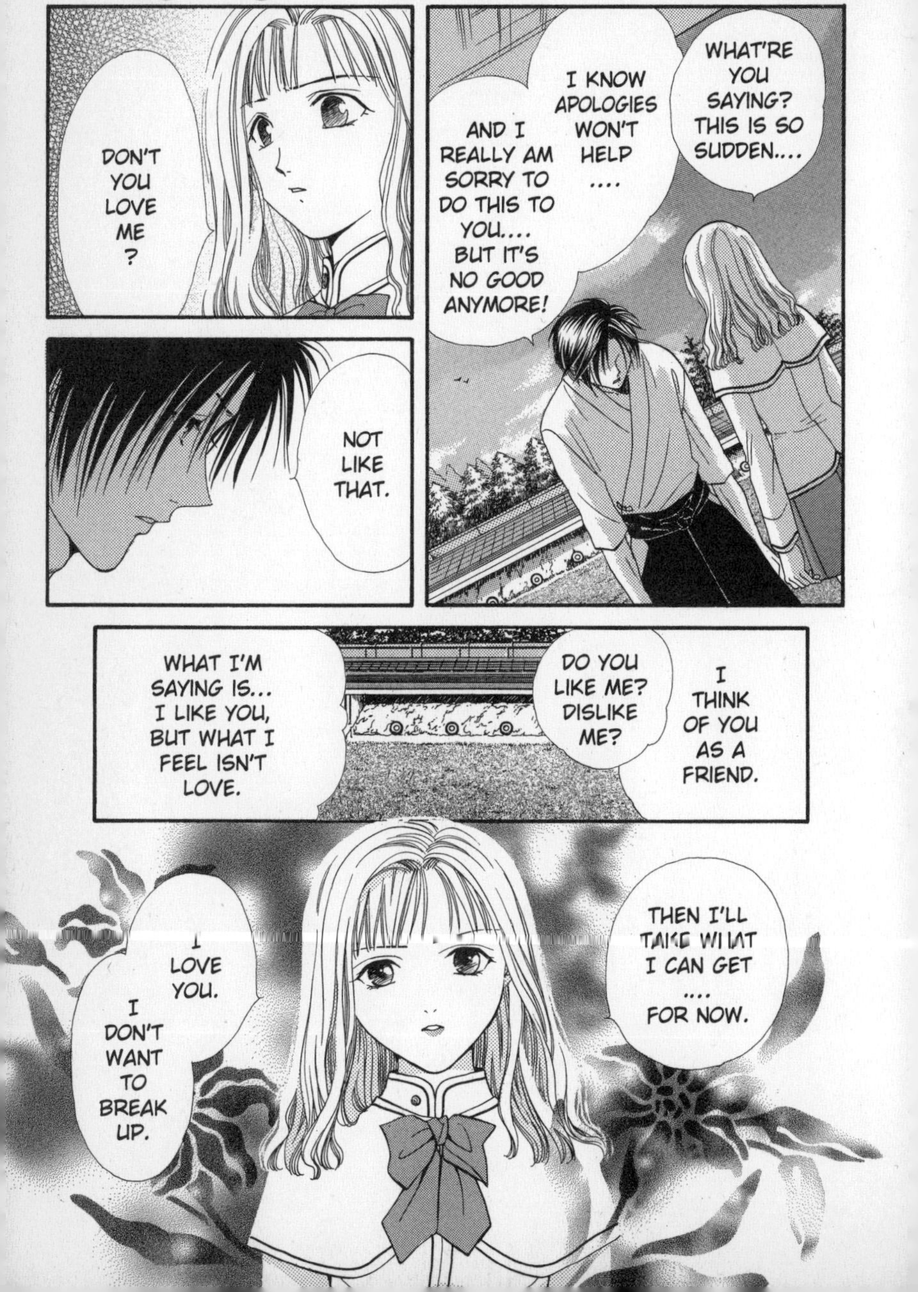
WHAT'RE YOU SAYING? THIS IS SO SUDDEN....
I KNOW APOLOGIES WON'T HELP ....
AND I REALLY AM SORRY TO DO THIS TO YOU.... BUT IT'S NO GOOD ANYMORE!
DON'T YOU LOVE ME ?
NOT LIKE THAT.
I THINK OF YOU AS A FRIEND.
DO YOU LIKE ME? DISLIKE ME?
WHAT I'M SAYING IS... I LIKE YOU, BUT WHAT I FEEL ISN'T LOVE.
THEN I'LL TAKE WHAT I CAN GET .... FOR NOW.
I LOVE YOU.
I DON'T WANT TO BREAK UP.

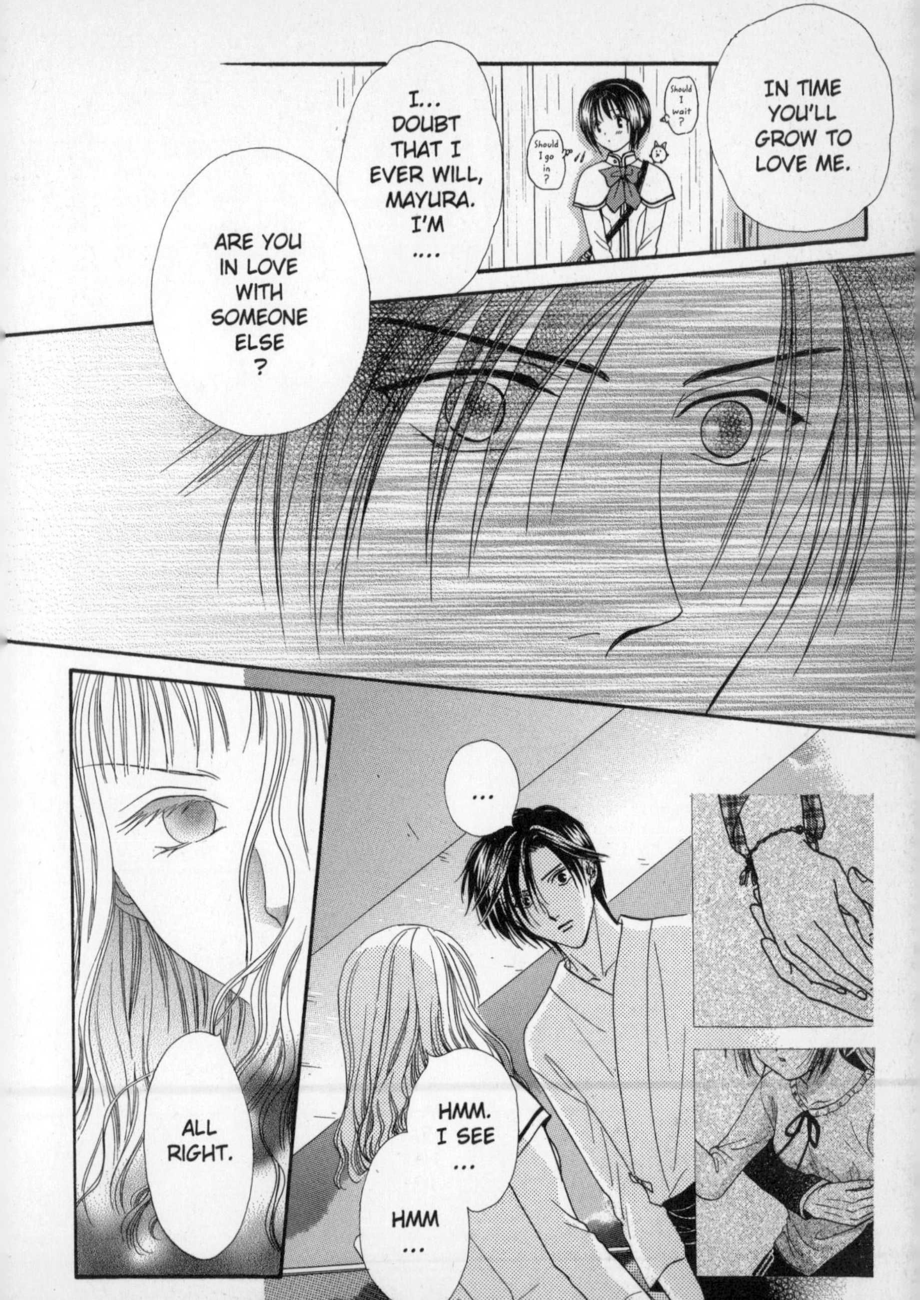
IN TIME YOU'LL GROW TO LOVE ME.
Should I wait?
Should I go in?
I... DOUBT THAT I EVER WILL, MAYURA. I'M ....
ARE YOU IN LOVE WITH SOMEONE ELSE?
...
HMM. I SEE ...
HMM ...
ALL RIGHT.

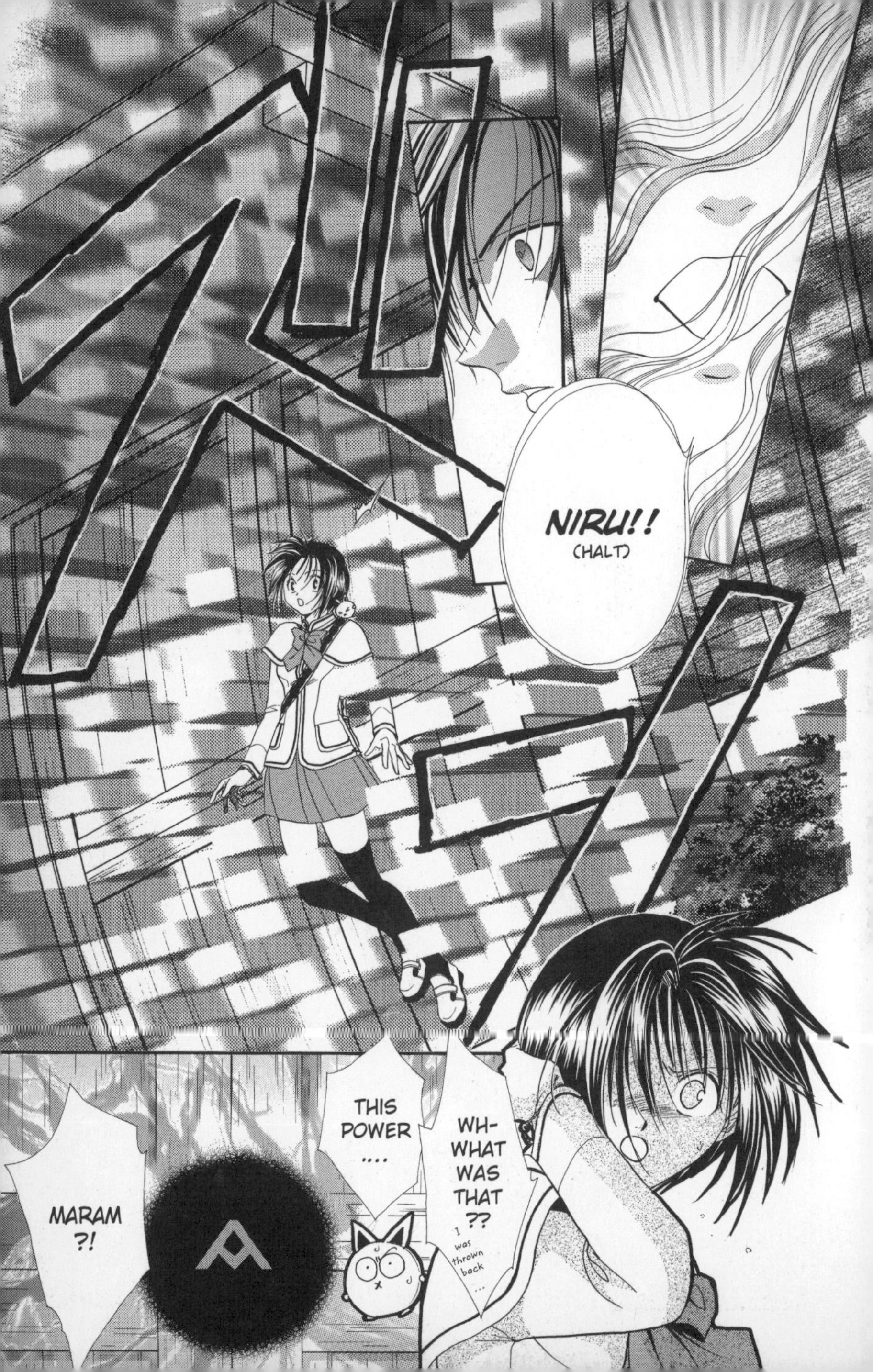
NIRU!!
(HALT)
WH-WHAT WAS THAT ??
I was thrown back ...
THIS POWER ....
MARAM ?!

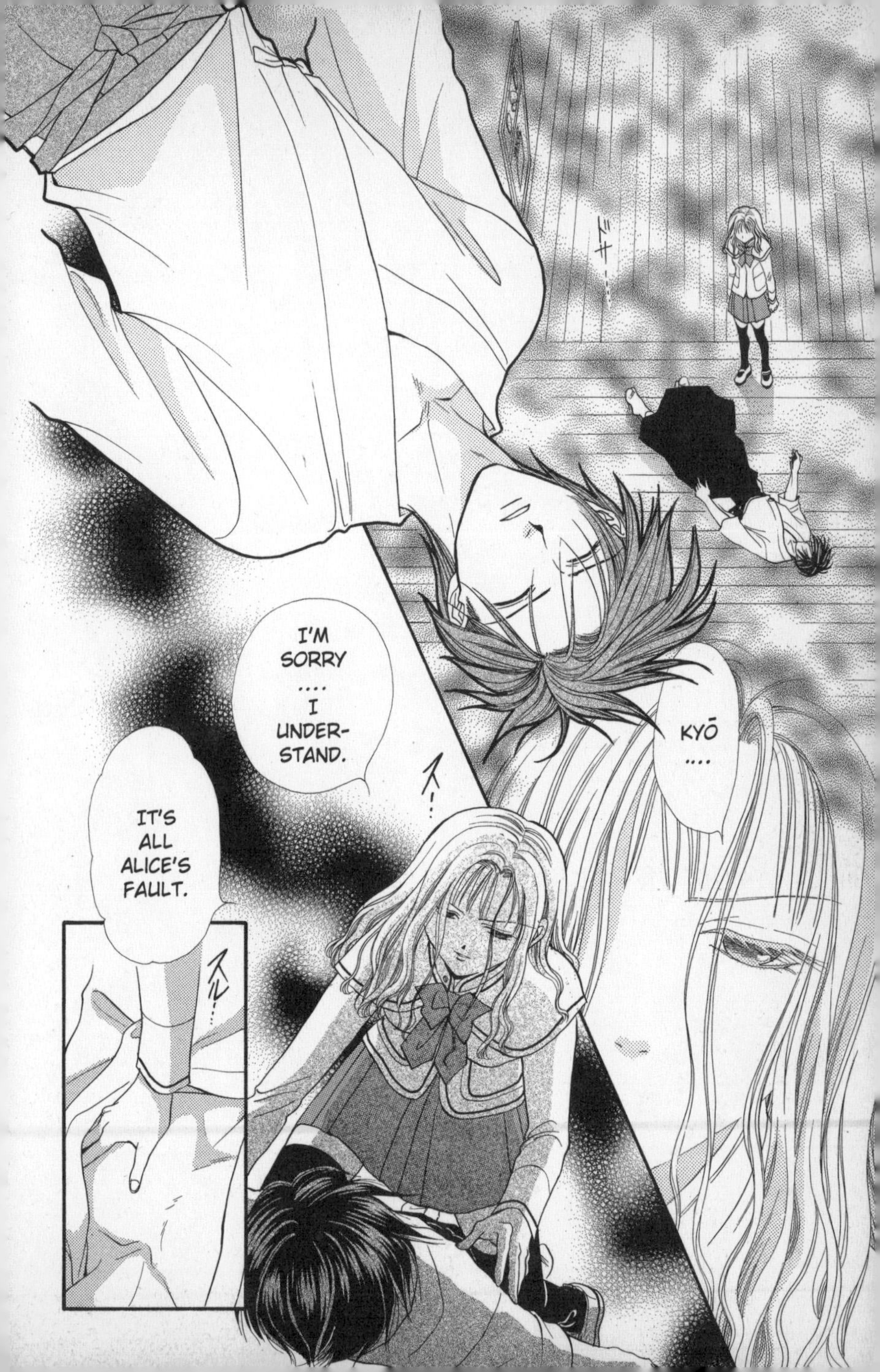
KYŌ ....
I'M SORRY .... I UNDER-STAND.
IT'S ALL ALICE'S FAULT.

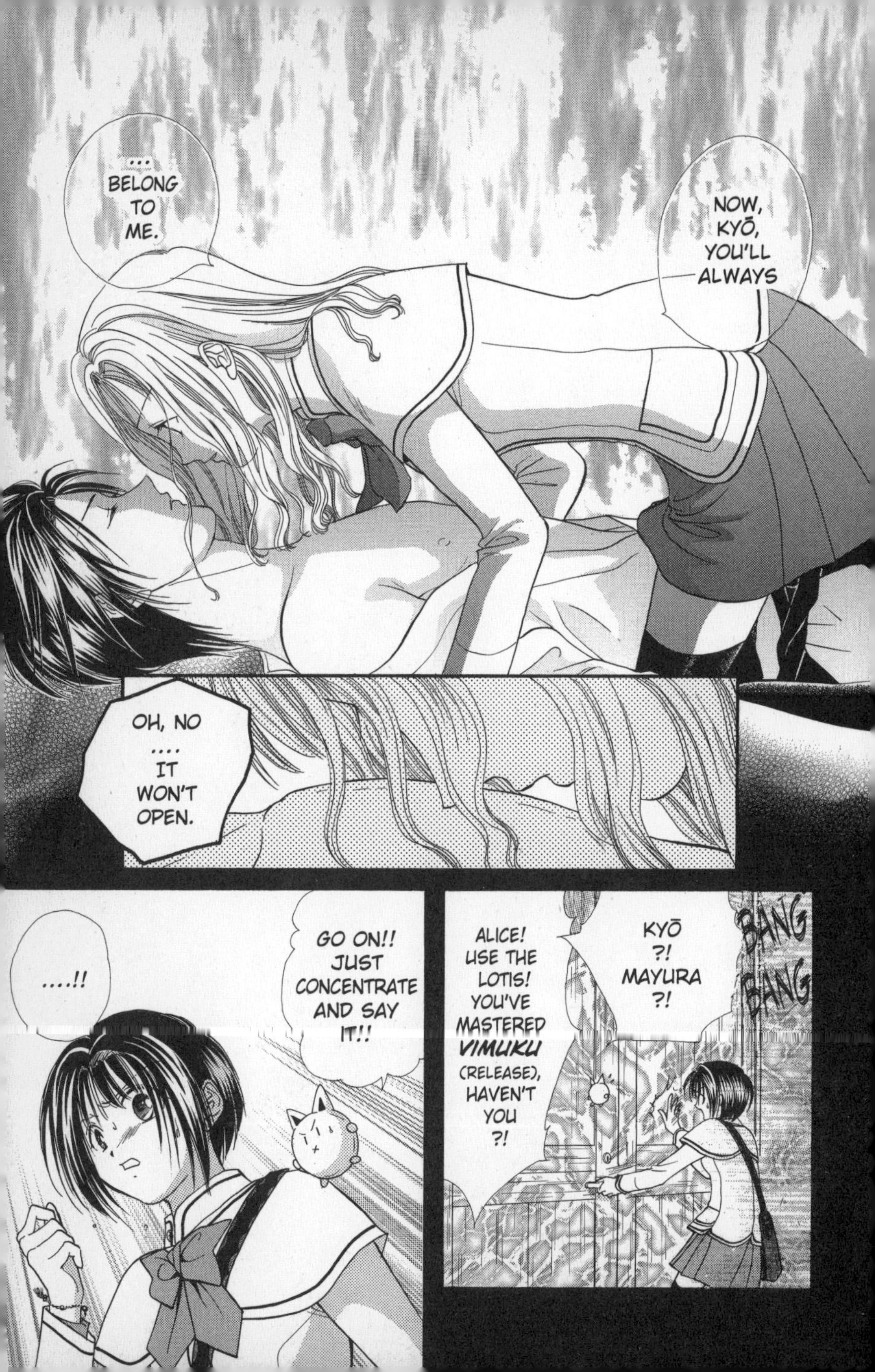
NOW, KYŌ, YOU'LL ALWAYS
... BELONG TO ME.
OH, NO .... IT WON'T OPEN.
BANG BANG
KYŌ ?! MAYURA ?!
ALICE! USE THE LOTIS! YOU'VE MASTERED VIMUKU (RELEASE), HAVEN'T YOU ?!
GO ON!! JUST CONCENTRATE AND SAY IT!!
....!!

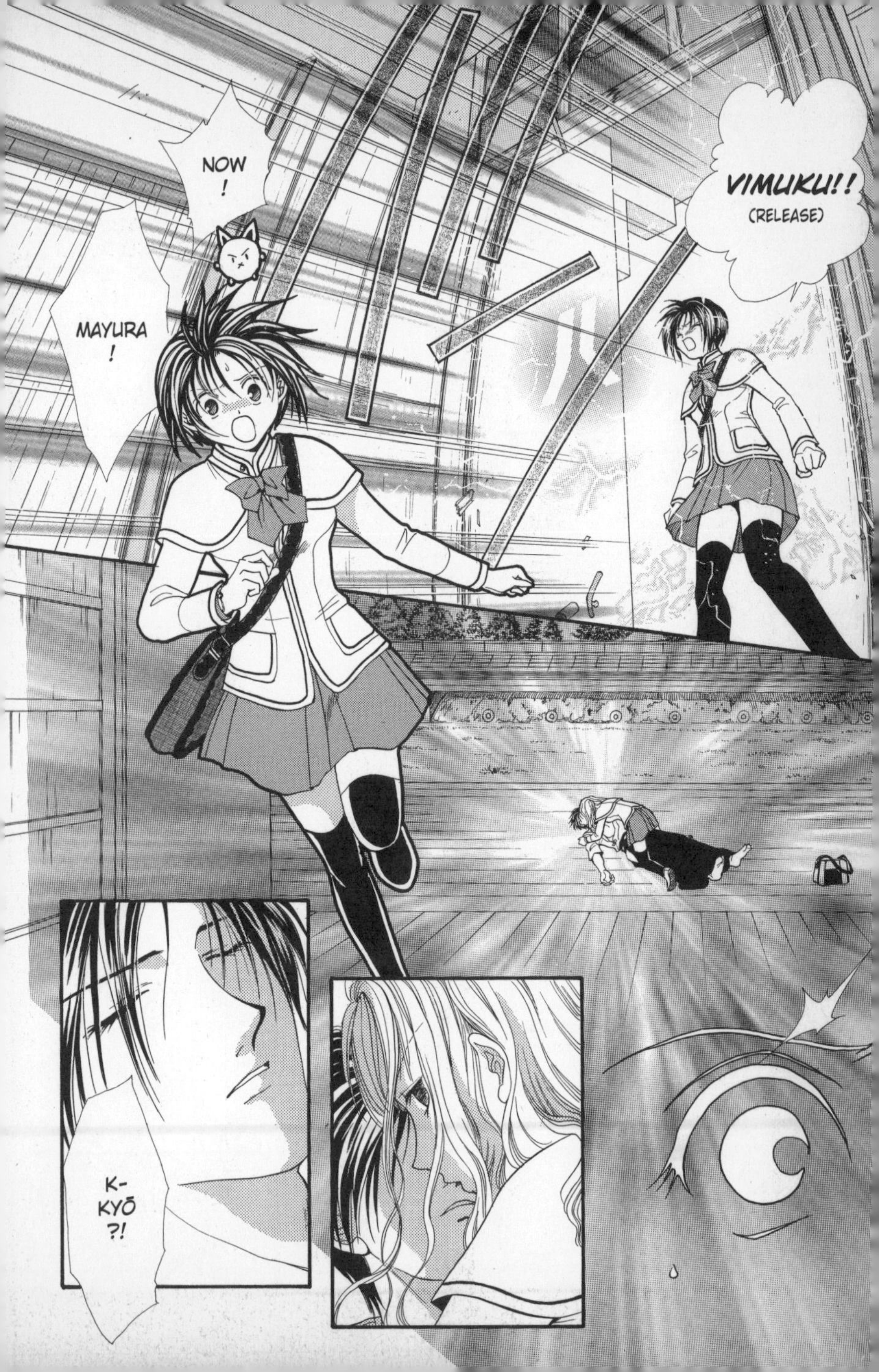
VIMUKU!!
(RELEASE)
NOW!
MAYURA!
K-KYŌ?!

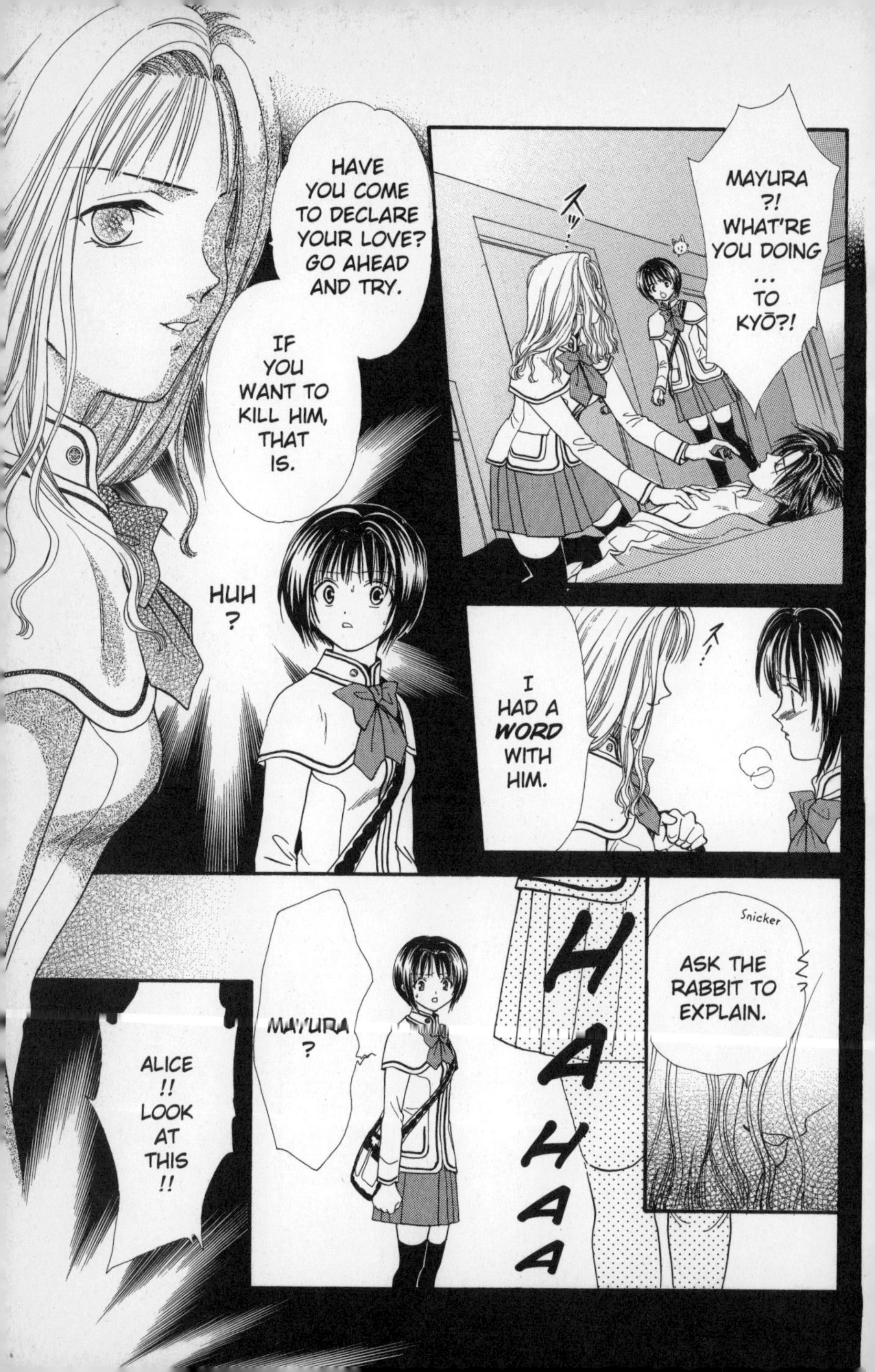
MAYURA ?! WHAT'RE YOU DOING ... TO KYŌ?!
I HAD A ***WORD*** WITH HIM.
HAVE YOU COME TO DECLARE YOUR LOVE? GO AHEAD AND TRY.
IF YOU WANT TO KILL HIM, THAT IS.
HUH ?
Snicker
ASK THE RABBIT TO EXPLAIN.
HAHAHAA
MAYURA ?
ALICE !! LOOK AT THIS !!

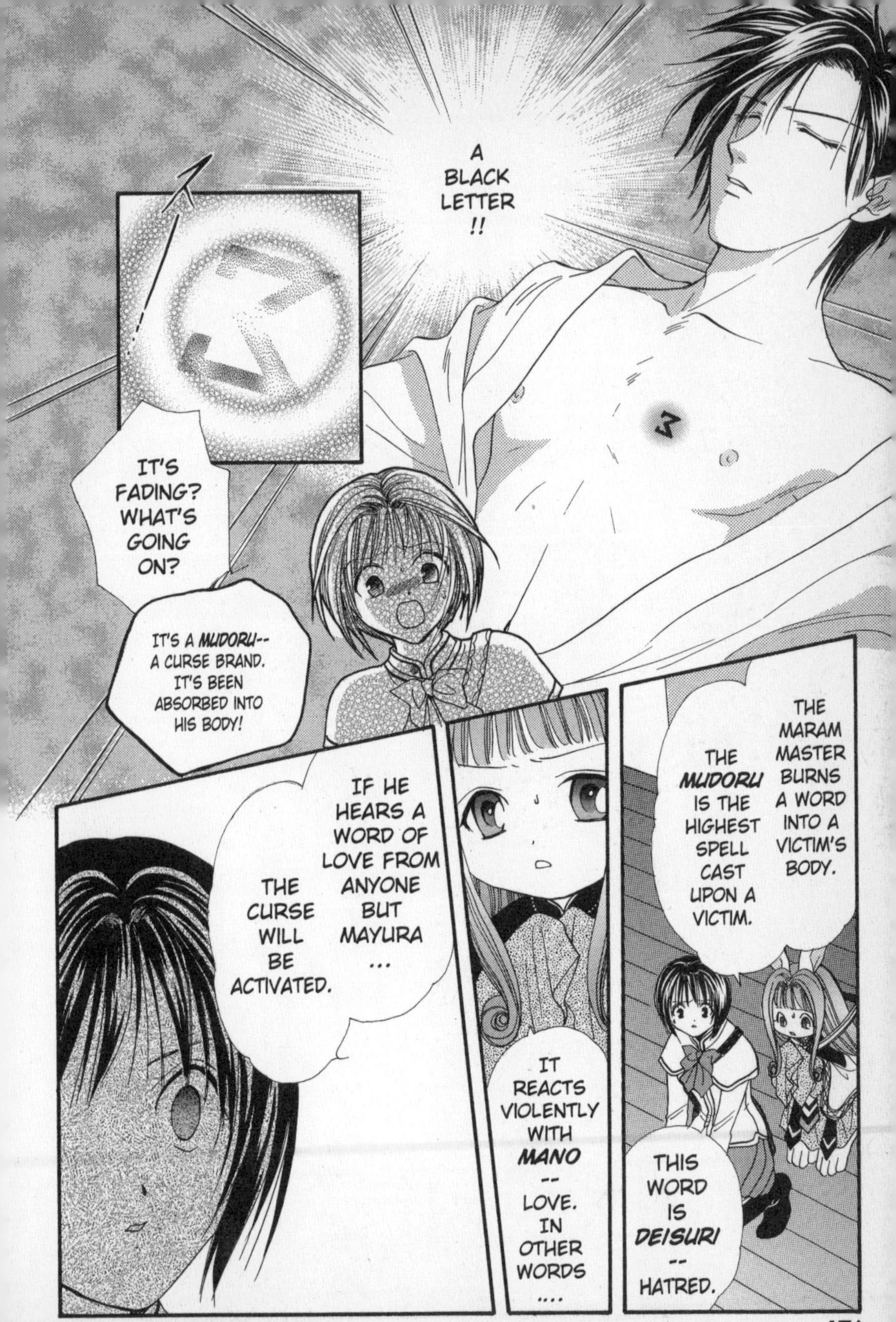
A BLACK LETTER !!
IT'S FADING? WHAT'S GOING ON?
IT'S A MUDORU-- A CURSE BRAND. IT'S BEEN ABSORBED INTO HIS BODY!
THE MARAM MASTER BURNS A WORD INTO A VICTIM'S BODY.
THE MUDORU IS THE HIGHEST SPELL CAST UPON A VICTIM.
THIS WORD IS DEISURI -- HATRED.
IT REACTS VIOLENTLY WITH MANO -- LOVE. IN OTHER WORDS ....
IF HE HEARS A WORD OF LOVE FROM ANYONE BUT MAYURA ...
THE CURSE WILL BE ACTIVATED.

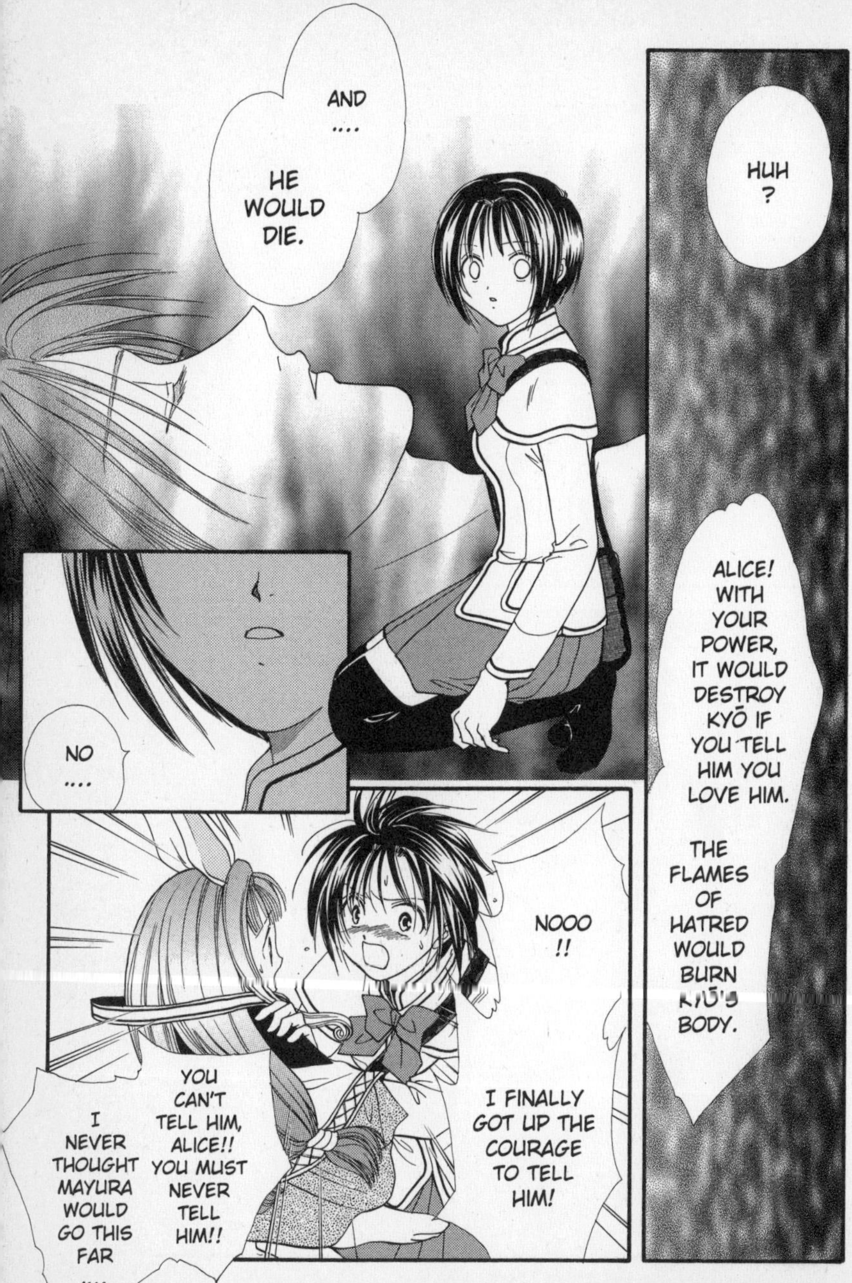
HUH?
ALICE! WITH YOUR POWER, IT WOULD DESTROY KYŌ IF YOU TELL HIM YOU LOVE HIM.
THE FLAMES OF HATRED WOULD BURN KYŌ'S BODY.
AND....
HE WOULD DIE.
NO....
NOOO!!
I FINALLY GOT UP THE COURAGE TO TELL HIM!
YOU CAN'T TELL HIM, ALICE!! YOU MUST NEVER TELL HIM!!
I NEVER THOUGHT MAYURA WOULD GO THIS FAR....

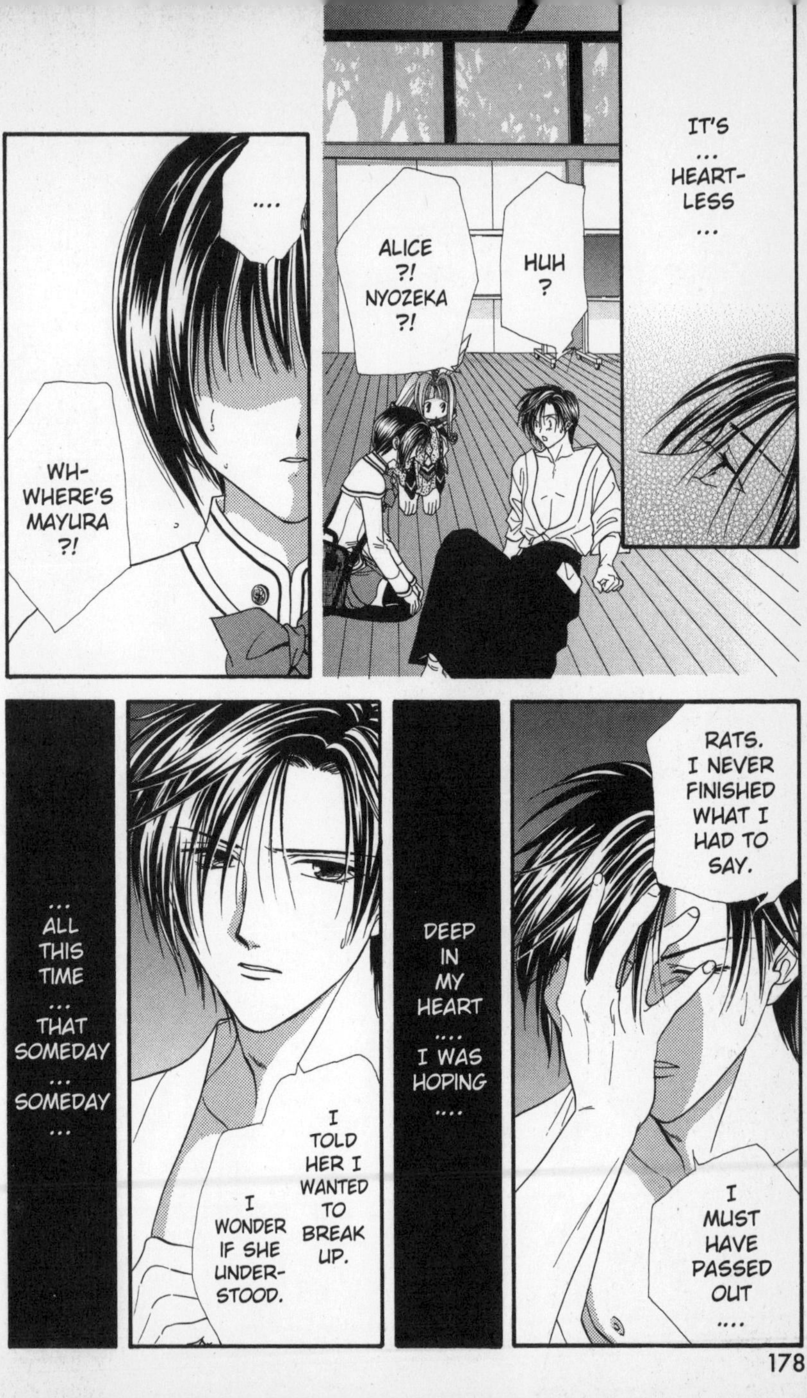
IT'S ... HEART-LESS ...
HUH ?
ALICE ?! NYOZEKA ?!
....
WH-WHERE'S MAYURA ?!
RATS. I NEVER FINISHED WHAT I HAD TO SAY.
I MUST HAVE PASSED OUT ....
DEEP IN MY HEART .... I WAS HOPING ....
I TOLD HER I WANTED TO BREAK UP.
I WONDER IF SHE UNDER-STOOD.
... ALL THIS TIME ... THAT SOMEDAY ... SOMEDAY ...

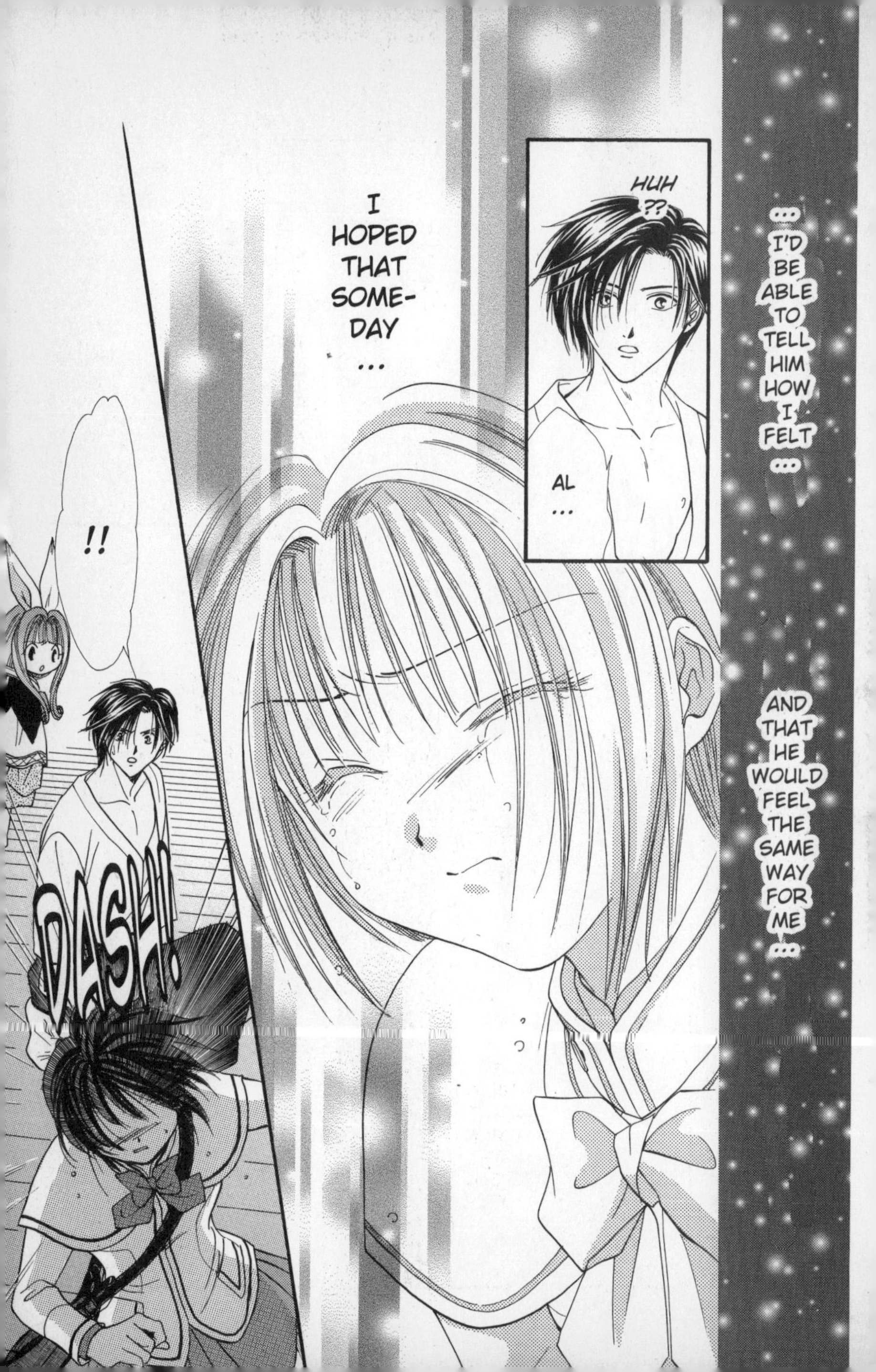
HUH ??
AL ...
I HOPED THAT SOME-DAY ...
... I'D BE ABLE TO TELL HIM HOW I FELT ...
AND THAT HE WOULD FEEL THE SAME WAY FOR ME ...
!!
DASH!!

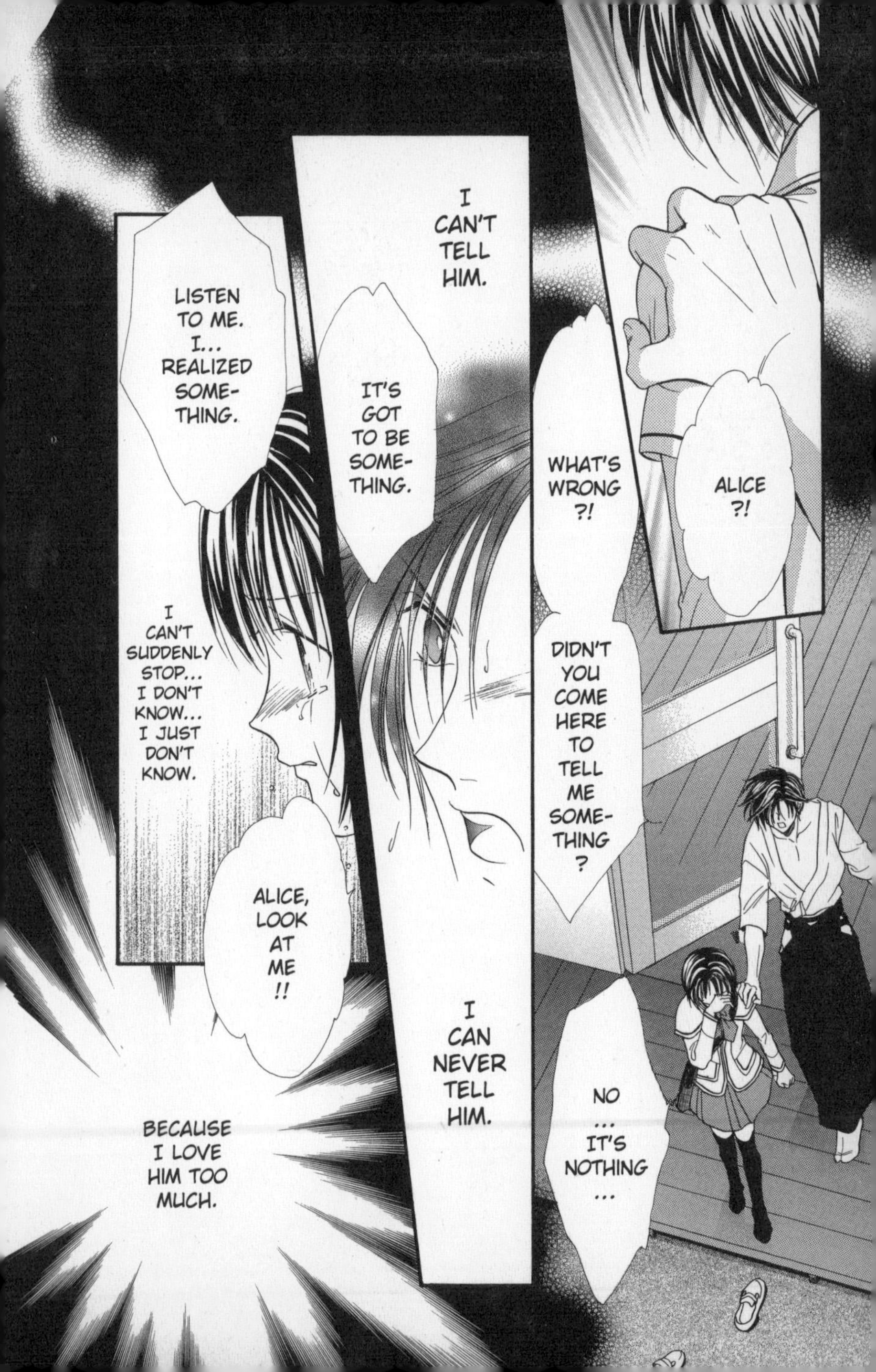
ALICE ?!
WHAT'S WRONG ?!
DIDN'T YOU COME HERE TO TELL ME SOMETHING ?
NO ... IT'S NOTHING ...
I CAN'T TELL HIM.
IT'S GOT TO BE SOME-THING.
I CAN NEVER TELL HIM.
LISTEN TO ME. I... REALIZED SOME-THING.
I CAN'T SUDDENLY STOP... I DON'T KNOW... I JUST DON'T KNOW.
ALICE, LOOK AT ME !!
BECAUSE I LOVE HIM TOO MUCH.

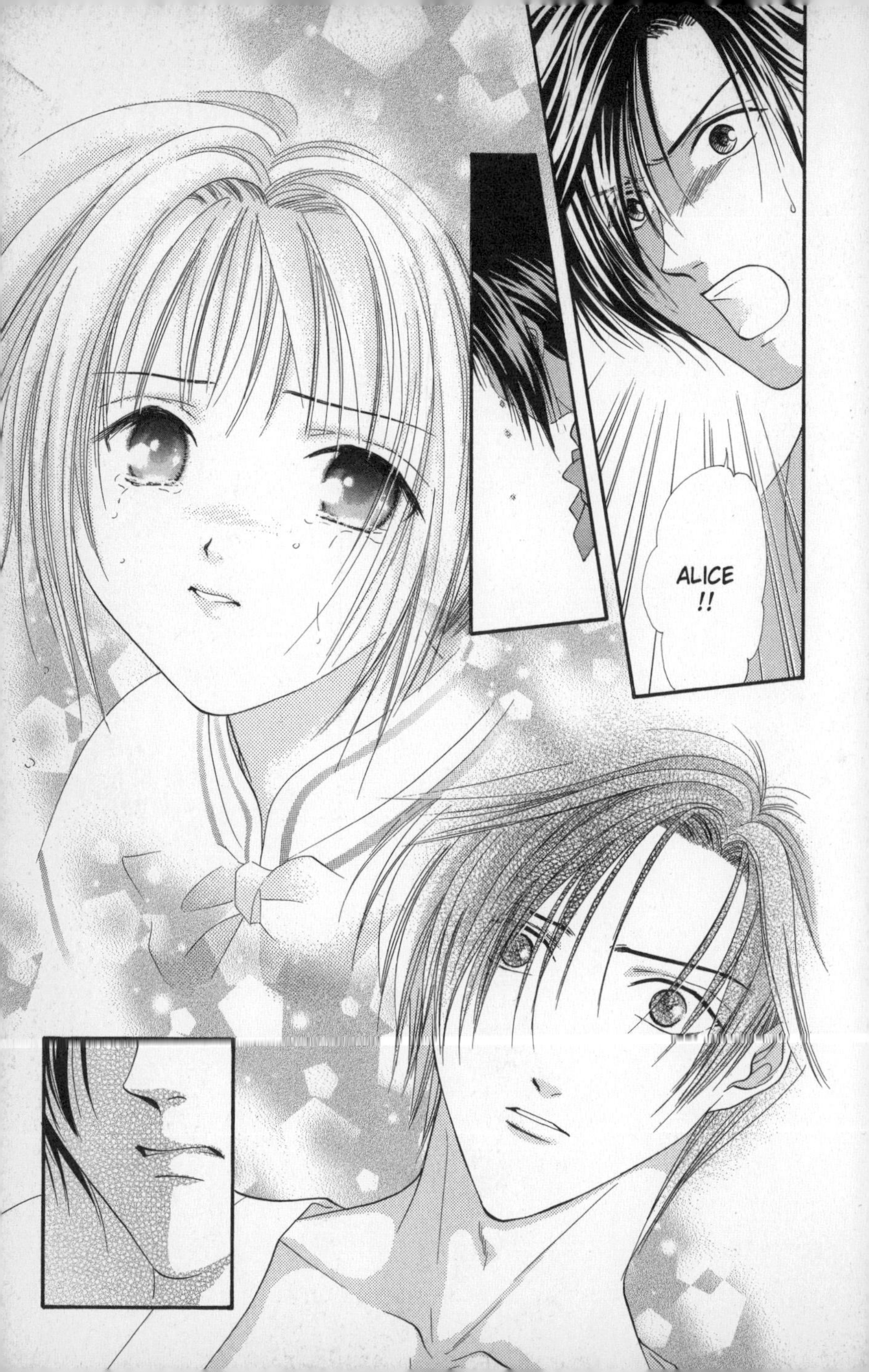
ALICE !!

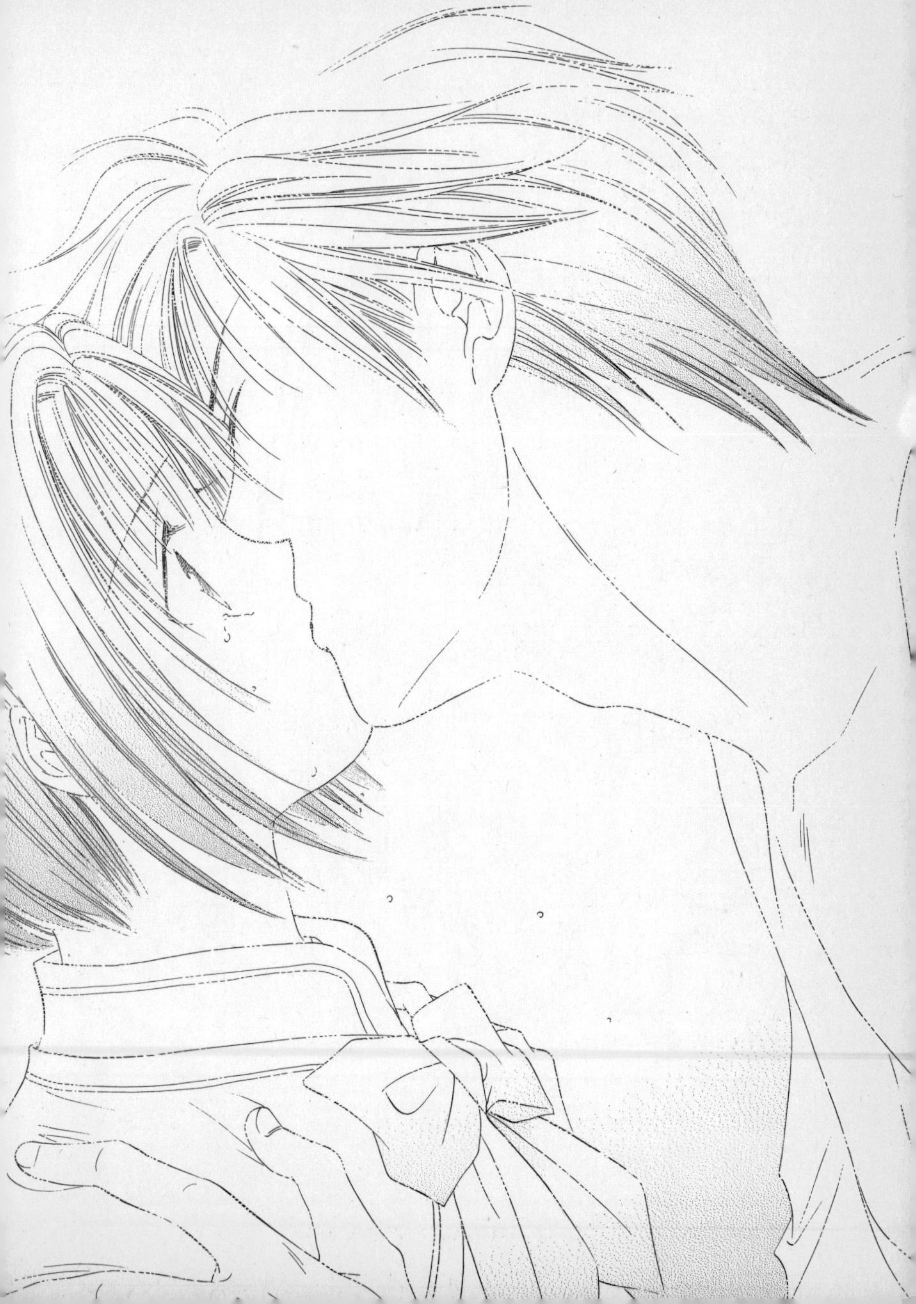

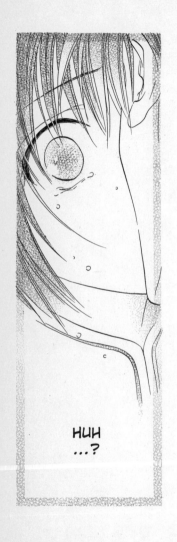

HUH
...?

TO BE CONTINUED IN VOLUME 4

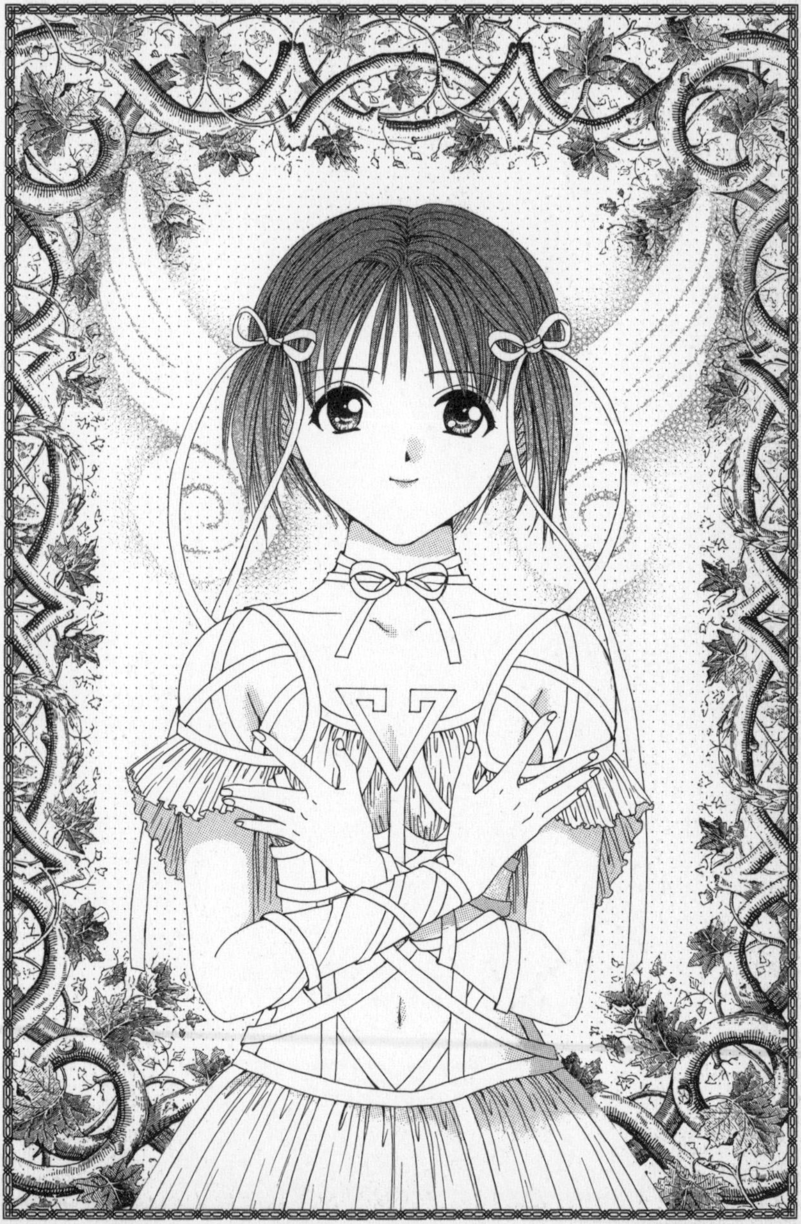

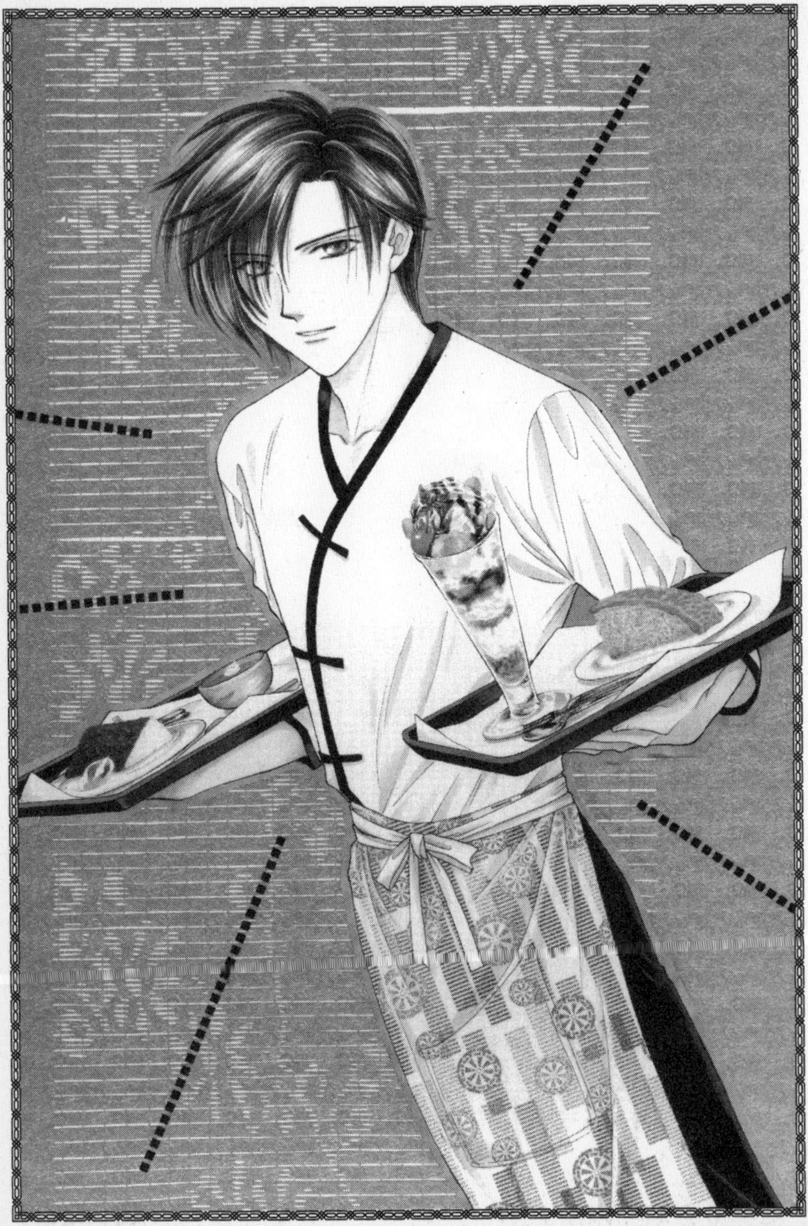

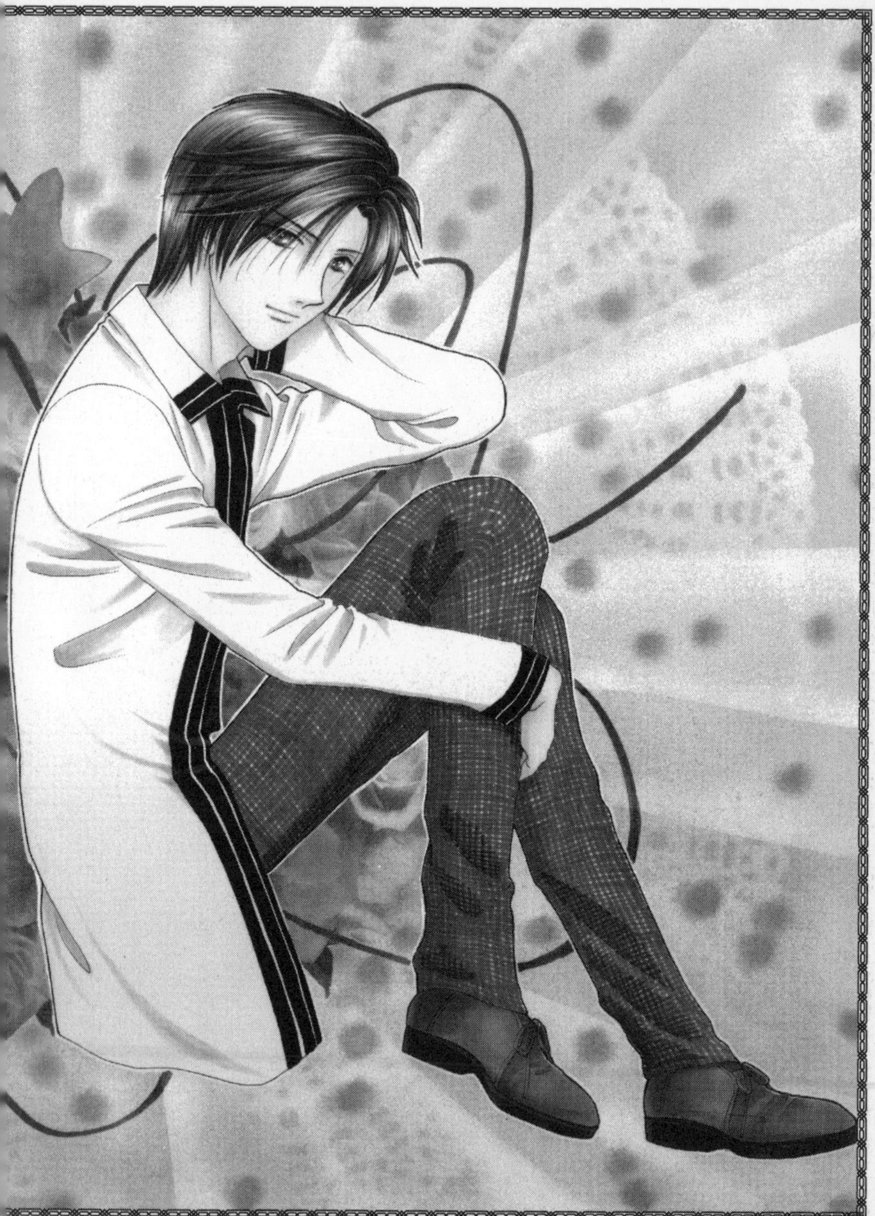

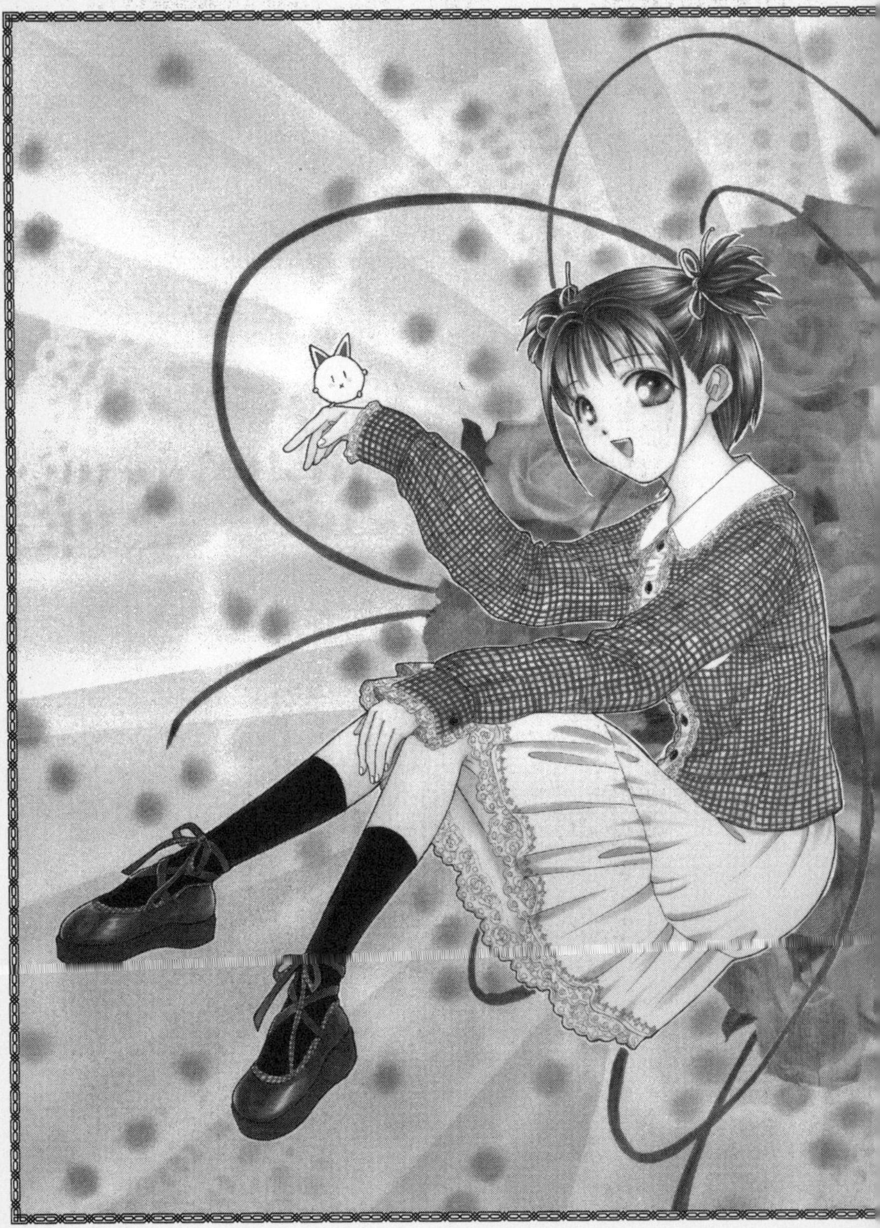

Editor Remarks:

Alice Seno uses the power of words to save the inner heart. She must search deep within herself to find the right words in order to become a true Lotis-master. Yû Watase did not take this ability lightly, making sure that Alice's power is authentic. It is probably Yû Watase's love for Norse mythology that brought Alice Seno such a meaningful power that all of us can use in real life.

It's been said that the ancient Norse God Odin sacrificed himself for nine days while hanging upside down from a world tree to understand the meanings of the rune (a.k.a. secrets). This enlightenment created rune stones that are symbols etched into rocks or slabs of stone that encompass formless and timeless meanings. Runes soon became incorporated into ancient Germanic alphabet, each symbol still holding a specific meaning behind them. Vikings used rune stones as a source of guidance and insight. It is believed that rune stones provide the ability to communicate to a higher being. They are still used today as a source of enlightenment and its practice is considered an alternative religion.

If you enjoyed this volume of Alice 19th then here are some manga that might interest you.

©1992 Yuu Watase / Shogakukan, Inc.

Fushigi Yûgi: The manga that brought Yû Watase into the shôjo spotlight. A beautiful shôjo fantasy series about a junior high school girl named Miaka Yuki who gets pulled into the world of a book called The Universe of the Four Gods. In this fictional world of ancient China she ends up falling in love, surviving danger and becoming the priestess of the god Suzaku and must find all seven of her Celestial-Warrior protectors. Adventure, romance and a good read ensue.

©1997 Yuu Watase / Shogakukan, Inc.

Ceres: Celestial Legend: Aya Mikage thinks she's just a normal girl in high school until she discovers that she can transform into a vastly powerful "celestial maiden" named Ceres.... But Ceres has a vendetta against Aya's family and is out for revenge! And because of the manifestation of Ceres, Aya's own family is out to kill her!

©1992 Yoko Kamio / Shuiesha, Inc.

Boys Over Flowers, Hana Yori Dango: Tsukushi Makino is a young girl who is entering a prestigious high school where only the richest most elite students from Japan get to attend, but she's from a modest family, with no riches to speak of and feels more than a little out of place. She is perfectly happy being a fly on the wall until one day she sticks up for her friend to the coolest most influential gang of the school, known as the F4. Now on their hit list, She's rejected by the entire school, rather than flee the scene, Makino fights for her rights and discovers her strength from within.

Glossary of Sound Effects, Signs, and other Miscellaneous Notes

Each entry includes: the location, indicated by page number and panel number (so 3.1 means page 3, panel number 1); the phonetic romanization of the original Japanese; and our English "translation"—we offer as close an English equivalent as we can.

24.3——FX: Gasa gasa (Busy cleaning up)

24.5——FX: Gasa gasa (Busy cleaning up)

30.1——FX: Boso (Quietly)

30.5——FX: Kata, kata, kata (Rattle)

30.5——FX: Gata, gata (Heavier rattling)

30.6——FX: Gata, gata, gata, gata (Heavier rattling)

31.1——FX: Zu, zu, zu! (Crack, crack, crack!)

31.2——FX: Za! (Door opens)

31.2——FX: Zu, zu, zu! (Crack, crack, crack!)

31.3——FX: Zu (Crash)

31.3——FX: Zu, zu (Crash)

31.4——FX: Zu (Crash)

32.4——FX: Zuzu (Rumble fading)

34.2——FX: Ring (Phone ring)

34.3——FX: Ring (Phone ring)

34.4——FX: Rrrrr (Phone ring)

34.5——FX: Ring (Phone ring)

35.1——FX: Za (Phone static)

35.2——FX: Za za (Phone static)

35.3——FX: Za (Phone static)

38.4——FX: Tsu, tsu, tsu (Hung-up beeping)

40.2——FX: Da! (Dash!)

7.3——FX: Gyurururu (Wheels skidding)

9.2——FX: Sha! (Bikes going. Swoosh)

9.4——FX: Shaka shaka shaka (Peddling)

9.5——FX: Gacha (Click. Door opening)

12.1——FX: Tossu (Thok! Arrow hits)

12.2——FX: Pyu (Blood spattering)

14.2——FX: Boko! (Bap!)

15.3——FX: Oro oro (Tremble in fear)

15.4——FX: Kacha (Door opening)

16.1——FX: Shaako shaako (Shuk, shuk. Rub. On ink slab)

16.4——FX: Doka, dosu (Bam! Thud)

16.4——FX: Baki (Whap)

16.5——FX: Ban! (Bam! Door)

17.5——FX: Kaa (Consternation)

18.1——FX: Kaa (Horror)

18.3——FX: Doh dadada! (Falling down stairs)

20.2—— "A Normal Mind"

20.4——FX: Su (Softly face emerges)

21.1——FX: Kasa kasa (Paper rustling)

22.1——FX: Kaa (Horror)

22.1——FX: Dosa (Thud. Fall on girl)

60.6 — Soft voice…

61.1 — FX: Za! (Appears)

62.3 — FX: Pi! (Punching number)

62.4 — FX: Pi! (Punching number)

62.5 — FX: Pi! (Punching number)

63.1 — FX: Pi! (Punching number)

63.2 — FX: Pi! (Punching number)

63.3 — FX: Pi! (Punching number)

63.4 — FX: Pi! (Punching number)

63.5 — FX: Pi! Pi! (Punching number)

70.2 — FX: Su! (Pass!)

70.5 — FX: Bashi! (Blam!)

72.5 — FX: Ta! (Dash!)

73.1 — FX: Doh! (Blam!)

73.3 — FX: Piku! (Poit! Ears perk up)

75.2 — FX: Goh! (Blast! Gross fog)

76.3 — FX Kururi (Fwip. Change into rabbit)

76.5 — FX: Shu! Shu! Shu! Shu! (Monster laugh)

77.4 — FX: Za! (Assume stance!)

78.5 — FX: Shururururu… (Twing,twing, twing. Arrow arms flying)

78.5 — FX: Yoro! (Wobble!)

79.4 — FX: Za! (Whip!)

79.6 — FX: Zu! (Slip!)

82.2 — FX: Yoro (Wobble)

82.4 — FX: Su (Bowstring drawn back)

40.5 — FX: Dokun, dokun, dokun, dokun (Heart beating)

41.2 — FX: Gacha. (Click. Door opening)

41.3 — FX: Blam!!

42.3 — FX: Ka (Glow)

42.5 — FX: Bari bari (Dissipating)

44.1 — FX: Dosa (Plop. Sits down)

45.1 — FX: Ka! (Bam!)

45.2 — FX: Su… (Sinking)

45.4 — FX: Su… (Sinking)

46.1 — FX: Ba! (Blam!)

47.2 — FX: Nyu! (Everybody pops up)

47.3 — FX: Shiin (Scene expands)

51.2 — Sana (Guide)

51.3 — FX: Boro boro (Crumble. Falls apart or fizzles)

51.4 — FX: Pi (Pip. Phone clicked on)

52.5 — FX: Zuru?! (Hah?!)

53.1 — FX: Pi (Pip. Phone clicks off)

53.1 — FX: Tsuu, tsuu, tsuu (Phone signal)

54.1 — FX: Haaaa (Monster)

54.1 — FX: Zuru (Creeping)

54.5 — FX: Pi! Pi! (Punching numbers)

54.5 — FX: Pi, pi, pi, pi (Punching numbers)

55.1 — Jiva (Heal)

57.3 — FX: Geho! (Cough)

57.3 — FX: Fura… (Sink wearily)

117.1 —FX: Su (Mara appears)

117.2 —FX: Su (Frey moves ahead)

119.2 —FX: Niya (Smirk)

119.3 —FX: Bo! (Hole opens)

122.2 —FX: Ba! (Flap! Wings)

123.3 —FX: Basa (Flap)

126.1 —FX: Chi chi chi (Chirp, chirp, chirp)

126.3 —FX: Kacha (Click. Door opens)

130.1 —FX: Pon (Hand on shoulder)

130.3 —FX: Doki! (Shock!)

132.5 —FX: Boka! (Bap!)

134.3 —FX: Furu furu (Shakes head)

138.4 —FX: Doso (Dash to Kyo)

139.1 —FX: Dotsu (Hits elbow)

139.1 —FX: Mukyu (Smish. Squash Nyozeka)

140.2 —FX: Zuki! (Shock!)

140.5 —Doki (Afraid)

142.1 —FX: Doki (!)

143.6 —FX: Su (Kyo's hand comes in)

145.5 —FX: Gura! (Twist!)

148.3 —FX: Su (Pass by)

148.4 —FX: Giku! (Startled!)

149.6 —FX: Batan! (Slam!)

150.1 —FX: Dokun dokun dokun (Heart beating)

150.1 — FX: Gacha (Lock door)

83.2 —FX: Go-o-o (Roar)

84.1 —FX: O-O-O (Roar)

84.4 —FX: Goh! (Blam!)

85.2 —FX: Gusha gusha (Noogie, noogie)

86.1 —FX: Doh! (Thok!)

87.2 —FX: Gyu (Glare. Stern look)

87.5 —FX: Zu (Slipping)

89.2 —FX: Biku! (Shock!)

89.4 —FX: Shu-u-u (Monster remains fizzle out)

91.4 —FX: Dou! (Chunk!)

94.3 —FX: Za! (Appears!)

94.4 —FX: Para (Hair billows)

99.1 —FX: Zun (Crash!)

99.2 —FX: Dosa (Thud. Dad falls)

100.2 —FX: Gu! (Gulp!)

102.2 —FX: Ba! (Blam!)

106.3 —FX: Su (Asleep)

106.5 —FX: Bo (Foom. Dad quietly appears)

106.5 —FX: Gaba! (Wakes with a start)

109. —FX: Gara, gara, gara (Crumbling sound)

109.2 —FX: Gara, gara, gara (Crumbling sound)

109.3 —FX: Gara, gara (Crumbling sound)

111.3 —FX: Bo! (Boot! Kicks stone)

113.6 —FX: Gakun (Legs give way)

116.2 —FX: Pan! (Pow!)

150.2—FX: Dokun (Heart beat)

151.1 —FX: Dokun! (Heartbeat!)

156.3—FX: Zawa! (Commotion!)

157.1 —FX: Pita (Mayura stops walking)

160.2—FX: Gacha (Door opens)

160.5—FX: Bashi (Whack)

162.4—FX: Zawa zawa (Yadda yadda)

164.4—FX: Sha-ko, sha-ko (Rubbing ink block)

165.1 —FX: Shobo (Teary)

165.4—FX: Gu (Grip)

166.1 —FX: Gu (Grip)

166.5—FX: Peko (Bow)

167.1 —Kuu kuu (Holding back sobs)

171.3—FX: Zun! (Voom!)

172.1 —FX: Dosa (Fall)

172.3—FX: Su (Bends over)

172.4—FX: Suru (Hand slides over chest)

174.2 —FX: Ban! (Blam!)

175.1 —FX: Su (Looks up)

175.2—FX: Su (Stands up)

176.2—FX: Su (Fading)

About the Author:

Yû Watase, the immensely popular writer and manga artist who currently resides in Japan. Her first work, **Pajama De Ojama** ("An Intrusion in Pajamas") was published in 1989 when she was only 18 years old. Since then, she has amassed a hefty body of work, producing more than 50 volumes of short stories and continuing series. Best known for her romantic stories based in a fantasy world like **Fushigi Yûgi: The Mysterious Play** and **Ceres: Celestial Legend.** She continues to work hard on upcoming projects, her latest, **Appare Jipangu**, is set in the Edo Period and is about a girl who cures people of their sadness.

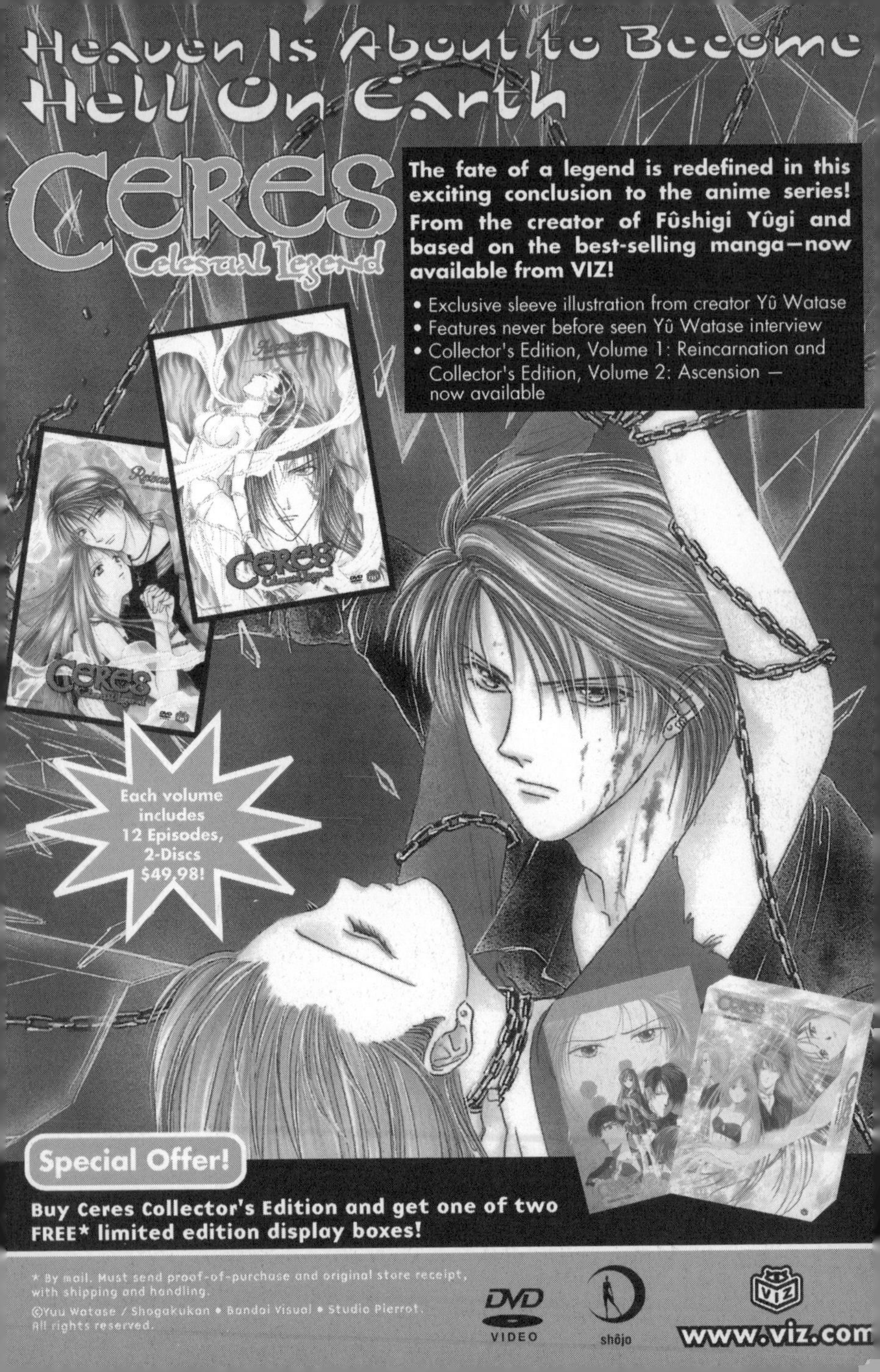
Heaven Is About to Become Hell On Earth
Ceres Celestial Legend
The fate of a legend is redefined in this exciting conclusion to the anime series! From the creator of Fûshigi Yûgi and based on the best-selling manga—now available from VIZ!
• Exclusive sleeve illustration from creator Yû Watase
• Features never before seen Yû Watase interview
• Collector's Edition, Volume 1: Reincarnation and Collector's Edition, Volume 2: Ascension — now available
Each volume includes 12 Episodes, 2-Discs $49.98!
Special Offer!
Buy Ceres Collector's Edition and get one of two FREE* limited edition display boxes!
* By mail. Must send proof-of-purchase and original store receipt, with shipping and handling.
©Yuu Watase / Shogakukan • Bandai Visual • Studio Pierrot. All rights reserved.
DVD VIDEO
shôjo
VIZ
www.viz.com

fushigi yûgi
The Mysterious Play

Seven Warriors... Four Gods...
Two Worlds... One Quest

Get drawn into the graphic novels today – only from VIZ!

"Yû Watase's art is lush and detailed." – Sequential Tart

Tough Love Was Never This Cute!

In a world where the wedding chapel is a war zone between good and evil, three young girls transform themselves into mighty morphin' warriors of love. Armed with magical powers borne from age-old wedding traditions, will the power of love help them save the day?

Only $9.95!

Start your graphic novel collection today!

A
PRISONER
of Society.

A
SWORDSMAN
Without Equal.

A
GIRL
With A Dream.

Written and Illustrated by
CHIHO SAITO

Story by
BE-PAPAS

Revolutionary Girl
UTENA

As seen in
ANIMERICA
EXTRA
the anime fan's comic magazine

Santa Fe Springs City Library
11700 Telegraph Road
Santa Fe Springs, CA 90670

COMPLETE OUR SURVEY AND LET US KNOW WHAT YOU THINK!

☐ Please check here if you DO NOT wish to receive information or future offers from VIZ

Name: _____

Address: _____

City: _____ State: _____ Zip: _____

E-mail: _____

☐ Male ☐ Female Date of Birth (mm/dd/yyyy): ___ / ___ / ___ (Under 13? Parental consent required)

What race/ethnicity do you consider yourself? (please check one)

☐ Asian/Pacific Islander   ☐ Black/African American   ☐ Hispanic/Latino

☐ Native American/Alaskan Native ☐ White/Caucasian   ☐ Other: _____

What VIZ product did you purchase? (check all that apply and indicate title purchased)

☐ DVD/VHS _____

☐ Graphic Novel _____

☐ Magazines _____

☐ Merchandise _____

Reason for purchase: (check all that apply)

☐ Special offer   ☐ Favorite title   ☐ Gift

☐ Recommendation   ☐ Other _____

Where did you make your purchase? (please check one)

☐ Comic store   ☐ Bookstore   ☐ Mass/Grocery Store

☐ Newsstand   ☐ Video/Video Game Store ☐ Other: _____

☐ Online (site: _____)

What other VIZ properties have you purchased/own? _____

_____

How many anime and/or manga titles have you purchased in the last year? How many were VIZ titles? (please check one from each column)

ANIME
- [ ] None
- [ ] 1-4
- [ ] 5-10
- [ ] 11+

MANGA
- [ ] None
- [ ] 1-4
- [ ] 5-10
- [ ] 11+

VIZ
- [ ] None
- [ ] 1-4
- [ ] 5-10
- [ ] 11+

I find the pricing of VIZ products to be: (please check one)
- [ ] Cheap
- [ ] Reasonable
- [ ] Expensive

What genre of manga and anime would you like to see from VIZ? (please check two)
- [ ] Adventure
- [ ] Comic Strip
- [ ] Science Fiction
- [ ] Fighting
- [ ] Horror
- [ ] Romance
- [ ] Fantasy
- [ ] Sports

What do you think of VIZ's new look?
- [ ] Love It
- [ ] It's OK
- [ ] Hate It
- [ ] Didn't Notice
- [ ] No Opinion

Which do you prefer? (please check one)
- [ ] Reading right-to-left
- [ ] Reading left-to-right

Which do you prefer? (please check one)
- [ ] Sound effects in English
- [ ] Sound effects in Japanese with English captions
- [ ] Sound effects in Japanese only with a glossary at the back

THANK YOU! Please send the completed form to:

NJW Research
42 Catharine St.
Poughkeepsie, NY 12601

All information provided will be used for internal purposes only. We promise not to sell or otherwise divulge your information.